CRY OF THE ENVIRONMENT
Rebuilding the Christian Creation Tradition

edited by
Philip N. Joranson
Ken Butigan

The Center for Ethics and Social Policy
Berkeley, California

TM

Bear & Company
Santa Fe, New Mexico

Chapter One, "Creation in the Bible," is adapted, and in important respects modified, from the article, "Creation," by Bernhard W. Anderson in Interpreter's Dictionary of the Bible, *Vol. I. Copyright © by Abington Press; used by permission of the publisher.*

Chapter Seventeen, "Process Theology and An Ecological Model," is reproduced by the kind permission of the Editorial Advisory Board of the Pacific Theological Review, *from Vol. XV, No. 2 (Winter, 1982), pp. 24-29. This article presents the substance of the 1981 T. V. Moore Lectures which Dr. Cobb and Dr. L. Charles Birch jointly delivered at the San Francisco Theological Seminary, San Anselmo, California.*

Typesetting—Casa Sin Nombre, Santa Fe
Cover Design—William Field, Santa Fe
Printed in the United States by BookCrafters, Inc.

TABLE OF CONTENTS

RESOURCES FOR THE MODERN-DAY TRANSFORMATION
OF THE CHRISTIAN CREATION TRADITION

FOREWORD

This volume is a major contribution to a task of critical importance: the exploration of religious and ethical resources for dealing with mounting environmental abuse. Its authors draw from many disciplines—ranging from science to theology, ethics, and the arts—in elaborating the basis for a new creation consciousness, one which is faithful to both biblical foundations and an ecological understanding of the natural world. It moves from ideas and attitudes to actions, looking at environmental policy and individual life styles, as well as patterns of worship, meditation, and education.

During the 1970s there was increasing recognition that environmental degradation is a product of basic attitudes toward nature. Two debates dominated the discussion. The first was touched off by Lynn White's assertion that "Christianity bears a huge burden of guilt" for the environmental crisis because it emphasized the separation of humanity and nonhuman nature. White pointed to the assertion in Genesis that humanity has been given dominion over other creatures, and he criticized the "Christian arrogance" of assuming that nature is intended only for our use. He also saw in Christianity a separation of God and nature—and an emphasis on transcendence over immanence—which reinforced an instrumental view of the natural world.

Critics of Lynn White's thesis were quick to reply that Christianity was not a major cause of environmental exploitation. They pointed instead to the use of modern science in which nature was viewed as a machine, and to technology which provided new power to control nature. They noted that in the emerging industrial capitalism, the environment was seen only as a source of raw materials and profits. They argued that institutions are more important than beliefs in molding behavior and insisted that the growth of industrial institutions was too complex to attribute to any one cause. This historical debate raised significant issues, but it made only a limited contribution to the reformulation of a positive Christian vision of the created order.

A second prominent issue during the seventies was the fear that concern for the environment might divert attention from social justice in the agenda of the churches. To some critics, the preservation of natural beauty seemed a luxury of the affluent in a world of poverty and malnutrition. The environmental movement was accused of middle-class elitism, a denial of the biblical call to side with the oppressed of the world. At the United Nations environmental conference in Stockholm in 1972, Third World delegates insisted that rich nations are responsible for most of the basic problem. By 1979, Third World delegates to the World Council of Churches' conference at MIT were more aware that developing nations have serious environmental problems too, but they still felt greater urgency about justice and participation than about sustainability as policy goals. In the early 1980s, during a period of recession and unemployment, many Americans felt that economic growth should have higher priority than new measures for environmental protection.

The present volume goes significantly beyond these two earlier debates. Most of its authors acknowledge that the Christian tradition has not given adequate attention to the natural world. The tradition has often been preoccupied with human salvation and has typically seen nature as an impersonal stage for the drama of human redemption. But this volume dwells less on the failures of the past than on the possibilities of the future, particularly through the recovery of neglected themes in the Bible and in subsequent history. The biblical understanding of the goodness and value of the created order can lead us to the celebration of our habitat. The biblical vision of our common origin and destiny under God can itself help to overcome the subsequent separation of human and nonhuman worlds. These chapters are devoted to rebuilding the Christian creation tradition, not to rejecting or defending it.

These essays also move beyond the dichotomy of environment versus justice. One of them points out that in the biblical view both nature and history are included in God's covenant and are fulfilled in the final Kingdom. Another argues that St. Francis' simple life style, his concern for the poor, and his sense of kinship with nonhuman creatures were jointly products of his dedication to the creator God. Still another delineates the common hierarchical assumptions and institutions which have led to the domination of nature and the domination of women. As one author puts it, there are common social structures which exploit the oppressed earth and the oppressed of the earth, producing the violence of both environmental and human abuse. A fine essay by Matthew Fox traces the links between ideas of the goodness of creation, the participation of all things in God, maternal images of God, and the call to justice. Again, concern on these pages about the growing inequalities in resource use between rich and poor nations is motivated as much by an ecological understanding of the limited carrying capacity of the environment as by commitment to social justice.

The authors represent a variety of theological positions, from Roman Catholic and Protestant to Unitarian and naturalistic. But three theological ideas recur as themes with variations. One is the idea of a covenant which includes both nature and history. In the symbolism of Noah's ark, all types of creatures are saved, and the covenant with all living things, indicated by the rainbow, pledges God's future faithfulness: Seedtime and harvest, summer and winter, shall not cease while the earth remains. Violation of the covenant affects both the nonhuman and the human community, according to later biblical thought; and both participate in God's redemptive activity. Several of these essays explore the possibility of such a "covenantal theology" for today.

A second recurrent theme is the idea of continuing creation. Creation is not to be identified with a remote event at the beginning of time, but with the world's continuing dependence on God. God sustains the world and is with it in creativity in every age. The world is a dynamic and interdependent whole in which new forms emerge. Neither nature nor humanity is complete. Several authors invoke Teilhard de Chardin's vision of an evolving cosmos and refer to his conviction that we must understand God in relation to a world of becoming, rather than to a static order of being.

A third recurrent note is the potential of process theology for expression both biblical and ecological understanding. Under the influence of Alfred North Whitehead, process thinkers hold that there are mental and physical aspects of all entities, much as Teilhard refers to inwardness and outwardness at all levels of reality. All beings are constituted by their relationships. This conceptual scheme starts from the interdependence of the web of life—rather than starting from separate beings which are only externally related. Human beings are part of an inclusive ecosystem; they have unique capacities, but the unfolding of their experience is not unlike that of other creatures. Process theologians portray a God of persuasion rather than coercion who is a creative influence in every aspect. Here is a vision of the organic unity and openness of creation.

The editors of this volume have wisely solicited chapters from several scientists, for current science is an important source from which a new creation consciousness can draw. Newtonian science was mechanistic, deterministic,and reductionistic. Contemporary science, in contrast, finds both lawfulness and indeterminacy at many levels, from atomic physics to evolutionary biology. Nature is seen not as a machine but as a dynamic historical process in which there is genuine novelty. The scientists and the theologians writing here share the conviction that human beings have a distinctive freedom and responsibility but are part of a long evolutionary history in which all creatures are our kin. From ecology, too, we can learn the interconnectedness of the web of life today, which we ignore to our own peril.

The editors have also included examples of more personal responses to the re-envisioned world in art and liturgy. The imaginative celebration of the created order can both express and engender new perceptions of the community of being. Another distinctive feature of this collection is the attention given to prayer and meditation as vehicles of creation consciousness. Meister Eckhart, Thomas Merton, Thomas Kelly, and Teilhard are held up as persons for whom union with God was sought through the world, not by flight from the world. For them, love for the world and love for God are not incompatible, for God is present in all things. In contemplation we are aware of the deep interrelatedness and mystery of being. In prayerful openness we can experience a harmony and unity with the natural world which escapes us when we try to control and manage it.

Ethical concerns and policy issues, which have arisen in almost all the earlier essays, are more systematically explored in the concluding chapters. Here we are dealing not just with ethical theories but with strategies for individual and social change. It is easy to be overwhelmed by the magnitude of the crises we face: a nuclear arms race which could destroy civilization and much of nature, a massive inequity in the distribution of scarce resources around the world, an increasing imbalance between growing population and dwindling forests, soils, and other natural resources. But a person can start with his or her own lifestyle and with involvement in organizations dedicated to peace, justice, and environmental sustainability. Local churches can express solidarity with both nature and humankind in their worship, educational programs, community outreach, and social action. In such ways they can be both true to the core of their own tradition and relevant to a world desperately in need of a new vision of the possibilities for life together on this amazing planet.

IAN G. BARBOUR

ACKNOWLEDGMENT

An interdisciplinary research and writing project must draw upon the contributions of many individuals; this is especially true when the project deals with a crucially important subject like the revision—and re-envisioning—of a religious tradition's attitude toward the natural environment. Such an undertaking demands the emergence of novel connections between the disciplines which have, at least in the modern West, been kept strictly apart except under what have generally turned out to be shady circumstances. Fortunately, the authors who are represented in the following pages have been able to forge these links; we applaud their insight and creativeness, and thank them for their generosity in taking on this assignment.

To the Center for Ethics and Social Policy, a research and education institute located at the Graduate Theological Union in Berkeley, we are grateful for the time, effort, and encouragement which it has showered on this project. In particular, we wish to thank Center directors Dr. Charles S. McCoy and Dr. Drew Christiansen for the valuable help they have given.

We thank the Pacific School of Religion, a member school of the Graduate Theological Union, for sponsoring the course, "Christian Faith and the Environment," which was the initial basis for this volume. The entire enterprise has also benefitted much from the encouragement and support it has received from Sylvia M. Joranson, since its inception in 1981.

It has been a pleasure to work with Barbara Clow, editor with Bear & Company; her counsel and assistance during the final stages of the manuscript preparation have been most helpful.

This project was made possible first by a small grant from Trinity Church (Episcopal) in New York City, which allowed us to begin work, and by three subsequent gifts from the Anne S. Richardson Fund, also in New York, which saw us through to completion. For each of these we extend our deep appreciation.

PHILIP N. JORANSON
KEN BUTIGAN, EDITORS

Introduction
TRANSFORMING THE CREATION
TRADITION
The Present Challenge

Philip N. Joranson and Ken Butigan

No one of us lives apart from the natural world. As children of the earth and sea and sky, we are nourished and sheltered by the world's lively goodness, its dynamic presence, and its continual creation and re-creation. We are the daughters and sons—but also the sisters and brothers—of the rich, abundant, destroying-and-preserving cosmos. On close inspection we discover that rather than being "trapped in the net of nature," we are a vital aspect and dimension of that infinitely various, mysterious and far-flung net. We are a colorful part of the webbing of the cosmos.

No one lives apart from the natural world. We repeat this simple phrase with emphasis only because we so often think and act contrary to its obvious truth. For us, nature is less often conceived as "creative matrix" and more often grasped, in the spirit of "realism" and "utility," as our property to be used and used up. We are finding today that, although this attitude—and the practices it has spawned—may have seemed "pragmatic" in the short-term, it has led to severe long-term problems, many of which are only now being clearly recognized.

This exploitation of the natural world has been possible on such a massive scale because humans have set themselves apart from it and have therefore been encouraged by the intoxication of this distance to dominate, control, and recreate nature in their own image. Nature has been scaled-down to fit humankind's physical, but also psychological, requirements. Asserting our "superiority" —rooted, perhaps, in a need to compensate for our all-too-obvious feelings of finitude and smallness when compared with the cosmos—we have "re-drafted" the physical landscape and our perception of nature. Alternating waves of the urge to dominate and the urge to sentimentalize have been substituted for a genuine awe and respect for the earth from which we come and through which we are sustained.

Faced with the prospect of environmental ruin, and thus our own destruction, it is necessary to engender a new reading of the text of nature and our relationship to it. It is for this reason that the authors of this volume choose to explore the creation tradition and the horizon of creation consciousness. Ecological renewal depends on political and economic shifts on a global scale, but these in turn depend on a far more profound shift in basic feelings and attitudes toward the environment. This shift will be both a return to some very ancient concepts and an invention—or, better, an improvisation—of new ideas adapted to the unique circumstances and problems which presently confront us, insights springing from a much greater understanding of the natural world. Fundamentally, this shift will signal a retrieval of the sense of immediacy of the natural world and our being intimately connected with that world; it will announce a crucial creativity in working out a much-needed program of "therapy" between humans and all creation so that they will spare each other common devastation and will, together, create a "wildly harmonious" tapestry of fecund, nurturing, abundant life.

Religion and The Environment

The massive problems besieging the natural environment did not disappear when the great world-wide interest in ecology of the late 1960s lapsed in the middle 1970s. Tragically, many of the problems which became the focus of heated debate and militant action a decade ago have been allowed—through both negligence and deliberate policy—to worsen in magnitude. The problems are still very much with us, and the prospect of ecological crisis becoming ecological catastrophe grows daily.

The recent wanton disruption of the earth's ecosystems— through galloping industrialization, through the rapid consumption of the planet's precious and finite resources, through the turning of the oceans, the soil, and the atmosphere into the sewers of humanity—raises the distinct possibility of the collapse of a fragile and increasingly burdened biosphere. Shaped over millions of years of planetary evolution to support its creatures, the earth is being grievously taxed in its ability to function as a viable habitat for the human species and the hundreds of thousands of other species it has sheltered for aeons. The earth heaves under the weight of our unplanned, unthought-out assault upon it. In its own subtle way it cries out for a moratorium of abuse and we, deaf to this plea, stumble ahead with increased consumption of resources, increased stripping of the land, and increased extinction of our fellow creatures, species which have been silent partners in the adventure of evolution since the beginning of the world.

What are the prospects of survival if the present rates of abuse are continued? "The Global 2000 Report"—a U.S. government study issued in 1980—shares with us a glimpse of what we might expect in a scant 16 years if ecological damage continues unabated. "If present trends continue," the report predicts, "the world in 2000 will be more crowded, more polluted, less stable ecologically, and more vulnerable to disruption than the world we live in now. Serious stress involving population, resources and environment is clearly visible ahead."[1]

It is apparent that any effort to reverse this gloomy situation will have to draw on a wide range of analysis and techniques. The expertise of natural and physical scientists, of population specialists, of energy specialists, and of policy-makers must be drawn together in a joint effort to deal realistically and forthrightly with the peril which threatens the life of our global home. Some efforts are being undertaken in each of these areas to address these complex and far-reaching problems. Nevertheless, most of the problems worsen each day, because the forces which create these massive difficulties for the biosphere rush ahead of the experts and specialists, bypassing their relatively puny attempts to reverse, or at the very least, slow the avalanche of environmental degradation.

The slaughter of planet earth will not cease strictly because of piecemeal policy proposals or legislation. This is true not merely because any legislation must be globally oriented and comprehensive—that is, it must embrace all of the world's interacting ecosystems. No, this is true more significantly because this worldwide environmental abuse is rooted in a set of ideas which have become the assumptions and axioms of modern human behavior—assumptions about technological progress, about an infinitely expanding consumption of raw materials, about the primacy of humankind in the world order, and about the unceasing maximization of "development." But these are not ideas which exist in a pristine intellectual vacuum—no, they are saturated with emotions of pride, confidence, advantage, winning and losing; in other words, a *mystique* of perpetual enlargement of human presence and will, and a perpetual enlargement of human appetite and satisfaction, infects these "organizing principles" which legitimate the policies of multi-national corporations and governments as they, thoughtlessly or not, carry out a "slash and burn" policy across the face of our planet. Thomas Merton once wrote that a mystique is "the emotional icing on an ideological cake," and it seems that his descriptive definition holds in this case—our reckless binge of development and digestion of the earth's finite treasures is carried along on a tidal wave of emotional self-justification which is bound up with the Industrial West's point of view about ownership and property, particularly what it regards as its *own* ownership and property. Business—and the ravages of land, water, and sky which it has instigated—has passed from the realm of simple transactions to that of protector of the West's "mission" to populate the world with docile producers and unsatisfied consumers.

Seen in this way, it becomes immediately clear that this set of "fundamental assumptions" wrapped in a package of highly charged emotions generated by a "property" ideology and mystique is not merely one among many competing outlooks. Rather, it is a foundational world view—or, more correctly, a faith. It offers a horizon of meaning. It grounds action. It provides an over-arching social structure by which one lives and for which one is willing to die—though it is rarely articulately in such "ultimate" terms, it harbors these "ultimate" connotations.

Given this perspective, the ecological crisis our species is presently facing will never be managed, let alone resolved, until we deal with the fundamentally religious character of that crisis. "Exponential growth", "limitless consumption", "maximization of development"—each of these modern economic watchwords implies a set of attitudes or values which is rarely formulated systematically but which saturates the policy decisions that invoke these hallowed phrases when a dam is built which will extinguish the life of a species or when the skin of the earth is flayed in order to extract enormous quantities of coal, which when burned, will foul the skies even more than they are fouled now. To undo the present ecological rout, it is not enough to treat specific symptoms of the problem—it is, rather, necessary to expose the assumptions on which such activity is based, to critique these presuppositions, to challenge and transform the patterns of behavior which they unleash upon an unsuspecting world, and to offer a new vision of living and being in relationship with all the earth. This is, at heart, a religious task.

This is a religious undertaking because it smokes out the inadequacies of one horizon of meaning—the perspective of the world as a "thing" to be exploited and used up—and embraces a more adequate horizon of meaning, one in which the earth is the nurturing, sustaining habitat in which we meet the presence of The Great Nurturer and Sustainer, the Spirit of God. Such a frame-of-reference is more adequate because it is more faithful to the vision and identity of the human species among other species on a planet among other planets in a galaxy among other galaxies.

The question, then, becomes less whether or not our attempts to prevent the ecocide of planet earth are at bottom a religious task generated from a religious impulse toward meaning and ultimacy, and more a question of the religous resources at hand to help us in our task. Are there religious insights, rituals, visions, practices and ways of life which both call into question the madness of ecological destruction and offer new paths out of that destruction and into a wise and harmonious relationship with the natural world? Are there religious perspectives of the planet which offer a far more constructive approach to life than one in which we are careening toward mass destruction? Are there world views which can reprioritize our values in such a way that we are able to linger long enough to appreciate the wonderful beauty and complexity of the cosmos, and therefore rediscover a long-exiled dimension of being human—the awareness of our fundamental place in a dynamic and ceaselessly flourishing universe?

Traditional societies, closest in feeling to the earth, offer many examples of a loving reciprocity with the planet and its myriad miracles planted in the stubborn but yielding heart of the "everyday." We have much to learn from the Native Americans, the peoples of the South Pacific, the Lapps living within the Arctic Circle, and the tribes in Southeast Asia about this significant and holy connectedness to the natural world. So too, in their unique ways, do the Sufis, the Buddhists, the Hassidim, and the Hindus have much to teach us about respecting the gentleness and fury of nature. As each of these traditions has emerged, it has more or less adequately dealt with the fact of the natural world, and has incorporated the ambiguity of ideas and feelings it has elicited, in an overarching vision of the nature-human relationship. This creative dialogue with the natural world has often been filled with rewards and problems, creating a dialectic that passes into the symbolism of the particular tradition and becomes a source of new understandings of the tradition itself.

In this book, we explore the Judeo-Christian view of the natural world. Why? Why scrutinize a religious tradition which has seemed to encourage, to legitimate—and, according to some analysts, even to spawn—the environmental degradation unleashed by our advanced technological society? Our answer is at least twofold. First, it is crucial that whatever legitimacy Christianity has offered to the calamity of environmental destruction be seriously investigated and challenged; if some of the roots of Western domination of the earth lie in this particular religious tradition, it is necessary to humbly acknowledge this fact and then attempt to work a new kind of influence, and to create *new* axioms and assumptions on which to base our environmental behavior. Second, it is absolutely essential to recover the elements of this tradition which seek to preserve and champion the earth. We can re-create the creation tradition, in part, by retrieving those aspects of this ambiguous tradition which seriously affirm and playfully celebrate our wondrous habitat. Both of these points draw us directly to grapple with and, where necessary, reshape Christianity's checkered attitudes toward the environment.

The fact is that Christianity's approach to the natural world has been mostly a tense, stormy affair from the beginning, and from the outset would seem to have little to offer in our present religious task, which includes the assessment of meaning, the cultivation of vision, the engendering of commitment, and the mobilization of constructive action. Nevertheless, a closer look reveals that the dominant tradition—which has generally either been indifferent toward the environment or outright hostile toward it—has obscured another tradition within the history of the church that reverenced the cosmos and discovered God there. Indeed, both views have competed with each other from the time of the primitive church. In this book a group of specialists will examine the negative and positive sides of the Christian appraisal of the natural order and, out of that task of "spiritual archeology," explore the value of a religious spirit informed by what has been recently called "creation consciousness" for our thoughts and actions on the present ecological disaster we are all facing. This volume explores the possibility of retrieving the positive aspects of the Christian attitude toward the environment and envisioning, in the light of a host of relevant scientific, artistic, political, and theological resources, the creation of a new awareness of the world we live in—a world which we are gradually, and not so gradually, destroying.[2]

Rebuilding The Judeo-Christian Creation Tradition

Twenty years ago, the Christian churches in America were just beginning to identify theological and ethical resources which would help them deal with the mounting environmental abuse which they were just then becoming aware of.[3] At that time, the senior editor of this book began a ten-year term as chairperson of a newly established interdisciplinary and interdenominational research group whose aim was to examine and develop these resources.[4] This was a time when the churches and the seminaries were coming face to face with the hard reality that, although the biblical vision of creation was rich and extremely relevant to the human understanding of and appropriate behavior toward the environment, this vision had been only very poorly grasped in the Christian tradition—in fact, researchers found that the tradition had often been turned against itself, seeing the natural world as enemy or as inert object fit only for manipulation.[5]

The negative side of the Christian vision of the natural world has been aired numerous times: God's Lordship over the earth is mimicked by humanity when it sets itself over against the natural, limiting meaning to human history and the "events of salvation"—a salvation, in part, from the realm of matter and into another world beyond this one. The God of heaven is far removed from mere earth, and so should his children be. This attitude spawned both asceticism and materialism, for the earth, disconnected from the Lord, was only an object which could be transformed as it pleased humanity. This, of course, caricatures the nuances of this negative tradition, but it has been the caricature which has persisted generally intact across the centuries and not the carefully reasoned and articulated philosophies which grounded it (eg., Neo-Platonism, Gnosticism, Hellenistic influences).

The positive side has been far less influential, but it has been there all along. The biblical affirmation of the environment, as recently summarized by theologian Durwood Foster[6], includes these elements:

1. God, as creator of the natural world, finds creation purposeful.

2. The goodness of creation is affirmed repeatedly.
3. The vision of the salvation—the "making whole"—of all creation, is intrinsic.
4. Jesus' incarnation is understood as the divine presence and agency dwelling in the midst of the creaturely reality.
5. Eternal fulfillment of creation as the final state of things is affirmed, as foreshadowed in the resurrection and transfiguration of the body.

What is the vocation of the Christian in the age of Verdun and Guernica, Auschwitz and Hiroshima, the Gulag and My Lai, Love Canal, Three Mile Island and the The Bomb? *It is to work and pray for justice; to liberate all those imprisoned by oppressive economic, political, and social structures; and to affirm the fundamental unity of our world by actively seeking to heal its deeply rooted divisions.* These cannot remain lofty and unattainable ideals—they must become increasingly central, for they define our fundamental identity as Christians in a world afflicted with great individual and systemic violence.

What, then, is our Christian vocation in the age of senseless and greedy destruction of the environment? *It is to work and pray for eco-justice, to liberate the earth from the threat and reality of its slow and steady execution at the hands of humanity, and to celebrate our awareness of the basic unity of our physical and living world by really behaving as if this insight were true.* The unity of humankind will never be achieved until we grasp the unity of the cosmos. To war against the earth is to war against the creatures of the earth, and—with the gruesome capabilities of the nuclear weapons we continue to produce at a rate of between three and five per day—the converse is true also: to war against the creatures of the earth is to war against the earth itself.

We must take this vocation extremely seriously, and allow its wide implications to settle into our bones, our heads, our hearts, and so to let ourselves be joined in an intimate way with a creative but suffering world that is crying out for liberation.

In 1982, novelist Alice Walker[7] delivered a powerful speech in San Francisco in which she worried that human beings—specifically white males—would soon export environmental destruction beyond the earth to other planets, and then cautioned her audience that "if we have any true love for the stars, planets, the rest of Creation, we must do everything we can to keep white men away from them. They who have appointed themselves our representatives to the rest of the universe. They who have never met any new creature without exploiting, abusing, or destroying it . . . What they have done to the Old, they will do to the New . . ." Over the pandemic condition of human greed and wanton consumption hangs a curse: the curse of total annihilation, a curse we set in motion when we exploit and destroy, instead of help and heal. Perhaps this curse will finally be unleashed, Walker conjectures; she wonders aloud whether "fatally irradiating ourselves may in fact be the only way to save others from what Earth has already become." But she finally cannot accept this, and declares:

> So let me tell you: I intend to protect my home. Praying—not a curse—only the hope that my courage will not fail my love. But if by some miracle, and all our struggle, the earth is spared, only justice to every living thing (and everything is alive) will save humanity. And we are not saved yet.
> *Only justice can stop a curse.*

"Only justice can stop a curse." Our indiscriminate assault on the earth—and our potential nuclear strike against the planet, as well as its creatures—represents an enormous curse of our own making, and, as Walker claims with such insight, that curse will not be lifted until justice is done in its place. This is our ecological, but also deeply religious, mandate in these days of first strike weapons, acid rain, deforestation, and the fouling of our planet's oceans and atmosphere. Only justice can relieve injustice.

This small attempt to revise and re-envision the way in which Christians interact with the natural world is motivated largely by the horrific abuse being heaped on that world at the present time and the strong desire to change this behavior and the attitudes which make this behavior possible, but it also comes out of the hope that we will reclaim a sense of the sacredness of *all* our relations with the environment. Let our eating and drinking again become sacraments of the dynamic pulse of the cosmos which is known in the natural cycles which make possible food and drink and which therefore link us again and again to this world (or, better, remind us that we are never separate from the world). Let our hygiene, our teaching and our learning, our crafts, our gardening—and our appreciation of the garden of the world— spark our awareness of the *presence* of the trembling life of the cosmos before us. Let this awareness inform our work, our professions, our relationships with others. Let a gradually growing Christian creation-consciousness transform all these relationships.

Years ago, well ahead of his time, theologian Bernard E. Meland wrote in *Modern Man's Worship*, "It is not enough to breathe, eat, and drink in accord with earthways; we must think, hope, and feel in accord with them. As creatures of the earth we must bring our total organism into accord with its sustaining ways."[8] This consciousness must now be cultivated and embodied, not merely because of its inherent aesthetic attractiveness, nor even because it is a key to our survival, but because it broadens our praise of, and participation in, the life of the One who makes and sustains all things. Let us begin to glimpse the subtle pattern in the texture and lining of life: an earth-and-cosmos ecosystem of Spirit, being actualized and released in every creaturely relationship.

Notes

1. Gerald O. Barney, *The Global 2000 Report to the President of the United States* (New York: Pergamon Press, 1980), p. 1.
2. Herman Kahn in his forthcoming book, *Global 2000 Revisited*—co-edited with Julian Simon and presenting essays by a number of contributors—challenges all the major conclusions reported in the summary of the *Global Report to the President of the United States*, also known as the *Global 2000 Report*. Constance Holden, in *Science* (vol. 221, no. 4608, July 2, 1983, pp. 341-343), reviews the book and presents an account of the controversy between Kahn's views and the thinking of those who support the conclusions of this study.

    Kahn, in contrast to the perspective of this volume, holds that: 1) left to its own devices, in the future the economy, population, and the environment will all achieve eventual equilibrium; 2) humanity must continue to dominate nature; and 3) religious perspectives are irrelevant to environmental behavior and policy.
3. Before this time, pioneering efforts of various kinds had been initiated by several groups. One of these was the Boston Industrial Mission. Among other activities, it conducted environmental ethics seminars for managers and engineers at local industrial plants, and programming was developed in cooperation with nearby seminaries and MIT. A program which had been underway for some time was the educational and worship observance of Soil Stewardship Sunday, an initiative of a number of Protestant and Roman Catholic rural life

agencies working in partnership with the National Association of Soil Conservation Districts and the USDA Soil Conservation Service.

4. This was the Faith-Man-Nature Group, related to the National Council of Churches. For a history of its activities and a listing of publications, see: Philip N. Joranson, "The Faith-Man-Nature Group and a Religious Environmental Ethic," *Zygon*, vol. 12, no. 2 S (June, 1977), pp. 175-79.

5. In this discussion, "creation tradition" refers to (1) the biblical elements of creation-related theology and ethics, and the Christian understanding of the natural environment as developed in the theological/ethical/spiritual literature of the tradition, and (2) the actual attitudes and relationships of Christians toward the environment throughout the church tradition.

6. A. Durwood Foster, from an unpublished manuscript offered during a presentation in a graduate course at Graduate Theological Union, Berkeley, Spring Quarter, 1983. The course: "Christian Faith and the Environment: Agenda for Updating the Creation Tradition."

7. Alice Walker, "Only Justice Can Stop a Curse," *Re-weaving the Web of Life,* ed. Pam McAllister (Philadelphia: New Society Publishers, 1982) pp. 262-265.

8. Bernard Eugene Meland, *Modern Man's Worship* (New York: Harper, 1934) p. 168.

Part I

THE JUDEO-CHRISTIAN
TRADITION
Problem and Resource

Creation consciousness will be fostered by a critical analysis and assessment of the Judeo-Christian creation tradition. Such an evaluation is indispensable in acquiring an adequate appreciation of the presuppositions, perceptions, and attitudes of our own time, and of how these modes of approach to the non-human creation have been molded. This evaluation has been late in coming. This has not been a primary concern of scholars who have sought to trace and understand the growth of Christianity, and one reason is clear: the creation-oriented impulse within the tradition has been overshadowed by the emphasis on human salvation. Consequently, faithfulness to the non-human creation—and to the special relationship which humankind enjoys with the non-human world—has for the most part been very weakly developed.

Over the past several decades, this conclusion has been gradually acknowledged in some quarters of the Christian community, owing chiefly to the studies of a small group of scholars.[1] The essays in the section which follows are shaped in light of this conclusion. Their purpose is to:

1. Identify the basic elements of creation-related theology and ethics in the Bible;

2. Elucidate factors which have had a negative effect upon the Christian tradition's view of the creation and humankind's relationship to it; and

3. Identify positive elements that have also appeared in the tradition, and that are recognized today as resources for the transformation of the tradition.

Elements of Biblical Creation Theology and Ethics and Their Expression in Biblical Times

Part of the evidence of the weakness of the inherited creation tradition is the relatively poor understanding of most Christians regarding its biblical roots. Faith that is at home in God's creation will be greatly nurtured by the understanding of the world that emerges in Genesis and Second Isaiah, in the Wisdom literature of Job and Proverbs, as worship in some of the Psalms, and in the New Testament, especially in the Gospels, Acts, Romans, Ephesians, Colossians, and Revelation.

In Chapter 1, Bernhard Anderson tells this story from the Bible. Then in Chapter 2, he analyzes Yahweh's covenant with Noah, understanding it as an integral feature of a connected history of God's activity that begins with the creation story in Genesis 1:28-2:4. He finds the covenant with Noah affirms the teachings of the creation story, and the covenant is intended to apply in the widest sense imaginable. A lifetime biblical scholar and teacher, Anderson has had a particular interest in creation theology and its bearing on human behavior in the environment.

Recent scholarship is shedding new light upon the way the creation was understood and related to by the Hebrews. The relatively recent introduction of the social sciences as tools for the biblical scholar promises new insights from the study of the cultural interfaces in biblical times between humankind and all otherkind.[2] The theological significance of the land has also received recent attention in Old Testament studies by Walter Brueggemann[3] and others, and adds an important dimension to our understanding of how Israel's relationship to the creation was conceived in covenantal terms.

The Course of the Judeo-Christian Creation Tradition in Western Christianity

As we have recognized at the outset, the Western creation tradition from the early church onward has been dominated by powerful influences that have resulted in a weak development, unworthy of the biblical heritage. However, we note also that there have occurred notable exceptions that are of special interest today. For example, Richard Woods in Chapter 3, Claude Stewart in Chapter 5, and Matthew Fox in the opening of Chapter 4, have identified formidable factors influencing the tradition in a variety of ways that have drastically thwarted its creative analyses. These chapters allow a discriminating and realistic appraisal of the tradition today.

A number of other factors figure in a negative view of the environment, including the influence of Francis Bacon, the undervaluation of Jesus' relationship to nature, and the relatively weak awareness of most biblical scholars, theologians, and ethicists towards the creation as it has been described by the natural sciences.[4] Because of this inadequate grasp of scientific understanding, the creation is not appreciated deeply in their professional work, and this inadequacy is reflected in their training of ministers and religious educators.

Factors which have thwarted a worthy development of the creation tradition deserve continuing research by scholars working in interdisciplinary cooperation. This inquiry can expose the presence of persistent influences which have devalued and undermined the creation dimension of Christian faith and have therefore not given that faith its proper scope and power. This inquiry will also reveal the influences which restrain initiative and activity in this field today, thus encouraging the ongoing discernment of effective strategies for the modern-day transformation of the tradition.

Part of this work involves bringing alive the powerful insights and vision found within the tradition which lend themselves to the development of creation consciousness. This means taking seriously the creation visions of Francis of Assisi, Meister Eckhart, Martin Luther, John Calvin, Thomas Merton, and an emerging school of eco-process theologians, as well as the strands of creation thought in Celtic Christianity and Eastern Orthodoxy. In Chapter 3, Richard Woods opens a window for modern Christians upon the creation-centeredness of Celtic Christian spirituality, comparing it with the spirituality of the Roman church in the same era. And his chapter is followed by Matthew Fox's essay on "Creation-Centered Spirituality from Hildegard of Bingen to Julian of Norwich: 300 Years of Ecological Spirituality in the West."

Notes

1. Much of this documentation may be found in the following publications:

   Ian G. Barbour, ed., *Western Man and Environmental Ethics: Attitudes Toward Nature and Technology* (Reading, Mass: Addison-Wesley, 1973)

Matthew Fox, O.P., ed., *Western Spirituality: Historical Roots, Ecumenical Routes*(Santa Fe, NM: Bear & Company, 1982).

Clarence J. Glacken, *Traces on the Rhodian Shore: Nature and Culture in Western Thought from Ancient Times to the End of the Eighteenth Century* (Berkeley: Univ. of California Press, 1967).

Charles Earl Raven, *Natural Religion and Christian Theology.* The Gifford Lectures, 1951. First Series: Science and Religion (Cambridge, England: Cambridge Univ. Press, 1953).

Eric C. Rust, *Nature and Man In Biblical Thought.* Lutterworth Library, Vol. 40. (London: Lutterworth Press, 1953).

Lynn White, Jr., "The Historical Roots of Our Ecologic Crisis." *Science*, Vol. 155, p. 1203-1207 (10 March, 1967). White is a Professor of History. His widely known article has stimulated much debate. It is reprinted in the Barbour volume, No. 1 as above.

2. The value of applying the methods of the social sciences in studies of the life of the Jewish people in Old Testament times is explained and illustrated in a substantial recent scholarly treatment. See Norman K. Gottwald, *The Tribes of Jawheh, A Sociology of the Religion of Liberated Israel,* 1250-1050 B.C.E. (Maryknoll, N.Y.: Orbis, 1979), 916 pp.

3. See Walter Brueggemann, *The Land: Place As Gift, Promise and Challenge in Biblical Faith* (Philadelphia: Fortress, 1977).

4. Concerning Jesus' relationship to nature, various considerations should lead us to expect that Jesus related to the creation during his ministry in far more intimate, intrinsic, and spiritually dynamic ways than we have hitherto noticed in the tradition. The gospels include a treasured scattering of sayings of Jesus which offer insight into how he personally understood and related to the creation during his ministry, and, though we must bring a critical hermeneutic to the layers of meanings of all sections of scripture, not enough has been done in taking seriously what the miracle stories tell us about Jesus' own grasp of creation and creation consciousness.

Chapter One

CREATION IN THE BIBLE

Bernhard W. Anderson

In the Bible the doctrine of creation presupposes and builds upon the ancient mythopoeic views of divine creation found in the ancient Near East, particularly Babylonia, Egypt, and Canaan. In the Old Testament, however, the inherited views were reinterpreted in the light of Israel's worship of Yahweh, the Holy God, whose saving power and commanding will were revealed in crucial historical experiences, preeminently the Exodus and the Sinai covenant. In the New Testament, faith in God the Creator, mediated to the church through the canonical scriptures of Israel, was reinterpreted christologically, that is, in the light of God's revelation in Jesus Christ and the "new creation" which through him has already begun in history. In both Testaments, the doctrine stresses the transcendence and freedom of God, the complete dependence of the whole creation upon the Creator, the reverence for all forms of life, especially human beings who are elevated to a supreme position of honor and responsibility, and the sovereign power and purpose of God which undergirds the whole earthly drama from beginning to end and which endows the cosmos, and everything in it, with ultimate meaning.

I. Creation and the Ancient World View

The New Testament inherits and transforms the Old Testament faith that God created all things (Acts 4:24; 14:15; 17:24; Eph. 3:9; Rev. 4:11; 10:6); and likewise the Old Testament creation faith, as expressed consummately in the creation stories of Genesis, the message of Second Isaiah (Isa. 40-55), various psalms of the Psalter (e.g. Pss. 8; 19; 104), and Israelite wisdom literature (especially Job) both presupposes and modifies the cosmological views of antiquity. The Old Testament affirms that Yahweh, the God known and worshiped in Israel, is the creator of heaven and earth. And since the meaning of God's personal name (identity) was given to Israel in her historical experiences as interpreted by a series of prophetic figures beginning with Moses, Yahweh's creative work was understood in a different sense from the prevalent creation beliefs among Babylonians, Egyptians, or Canaanites.

Ancient Cosmology and Mythology.   In a formal sense there are numerous points of contact between Israel's creation faith and the cosmological views of antiquity. The Bible takes for granted a three-storied structure of the universe: heaven, earth, and underworld (Ex. 20:4). According to this *Weltbild*, the earth is a flat surface, corrugated by mountains and divided by rivers and lakes. Above the earth, like a huge dome, is spread the firmament which both holds back the heavenly ocean and supports the dwelling-place of the gods (Gen. 1:8; Ps. 148:4). The earth itself is founded upon pillars which are sunk into the subterranean waters (Pss. 24:2; 104:5), in the depths of which is located Sheol, the realm of death. In this view, the habitable world is surrounded by the waters of chaos which, unless held back, would engulf the world, a threat graphically portrayed in the Flood Story (Gen. 7:11; cf. 1:6) and in various poems in the Old Testament (e.g. Pss. 46:1-3; 104:5-9).

In various ways ancient peoples affirmed that the world emerged out of primordial chaos. In Babylonian mythology the origin of the three-storied universe was traced to a fierce struggle between divine powers that emerged from uncreated chaos— Marduk the god of order and Tiamat the goddess of chaos. Victorious in the struggle, Marduk split the fishlike body of the monster down the middle, thus making a separation between the upper and lower parts. In Canaan there was a similar myth of the victorious struggle of Baal, the god of storm and fertility, against Yamm ("Sea"), the god of chaos. Apparently Canaanite mythology does not deal with creation in the cosmic sense but with the maintenance of the created order in the face of the periodic threats of chaos. The gods and goddesses, whose loves and wars dramatize the conflicts of nature and the cyclical movement of the seasons, are personifications of natural forces.

The Old Testament contains reminiscences of these ancient myths of creation against chaos.[1] We hear of Yahweh's primordial battle with sea monsters named Rahab or Leviathan (Job 9:13; Pss. 74:13-14; 89:10; Isa. 27:1; 51:9) and of Yahweh's action in "dividing" the upper and lower waters (Gen. 1:6-8) and in setting bounds for the

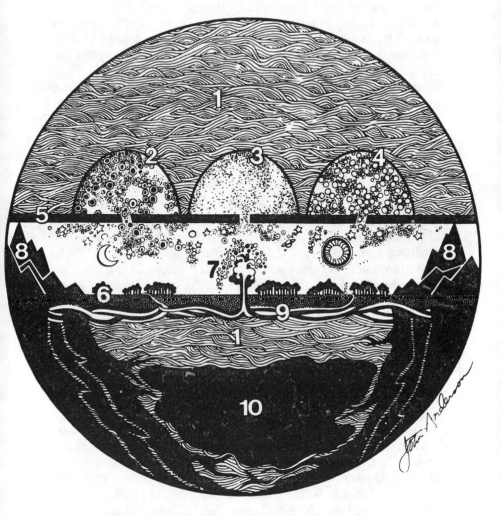

The Ancient Pictorial View of the Universe

1. The waters above and below the earth
2-4. Chambers of hail, rain, snow
5. The firmament with its "sluices"
6. The surface of the earth
7. The navel of the earth: "fountain of the Great Deep"
8. The mountain-pillars supporting the firmament
9. Sweet waters (rivers, lakes, seas) on which the earth floats
10. Sheol, the realm of Death (the "Pit")

sea (Ps. 104:7-9; Prov. 8:27-29). But these are very distant echoes. Although the Bible takes for granted the contours of ancient cosmology, it has demythologized ancient cosmological views. The Old Testament contains no theogony, no myth which traces the creation to a primordial battle between divine powers, no ritual which enabled people to repeat the mythological drama and thereby ensure control over the conflicting forces of the natural world. Mythological allusions have been torn out of their ancient context of polytheism and nature religion, and have acquired a new meaning within the historical syntax of Israel's faith. The pagan language survives only as poetic speech for the adoration of Yahweh, the creator of the world and the ruler of history (Ps. 33).

The Origin of Israel's Creation Faith.   The creation stories of Genesis 1 and 2 must be considered, not only in terms of the date of their literary composition, but also in terms of the age of the tradition they preserve. The old Epic [J] story (Gen. 2:4b-25), although it actually does not deal with creation in the broadest sense, dates back at least to the time of the early monarchy, probably Solomon's reign; and it is not impossible that its terse reference to "the day that Yahweh God made the earth and the heavens" implies a longer account of the creation of the earth which has been superseded by the Priestly [P] account (Gen. 1:1-2:3). Creation is dealt with most comprehensively and intensively in the latter story. The Priestly account is usually dated in the time of the Exile (ca. 550 B.C.), but careful study of its form and content indicates that the present version is the end result of a tradition whose development extended over a considerable period of time.

Various biblical texts indicate that Yahweh was acclaimed as creator in the Jerusalem temple during the period of the monarchy. Although the date of Genesis 14 is uncertain, it is noteworthy that in this passage, which is placed in a pre-Davidic Jerusalem setting, the title 'El 'Elyôn, "Maker [gônē] of heaven and earth," is applied to Yahweh (vs. 19, 22). The title has been appropriated from Canaanite religion, as evidenced by the occurrence of the verb in the Ras Shamra mythological texts and the expression 'El qn 'rs [El, creator of earth] in the Phoenician inscription of Karatepe. Furthermore, an old poetic fragment found in Solomon's temple address affirms that "Yahweh has set the sun in the heavens" (I Kings 8:12; text reconstructed on the basis of the LXX). Also, some scholars hold that in the pre-exilic period Yahweh's creative work was celebrated at the fall New Year's Festival, just as Marduk's victory over Tiamat was celebrated in the liturgy of the Babylonian New Year's Festival, and that several psalms reflect that cultic situation (Pss. 24; 47; 93; 95-99). Whether or not a parallel festival was held in Israel, these psalms indicate that in the Jerusalem cult Yahweh was acclaimed as the cosmic King who "established" the earth, that is, ordered it as a human dwelling (Ps. 93:1), and who sustains the world in the face of threats of chaos. Yahweh's greatness as celestial King is summed up in the affirmation that "all the gods of the peoples are idols, but Yahweh made the heavens" (Ps. 96:4-5).

Some scholars maintain that even before the period of the monarchy, and indeed at the beginning of Israelite traditions, Yahweh was acclaimed as Creator. This view rests heavily upon an interpretation of the tetragrammaton, the four consonants of the divine name (YHWH) introduced in Ex. 3:14. The tetragrammaton, it is argued, was originally a causative verbal form (*yahweh* = "He causes to be") meaning "He causes to be what comes into existence," i.e. creates, and in the patriarchal period was part of a larger litanic formula in which the ancestral god was praised as the creator of the cosmos, just as in Canaanite circles the high god *'El* was acclaimed as "creator of creatures."[2]

It is striking, however, that in the narrative context of Exodus, chapter 3, where an etymology of the divine name is given, Yahweh is presented as the liberating God rather than the creator. Furthermore, in early Israelite poetry, which apparently comes from the pre-monarchic period, the emphasis falls upon divine liberation, even when ancient mythopoeic creation language is used. This is the case in the Song of the Sea (Ex. 15:1-18), which is redolent of the mythopoeic language of the chaos myth and which follows essentially the movement of the mythical drama: the Divine Warrior (Ex. 15:3) encounters the powers of chaos, marches triumphantly to the sacred mountain (temple), and there is acclaimed as cosmic King (15:18). At one point the poet speaks of "the people whom you [Yahweh] have created" (15:16b, translating the verb *qānā* as "create;" cf. Gen. 14:19-20, 22).[3] In another ancient poem, "The Song of Moses" (Deut. 32:1-43), the poet uses this verb and other creation verbs to speak of the creation of a people.[4]

Is not Yahweh your Father, who created you,
    who made you and established you?   (Deut. 32:6b)

It seems, then, that Israel's earliest traditions did not refer to

Yahweh as creator in a cosmic sense but concentrated, rather, on Yahweh's "mighty deeds" of liberation, through which the Holy God became known and formed Israel as a people out of the chaos of historical oblivion and oppression. To be sure, ancient Israelites confessed that the God who is mighty in history could also make the forces of nature serve a redemptive purpose. Yahweh prepared a path for fugitives through the Reed Sea, preserved wanderers in the wilderness by performing signs and wonders, and rescued embattled Israelites at Megiddo by causing the stars to fight on their side and the River Kishon to overflow its banks (Judg. 5:20-21). Nevertheless, from the first, Israel confessed her faith by telling a story—the story of Yahweh's mighty acts of salvation (cf. Deut. 26:5-10). The theme of the creation/liberation of a people is a major motif of Mosaic tradition, whose trajectory can be traced throughout the Old Testament (Pss. 95:6-7; 100:3; Isa. 43:15; 45:11) and into the New.

The Old Testament theologian, Gerhard von Rad, has argued forcefully that Israel's faith from the very first was primarily concerned with historical redemption and that creation, as an independent doctrine, came into Israelite tradition relatively late through the influence of the wisdom movement.[5] There is some support for this view in Israel's premonarchic poetry in which, as we have seen, creation is understood soteriologically: the creation of a people. But this view does not do justice to theological developments in the early monarchy. Creation in the cosmic sense was introduced into the mainstream of Israelite life and thought by Davidic theologians who maintained that Yahweh made a "covenant in perpetuity" [bêrîth ôlām] with David (II Sam. 7; Ps. 89) and chose the Jerusalem temple as the divine dwelling place (Pss. 78; 132).[6] In this view, king and temple belong to a pattern of symbolization which relates the cosmic order of creation to the mundane order of history. The security, harmony, and peace of society depend upon the cosmic, created order, whose saving benefits are mediated to the social order through the divinely elected king, the "son of God." Accordingly, in a hymnic passage in Psalm 89, where the poet elaborates Yahweh's "covenant in perpetuity" with David, Yahweh is praised in mythopoeic language as the victor in the Chaoskampf (Ps. 89:9-12); and the psalmist goes on to say that the Davidic king, as the representative of the deity, will be victorious over the mythical "sea" or "floods" (Ps. 89:24-25).

The royal covenant theology, which placed the Davidic kingship in the vertical axis of the cosmic and the mundane, of macrocosm and microcosm, is compatible with psalms of the Zion temple (mentioned previously) which celebrate Yahweh's enthronement as cosmic Creator and King. Other psalms from the period of the monarchy show that reflection on creation was encouraged by Israel's sages (Ps. 104)[7] and by theologians and liturgists connected with the Jerusalem temple (Pss. 8, 33, 136, 148). The first prophet to reckon seriously with the doctrine was Jeremiah; he declared that divine sovereignty over history is underscored by the fact that Yahweh is Creator (Jer. 27:5; cf. 32:17) and perceived in the constancy of nature a pledge of Yahweh's covenant faithfulness (5:22-24; 31:35-36). Aside from the Priestly account (Gen. 1:1-2:3), the doctrine of creation finds its deepest expression in the message of Second Isaiah (Isa. 40-55) during the Exile (see III below). As evident from the devotional, apocalyptic, and wisdom literature of the postexilic period, the doctrine came to be a cardinal tenet of Judaism.

Creation and the Beginning of History.   In the book of Genesis creation does not stand by itself as though it were a prescientific attempt to explain the origin of the cosmos. Rather, as indicated by the position of the creation stories at the opening of the Bible, creation is the prologue to history. It sets the stage for the unfolding of the divine purpose and inaugurates a historical drama within which Israel and, in the fullness of time, the church were destined to play a key role. Thus the creation stands in an inseparable historical relation to the ensuing narratives that span the generations from Adam to Noah (Gen. 5), from Noah to Abr[ah]am (Gen. 10; 11:10-26), and from Abraham ((11:27-32) to Joseph. In the old Epic tradition (J), the story of the creation of humanity, together with the stories of primeval history, is the prologue to the sacred history that unfolds with the call of Abraham, the deliverance from Egypt, the guidance through the wilderness, and the entrance into the Promised Land. In this context, creation provides the background and setting for the vocation of God's people. The Priestly creation story, too, does not stand in isolation but prepares the way for a series of historical covenants: the ecological covenant with Noah (Gen. 9), the land-covenant with Abraham (Gen. 17), and the climactic revelation of God under the cultic name Yahweh in the Mosaic period (Ex. 6). Each of these covenants—the Noachic, the Abrahamic, and the Mosaic—is understood as a "covenant in perpetuity (*berit'h 'olam*), signifying God's unconditional commitment to human beings, as well as the earth and the whole non-human creation.[8]

Just as the creation points forward to the Exodus and the making of the covenant with Sinai, so the covenant faith reaches backward and includes the creation. Contrary to the present arrangement of the biblical drama, the theological movement is not from the confession "God is the Creator" to "Yahweh, the God of Israel, is the Redeemer," but in just the opposite direction. In the formulation of the traditions now included in the Pentateuch, the Exodus, together with historical events immediately associated with it, had decisive significance for the historical interpreter. This is evident, above all, in the old Epic tradition (J). From the standpoint of faith provided by Exodus and Sinai, "the saving experience" and "the commanding experience,"[9] Israelite narrators undertook the task of interpreting the whole human drama, right from the beginning. The story of Israel's life, which began with the call of Abraham (Gen. 12:1-3), was expanded to include not only the ancestral period (Gen. 12-50) but the previous world history portrayed in stories dealing with primeval times (Gen. 2-11). Thus an historical line was traced from the faith situation of Israel to the remotest historical beginnings imaginable, with the result that all human history was seen in the light of the revelation given to Israel and was embraced within the saving activity of Yahweh. The Priestly theologians, who have given us the Torah in its final form, have incorporated this enlarged story in the framework of a periodized history which moves from creation to the events that constituted Israel as a worshiping community: the Exodus and the Sinai revelation. In a similar manner, the New Testament church, convinced of the decisive character of God's revelation in Jesus Christ, understood the total sweep of historical time and whole creation in a christological perspective (Eph. 1:9-10; see IV below).

In Israel's understanding, then, creation and history are inseparably related. Creation is the foundation of the covenant; it provides the setting within which Yahweh's saving work takes place. But it is equally true that creation is embraced within the theological meaning of the covenant. Therefore, psalmists may regard creation as the first of God's saving deeds (Ps. 74: 12-17) and in the recitation of the *Heilsgeschichte* may move without a break from deeds of creation to historical deeds of liberation (Ps. 136).

In view of the inseparable relation between creation and history, it is not surprising to find that Yahweh's historical deeds are regarded as creative acts and, indeed, may be described by the same verbs as are applied to the original creation (*yāṣār* = "form;" *bārā'* = "create," *'āsā* = "make"); and this is true, above all, of Yahweh's creation of Israel (Isa. 43:1, 7, 15, 21; 44:2, 21, 24; 45;11) or the Servant (49:5). No prophet grasps as profoundly as Second Isaiah the soteriological meaning of creation and the creative significance of redemption. He appeals to the Creator's wisdom and power in order to demonstrate to despairing exiles that Israel's God is sovereign over the whole course of history and therefore can and will redeem the people (Isa. 40:12-31; 43:1-7; 45:9-13; 48:12-13). Furthermore, he declares that Yahweh's imminent coming to redeem the chosen people will result in nothing less than a new act of creation.

This view of creation in relation to a temporal movement displays a distinct break with the religions of antiquity. The gods of the ancient world had a story (*mythos*) but not a "history." In the perspective of the history of religions, creation is a timeless event—timeless in the sense that it belongs within a cyclical pattern of myth and ritual which must be re-enacted each year, as in the case of the Babylonian New Year ritual or the Ras Shamra (Canaanite) mythical drama. So pervasive and appealing was this mythology, especially in the agricultural setting of Canaan, that Israelites were tempted to turn to the *mythos* of the Canaanite gods and goddesses which assured fertility of the soil (Hos. 2:8) and to "forget" the story which identified Yahweh as their liberator (Jer. 2:4-13). It was no simple task for Israel's interpreters to insist that Yahweh alone is the sole Power, the fountain of life's meaning and vitality (Jer. 2:13) and the source of all that is. The ancient views of creation had to be demythologized and brought into theological relationship with the story of Yahweh's historical actions. When this was accomplished, as in the Priestly creation story, the foundations of the ancient mythological world view were shaken. No longer was creation a timeless event—timeless in the sense that it belongs within a cyclical pattern of recurrence ("the myth of the eternal return").[10] Rather, incorporated into Israel's sacred history, creation was a "once for all" event that marked the beginning of history.

II. The Sovereignty of the Creator

The Bible does not have the equivalent of the Greek term *kosmos*, which suggests the view of the universe as a rationally constituted and self-sustaining structure of reality. Instead, it speaks of the relationship between the Creator and the creation, a relationship which is essentially that of the covenant. For the belief that "heaven and earth" or *kōl*, "everything" (Ps. 8:6—H 8:7; Isa. 44:24), is dependent upon Yahweh, the Creator, is a corollary of Israel's understanding that her whole life is dependent upon Yahweh, her savior and judge, to whom they are bound in covenant relationship. The covenant, rather than a rational principle, is the ground of the unity of creation. Hence psalmists exclaim that divine *ḥesed* or covenant loyalty embraces all God's works (see the antiphonal refrains in Ps. 136).

The doctrine of creation, then, is preeminently an affirmation about the sovereignty of God and the absolute dependence of the creatures. To say that Yahweh made the earth is to confess that it belongs to its Maker; Yahweh is its Owner (Pss. 24: 1-2; 89:11-H 89:12; 95:5).[11] Nothing in the realm of creation should be glorified, for the creation points beyond itself to the God who is high and lifted up and therefore is worthy of the praise of human beings and all other creatures. Thus the proclamation that Yahweh is creator is a summons to worship, for the creation testifies to God's wisdom and power (Ps. 104:24; Prov. 3:19-20; Jer. 10:12-13), God's faithfulness (Ps. 136:4-9), and God's incomparable majesty shared with no other (II Kings 19:15; Neh. 9:6; Isa. 40:25-26). To be sure, the creation does not witness to the Creator so clearly that faith is unnecessary. In the wisdom books, Ecclesiastes and Job, the rational mysteries of the Creation witness to divine sovereignty which is beyond human understanding (see especially Job 38:1-7); and even in other contexts, where Yahweh's historical revelation provides the standpoint of faith, the Israelite is aware of the hiddenness of God (Isa. 45:15). Although the language of creation was often mysterious, it was nonetheless sufficiently intelligible to enable those who stood within the covenant to exclaim that the heavens declare the glory of God (Ps. 19:1-4—H 19:2-5). Thus the sovereignty of God, manifest in the works of creation, is the motive for worship and service (Ps. 95; Isa. 40:27-31).

Creation by the Word.   The creation stories of Genesis 1 (Priestly) and 2 (old Epic) have their differences, but they agree in ascribing creation to the free and spontaneous initiative of God. The personal relation between God and the creation is vividly portrayed in the old Epic account. In this story Yahweh is portrayed as a Potter who "forms" (*yāsār*) a human being from moist soil and then provides an environment suitable for the creature. The strong anthropomorphism of the story, however, does not reduce the Creator to the human level or exalt the creature to a plane of equality with God (cf. Gen. 3:22). Elsewhere the image of the divine Potter expresses the sovereignty of God over all creatures (Isa. 29:15-16; 45:9-13; Jer. 18:1-6; Rom. 9:20-21).

The sovereignty of God is expressed more forcefully in the Priestly account, which bears the marks of profound theological reflection about creation in the cosmic sense. In this account, God is exalted and transcendent. The Creator's only point of contact with the creation is the uttered command, which punctuates the creative drama with the refrain: "And God said . . . And it was so." The same thought is echoed by a psalmist:

Yahweh spoke, and it came to be;
he commanded, and it stood forth.
(Ps. 33:9; cf. v. 6)

and in other Old Testament passages (Ps. 148:5; cf. Isa. 45:12). Creation by the Word came to be the normative expression of the mode of God's creative work (Ecclus. 42:15; Syr. Apocalypse of Bar. 21:4ff; John 1:1-3; Heb. 11:3; II Pet. 3:5-6). It is noteworthy that this view was found also in the theology of ancient Memphis, according to which the God Ptah conceived the elements of the universe with his "heart" (mind) and brought them into being with his "tongue" (commanding word).[12]

As Israel learned in her historical experience, the Word of God is the sovereign power that shapes people's lives and controls the course of history. Yahweh's word is active and dynamic; it is the means by which the divine will is accomplished. The "word of Yahweh," when put in the mouth of the prophet, makes the prophetic spokesman sovereign over nations and releases a divine power which both overthrows and rebuilds (Jer. 1:9-10). As the rain and the snow descend from heaven and do not return thither until they have made the earth fertile, so the word that goes forth from Yahweh's mouth does not return empty, but accomplishes Yahweh's purpose and effects Yahweh's will (Isa. 55:10-11). God's word is "living and active, sharper than any two-edged sword" (Heb. 4:12; cf. Rev. 19:13-15). In these instances, it is clear that the Word is not a sound or even an idea. God's word is an act, an event, a sovereign command, which accomplishes a result. The creation story affirms that God's word, mighty in history, is also the very power which brought the creation into being. Since the creative

Word establishes a personal relationship between the Creator and the creation, the Christian faith affirms with theological consistency that the Logos (Word) became flesh in a person (John 1:1-18).

Creation ex nihilo.   In later theological reflection upon the meaning of creation, the sovereignty of the Creator was further emphasized by the doctrine that the world was created out of nothing (II Macc. 7:28; cf. Rom. 4:17; Heb. 11:3). It is doubtful, however, whether this teaching is found explicitly in Gen. 1 or anywhere else in the Old Testament for that matter. The statement in the book of Job that God "hangs the earth upon nothing" (Job 26:7) is poetic hyperbole, as the mythopoeic context shows.

The Genesis creation account opens with a statement that refers to God's transcendence of time and space and seems to point to an absolute beginning (Gen. 1:1). To be sure, there is some ambiguity in the Hebrew text which grammatically may be translated as a temporal clause that introduces a main sentence beginning with v. 2 or v. 3, as in some modern translations (e.g. The American Bible, The New English Bible, The Jewish Torah), or as a declarative sentence, as in the oldest translation (Septuagint) and most modern translations (e.g. Revised Standard Version, New International Version). A possible parallel with the Babylonian creation story, which begins with a temporal clause (*enuma elish*, "When on high. . .") makes it tempting to construe the first three verses as describing a temporal process. Stylistic and contextual considerations, however, favor the view that Genesis 1:1 is an independent sentence which serves as a preface to the entire creation account.[13] On this view, the story actually begins in v. 2 with a portrayal of uncreated chaos as the presupposition and background of God's creative work. The notion of creation out of nothing was undoubtedly too abstract for the Hebraic mind and, in any case, the idea of a created chaos would have been strange to a narrative which is governed by the view that creation is the antithesis to chaos (cf. Isa. 45:18).

The main intention of the writer is to emphasize the absolute sovereignty of God. There is not the slightest hint that God is bound or conditioned by chaos, as in the Babylonian *Enuma elish* myth, which portrays the birth of the gods out of the waters of chaos. Nor does God have the character of a demiurge who works with material that offers some resistance or imposes limitations (see IV below). On the contrary, God creates with perfect freedom by the commanding word—a view which is underscored by the use of the verb *bārā'*. In the Old Testament this verb is used exclusively of God's action and expresses the effortless divine creation which surpasses any human analogy such as the potter or the architect (cf. Pss. 51:10—H 51:12; 104:30; Isa. 43:1, 7, 15; 48:7). Since, however, this verb is used in connection with the verb *'āsā* (make) in Genesis 1:16-17, and elsewhere is linked with *yāsạr* (mold) as in Isaiah 43:1; 45:18, it was undoubtedly employed to support the view of creation by the Word, rather than creation *ex nihilo*.

The harmony and goodness of the creation.   God's creation is characterized by order. This order, however, is not that of Greek *kosmos*, harmonized by reason, but rather a divinely decreed order within which each creature fulfills the Creator's will. The Creator commands, and thereby not only brings a creature into being but also designates its peculiar nature and assigns to it a specific task. The heavenly bodies, e.g., are not independent deities who control human life, as was supposed in antiquity, but are servants of God whose appointed function is to designate the seasons and to separate the day and the night (Gen. 1:14-19). Earth is not just the fertile "Mother," from whose womb all life proceeds and to which it returns (Job 1:21; Ecclus. 40:1), but is God's creature who produces vegetation and animals at God's command (Gen. 1:11-12, 14-15). The idea of "nature" as an autonomous sphere governed by natural law or set in motion by a First Cause is not found in the Old Testament. The creator stands in personal relationship to the creation. It is the divine decree (*hōq*) that determines order (Job 38:33; Pss. 104:9; 148:6; Jer. 5:24; 31:35-36), and it can even be said that Yahweh has made a covenant with the day and the night (Jer. 33:20). At any moment the Creator could allow the creation to fall back into chaos, for God's continuing power is necessary to uphold and renew the creatures (Ps. 104:29-30). The regularities of nature, as expressed in the promise to Noah (Gen. 8:22; cf. 9:13-17), are expressions of Yahweh's covenant faithfulness.

When God looks upon the finished creation, seeing that each creature corresponds to the divine intention and fulfills its assigned function, the verdict is pronounced, "Very good" (Gen. 1:31). This is an esthetic judgment in the sense that in the view of the Cosmic Artist all creatures function perfectly in a marvellous whole which is without fault or blemish. The essential goodness of

God's creation is a recurring theme in Israel's praises. Yahweh's name (identity) is majestic throughout all the earth (Ps. 8:1—H 8:2), for those who have eyes to see may behold the Creator's handiwork, and those who have ears to hear may listen to an anthem of praise sung by all creatures (Ps. 19:1-4-H 19:2-5; Rom. 1:20). The creation faith demands a repudiation of all metaphysical dualism which leads one to suppose that the created world is evil and to seek a pathway of escape into a higher realm of pure Being. Likewise it calls for the surrender of ascetic practices, "for everything created by God is good, and nothing is to be rejected if it is received with thanksgiving" (I Tim. 4:4). The positive view of human life on earth, including bodily pleasures, is expressed admirably in Ps. 104, which climaxes with the prayer that God may "rejoice" in the manifold works of creation. This psalmist, whose poem is an exuberant commentary on the "very good" of the creation story, sees only one cloud that mars the beautiful picture: the human "wickedness" mentioned at the very end (Ps. 104:35). A similar observation prompted the Priestly redactors of the Pentateuch to supplement the Priestly creation story with the story of "Paradise Lost" (the so-called "Fall" of humanity; see "Threats of God's Creation" in Part III below).

Humanity's Position of Honor.   It is striking that in Psalm 104, which displays affinities with Genesis 1, both humans and animals are put on a level of equality in God's creation. The poet says that "all of them" (i.e. humans and animals, v. 27) depend upon the Creator for their livelihood and are animated by the divine *rûah* (spirit, breath) which renews them day by day in a *creatio continua* (vs. 27-30). On the other hand, the two creation stories affirm, although in different ways, that human beings are elevated to the highest place in God's earthly estate. In the old Epic (J) story the human being (*hā'ādām*) is formed from the ground (*hā'adāmā*) and must return to the ground at death (Gen. 2:7; 3:19). But the special status of humanity is symbolized by saying that *'ādām* was created first (contrary to the Priestly account), that a portion of the earth-wilderness was converted into a garden for human beings to tend and enjoy, and that the animals were created with a view toward providing human companionship. The special relation of the human being to God is symbolized by the animation of the human body with the divine breath (Gen. 2:7), and human superiority over the animals is indicated by the authority to give them names (2:20). Above all, *'ādām* is the creature who lives vis-à-vis God, and whose life is incomplete apart from the woman, the human person who stands vis-à-vis as a partner (2:18, 21-24; cf. the "male and female" of Gen. 1:27; 5:2).[14]

In the Priestly account the creation of humankind occurs at the climax of the creative drama. The plants and the animals stand in only an intermediate relation to God, for they are brought forth by the earth in response to the divine command (Gen. 1:11, 14). But the immediate relation of human beings to God is symbolized by a solemn decision, announced in the heavenly council: "Let us make humanity in our image, after our likeness" (1:26-27; cf. 5:1; 9:6). The anthropomorphism of this statement should not be toned down by attempting to define the "image of God" as something *in* the human body: "spiritual nature," "soul," "rationality," "freedom," "self-transcendence," etc. The application of the same language to Seth, a son in Adam's image (5:3; cf. v. 1), indicates that human beings, in their total bodily (psychosomatic) existence, are made in the image of the parent, although in Genesis 1:26-27 the immediate reference is probably to the divine beings (angels) who surround God in the celestial realm (cf. Ps. 8:5—H 8:6).

In Genesis 1, however, the intention is not to define the essence of humanity or the essence of God, but rather to indicate the task of human beings and their relationship to God. As God's living image on earth, human beings—"male and female"—are to act as God's representatives. They are drawn into God's cosmic administration as overseers of God's earthly estate. Hence the thought quickly moves from the "image" to the announcement that God has given human beings a special blessing and has commanded them to exercise dominion over the earth (1:28). Likewise in Psalm 8 the thought that human beings have been placed slightly below God (or reading with the Septuagint, "angels") is quickly followed by the thought that Yahweh has crowned them with royal rank and has put all things under their feet (Ps. 8:6-8—H 8:7-9). Human beings are to exercise sovereignty within God's sovereignty, so that all earthly creatures may be related to God through them and thus join in the creation's symphony of praise to the Creator.

God crowns human beings with glory and honor, not only by investing them with rulership in God's earthly empire, but also by singling them out for special concern. To the psalmist, the vastness of God's creation prompts the wondering query as to why the Creator chooses to notice and care for human persons, so insignificant and transient in the cosmos. (Ps. 8:3-4—H 8:4-5). Human beings are made to have fellowship with God. They are the only creatures who can answer God, either in defiance or in trust. Although all God's creatures are summoned to praise their Creator, human beings are the only earthlings in whom praise can become articulate. They are made for conversation with God, for a dialogue in an I-and-thou relation, and as Augustine remarked in his *Confessions*, they are restless until they find rest in God. According to Second Isaiah, Israel is Yahweh's "chosen people" — "the people whom I [Yahweh] formed for myself that they might declare my praise" (Isa. 43:21). Israel's calling is to vocalize the praise that wells up from all peoples and nations.

The Good Earth.   Israel's creation faith endorses a positive this-worldliness, one may even say a healthy materialism. For the natural world is the God-given habitat in which human beings are to find joy in the service of their Maker. Accordingly, the earth and all its resources are put at human disposal, not to exploit and ravish, but to explore, to enjoy, and to use within the limits of the wisdom that is based on the "fear [reverence] of Yahweh" (Job 28:28).

As mentioned previously, Israel was tempted to turn to a religious naturalism (the worship of Baal) to satisfy the needs of farmers who live close to the soil and are dependent on the earth's seasonal regularities. Prophets who criticized the people for yielding to the allurements of Canaanite religion, however, did not advocate a repudiation of earthly existence and a flight into an otherworldly faith. On the contrary, they were "down to earth" in their preaching. They only summoned the people to recognize that Yahweh, their liberating God, was the source of all earthly benefits. Jeremiah, for instance, speaks of the "land" (*'eretz*) as "Yahweh's land," "Yahweh's heritage" which the people have polluted with their false way of life (Jer. 2:7). Repentance, that is, turning away from false loyalties (spurious values), and clinging in faith to Yahweh, is the basis for human welfare on "the good earth." In the Mosaic tradition, as represented by the book of Deuteronomy, the people of Israel will be providentially ushered into "a good land, a land of brooks of water, of fountains and springs, flowing forth in valleys and hills, a land of wheat and barley, of vines and fig trees and pomegranates, a land of olive trees and honey, a land in which you will eat bread without scarcity, in which you will lack nothing, a land whose stones are iron, and out of whose hills you can dig copper" (Deut. 8:7-9). The one condition, however, is that the people must realize that "the good land," with all its resources, is God's gift—a gift which can be forfeited by false and irresponsible behavior.

Thus the doctrine of creation liberates from the alternatives between which human thought often moves: either the materialistic enjoyment of the natural world for its own sake, or the verdict that the world of change and decay is essentially meaningless. It is significant that prophetic portrayals of God's future are sketched, not in unearthly terms, but in terms of a transformed earth in which justice and peace will prevail (Mic. 4:1-4); cf. Isa. 2:2-4).

III. Beginning and End

Just as Israel traced a historical line back to the Creation, so she looked forward in hope toward the end when the Creator's purpose would finally be realized. The purpose of human history is grounded transcendentally in the will of the Creator who, in the language of Second Isaiah, is "the First and . . . the Last" (Isa. 44:6; 48:12). Creation is basically an eschatological doctrine in the sense that it has a future horizon. This is clear in the final Priestly edition of the primeval history in which the movement is from creation to the new beginning after the Flood. The opening words of Genesis, "In the beginning God," correspond to the prophetic expectation, "In the end God."

Threats to God's Creation.   Although the Creator's work was finished in the beginning (Gen. 2:1), the Bible also speaks of threats to God's creation which must be overcome before the divine purpose is finally realized.

The first threat is that of chaos. The Priestly creation story, which is influenced by the mythopoeic thought of the ancient world, portrays a creation out of chaos—the primeval waste and void (*tōhû wābōhû,*Gen. 1:2) and the darkness of the Deep or Abyss (*tehôm*). God's work of creation did not destroy the chaos and darkness but pushed them back, so to speak. Light was separated from the primeval uncreated darkness (vs. 3-5), a firmament separated the upper and lower waters (vs. 6-8), and the waters under the heaven were gathered together in one place so that the dry land might appear (vs. 9-10). According to this mythopoeic view, chaos surrounds the habitable world on every hand. We can best understand this portrayal as one which comes out of experience, rather than speculative, rationalistic inquiry. Ancient people knew existentially that human life is precarious and contingent;

it is suspended over the formless Abyss and hemmed in by the waters of chaos which threaten to engulf the world.

Chaos imagery recurs throughout the Old Testament, especially in poetic contexts. A psalmist affirms that the earth belongs to Yahweh who "has founded it upon the seas, and established it upon the rivers" (Ps. 24:2; cf. 136:6). God has made the firmament strong and assigned boundaries to the primeval sea (Job 38:8-11; Pss. 33:7; 104:7-9; Prov. 8:27-31; Jer. 5:22). Indeed, God watches over chaos (Job 7:12), and if the rebellious waters lift up, God rebukes them and they flee (Pss. 18:15—H 18:16; 77:16; 104:7).

Poets also affirm that God is victorious over the chaos monster, Rahab or Leviathan (Job 9:13; Pss. 74:13-14; 89:9-10—H 89:10-11), and commands the serpent that lurks in the subterranean depths of the sea (Amos 9:3). Chaos imagery figures prominently in apocalyptic literature, as illustrated by a passage from "the little apocalypse of Isaiah" (Isa. 24-27) which echoes ancient Canaanite (Ras Shamra) mythopoeic language: "In that day Yahweh with his hard and great and strong sword will punish Leviathan the fleeing serpent, Leviathan the twisting serpent, and he will slay the dragon that is in the sea" (Isa. 27:1, RSV). In the New Testament a seer declares that in the end time, when God's redemptive work is complete, the sea will be no more (Rev. 21:1) and there will be no more night (22:5). In the meantime, the Creator's work must continue. For unless God's power upholds the creation, the waters of chaos would sweep in and the earth would return to the precreation watery void, as at the time of the Flood (Gen. 7:11; 8:2). In a time of insecurity, when the very foundations of the world tremble and the earth seems about to lapse into the waters of chaos, people of faith confess that God alone is their refuge and strength (Ps. 46:1-3—H 46:2-4).

To Israel's prophets, the work of God is threatened especially by misused or misdirected human freedom (sin). Curiously, the view of a "fallen creation"—not only the "fall" of humankind but also the "fall" of heavenly beings (Gen. 6:1-4)—had little influence upon Old Testament tradition. In old Epic tradition (J), the story of human banishment from the Garden of Eden (Gen. 3) is intended as a background and preparation for the call of Israel, as personified in Abraham (Gen. 12:1-3). Neither the Priestly creation story nor the creation psalms (Pss. 8; 19; 33; 104) contain the somber note that "every imagination of the thoughts of the human heart was only evil continually" (Gen. 6:5). Although the Priestly version of the Flood portrays almost complete divine judgment upon the creation, owing to the spread of "violence" (Gen. 6:11-13), the creation still bears the signature of God, and the divine image is not effaced (cf. Gen. 9:6). But if the Old Testament is reticent to speak of a fallen creation, some of its prophets speak of Israel's fallen or perverted history, whether the tragedy is traced to the entrance into Canaan (Hosea, Jeremiah) or to the time of the people's beginning in Egypt (Ezekiel). Their diagnosis of Israel's sickness is not based upon a general teaching about human sinfulness, but upon the empirical reality of Israel's persistent blindness and rebellion as evident in her false lifestyle. Sin, it was said, is "unnatural," a mysterious fault that characterizes only the human heart (cf. Jer. 17:9). The animal knows its master, but Yahweh's children rebel against the One who nurtured them (Isa. 1:3)! The birds follow their homing instincts, but Israel does not know Yahweh's ordinance (Jer. 8:7)! Even the realm of nature, according to Hosea, has been affected by the corruption of Israel's sin (Hos. 4:3). In a moving poem Jeremiah envisions Yahweh's judgment falling so heavily upon the people that the earth is on the verge of returning to pre-creation chaos (Jer. 4:23-26; the language in v. 23 echoes Gen. 1:2).

From Jewish scripture the rabbis derived the view that the human heart is the arena of conflict and decision between two tendencies, the "evil impulse" and the "good impulse"(cf. Ecclus. 15:14-15). It remained for Christian interpreters to view historical tragedy in the dimension of a fallen creation. The way was prepared, however, especially in the apocalyptic circles of Judaism, by the myth of Satan's rebellion against the Creator and his fall from status within the heavenly council. Viewed in apocalyptic perspective, history is the scene of a cosmic struggle between God and Satan, the ruler of the present evil age, who seeks to establish a rival kingdom and to seduce human beings into his service. But even this view reflects an historical, rather than a metaphysical, dualism. Satan is not coeternal with God, but is a parasite on God's creation. His rule will last only as long as people are deceived by him; and in the last day, when God's victory is complete, he will be eliminated.[15]

The New Creation.   According to Israel's prophets, once divine judgment has been accomplished, God will make a new beginning, giving human beings a new heart (Ezek. 36:26-28) and bringing them into a new covenant relationship (Jer. 31:31-34; cf. Hos. 2:18-23—H 2:20-25). Not only will humankind enter a new history, but the nonhuman creatures, who are also embraced

within God's covenant (Gen. 9:8-17), will be quickened and transformed (Isa. 11:6-9; Hos. 2:18—H 2:20). Thus prophetic eschatology moves toward the vision of the new creation—"the new
heaven and the new earth" (Isa. 66:22)—which figured
prominently in apocalyptic theology of the postexilic period.

The theme of the new creation dominates the message of
Second Isaiah, who grasps profoundly the interrelation of creation
and history.[16] At one level of thought, Yahweh's power and wisdom
in creating heaven and earth are the ground for the proclamation
of divine redemption (Isa. 40:12-31; 42:5-9). At another level,
however, confidence in Yahweh, the cosmic Creator and King,
leads the prophet to announce that the new beginning in Israel's
history will be God's new act of creation. In a striking passage, he
interprets the old myth about the Creator's triumph over the chaos
monster in historical terms (51:9-11). The divine victory over
Rahab once occurred at the beginning of Israel's history, when Yahweh created Israel as a people (cf. 43:1). At that time Yahweh dried
up the waters of the "great deep" (*têhōm rabbā*), that is the
Reed Sea, so that the redeemed people could pass over (cf. Ps.
77:16-20—H 77:17-21). In prophetic imagination, this creative/re-
demptive event was the paradigm of the "new thing" that God
was about to do or create (see Isa. 43:18-21): a "new exodus of salvation" that Israel would experience and that would have saving
benefits for all nations and peoples. In the prophet's vision, even
nature would be marvellously transformed (41:17-20; 43:18-21) as
it is taken up into the new beginning in the history of God with
Israel and with the creation (a note sounded later by Paul in Rom.
8:19-23).

It is characteristic of eschatology that the visions of the end time
are drawn in terms of the pictures of the first things. Creation anticipates the consummation; and the consummation is the fulfilment of the beginning. The goal of history will be a return to the
beginning, not in the sense of a historical cycle which repeats
itself, but in the sense that the original intention of the Creator,
frustrated by creaturely rebellion and threatened by the insurgent
powers of chaos, will be realized.

IV. Creation Viewed Christologically

During the Hellenistic period (after the death of Alexander the
Great in 332 B.C.) the doctrine of creation was a cardinal tenet of
faith which distinguished Judaism from other religions and philosophies. The early Greek translation of Israel's Scriptures known

as the Septuagint avoided using the Greek verb *demiourgeo* with respect to God's creative action, owing to its association with the idea of a worker who manufactures or produces things out of previously existing material. The Creator is not the demiurge of Gnostic thought. The translators chose instead other verbs, especially *ktizo* which express the absolute sovereignty of God. The New Testament likewise avoids using *demiourgeo* (although the substantive form occurs in Heb. 11:10) and prefers *ktizo* and its derivatives. The Christian faith is at one with Judaism in affirming that God alone and by the sovereign Word created the world and determines its purpose from beginning to end. Frequent reference is made to the original creation (Mark 10:6 = Matt. 19:4; Mark 13:19 = Matt. 24:21; Rom. 1:20; II Pet. 3:4) or to that which happened "from the foundation of the world" (Matt. 25:34; Luke 11:50; John 17:24; Eph. 1:4; Heb. 4:3; I Pet. 1:20; etc.). The apocalyptic vision of the Creator enthroned in glory, while many creatures raise their voices in praise (Rev. 4-5), vividly expresses God's sovereignty over the whole course of history.

Christ and Creation. Just as in the Old Testament creation is viewed in the perspective of Israel's covenant faith, so in the New Testament the church understands creation christologically—i.e. in the light of God's action in Jesus Christ, who is the fulfilment of Israel's sacred history and the inaugurator of the New Covenant. Since Christ is the center of history, he is also the revelation of God's purpose which undergirds the whole creation. The unity of creation is not disclosed in a rational principle but in God's purpose "which he set forth in Christ as a plan for the fullness of time, to unite all things in him, things in heaven and things on earth" (Eph. 1:9-10). In Christ all things cohere or "hold together" (Col. 1:17) and, indeed, he "upholds" the universe by his word of power (Heb. 1:3). He is the bearer of the meaning of history and creation. Therefore, people of faith, convinced of the decisive character of God's action in Jesus Christ, could confess that human salvation was predestined in Christ before the foundation of the world (Matt. 25:34; Eph. 1:4; I Pet. 1:20; Rev. 13:8; 17:8).

By making use of the notion of pre-existence, an important further step was taken in Pauline and Johannine circles: God created the world through Christ. The Old Testament background for this view is the conception of Wisdom as the first product of God's creative work. Israel's sages not only declared that wisdom is one of the supreme traits of God, but they also regarded "her"[17] as the form of God's creative activity and, indeed, the personal agent of the Creator (Job 28:12-17; Prov. 8:12-36). Thus their thought moved in the direction of hypostatizing Wisdom (Wisd. Sol. 7:22-8:1). Furthermore, the doctrine of creation by the Word (see II above) was the decisive line of theological thought in the Old Testament. These two views—pre-existent, creative Wisdom and creation by the Word—converge in the Prologue to the Fourth Gospel, which declares that the redeeming Christ is none other than the Logos of creation (John 1:1-18; cf. I John 1:1-3; 2:13-14).

By his juxtaposition of the prepositions "from" and "through," Paul makes a similar affirmation. There is one God "*from* whom are all things and for whom we exist," even as there is one Lord, Jesus Christ, "*through* whom are all things and *through* whom we exist" (I Cor. 8:6). A deutero-Pauline writer says of Christ that "in him all things were created, in heaven and on earth," for he is "the image of the invisible God, the first-born of all creation" (Col. 1:15-17; similar language is found in Heb. 1:2-3). Everything has its center in Christ, through whom God creates, upholds, and redeems the world.

The doctrine of creation, then, underlines and validates the truth that history, from beginning to end, is under the sovereign purpose of God as revealed in Jesus Christ. The Fourth Gospel begins by echoing the opening words of Genesis: "In the beginning" and speaks about the light shining in darkness (cf. II Cor. 4:6). And even as Christ was in the beginning, so he will triumph at the end (I Cor. 15:24-28; Revelation). Indeed, the very title which Second Isaiah applied to God is ascribed in the book of Revelation to Christ: he is "the Alpha and the Omega," "the first and the last," "the beginning and the end" (Rev. 1:17; 22:13; cf. 3:14). The whole sweep of history, from creation to the new heaven and the new earth, has its fulcrum in him.

The New Creation in Christ.   The heart of the New Testament gospel is the proclamation that in Christ, the Kingdom of God has already been inaugurated, the New Age anticipated by Old Testament prophets has already been introduced. Echoing the message of Second Isaiah, the New Testament declares that the new creation has already begun. At the same time, however, the new creation is a promise and foretaste of the end time, when there will be a new heaven and a new earth, free from the corruption of evil and death (Rev. 21:1-4), and when all creatures in heaven and earth will join in an anthem of praise to the Creator (Rev. 4:8-11;

5:13). Wherever God's action in Christ is effective for human salvation, God is creatively at work, after the manner of the original
creation. Thus Paul, commenting on the transformed life of
persons of faith, exclaims that God's redemptive deed is nothing
less than a new act of creation: "For it is the God who said [at the
dawn of creation, Gen. 1:3], 'Let light shine out of darkness,' who
has shone in our hearts to give the light of knowledge of the glory
of God in the face of Christ" (II Cor. 4:6). In another context Paul
declares that the new life of faith has its source in the grace of God
who creates *ex nihilo* by calling into existence the things that do
not exist (Rom. 4:17).

The light of God's new creation, however, breaks forth in the
darkness, which is the essence of the "world" (John 1:5, 10; 3:19;
8:12; 12:35-36, 46; I John 1:5-6; 2:8-9, 11). In both Pauline and
Johannine writings *kosmos* occasionally designates the world as
God's creation (e.g. John 17:4; Rom. 1:20; Phil. 2:15), but usually
it means the historical sphere—not only the earthly stage of
human history, but the context of social relationships in which
persons live and move and have their being. In the latter sense, the
kosmos is a fallen world, for it is characterized by enmity to God
and lies under the dominion of evil powers (John 12:31; 16:11; I
Cor. 1:21; Gal. 4:9; I John 5:19; etc.). Moreover, Paul goes so far as
to say that the whole created order, affected by human sin, groans
under the bondage of corruption, waiting eagerly for the creative
and redemptive act that will reveal the children of God (Rom.
8:19-23). But the promise of the coming redemption, not only of
humanity in the fullest sense but of the whole creation as well, has
already been given to those who receive the "first fruits of the
Spirit." Through Christ, God has already won the decisive victory
over the world, and thereby has initiated a new history, a new
humanity. To be "in Christ" is to be "a new creature," for "the old
has passed away, behold, the new has come" (II Cor. 5:17; cf. Gal.
6:15). And this newness is manifest in a new way of viewing people
(II Cor. 5:16-17) and in a community where old barriers have been
broken down and there is unity in Christ (Gal. 3:28; 6:15).

In Jesus Christ, then, God has restored the human pattern intended at the original creation. He is the *'ādām*, of whom Adam
was a foreshadowing type (Rom. 5:12-14; cf. I Cor. 15:21-22). He is
the "likeness of God" (II Cor. 4:4) and the "image of the invisible
God, the first-born of all creation" (Col. 1:15)—this language
recalls the "image of God" of Gen. 1:26, just as Heb. 2:5-9 interprets the "man" who is "crowned with glory and honor" (Ps.

8:4-6) christologically. He is the beginning of the new humanity into which any person may be born, not through biological parentage, but by free decision in response to divine grace. To be sure, the old human nature (*'ādām,*) lives on, the flesh wars against the Spirit, the world presents its temptations and frustrations; but the new has come and the old is passing away, for "we all, with unveiled face, beholding the glory of the Lord, are being charged into his likeness from one degree of glory to another" (II Cor. 3:18). Through Christ, says a deutero-Pauline writer, persons may put on the "new nature, which is being renewed in knowledge after the image of its creator" (Col. 3:10; cf. Eph. 4:24). The new person, "created in Christ" (Eph. 2:10, 15), lives in a new relation to God and therefore in a new relation to fellow human beings. Humankind, separated by dividing walls of hostility, is reunited by God's reconciling action in Christ (Eph. 2:11-22) and people begin to walk in "newness of life" (Rom. 6:4). The new community, which is "in Christ," is a frontier of the New Age, indeed, "a new creation" (Gal. 6:15), in which separating barriers are being broken down; for "there is neither Jew nor Greek, there is neither slave nor free, there is neither male nor female; for you are all one in Christ Jesus" (Gal. 3:28; cf. Rom. 11:6).

Thus the Christian community, from the standpoint of faith given by God's revelation in Christ, looks both backward and forward. It traces God's purpose to the first creation, saying: "In Christ all things were created;" and it lives toward the future, saying: "God will sum up all things in Christ." The full disclosure of the new creation lies in God's future, when the New Age will fully come and there will be a "a new heaven and a new earth." Even as the dramatic story of Genesis 1 is not a scientific account of the origin of the universe, so the poetic visions of Revelation are not a speculative projection into the future. The truth of both is perceived by those who participate in the new creation in Christ and who know in faith that the whole span of history, from beginning to end, is embraced within the sovereign purpose of the Creator and Redeemer.[18]

Notes

1. See Hermann Gunkel, "The Influence of Babylonian Mythology Upon the Biblical Creation Story," trans. Charles A. Muenchow, in Bernhard W. Anderson, ed., *Creation in the Old Testament* (Philadelphia:

Fortress Press, 1984), 25-52; also Anderson, *Creation versus Chaos: The Reinterpretation of Mythical Symbolism in the Bible* (New York: Association Press, 1967), Chap. 1.

2. This is the view of W. F. Albright and his students; see Frank M. Cross's new interpretation in *Canaanite Myth and Hebrew Epic* (Cambridge: Harvard Univ. Press, 1973), 60-75.

3. See Frank M. Cross, "The Song of the Sea and Canaanite Myth," in *Canaanite Myth and Hebrew Epic*, 112-44.

4. Ancient poetic texts are discussed by Dennis J. McCarthy, S.J., "Creation Motifs in Ancient Hebrew Poetry," CBQ 29 (1967), 393-406; revised edition included in *Creation in the Old Testament* (cited above), 74-89.

5. Gerhard von Rad, "The Theological Problem of the Old Testament Doctrine of Creation," in *The Problem of the Hexateuch and Other Essays*, trans. E. W. T. Dicken (New York: McGraw-Hill, 1966), 131-43; included in *Creation in the Old Testament* (cited above), 53-65.

6. See further my essay, "Mythopoeic and Theological Dimensions of Biblical Creation Faith," in *Creation in the Old Testament*, 1-24, especially 7-11.

7. See Hans-Jürgen Hermisson, "Creation Theology in Wisdom," *Israelite Wisdom*, essays in honor of Samuel Terrien, ed. J. G. Gammie *et al.* (Missoula, Mont.: Scholars Press, 1978), 43-57. Included in *Creation in the Old Testament*, 118-34.

8. The covenantal context is discussed further in my essay, "Creation and the Noachic Covenant," in this volume. For fuller discussion, see "Creation and Ecology," in *Creation in the Old Testament*, 252-71.

9. These "root experiences" are discussed illuminatingly by Emil Fackenheim, *God's Presence in History: Jewish Affirmations and Philosophical Reflections* (New York: Harper and Row, 1970), especially chap. 1.

10. Mircea Eliade, *Cosmos and History, The Myth of the Eternal Return* (New York: Harper Torchbook, 1954).

11. On this motif, see "The Earth is the Lord's: An Essay on the Biblical Doctrine of Creation," revised edition of my 1955 essay (*Interpretation* 9:3-20) in Roland M. Frye, ed., *Is God a Creationist? The Religious Case Against Creation-Science* (New York: Scribners, 1983), 176-196.

12. The Egyptian text is found in *Ancient Near Eastern Texts Relating to the Old Testament* (Princeton, N.J.: Princeton Univ. Press, 1955), "The Theology of Memphis," 4-6

13. See Walther Eichrodt, "In the Beginning: A Contribution to the Interpretation of the First Word of the Bible," in *Israel's Prophetic Heritage*, essays honoring James Muilenburg, ed. B.W. Anderson and Walter Harrelson (New York: Harper & Row, 1962), 1-10; reprinted in *Creation in the Old Testament*, 65-73. The case is presented on stylistic grounds in my essay, "A Stylistic Study of the Priestly

Creation Story," in *Canon and Authority,* ed. G. W. Coats and B. O. Long (Philadelphia: Fortress Press, 1977), 148-62.

14. On the relation between "man" and "woman" in the creation stories, see Phyllis Trible, *God and the Rhetoric of Sexuality* (Philadelphia: Fortress Press, 1978), "The Topical Clue," 12-13, and "A Love Story Gone Awry," 72-143, A different hermeneutical slant is provided by Phyllis Bird, "Male and Female He Created Them: Gen. 1:27b in the Context of the P Account of Creation," *Harvard Theological Review* 74 (1981),, 129-59.

15. On the myth of Satan, see further Bernhard W. Anderson, *Creation versus Chaos,* chap. 5, especially 160-170.

16. Under the stimulus of Gerhard von Rad's seminal essay (referred to above, n. 5), numerous essays on creation theology in Second Isaiah have appeared. The central theological issue is posed in P.B. Harner, "Creation Faith in Deutero-Isaiah," *Vetus Testamentum* 17 (1967),298-306.

17. In Hebrew "wisdom" (*hokmā*) is feminine, and in the book of Proverbs is personified as a woman who speaks prophetically to human beings (Prov. 1:20-33).

18. An extensive bibliography on the subject of the biblical doctrine of creation is provided at the end of *Creation in the Old Testament,* 172-178.

Chapter Two

CREATION AND THE NOACHIC COVENANT

Bernhard W. Anderson

The superb forty-sixth psalm, which was the basis of Martin Luther's well-known hymn of the Reformation, contains a line that rings with both unshakable trust and ominous foreboding. Right after the affirmation that God is a "mighty fortress," "a bulwark never failing," as Luther paraphrases, comes the confession in the familiar King James Version:

Therefore will not we fear, though the earth be removed,
and though the mountains be carried into the midst of the sea.

This poet's contemplation of the ominous possibility that the earth will undergo such profound changes that chaos will return finds a sympathetic response in our technological world. Gradually it is dawning upon us that the earth's resources are not inexhaustible, and that we cannot continue the exploitation of our natural environment much longer without suffering nature's severe backlash. Furthermore, modern technology, conscripted for military service, has brought about a historical crisis in which nuclear disaster could reduce the earth, or large portions of it, to a radioactive wasteland. As this essay is being written many people in various parts of the world, awakened to this frightening possibility, are demonstrating against the nuclear arms race.

The crisis, of which scientists are often more aware than theologians and practitioners of religion,[1] is totally inclusive: it affects humanity, nonhuman forms of life, and the good earth itself. Inevitably people raise the question: who or what is to blame for this unprecedented ecological crisis? In a celebrated essay Lynn White, Jr. ventured to say that the Judeo-Christian tradition bears "a huge burden of guilt" for having espoused a view of creation which places humanity at the peak of God's creation and endows it with dominion over the earth. He even nominated St. Francis of

Assisi, "the greatest spiritual revolutionary in Western history," to
be the patron saint of the ecological cause, for in vain "he tried to
substitute the idea of the equality of all creatures, including man,
for the idea of man's limitless rule of creation."[2] Since, however,
the Bible is inevitably read and interpreted in a particular social
location, it makes more sense to trace the roots of the crisis to the
economic and political revolution that marked the transition from
medieval life to the modern age. At one point Karl Marx could
express reserved appreciation for capitalism which introduced a
sharp dichotomy between human beings and their natural
environment.

> Nature becomes for the first time simply an object for mankind,
> purely a matter of utility; it ceases to be recognized as a power in its
> own right; and the theoretical knowledge of its independent laws
> appears only as a stratagem designed to subdue it to human require-
> ments, whether as the object of consumption or as the means of
> production.[3]

Given the sociological matrix of biblical exegesis, it is understandable that in the new age dominated by technology and free enterprise many people have turned to the Bible to find warrants for the
new way of life which some nations, especially the United States,
now enjoy to the full.

In any event, the time has come to seek liberation from a "root
metaphor" that is mechanistic and technological to regain an
artistic appreciation of creation and the dwelling of human and
nonhuman beings in it.[4] If this is to happen, we will also have to be
liberated from a literalistic (and hence rationalistic) view of the
biblical creation tradition, which in the past has led to unnecessary conflict between science and religion, as in the recent controversy over "creationism." The rediscovery and refurbishing of
the biblical creation tradition can only take place if we reject a
hermeneutic which accommodates to a rationalistic, technological world and instead cultivate an artistic, poetic appreciation of
the creation story. Viewed as story or narrative, the creation tradition opens up new horizons of ecological, ethical, and philo-
sophical/theological understanding.

I. Creation and Covenant

To begin with, the story of creation found in Genesis 1:1-2:3
belongs to and functions within a larger narrative context, the so-
called Primeval History [Story] set forth in the opening chapters

of Genesis (Gen. 1-11). It may be, as some scholars maintain, that the creation story once circulated independently and served as a liturgical reading for a religious festival, perhaps the celebration of the New Year. Whatever its prehistory, the literary piece has been placed within a scriptural setting. Its meaning is dependent upon its function in the larger setting of the Torah which has been given to us in final form by so-called Priestly redactors. Too often, the creation story has been torn out of its native scriptural context and has been used as a warrant for ethical or philosophical views arrived at on other grounds. This "modern use of the Bible" should be avoided. The basic interpretive rule is: read the creation story in its own narrative context.

When the creation tradition is read in this manner, it is clear that creation belongs to a "story" or "history" that moves dramatically from the "first things" to a universal, ecological crisis; from creation "in the beginning" to the Flood in the days of Noah—and beyond. The literary and theological correspondences between the creation story and the flood story, both of which come from Priestly writers in their final form, are striking.[5] It is instructive to read the key theological passages, Genesis 1 and Genesis 9:1-17, side by side, so that the connections may be sensed. According to the Priestly creation story, the habitable earth was created out of chaos—the watery, turbulent abyss portrayed in Genesis 1:2; in the corresponding story the flood (*mabbul*, a technical term for cosmic waters) is portrayed as a cosmic catastrophe that threatened to return the earth to watery chaos. Genesis 1 portrays the Creator making a living-space for humans and animals by pushing back the waters so that the dry land may appear; correspondingly, the flood story portrays the renewal of the earth when God caused a wind (8:1; cf. the "Wind of God" in Gen. 1:2) to blow over the chaotic waters with the result that the dry land appeared and the earth began to green again. Moreover, both stories emphasize the God-given blessing upon human-kind and the commission to have dominion over the earth. Indeed, the blessing upon Noah and his descendents, "Be fertile, multiply, and fill the earth" (9:1, 7), is linguistically the same as the blessing given at creation (1:28). Also, the motif of the *imago Dei*, which appears in both stories (1:26-27 and 9:5b-6), provides an important link of continuity. There are numerous other linguistic affinities between the two passages which become evident when one studies them carefully, especially in the original language. Clearly the Priestly tradent intends that the two should be taken together, as the obverse and reverse of the same coin. The covenant between the Creator and Noah, with which the flood story culminates, is the narrative goal that is in view. The story starts with the creation of the habitable earth out of chaos; it moves to a cosmic catastrophe in which the earth was on the verge of returning to pre-creation chaos; and it reaches a climax with the new beginning, indeed, the new creation based on the Creator's covenant pledge which opens a future for human beings, animals and birds, and the whole earth.

When the creation story is interpreted contextually, several matters leap to attention. First, the Creator's purpose is to provide living space for a great variety of living beings. Stylistically the creative drama is composed in two movements, in each of which the movement is from heaven to earth (*'eretz*, a word that stands in the emphatic position in the prologue to the creative acts, 1:2).[6] The first movement, consisting of four creative acts in three days, culminates in the greening of the earth with vegetation (Gen. 1:3-13). The second movement, likewise consisting of four creative acts in three days, reaches a climax in the appearance of earth-creatures, animals and humans (1:14-27). The wonderful order and regularity of the cosmos, in which every creature, animate and inanimate, has its assigned place and function in a marvelous whole, evokes esthetic feelings of wonder and reverence. Indeed, the narrator observes that the Creator, like a cosmic artist, surveyed the symmetry and design of the completed work and perceived it to be *tob me'od*, "very good" (1:31). The beauty of the earth, however, lies primarily in its functional value. The story intends to show that the Creator's purpose is to provide the earth, and its surrounding cosmic environment, as a well-ordered and well-furnished habitat for living beings to appear and flourish. The Creator's activity is directed toward order, not chaos. This theme would have had special appeal in the period of the Exile, when the Priestly Torah was given its final literary shape. Speaking to a people in exile, who were threatened with the powers of meaninglessness and chaos, an Exilic prophet proclaimed that Yahweh, the God of Israel,

> who created the heavens (he is God!),
> who formed the earth and made it (he established it!),

"did not create it [the earth] a chaos, but formed it to be inhabited," and did not say to people "seek me in chaos" (Isa. 45:18-19). The earth, then, is a God-given habitat, an *oikos* ("house")—to use the Greek word from which our word "ecology" is derived—designed for use by living beings.

Second, the story shows that the earth is created as a habitat for both human and nonhuman creatures equally. The emphasis falls, not so much on anthropology, as on ecology, that is, the earthly habitation which human beings share with other forms of "living beings" (*nefesh hayya*). It is striking that the creation account applies the expression "living being," not to the vegetation which greens the earth at the end of the first movement of the creative drama, but to the new forms that appear in the second movement. The reader senses that something radically new appears in the case of the water-beings (fish, sea monsters) and the flying creatures that soar over the waters (birds, winged creatures). For the first time in the story, these creatures are called "living beings" (*nefesh hayya*, Gen. 1:20), and this novelty is signalled by a special divine blessing which grants dominion to these creatures in their medium of water or air (1:22). The narrator's climactic interest, however, is reserved for the *nefesh hayya* created on the sixth day: the animals according to their species (*min*, "kind"; see 1:24-25) and the supreme earthling known as *'adam*, human being, humanity (1:26-27). Even though th story reaches its climax in the creation of *'adam*, and reserves the divine blessing for this earth-creature, the narrator shows in various ways that animals and humans belong together and share a common "house." For one thing, it is significant that, according to the dramatic sequence, animals and humans are created on the same day, a subtle literary indication of affinity. Moreover, at the conclusion of the story we read that animals and human beings are to share the same table: the vegetation provided in the first movement of the creation drama (1:29-30). Indeed, it should be noted that the Creator initiated a "peaceable kingdom" in which there was no violence, not even the killing of animals. When the narrative moves from creation to flood, again we find that humans and animals share the same "house," the ark or houseboat in which all living beings according to their species huddle together to escape the waters of chaos. To be sure, God's special favor is bestowed upon Noah, who is the representative ancestor of humankind according to ethnic groupings. But with a fine literary touch the narrator portrays the animals turning to Noah, as though led by their native attraction to human beings, in the face of catastrophe.

> Two by two they came to Noah into the ark, male and female,
>   Just as God commanded Noah.   (Gen. 7:9)

The fish, of course, are not mentioned because they live in another habitat and, in any case, are not threatened by water. This picture of a remnant of animals, birds, and human beings living together in a house that tosses on the cosmic waters of chaos (the *mabbul*), is not far removed theologically from Paul's testimony in the New Testament that the non-human creation longs to share with humankind the redemption from "the bondage of corruption" (Rom. 8:19-23).

Third—and this has already been anticipated—when the creation story is read in its scriptural context it becomes clear that the whole of creation is embraced within God's covenant. In the Priestly scheme that governs the Torah in its final form, the genealogical movement from creation through the times of primeval and ancestral history and on to the Sinai sojourn is periodized into a sequence of covenants.[7] Three major periods, from creation to Noah, from Noah to Abraham, from Abraham to Moses are concluded with a covenant, each of which is characterized as a *berith 'olam*, an "everlasting covenant" or covenant in perpetuity. The first period, the one with which we are concerned here, culminated in the Noachic covenant, the covenant in perpetuity between the Creator and Noah along with his sons, who are regarded as the ancestors of the major ethnic groupings that populated the earth. This covenant, it should be noticed, is anticipated at the opening of the Priestly flood story (Gen. 6:18) and is actualized at the conclusion (9:8-17), thereby forming a literary and theological *inclusio* that unifies and rounds off the story. Notice that this covenant not only includes all humankind, for—as we have seen—Noah and his wife are regarded as the ancestor and ancestress of all peoples that dwell on earth (cf. 10:1), but it embraces "every living being of all flesh" (6:19), that is, all creatures that are regarded as *nefesh hayya*, "living being." We read:

> Then God said to Noah and his sons who were with him:
> "As for me, I am establishing my covenant with you,
>   and with your posterity to come,
> and with every living being with you—
> the birds and the animals and all the wild beasts
> that are with you,
> all that came out of the ark..." (Gen. 9:8-10)[8]

The Noachic covenant, then, is universal in the widest sense imaginable. It is fundamentally an ecological covenant that includes not only human beings everywhere but all animals—"every living being [*nefesh hayya*] of all flesh that is upon the earth'' (9:16, repeating what was said in 6:19). Furthermore, this covenant includes the earth itself, for it is based on a solemn divine pledge never again to disturb the constancy of "nature" so radically that pre-creation chaos almost returns. In this regard the Priestly narrator has built upon old Epic tradition which included a poetic passage:

> Throughout all the days of the earth,
>> seedtime and harvest,
>> cold and heat,
>> summer and winter,
>> day and night,
> Shall never cease.   (Gen. 8:22)

The regularities of "nature," then, are not based on the mechanical laws of an autonomous self-contained system (a "cosmos" in the Greek sense) but are the constancies that express the Creator's covenant faithfulness. Living beings flourish in an environment that is dependable and trustworthy because, as a prophetic interpreter puts it, God has established "a covenant with day and night and the orders of heaven and earth" (Jer. 33:25).

II. The Creator's Covenant Commitment

So far we have seen that the creation story belongs to a larger narrative which reaches its theological climax with the Noachic covenant and that, in this narrative perspective, creation is embraced within covenant. The word "covenant," of course, symbolizes commitment of one party to another. What is the nature of God's commitment to the creation?

Earlier we noticed that the Noachic covenant, according to the Priestly scheme that governs the Torah, is classified as an "everlasting covenant" (*berith 'olam*) or covenant in perpetuity. This is a different type of covenant than the Mosaic covenant as interpreted by Deuteronomic theologians who have given us the book of Deuteronomy and have edited the history work extending from Joshua through II Kings (the so-called Deuteronomic History). The Deuteronomic covenant is one in which a party is bound to the covenant maker who imposes conditions and sanctions (blessings for obedience, curses for disobedience). It is a covenant of grace, to be sure, that is initiated by a powerful party who extends help and protection to the weaker one, but it is a reciprocal relationship and, above all, is conditional upon faithfulness to legal stipulations. The Priestly covenant, however, is one in which God is bound by God's own commitment, regardless of the actions of the covenant recipient.[9] To be sure, legal obligations are given in the Noachic covenant, as we shall see, but the permanence of the covenant is based upon the unconditional commitment of God to the human and nonhuman creation, for better or for worse. Hope for the future, in this view, does not rest upon human performance or improvement, a weak reed on which to lean since human beings do not seem to change, a somber note that was struck in the old Epic flood tradition (Gen. 8:21) and which reverberates in today's wars and rumors of wars.[10] Rather, hope is based on God's absolute commitment to the creation.

The Creator's unconditional commitment to the creation, according to the biblical narrative, is made in the face of violence that threatens the earth with chaos. The Priestly recension of the flood story begins with the solemn announcement:

> Now, the earth was corrupt before God,
>   the earth was filled with violence,
> God saw how corrupt the earth was,
>   ·for all flesh had corrupted its way on the earth.
>   (Gen. 6:11-12)

In the narrator's view the world-wide catastrophe of the flood was not unmotivated, nor was it a capricious natural calamity (an "act of God" in the sense of modern insurance policies). Rather, violence had so marred and corrupted the earth that God's judgment came for the purpose of cleansing the earth and making a new beginning.

We read that "all flesh" had corrupted its style of life and that "through them the earth is filled with violence" (6:13). In Priestly vocabulary the expression "all flesh" refers to all that is fleshly, including birds, animals, humans, as in God's resolution "to exterminate all flesh under heaven that has the spirit of life" (6:17) or God's final vow to "remember the everlasting covenant between God and every living being of all flesh that is upon the earth" (9:16). The language suggests that violence is a disease, as it were, that contaminates all those beings, human and nonhuman, that live in the same earthly *oikos*. A lifestyle based on violence, as we well know today, cannot be contained or confined. Violence affects human beings, it permeates the nonhuman realm of animals, birds, and fish; it pollutes the earthly environment. We are dealing here with the problem of power—power that corrupts.

Although the story indicates that violence corrupted "all flesh," that is, the human and the nonhuman creation, there is no suggestion that violence is rooted in "nature," the nonhuman creation. In the natural realm, of course, there is tremendous violence: "nature red in tooth and claw"; earthquake, wind, and fire; disease, plague, and pestilence. Indeed, according to a modern view of nature, violence (power) belongs essentially to the evolutionary process in which the fittest struggle to survive. In the biblical narrative, however, the violent face of nature receives virtually no attention. Even the flood itself, which may be reminiscent of a natural calamity caused by the rampaging waters of the Tigris and Euphrates rivers, is not recounted to illustrate natural evil but to symbolize narratively the severity of God's judgment. Furthermore, the biblical narrative provides not the slightest hint that animals were driven by their predatory instincts into conflict with human beings for living space and for survival. Indeed, as we have seen, the picture presented in the creation story is that of a paradisaic peace in which humans and animals live together and share earth's resources. The biblical story makes the reader face one uncomfortable truth: the violence that corrupted "all flesh" is traced to the noblest creatures of God's creation, those whom God elevated to the highest position of honor and responsibility.

Here we cannot go into the details of the dramatic biblical story as it unfolds from creation to flood. Suffice it to say that the Priestly tradent, who has given us the Primeval History in its received form, shows what violence is by including illustrative episodes from old Epic tradition. Violence is shown by the story of the Garden of Eden: a human couple who, desiring to be like God, rebel against their Creator and, in doing so, disrupt their relationship with each other and to the soil from which they were taken and to which they return (Gen. 2:4b-3:24). Violence is shown by the story of Cain who polluted the earth with the blood of his murdered brother (4:1-16). Violence is shown by Lamech, the ancestor of those who originated civilized skills (agriculture, music, metallurgy), whose lust for power prompted him to boast of measureless revenge (4:17-24). And violence is shown by that strange story which almost defies understanding, about the heavenly beings, the "sons of God," who breached the Creator's distinction between heaven and earth and seized and had intercourse with beautiful human maidens (6:1-4). These episodes are only illustrations taken from a much wider human tradition that could easily be extended into the present. Enough illustrations are given, however, to show that the problem of violence is rooted in the misuse of God-given freedom, that this perversity is manifest especially in humankind's exercise of power, and that the corruption of power spreads from the human to the nonhuman sphere, so that it may be said of "all flesh" that "through them the earth is filled with violence" (Gen. 6:13).

The total sweep of the biblical story from the original beginning to the new beginning after the flood brings before the reader an important dimension of the biblical doctrine of creation, namely, that the "deed/consequence" syndrome belongs not only to the social order but to the creation, and that the created order cannot be violated without severe consequences which, in religious perception, signify the judgment of God.[11] The flood story vividly portrays the paradox of human culpability and divine judgment. On one hand human beings bring upon themselves catastrophe by their false lifestyle and violent ways; yet, on the other, this consequence is seen to be the judgment of God. The prophet Jeremiah also dealt with this paradox of human freedom and divine sovereignty. Catastrophe, he proclaimed, is indeed the consequence of human actions. "Have you not done this to yourself," he asked, "by forsaking Yahweh your God?" (Jer. 2:17). Yet he could also perceive the consequences of human action to be the judgment of God, a backlash so severe that, as in the case of the flood story, the earth seemed to be on the verge of returning to pre-creation chaos. His poetic vision is not alien to the experience of many modern people.

> I looked upon the earth, and lo, chaotic waste [*tohu wa-bohu*],
>   and unto the heavens, and their light was gone.
> I looked on the mountains, and lo, they were quaking,
>   and all the hills were trembling.
> I looked, and lo, there was no human being,
>   and all the birds of the air had vanished.
> I looked, and lo, the fertile land was wilderness,
>   before Yahweh, before his fierce indignation.
>   (Jer. 4:23-26)

A commentator on the Revised Standard Version translation of this poem appropriately remarks at this point: "As if struck by a mighty nuclear bomb, the earth has been returned to its primeval state: waste and void," the *tohu wa-bohu* portrayed in Gen. 1:2.[12]

The biblical storytellers and poets are realists, not dreamers. As the biblical story shows, human beings do have the terrible power to pollute the earth with their lifestyle. They do have the capacity for violence to the degree that the earth is threatened with a return to chaos. This is the precarious possibility of human history. Nevertheless, and this "nevertheless" is characteristic of the Noachic covenant, the Creator remains unconditionally committed to the creation, and moves history from chaos toward a new age, indeed, a new creation in which the relations between human beings, nonhuman creatures, and their environment will be reordered. The rainbow, which is the sign of the new age of God's covenant promise, has an ambivalent poetic meaning. In one sense, the rainbow is a natural phenomenon, visible after a storm as a sign of the dawning of a new day. In another sense, the bow symbolizes a weapon of war, which God has, so to speak, laid aside as a sign of peace. One of my students has put it very well: "By this act of unilateral divine disarmament, God casts judgment on the arrogant and petty violence of man and woman, of which the *Ur*-history (and beyond) provides numerous examples."[13]

III. Human Responsibility within the Noachic Covenant

The biblical story, then, moves toward a new age and a new humanity, of which Noah is the representative. The final question is: what is the role of humanity within the Creator's covenant with creation? We have already seen that in one sense there is equality between human beings and nonhuman creatures. Both are *nefesh hayya*, living being; both share the same earthly habitat; both depend upon earth's regularities and resources. Yet equality of status before God does not mean equality of position and responsibility. To quote the well-known words from George Orwell's *Animal Farm*, "All animals are equal, but some animals are more equal than others." In the biblical story, the being who is "more equal" than other earth-creatures is '*adam*, "human being" consisting bisexually of "male and female." The creation story, articulated into two movements, reaches a dramatic climax with God's resolution (Gen. 1:26):

> Let us make '*adam* [humanity] in our image,
>   after our likeness,
> and let them have dominion over the fish of the sea,
>   over the birds of the air,
>   over the cattle and over all wild beasts,[14]
>   and over all crawling things that move on the earth.

The special status of *'adam* is also a special commission. For no sooner is the divine intention realized in a creative act than a divine blessing empowers man and woman, who together share the divine image.

> Be fertile, multiply,
>> Fill the earth and subdue it!
> Rule over the fish of the sea,
>> over the birds of the air,
>> and over every living creature that moves on the earth.
>>>>> (Gen. 1:28)

As we have seen previously, this theme of the creation story is recapitulated at the climax of the Primeval History, when the earth emerges from the waters of chaos and a new creation dawns. At this juncture the divine blessing upon humanity is repeated in practically the same language (9:1, 7; cf. 1:28), and once again the truth is underscored that *'adam*, made in the image of God, has a special status and function in God's creation (9:6; cf. 1:26-27).

The expressions "image of God" and "likeness of God" occur only in the Priestly recension of the Primeval History (but cf. Isa. 40:18). This is not the place for an extended discussion of these terms; suffice it to say that they intend to affirm that *'adam* is created to be God's representative on earth, just as a child represents the parent on a family estate.[15] A helpful parallel is found in ancient Babylonian and Egyptian texts which describe the king in similar language. For instance, in an Egyptian text the deity addresses Pharaoh Amenhophis III as follows:

> "You are my beloved Son, produced from my members, my image which I have established on the earth. I have made you to rule the earth in peace."[16]

Here the emphasis is on the king's role in the royal office, his function *ex officio*. Analogously, in the biblical texts the image is not something *in* human nature (reason, will, conscience, immortal soul, etc.) but it refers to the role of *'adam*, consisting of male and female, in their bodily, historical being. Viewed in this perspective, *'adam* is not an autonomous being, at liberty to rule the earth arbitrarily or violently. On the contrary, human dominion is to be exercised wisely and benevolently so that God's dominion over the earth may be manifest in human action. In his commentary on the book of Genesis, the Old Testament theologian Gerhard von Rad writes:

> Just as powerful earthly kings, to indicate their claim to dominion, erect an image of themselves in the provinces of their empire where they do not personally appear, so man is placed upon earth in God's image as God's sovereign emblem. He is really only God's represent- ative, summoned to maintain and enforce God's claim to dominion over the earth. The decisive thing about man's similarity to God, therefore, is his function in the non-human world.[17]

Humanity did not forfeit or lose this God-given role in the period "after the Fall," to use the language of Christian theology. To be sure, the new creation after the flood was not just a repetition of the original creation. The narrator shows that the new creation bears the marks of tragedy owing to the misuse of human freedom and the spread of violence. Therefore, there must be a reordering of relations between the human and nonhuman creation which contrasts with the peaceable kingdom that prevailed at first. This reordering is spelled out in a passage which comes between the *inclusio* of 9:1 and 9:7 where the divine blessing given at creation is renewed. Here we find that animals, who once lived in harmony with humans, are now overcome with "fear and dread" of human dominion; and they are regarded as rivals and predators who are to be held responsible for the blood of *'adam* (9:2-5a). Further- more, human beings, to whom the earth was given to manage as children inherit a parental estate, are now at such odds with one another that a strict, apodictic law, predicated on the *imago Dei*, has to be issued against murder (9:5b-6; cf. Lev. 24:17). Neverthe- less, even in this new situation, in which may be heard the "groan- ing of creation" (cf. Rom. 8:22-23), human beings do not cease to be who they are: creatures who are made in the image of God and who are therefore called to the high responsibility of representing or "imaging" God's rule on earth.

Notice that in this new situation a new word is spoken which contrasts with the even-handed treatment of humans and animals at the time of creation (1:29-30). The new word of God is: "Into your power they are given" (9:2, end of verse); "I give you every- thing" 9:3, end of verse). This extension of human dominion, how- ever, is immediately qualified by two heavy restrictions, each of which is introduced by an emphatic particle (Hebrew: *'ak*, "only," "however," at the beginning of verse 4 and 5). First, there is a prohibition against eating animal flesh with its blood. Meat may be eaten only if an animal is properly slaughtered, for blood is regarded as sacred to God. The life of any *nefesh hayya* is precious, not because it has value in itself but because of its relation to the

Creator. And second, there is a prohibition against the violent shedding of human blood on the ground that 'adam is made in the image of God. Both animals and humans are held responsible before God for the taking of human life.

Thus human beings are reminded in the strongest terms, precisely at the time when their dominion over the nonhuman creation is extended, that their power is not absolute but is subject to the judgment of God. Indeed, the Noachic covenant demands a reverence for life, for every *nefesh*, animal or human, has value by virtue of its relation to God. It may well be, as some have suggested, that in our time, when meat has become a necessary staple for many human beings, some way must be found to express reverence toward animals, consonant with the demand of the Noachic covenant. For, as the creation story shows, animals also have a place, along with human beings, in the *oikos* that God has created and furnished, and they have value in relation to the Creator. Above all, the Noachic covenant demands respect for the sanctity of human life. Each person, each human *nefesh* is precious, not because of intrinsic value but because of the Creator's relation to and claim upon human life as expressed in the *imago Dei*. The Noachic covenant has far-reaching ethical implications, especially in our time when many people have become inured to violence and when indiscriminate bloodshed can mount to genocide. It is inconceivable that a nuclear holocaust, in which multitudes of human beings would be vaporized and the remainder subjected to the torture of slow, agonizing death, could be squared with the permissions and prohibitions of the Noachic covenant.

In summary, the Noachic covenant endorses the call to human responsibility that is inherent within the creation story. To be sure, hope for the future is not grounded in human ability or human wisdom, for the biblical story, both in old Epic tradition and the Priestly reworking of that tradition, shows that there is a stubborn perversity in human nature (see Gen. 6:5 and 8:21). Nevertheless, God is committed irrevocably and unconditionally to the creation, and God's will and purpose is that there should be order, not chaos on the earth. Human beings, created in the image of God, are commissioned to represent God's will for *shalom* (peace, well-being, harmony) on earth.

The biblical story, as far as we have traced it in the so-called primeval history, is unfinished. The story unfolds into a continuing history, an open-ended future in which God not only upholds the order of creation but continues to work creatively in the history that takes place on earth. God, who created in the beginning, creates the "new thing." The prophet of the exile, so-called Second Isaiah, announced that one should not even look backward but forward, for Yahweh does the *Novum*.

Don't remember the beginning things,
 the things of old don't consider!
Behold, I am going to make something new;
 now it sprouts up, don't you perceive it?
(Isaiah 43:18-19a)

Within the spacious horizons of the Noachic covenant, to which this prophet also refers in exquisite poetry (Isa. 54:9-10), the future is not closed, but open. Standing under the rainbow arch of God's promise, whose source is lost to human view at both the beginning and the end, human beings are called to responsibility as God's representatives. Indeed, they are summoned to participate actively in God's continuing creation.[18]

Notes

1. An issue of the *Boston Globe* (Jan. 14, 1981) announced that the "Doomsday Clock," created by the Educational Foundation for Nuclear Science in Chicago, was moved to four minutes to midnight because "as the year 1980 drew to a close, the world moved inexorably closer to nuclear disaster." Reportedly this clock has been ticking ominously on the cover of *The Bulletin of the Atomic Scientists* since 1947 and has been moved up or back slightly, depending on political developments.
2. Lynn White, Jr., "The Historical Roots of Our Ecological Crisis," *Science* 155 (1967): 1203-07; reprinted in *The Environmental Handbook*, ed. Garrett de Bell (New York: Ballantine Books, 1970), pp. 12-26. For a biblical-theological response to this thesis, see my essay "Human Dominion over Nature," *Biblical Studies in Contemporary Thought*, ed. Miriam Ward, R.S.M. (1975), pp. 27-45.
3. Quoted by Spencer Pollard in his review of Marx's *Grundrisse*, *Saturday Review* (August 7, 1971), p. 27.
4. See Gibson Winter's provocative book, *Liberating Creation: Foundations of Religious Social Ethics* (New York: Crossroad, 1981), where this challenge is set forth forcefully.
5. "Story" and "history," both covered by one word in some languages (as in German *Geschichte*), are closely related. Here I cannot go into the question of whether or how far "historical" elements are present in, e.g., the flood story.

6. The literary pattern is worked out in detail in my essay, "A Stylistic Study of the Priestly Creation Story," *Canon and Authority* (Philadephia: Fortress Press, 1977), ed. by G. W. Coats and B. O. Long, pp. 148-162.

7. See Frank M. Cross, "The Priestly Work," in *Canaanite Myth and Hebrew Epic* (Cambridge: Harvard Press, 1978), pp. 293-325. This matter is elaborated in my essay, "From Analysis to Synthesis: The Interpretation of Gen. 1-11," *Journal of Biblical Literature* 97 (1978): 23-29.

8. At the end of the verses quoted, where I have placed some dots, the received Hebrew text adds the phrase "every beast of the earth," thus stressing the involvement of nonhuman creatures in the Noachic covenant. The repetitious phrase, however, is lacking in the Greek translation of the Old Testament (Septuagint) and has probably crept into the text by scribal error.

9. For a discussion of these two kinds of covenant, see George E. Mendenhall, "Covenant," *Interpreter's Dictionary of the Bible* I (New York: Abingdon, 1962). He distinguishes between covenants in which God is bound and covenants in which the people are bound.

10. "Surrender in the Falklands," according to an editorial in the *Boston Globe* (June 16, 1982), "ends a war that demonstrated that even in this nuclear age men don't change, that on the tiniest speck of land in the most remote part of the earth armies can battle for the most contrived and anachronistic reasons of national honor and for the basest reasons of domestic politics."

11. This is the thesis of Hans Heinrich Schmid in his essay, "Schöpfung, Gerechtigkeit und Heil," *Zeitschrift für Theologie und Kirche* 70/1 (197): 1-19. By concentrating on this dimension of creation he is able to claim that "creation theology" is the full, encompassing horizon of biblical theology.

12. *The New Oxford Annotated Bible* (1973) on Jer. 4:23-26. The commentator is Victor R. Gold.

13. Hugh J. Matlack, a Th.M. student at Princeton Theological Seminary, in an essay on Genesis 9:1-17, Spring 1982.

14. The received text reads here "and over all the earth." The notion of *dominium terrae* certainly fits the context, but at this point the text requires an animal sequence, not a general reference. Accordingly, following the Syriac, I read here "all wild beasts."

15. The same language is found in the Priestly genealogy in Genesis ch. 5 where it is said that Adam fathered a son "in his own likeness, after his image" (5:1). Here the idea is not just physical resemblance. The son, as the heir, not only looks like but acts like the father.

16. Cited and discussed in my essay, "Human Dominion over Nature, *loc. cit.*, pp. 41-42.

17. Gerhard von Rad, *Genesis,* rev. ed. (Philadelphia: Westminster, 1972).

18. Elements of this essay have been derived from my paper, "Creation and Ecology: The Relation between the Human and the Nonhuman Creation in the Biblical Primeval History," published in *The American Journal of Theology and Philosophy* (forthcoming).

Chapter Three

ENVIRONMENT AS SPIRITUAL HORIZON
The Legacy of Celtic Monasticism

Richard Woods, O.P.

As the second millenium after Christ draws to its end, apocalyptic visions of desperate proportions appearing in scientific journals and political predictions have begun to equal if not surpass the jeremiads that in the Christian West traditionally presage the termination of centuries and especially of millenia.[1] But a technological rather than theological doom now clouds our horizon, arising, first of all, from the menacing possibility of thermonuclear war and its wake of "nuclear winter"—with the consequent destruction of most of the living systems on earth. Only marginally less cataclysmic are spectral projections for the coming decades of worldwide famine, industrial devastation of the planet's environment, rapid dissipation of energy resources and increasing global economic deterioration.[2]

Western civilization and American culture in particular have entered upon a threshhold situation. Undeniably positive aspects beckon toward a future bright with the promise of developing global awareness and the possibility of a true world community sharing what John Dewey called a common faith. Poised on the edge of space and the exploration of the universe, humankind has become conscious of its potential to develop as a whole—or not at all.

Whether the human race realizes this potential or falls victim to the unprecedented destructiveness of modern war and civil conflict, material lack, spiritual need, and environmental deterioration depends largely on the success or failure of creative imagination, that is, the power to envision alternatives.

A Search for Paradigms

It is understandable, perhaps inevitable and surely wise at such a juncture of possible destinies to scour the past for similar situations, hoping to glean examples, paradigms, and models of response that can enable us to endure and even flourish. We want to know why we are where we are now in history and what that means.

In one such effort, the Italian economist and philosopher Roberto Vacca described the transition period we are now entering as a "Dark Age," a period of decline optimally heralding a new renaissance of civilization. In remarkably prescient terms, he maintained that if the world manages to avoid the terminal conflagration feared by a growing number of scientists and other observers of the world situation, the West will still require a host of widespread "conservers of civilization and catalysts of a future renaissance" in order to survive the deeper crisis, now only in its early stages. Looking back more than a millenium to the first age dubbed "dark" by Renaissance writers impatient for a return to the glory of classical Rome, Vacca proposed for this role a new kind of monasticism modeled on the Celtic institutions which preserved the learning and culture of the West from the 5th to the 10th centuries.[3]

The Monastic Heritage

At first glance a new form of monasticism seems a rather bland if not inept agency for coping with Western civilization's present and future crises, particularly with regard to environmental problems. The negativity of early Christian attitudes toward nature and Christianity's historical culpability for environmental deterioration have been acknowledged by some for over a decade, often to the particular detriment of patristic and monkish approaches.

However, a turning point occurred in this regard as a result of the "debate" between René Dubos and Lynn White, Jr. concerning the differences between the Benedictine ideal of stewardship and the Franciscan ideal of conservation.[4] Regrettably, much of the discussion rested on a superficial acquaintance with both traditions.[5] But recent scholarship has also shown that the patristic bias against nature alleged by E. R. Dodds, among others, represented a one-sided consideration of the relevant literature.[6] Thus, the judgment that Christian theologians of the first millenium set a tone which culminated in wanton destruction of the environment abetted by the Church in later years now appears to have been at least premature.[7]

On the contrary, a reappropriation of certain patristic and monastic values could do much to offset present and especially future Christian complicity in the rape of the natural world. This is especially true with regard to the legacy of Celtic monastic spirituality, which even more than the Benedictine tradition revered nature as a divine theophany and for almost a thousand years lived in peaceful harmony with the living environment as a whole.

Through Fall and Decline: The Early Patristic Period

Christianity emerged from the era of persecution and its understandably fledgling and apologetic efforts to construct a theology out of its primitive faith into what E. R. Dodds accurately described as an age of anxiety.[8] Constantine's Edict of Toleration in 313 came at the onset of the very real decline and fall not only of the Roman half of the Empire, but with that, much of the culture and civilization of the West.

In 331, Constantine removed the seat of the Roman Empire to the Greek city of Byzantium which he renamed after himself. A decade later, the Empire was formally divided between Constans in the West and Constantius II in the East. Beginning scarcely a decade afterwards and lasting until approximately 950, Europe was subjected in every quarter to waves of recurrent invasion by barbarian tribes—Huns, Picts, Goths, Saxons, Franks, Slavs, Magyars, Lombards, Vikings—and, eventually, the armies of Islam. The Eastern Emperor Valens was himself killed in 378 battling the Visigoths in Thrace.

By 383, the legions began to be withdrawn from Britain to defend central and southern Europe. The Visigoths nevertheless invaded Italy under Alaric in 401 and sacked Rome itself nine years later. St. Augustine's mournful *City of God* was in effect written by the light of flames. And perhaps only in that ruddy glow can Augustine's bitter struggle with the humanistic theology of the Celtic expatriate Pelagius truly be understood. For to many the place, value, and purpose of both the human person and society were suddenly neither clear nor a matter of mere speculation. All that was again a matter of survival as well as faith.

In 455 the Vandals again sacked the Holy City. Finally, in 476 the last Roman Emperor of the West, Romulus Augustulus, whose diminutive name adequately reflects his historical importance, was simply deposed by Odoacer. He was not considered significant enough to be executed.

Although the Roman Empire crumbled, Byzantium proved impregnable, if sometimes barely so, to both barbarians and Islam for an additional millenium. And while the lamp of learning grew dim or was all but extinguished in the Latin West, Eastern Christianity entered upon a luminous age of theological speculation and spiritual growth.

Theophany: Nature in Theology and Praxis

As it had been for every preceding generation, nature was still the primordial "given" in the ordinary experience of the early Christians of both East and West—the uncontrollable, most often unpredictable, inescapable, mysterious, and sometimes hostile context of all personal and social life, religion, and commerce. The world of nature could neither be taken for granted nor, interpreted as the creation of a benevolent God, be despised. What is surprising in an era of classical philosophical distrust of nature is the highly positive light in which nature was regarded by Greek theologians and mystagogues. Indeed, for them like the Jews of old, nature was in belief and fact a revelation of that good and loving Presence, not merely a material product of God's creative activity.

What then of the pall of pessimism that Dodds saw hanging over the accomplishments of the Alexandrian theologians and desert monks, the world-weariness wont to disparage the natural as well as the social world as transient, feeble, and prone to decay? Their mysticism, we are told, while often acute, was otherworldly, embued with a Platonic longing for an ideal realm of pure ideas and spiritual essences, far removed from the material exigencies of the phenomenal world and even the body. Dodds observes, ". . . St. Anthony blushed every time he had to eat or satisfy any other bodily function. Because the body's life was the soul's death, salvation lay in mortifying it; as a Desert Father expressed it, 'I am killing it because it is killing me.' "[9]

That the early Fathers generally entertained a grim view of the natural world has been, as mentioned above, a common assumption. Dodds describes their contribution succinctly as "the progressive devaluation of the cosmos in the early Christian centuries (in other words, the progressive withdrawal of divinity from the material world), and the corresponding devaluation of ordinary human experience."[10]

Such an interpretation is, however, so one-sided as to become erroneous, especially when attributed to the Greek theologians in general. D. S. Wallace-Hadrill has recently demonstrated in opposition to Dodds' view that clearly "to many of the Greek fathers the world appeared interesting, enjoyable and important. . . ."[11] The major theologians of the first four centuries tended as a whole to "exhibit an interest in the structure of the physical world and its inhabitants which in many cases amounts to fascination."[12]

Among the subject areas observed and studied by the Greek Fathers were cosmology, astronomy, meteorology, botany, horticulture, zoology, human anatomy, physiology, and medicine. Basil and Nemesius even seem to have undergone medical training.[13] Gregory of Nyssa and Basil the Great were "filled with wonder" at the stars, planets, and comets.[14] "Even the abyss, says Basil, contributes to the praise which the whole universe offers to God."[15] It was not nature, but the sometimes exaggerated claims of science that they doubted.

Further, despite ascetical excesses on the part of some of the early hermits, early theological writers such as Irenaeus, Origen, Athenagoras, and Theodoret generally express a positive attitude toward the human body. Even Clement of Alexandria, "for all his severe moral demands, insists that God is the creator of man's body, 'flesh and marrow, bones, nerves, veins, blood, skin, eyes, *pneuma*, righteousness, immortality.' "[16] And, as Wallace-Hadrill observes, "The emphasis upon the wholeness of man consisting in the union of body and soul receives its most forceful and consistent expression in the unanimity of the Greek Fathers on the resurrection of the body."[17]

Nor in their study of nature were the Greek theologians engaged in detached, merely scholarly investigation. Citing a host of texts from Clement of Alexandria, Origen, Gregory of Nyssa, Gregory of Nazianzus, Cyril of Jerusalem, and Basil, Wallace-Hadrill concludes: "If it is true that the Greek fathers displayed deep interest in the natural world, it is equally true that they enjoyed it."[18]

But again like the Jews before them from whom they took their model and inspiration, the early theologians avoided any suggestion of pantheism while displaying a fundamentally mystical attitude toward creation: "The Greek fathers, for all their intense appreciation of nature, for all their interest in the structures and processes of nature and their insistence upon nature as a means by which God reveals his nature, nevertheless hold that God and nature are not identical, and that the mind must penetrate nature to find God."[19]

Thus, as the visible manifestation of the creative presence and power of God, to the Greek theologians nature was fundamentally a system of theophanies. A lasting tenet of Eastern theology passed over scantingly by the Western Fathers, this mystical view of nature would nevertheless find a positive echo in the great philosophical and theological system of the Irish scholar John Scottus four centuries later. And although Scottus derived his teaching from a study of Gregory of Nyssa and Maximus the Confessor, it is by no means absent, as we shall see, from the poetic spirituality of his Celtic forebears.

The Phenomenon of Monasticism

The religious response to the disintegration of sacred and secular culture varied in fifth century Europe much as it does today. Among this variety, the most noticeable, enduring, and constructive innovation was the development of monasticism. Its origins are to be found in the previous century among the desert saints of Egypt such as Anthony and Pachomius, and perhaps as far back as first century Jewish mystics, if Philo's description of the Therapeutae refers to historical fact.[20] Its Eastern roots help explain not only the early monks' practical attitude toward nature, but also their theological interpretation of creation. In fact, St. Basil, John Cassian, St. Augustine, and Cassiodorus themselves founded orders of monks. Many others flowered in Africa, Palestine, and Gaul, as we learn from the descriptions of Cassian. None, however, ever enjoyed the preeminence of the Order founded by St. Benedict of Nursia about the year 525.

Benedictine Monasticism

The historian Sir Richard Southern aptly observed, "Any account of medieval religious Orders must begin with the Order of St. Benedict. Not only is it the first of the great western Orders in time, but it held the field almost alone for several hundred years. . . ."[21] Incidentally, it is to this first, primitive phase of Benedictine history, with its comparatively simple and ecologically constructive intent, that Professor Dubos' favorable remarks most accurately pertain.

By the fifth century, the ecology of the late Roman Empire had been stretched to the breaking point by the increased demands of steady expansion. Deforestation and overgrazing had long since taken their heavy toll. Large estates had swallowed up most farms; tilth was under maximum cultivation. Barbarian invaders were held back only by dint of greater taxation and forced labor. And although a greater agricultural work force was needed to offset increased food requirements for the army and civil bureaucracy, the birth rate in fact began to decline. Incessant warfare accelerated the death rate, largely through the consequences of famine and disease. Even the climate worsened.[22]

Finally, although a series of "pestilences" had intermittently ravaged parts of the Empire since the end of the second century A.D., a devastating epidemic of bubonic plague erupted in the middle of the sixth century. It first appeared in Constantinople in 542 and quickly spread West. In 547 it reached Britain and in 590, Rome. By 594, it had halved the population of Europe, a global calamity unsurpassed until the Black Death of 1347.

The retraction of the Empire and its eventual capitulation to the barbarian populations pressing against the frontiers did not retard the sharp decline of already overburdened land and resources. The more primitive slash-and-burn agrarian techniques employed by the victorious *pagani* merely extended the damage.[23] Marsh, swamp, and forest began to reclaim the fields that once fed an Empire. Into this worsening, even desperate situation the thrust of Benedictine spiritual and agricultural reform brought new life and hope.

But despite its auspicious beginnings at Monte Cassino, recurrent invasions, plague, and the vicissitudes of time brought the history of early Benedictine monasticism to a close by the end of the eighth century. During the Carolingian renaissance of the ninth and tenth centuries the Order was virtually refounded. In increasing contrast to the primitive Order, the Carolingian monastic ideal was now "a mixture of the *Rule for Monks (Regula monachorum)* composed by Benedict of Nursia in the sixth century; the Cassiodoran view (from the same period) of the monastery as a bastion of erudition; Germanic notions of authority in which princely and spiritual powers were closely linked; and a hierocratic vision of society, based on function, that exalted the liturgical role of the monks and thus placed them well above the peasants who had the task of working the monastic lands."[24]

Many European kings established, patronized, and richly endowed Benedictine abbeys for religious as well as political reasons. In turn, they were often entombed there. Little observes that "More numerous than the kings were the dukes, counts, and other high-ranking nobles who built, protected, prayed in, retired to, and were buried in the new and renewed monasteries."[25] As a result, the monasteries grew rich and powerful, accumulating both treasure and land.

With land came rights—to fishing, as well as "rights over mills, houses, bakeries, animals, servile labour, and churches (with their tithes). Monasteries assumed or were given franchises for conducting fairs. Norman and Anglo-Saxon monasteries provided knights for ducal and royal armies respectively. Not least important was the jurisdiction that so often accompanied the land."[26] And thus, "in region after region the monastic order was one of the principal landlords."[27]

Franciscans, Dominicans, and other mendicant Orders of the high Middle Ages were hardly immune to the lure of wealth, property, and power despite the clear intentions of their founders, pre-eminently St. Francis.[28] In terms of landownership, wealth, and power, however, the Benedictines knew no equal. Their estate steadily expanded along with the wealth and power of the great abbeys—Montecassino, Nonantola, Farfa in Sabina, Subiaco in Latium, Saint-Martin of Tours, Cluny in Burgundy, Saint-Martial of Limoges, Reichenau, and, later, Battle Abbey, Canterbury, and Glastonbury. Many monasteries also had urban holdings.[29]

By the eve of the Protestant Reformation, the Order was in many respects spiritually moribund and from an environmental perspective a despoiler rather than conserver of the land.[30] But in fact Benedictine spiritualiy was by no means the only significant monastic influence between the fall of the Empire and the Reformation.

Celtic Monasticism: The Forgotten Tradition

It is perhaps typical of Anglo-Saxon and Frankish historians to pass over the only form of monasticism old enough, strong enough, and large enough to rival the Order of St. Benedict, which had indeed supplanted it by the thirteenth century. Not the least reason for such slight treatment concerns the particular ways in which Celtic monasticism differs from other Western forms. To appreciate these differences, and the lasting contribution of Celtic monasticism, it is necessary to consider something of the Celtic way of life itself.

The first mention of the "Keltoi" is by Greek historians of the sixth century describing a welter of Aryan peoples sharing a family of languages rooted in a lost ancestral tongue remotely related to Greek.[31] Perhaps significantly for understanding Celtic character, McNeill observes that "Plato mentions them in a list of nations addicted to drunkenness, and Aristotle notes their reckless indifference to danger, even of earthquakes and raging seas."[32]

They were pastoral and nomadic peoples, less given to agriculture than to heroic exploit, horsemanship, and the celebration of life in song and story. Closely attuned to nature, they developed a lasting affinity to the sun, water, and animals, aspects of which figure prominently in the character of their religious consciousness—both pre-Christian and Christian.

The Spirit of Celtic Christianity

By the beginning of the Christian era, continental Celtic tribes had established themselves in Spain and Gaul, while British and Irish tribes and the outlandish Picts settled in the islands at the northwestern edge of the world. The "Celtic Church" itself began in the obscurity of the second, possibly even the first century and lasted a thousand years, ending officially with the Synod of Kells in 1152 after the Norman invasion of Ireland. At the time of its final absorption into full Anglo-Roman character, the British Church was nearly one thousand years older than any Protestant denomination today and almost as venerable as any patriarchate of East or West. To the medieval imagination, the ancient origins of the Church in Britain were suitably expressed in the legend, ancient itself, that the faith had arrived there in the person of Joseph of Arimathea.[33]

The withdrawal of the legions from Britain in 410 left that largely Christian realm open to increasing attack from pagan Irish, Saxon, and Pictish pirates, severely weakening the long-standing ties of cultural and civil society. The Christian Church was the sole institution left to preserve the vestiges of civilization. Then, in 476, with the deposition of the Emperor, the Western Empire came to its inglorious end. The Western Church, too, began a long winter of organizational and especially administrative decline, not least because it had availed itself of the legal and governmental structures and even the territorial divisions of the empire. (The term *diocese* itself originally referred to an administrative unit of civil government.[34]) Providentially, there had already appeared a new spiritual force only provisionally indebted to the imperial model.

Irish Christianity and its Monasticism

There were Christians in Ireland and possibly even bishops before Palladius and Patrick came. But there was as yet no recognizable church. Even Patrick's mission, following the brief and largely failed attempt by Palladius in 431, was not an immediate success. But, assisted by several companions, probably monks ordained and functioning as secular clergy, he eventually managed to win sufficient converts to organize a stable organization. He set up Roman diocesan structures in fact, including a hierarchy of bishops, priests, and deacons.[35] He did not found monasteries. Nevertheless, within a century, the dominant form of Irish and British Christianity was not diocesan but monastic in form, and its spirituality was familial, personal, and democratic rather than curial, legal, and republican. As an extension of Celtic tribal society, it was also inescapably political.[36]

For almost six hundred years, the monastic movement virtually typified Celtic spirituality as a whole, largely because the Celtic form of monasticism, with its close-knit, almost tribal character more closely resembled the ordinary life of the people. Unlike Benedictine monasticism, especially in its later form, there was little if any trace of aristocratic distinction between the monks and the lay members of the monasteries or even those outside.

Even more than Benedictine monasticism, the Celtic form was decentralized, pluralistic, and loosely organized. More like settlements or small villages, many monasteries admitted both men and women, married lay persons as well as celibates, and a variety of support personnel. Many abbots were married, and leadership was often handed down through families for generations.

At the height of their development in the eighth and ninth centuries, Celtic monasteries extended from Iceland to Italy. The lifestyle tended to be coenobitical, that is, the monks lived in separate cells or huts but participated in common prayer, meals, and other functions. However, there was also a tendency among the more austere ascetics to become hermits in the strict sense, separating from others to undergo what came to be called "the green martyrdom," living in remote, isolated places alone with God.

This quest for an intense, self-sacrificing form of testimony was further expressed by the "white martyrdom," voluntary exile and death in an alien land out of love for the homeless Christ. In its extreme form, the white martyrdom meant a life of perpetual pilgrimage.

Lives of the Celtic Saints

Great saints appeared at the beginning, during its flowering, and even during the decline of the Celtic Church: Ninnian, David, Winifred, Illtyd, Patrick, Brigid, Ita, Brendan, Kevin, Columcille,

Columban, Malachy and hundreds more. There exists a surprisingly considerable body of hagiographical lore concerning these early British and Irish figures. Although largely compiled in the middle ages, most of the source material is of far greater antiquity.[37] While their intention was to edify and sometimes to establish property rights and lines of religious authority, the Lives also indirectly provide valuable historical information about the times, places and persons of the time they were written.[38] They also supply a vast amount of information about the character and attitudes of the Celtic Christians, particularly for present purposes concerning the natural world.

Excepting the "Confession" of St. Patrick, which is not a "life" in the hagiographical sense of later accounts, the earliest of these is probably Cogitosus' Life of Brigid, written about 650.[39] Brigid's harmony with nature is an important theme in the Life, not least because of her connection in the popular mind with the pagan goddess of the same name. As Hughes observes, "She can hang her cloak on a sunbeam, the wood supporting the altar at which she kneels when taking the veil burgeons into life."[40]

Patrick

Muirchú's Life of Patrick,[41] written shortly after 680 and found in the Book of Armagh, understandably dwells less on nature themes than political issues, although the ground has already been tilled for later extrapolations, particularly concerning the saint's confrontation with the druids, in works such as the tenth-century Tripartite Life. In that, for instance, has been interpolated the much older Lorica, long attributed to Patrick but probably not from his own hand. There we find him praying,

> I arise today
> Through the strength of heaven:
> Light of the sun,
> Radiance of moon,
> Splendor of fire,
> Speed of lightning,
> Swiftness of wind,
> Depth of sea,
> Stability of earth,
> Firmness of rock.[42]

The ancient and charming "Rune of St. Patrick" contains even more explicit references to nature, on which, like heaven itself, the saint calls in his hour of need:

Tara today in this fateful hour
I place all heaven with its power,
and the sun with its brightness,
and the snow with its whiteness,
and fire with all the strength it hath,
and lightning with its rapid wrath,
and the winds with their swiftness along their path,
and the sea with its deepness,
and the rocks with their steepness,
and the earth with its starkness;
all these I place,
by God's almighty help and grace,
between myself and the powers of darkness.[43]

Muirchú's Life includes the following story, which greatly resembles episodes from later saints' lives illustrating their tender attitude toward animals: when Patrick had been given land by King Daire for his residence, they went to inspect it. "...and they climbed up to that high ground and found a hind with her little fawn lying on the spot where now there is the altar of the North church in Armagh. And Patrick's companions wanted to take hold of the fawn and kill it, but the saint refused and did not allow it; indeed the saint himself took the fawn, carrying it on his shoulders; and the hind followed him like a very gentle, docile ewe, till he had let the fawn go free in another wood lying to the north side of Armagh, where the knowledgeable say there are some signs remaining to this day of his miraculous power."[44]

Animal Friends

Plummer considered that the great love for and importance of nature attributed to the Irish saints represented a continuation of pre-Christian Celtic nature-worship. Whatever its provenance, such a sensibility is pervasive. Some anecdotes are almost certainly based on fact, particularly the accounts of the saints' ordinary animal companions. Other features of early Irish hagiography clearly appear to depend upon ancient religious symbolism and folklore, their insertion functioning to locate the Christian saints within the accepted protocols of religious authority.

Many of the Celtic saints attracted animal companions, whether domestic or wild. Sea otters, for instance, were seen to have helped warm the saint's feet after Aiden's strenuous bouts of prayer submerged to his chin in the icy waters of the North Sea. Columban was known to have acquired a host of wild friends.

Plummer cites a charming instance in the life of Ciaran of Saigir "with his woodland monks, brother Fox, and the rest. And the story how the Fox stole his abbot's shoes, and the badger, as being skilled in woodcraft, was sent to fetch him back, and how brother Fox asked forgiveness and did penance by fasting is one of the most delightful things in hagiographical literature. Often does the saint interpose to save a hunted animal from its pursuers, or renders fierce animals tame, or feeds starving wolves out of the herds which he tends."[45]

Other wild animals that are helpful and friendly to the saints include stags, does, seals, and wild boars.[46] More "conventional" pets are also important in the lives of the Irish saints.[47] Plummer concludes,

> apart from all mythological and magical associations there seems evidence that the early and medieval Irish were really lovers of animals, and that the saints shared this quality to the full. The benevolence of Ciaran of Clonmacnois embraced the whole irrational creation, the little bird lamented Molua who 'never had worked the woe of living thing.' The same Molua had a tame partridge, Cronan a tame stag, Moling a tame fox. Cainnech inflicted a terrible penance on a woman for cruelty to a dog. The swans on Killarney come at the call of Cainnach, and those on Lough Foyle at the call of Comgall. Swans carry Columba of Terryglass from island to island, or sing to Colman Ela and his monks to console them at their work; and sea birds wing their flight to save a drowning child. Wild animals would gather round the hermit saints as they have done round many an Indian ascetic in earlier and later times. Even the blackbird that built on St. Coemgen's outstretched hand, or the wren that nested in St. Malo's cowl could probably be paralleled from the annals of Indian asceticism. We may well believe many of these things to be true, without supposing them to be miraculous; though we may agree with the spirit of Bede's remark, that the more faithfully man obeys the creator, the more he will regain his lost empire over the creature.[48]

Power over Nature

Other elements of nature figure importantly in the saints' Lives, their power over them, or, rather, powerful sympathy *with* them manifesting their sanctity as well as their unmistakably national identity. Prominent among these elements are those particularly sacred to the ancient Celts.

The sea, rivers, lakes, fountains, and wells are responsive to the saints' presence and command.[49] Their association with trees is clearly reminiscent of the sacred trees of pagan Celts:

> In many ways the trees do homage to the saints; their leaves make melody for Coemgen, they lie down to give him passage, and lift themselves up when he has passed. Fallen trees are raised at the bidding of the saints; fruitless trees bear fruit, sour fruits are made sweet, and fruits are produced or preserved out of due season; a dry stick becomes a green tree, and blossoms, and bears.[50]

Sacred as well as ordinary stones similarly respect and obey.[51] Finally, the saints are a potent source of help during the rigors and perils of birth, death, healing, and cursing.[52] Such powers and prerogatives, including reputed psychic and even magical skills, clearly identify them as the successors of the druids. And if the monk-saints succeeded the druids, the monk-poets similarly continued the traditions of the tribal poets, the *filidh*, for whom also nature was an unfailing source of image and inspiration.

The Poets

While the earliest poets writing in Welsh were the bards of the early sixth century, pre-eminently Taliesin, Aneurin, and Llywarch Hen—all secular writers,[53] the earliest Irish poetry was penned epigrammatically by monks in the margins of the manuscripts they so beautifully illuminated:

The Pilgrim at Rome

> To go to Rome
> Is much of trouble, little of profit:
> The King whom you seek there,
> Unless you bring him with you, you will not find.[54]

Longer poems soon appeared as well, their theme almost always some aspect of nature, as in this Haiku-like example from *Maytime:*

> The harp of the wood plays melody,
> its music brings perfect peace;
> color has settled on every hill,
> haze on the lake of full water.[55]

In both religious and bardic poetry, nature is a typical and fond subject. Speaking of Irish poetry, Eleanor Knott observes, "The early religious verse is mainly lyrical and contemplative. It has spontaneity and freshness of expression as well as an easy grace of form. As a whole it reflects clearly the ascetic and mystical yet deeply charitable character of early Irish Christianity. Especially frequent are poems which express the craving of the religious for solitude, to be alone with God and nature, and to rejoice in a life of innocence and repentance.''[56]

Even the more severe saints are known for their poems; four are ascribed to Columban, and many more to the lyrical favorites such as Columcille. The more scholarly scribes sometimes broke through the tedium of etymological discursions, as in the justly famous poem attributed to the learned Sedulius Scottus:

Pangur Ban

I and Pangur Ban my Cat,
'Tis a like task we are at:
Hunting mice is his delight,
Hunting words I sit all night.

Better far than praise of men
'Tis to sit with book and pen;
Pangur bears me no ill will,
He too plies his simple skill.

'Tis a merry thing to see
At our tasks how glad are we,
When at home we sit and find
Entertainment to our mind.

Oftentimes a mouse will stray
In the hero Pangur's way;
Oftentimes my keen thought set
Takes a meaning in its net.

'Gainst the wall he sets his eye
Full and fierce and sharp and sly;
'Gainst the wall of knowledge I
All my little wisdom try.

When a mouse darts from its den
O how glad is Pangur then!
O what gladness do I prove
When I solve the doubts I love!

So in peace our tasks we ply,
Pangur Ban, my cat and I;
In our arts we find our bliss,
I have mine and he has his.

Practice every day has made
Pangur perfect in his trade;
I get wisdom day and night
Turning darkness into light.[57]

Nature in the Thought of John the Scot

With Sedulius Scottus, we enter the realm of the scholarly inheritance of the Celtic Church, which included outstanding figures in medïeval theology, philosophy, and spirituality such as Alcuin, John Scottus Eriugena, Sedalius himself, and, at the end, Richard of St. Victor and Duns Scotus.

Among this illustrius band, the mystical appreciation of nature shown by the saints and poets was most perfectly translated into philosophical and theological terms by John Scottus Eriugena, the outstanding sage of Europe between Augustine and Aquinas.[58] His teaching stands out "like a lofty rock in the midst of a plain" (Copleston). One biographer describes him as one of the greatest metaphysicians of all time, "an outstanding figure in the history of thought, a favourite of the mystics and one who may provide for the future a Christian synthesis, at once purified of anthropomorphism and capable of bringing ideas of evolution, the continuum and the relative to the focus of Infinite Being: this after all is what Eriugena attempts to do."[59]

Scottus's major and perhaps most original work is the *Periphyseon* (De Devisione Natura), written in 867 and consisting of five books in a quarter million words. Even a brief discussion of his complex, brilliant system far exceeds the scope of this discussion. But it should be noted that in it John Scottus boldly attempted to reconcile the thought of Augustine with the mystical theology of Gregory of Nyssa and Maximus the Confessor in a sweeping and dynamic dialectic of creation. Like Eckhart almost five hundred years later, and whose thought his closely resembles, Scottus was rewarded for his efforts with additional centuries of misunderstanding, suspicion, and condemnation.

Central to Scottus's teaching is the mystery of creation, all of which he interprets as theophany, a revelation of God's nature which permeates the universe, drawing all things to itself in an infinite process of flow and ebb. "We should not understand God and the creatures as two things removed from one another," he tells us, "but as one and the same thing. For the creature subsists in God, and God is created in the creature in a wonderful and ineffable way, making himself manifest, invisible making himself visible.'"[60] For Scottus, like Eckhart, "God is all in all. All things that are in God, even are God, are eternal." He insists that "We should not understand God and the creatures as two things removed from one another, but as one and the same thing."

Potter comments,

> since nothing is outside God, creatures are in Him and not He in them. This does not mean Eriugena is a pantheist, for it is precisely God's transcendence that makes such language possible. He can also say that God is the substance of all things, He 'makes Himself' in the primordial causes, but this is not to deny the reality of the creature. Rather, it expresses the fact that He is their abiding principle without which they would be nothings.[61]

While drawing on the thought of the patristic theologians of East and West, John Scottus remained a highly original thinker. In Book Three of the *Periphyseon*, he not only transcends conventional cosmogony but returns indirectly, perhaps unknowingly, to his Celtic roots. He asserts, for instance,

> that [the celestial bodies] too are mixtures of accidents which came into visible existence through man's fall. Drawing upon Martianus Capella, but going beyond even his explanations, Eriugena argues that Jupiter, Mars, Venus and Mercury do not revolve around the earth but are satellites of the sun. Plato's world soul is invoked to show that nothing, not even a rock, is devoid of life, and from Pliny the Elder he borrows edifying details of animal behavior to show that they too have immortal souls.[62]

Conclusion

Dubos's extolling of Benedict as the patron of the ecology movement at the expense of St. Francis, although based on a distortion, suggests a major criterion for Christian ecological responsibility: mere love of nature without active care is inadequate. The early Benedictines did in fact exercise a constructive stewardship over "brute" creation, managing the wilderness to make it more productive and humanely habitable. The Celts and especially the monks were less inclined toward large-scale projects. But there is evidence in legend and tradition that the British erected dams and sea walls—often with later, tragic results when human management failed. The most notable example of such negligence concerns the devastating flood caused by the drunkenness of Seithennin, the steward of Gywddno Garanhir, according to legend the father of Elphin, the friend and patron of the first bard, Taliesin. As told in the tradition, Seithennin's failure to close the sluice-gates allowed the storming sea to overwhelm Gwyddno's entire kingdom, which now lies at the bottom of Cardigan Bay.[63]

Such stories may represent folk memories of actual events or even recall the eventual collapse of agricultural and engineering projects undertaken by the Romans during their four-century occupation of the Celtic realm. In effect, as cautionary tales, they remind us that reverence for nature in all its forms and especially a non-exploitative attitude toward the land over which we are mere stewards is a moral and religious imperative. This attitude, moreover, is not a peculiar characteristic of Celtic spirituality if a primary one; it is deeply rooted in the ancient theology and primitive monastic ethos of Christianity.

Thus Lynn White, Jr., merely caricatured the Christian view of nature by citing the example of Ronald Reagan as typical:

> The newly elected Governor of California, like myself a churchman but less troubled than I, spoke for the Christian tradition when he said (as is alleged), 'when you've seen one redwood tree, you've seen them all.' To a Christian a tree can be no more than a physical fact. The whole concept of the sacred grove is alien to Christianity and to the ethos of the West.[64]

Even a short review of the patristic view of nature, and especially a consideration of the spirituality of Celtic monasticism, substantially refutes such a narrow interpretation. Benedict of Nursia and Francis of Assisi certainly did not stand alone as champions of nature, but within a cloud of witnesses for whom every grove of trees is sacred and for whom humankind, the creative masterwork of God, is not the despoiler but the tender of Eden, the shepherd of being. It is to this authentic tradition of ecological responsibility that the present crisis calls us to return.

The spirituality of Celtic monasticism reminds us that to continue ignoring the intimate implications of the social, biological, and physical systems that constitute our environment, and the delicate balance that prevails between them to make this a habitable planet, is to worship death. It reminds us that no nation that relies primarily on military strength for its security will itself endure long nor leave to coming civilizations a heritage much worth preserving.

Notes

1. For an historical account of millenial panic, see Henri Focillon, *The*

Year 1000, trans. by F. D. Wieck (New York: F. Ungar Pub. Co., 1969), and Norman Cohn, *The Pursuit of the Millenium* (New York: Oxford University Press, 1970 ed.).

2. For a consideration of the implications for spirituality of the global crisis, see Richard Woods, O.P., *Symbion: Spirituality for a Possible Future* (Santa Fe, New Mexico: Bear and Co., 1983).

3. "These groups I am contemplating. . . should have characteristics in common with the monastic fraternities, if only because they would have to differ profoundly in constitution and purpose from the way of life, the distress, and the disorder prevailing in society outside." Roberto Vacca, *The Coming Dark Age* (Garden City, NY: Doubleday Anchor, 1978), pp. 210-211.

4. Lynn White, Jr., "The Historical Roots of Our Ecological Crisis," *Science* 155: 1203-1207 (10 March 1967). Reprinted in Jackson, pp. 22-30. René Dubos, "Franciscan Conservation versus Benedictine Stewardship," *A God Within* (New York: Charles Scribner's Sons, 1972).

5. See Chapter Seven in this collection by Paul Weigand.

6. E. R. Dodds, *Pagan and Christian in an Age of Anxiety* (New York: Cambridge University Press, 1965).

7. A number of able studies of constructive Christian approaches to environmental crises have appeared during the last decade, among them David and Eileen Spring, *Ecology and Religion in History* (New York: Harper and Row, 1974); Frederick Elder, *Crisis in Eden: A Religious Study of Man and Environment* (Nashville, Abingdon Press, 1970); H. Paul Santmire, *Brother Earth: Nature, God and Ecology in Time of Crisis* (New York: Thomas Nelson, Inc., 1970); Cf. also Carl O. Sauer, "Theme of Plant and Animal Destruction in Economic History," Shephard and McKinley, pp. 52-60; Francis A. Schaeffer, *Pollution and the Death of Man: The Christian View of Ecology* (Wheaton, IL: Tyndale House Publishers, 1970); Conrad Bonifazi, *A Theology of Things* (Philadelphia: Lippincott, 1967); Charles Francis Digby Moule, *Man and Nature in the New Testament* (Philadelphia: Fortress Press, 1967); George H. Williams, *Wilderness and Paradise in Christian Thought* (New York: Harper and Row, 1962); Eric Charles Rust, *Nature and Man in Biblical Thought* (London: Lutterworth Press, 1953).

8. Dodds, *Pagan and Christian in an Age of Anxiety* (New York: Cambridge University Press, 1965).

9. Ibid., p. 29-30. For similar examples, cf. pp. 33f. Dodds does, however, acknowledge the opposite attitude in Clement of Alexandria and Origen, p. 29 n. 3.

10. Ibid., p. 37.

11. David Sutherland Wallace-Hadrill, *The Greek Patristic View of Nature* (New York: Barnes and Noble, Inc., 1968), p. vii. Wallace-Hadrill summarizes the objective of his study in terms of general theses commonly brought against Patristic theology: "to counteract

the idea that Christianity necessarily ignores this world in favour of the next; that it necessarily involves denigration of the world and the flesh, and inevitably completes the satanic triad by associating them with the devil; that beauty is associated in the Christian mind with moral debility, and is therefore to be shunned." p. 9.

12. Ibid., p. 8. Cf. p. 9.
13. Ibid., pp. 9, 3.
14. Ibid., pp. 9f.
15. Ibid., p. 21 n. 4. The reference is to *Hex.*, iii.9.76c.
16. Ibid., p. 68. The reference is to *Protrep.*, x.98.2.3.
17. Ibid., p. 69.
18. Ibid., p. 82. Cf. p. 93: "The beauty of the natural world the Greek fathers gratefully acknowledge; the beauty of the human form they recognize, but approve only with reservations concerning its moral implications; beauty of building and of the plastic arts they approve as an aid to worship; beauty of literary style they hardly approve at all."
19. Ibid., p. 129.
20. Philo, "On the Contemplative Life *(De Vita Contemplativa),*" trans. by F. H. Colson (Vol. IX, Loeb Classical Library) (London: William Heinemann Ltd., 1941), pp. 151-169.
21. Richard William Southern, *Western Society and the Church in the Middle Ages* (New York: Penguin Books, 1970), p. 217.
22. "Scattered but consistent evidence indicates that the last centuries of antiquity and the first ones of the early Middle Ages were especially cold and wet. This might not in itself have been disastrous for the normally warm and dry Mediterranean world, but it made the traditional techniques of dry farming less successful and accelerated the already advanced process of erosion." Robert Lopez, *The Commercial Revolution of the Middle Ages* (New York: Cambridge University Press, 1976), p. 12.
23. Cf. Lopez, op. cit., p. 14.
24. Lester K. Little, *Religious Poverty and the Profit Economy in Medieval Europe* (Ithaca, New York: Cornell University Press, 1978), p. 61.
25. Ibid., p. 63.
26. Ibid.
27. Ibid.
28. "Upon the approach of death, knights and noble ladies would have themselves clad in the Franciscan habit, believing that if they died and were buried in it, they could not go to hell. . . .The Order acquired lands and riches, built itself churches and cloisters, developed its own hierarchy—all the opposite of the founder's intent." Barbara Wertheim Tuchman, *A Distant Mirror: The Calamitous 14th Century* (New York: Alfred A. Knopf, 1978), p. 31. Cf. also p. 32.
29. "The monks of Christ Church, Canterbury, . . .drew a considerable

income from the shrine of Thomas Becket, but they received higher amounts from the rents on their urban property holdings. By the end of the twelfth century, the monks had become lords of between one-third and one-half of the domestic property of the town of Canterbury, with over 400 separate holdings. They owned 25 dwellings in London and ten in Dover." Little, op. cit., p. 66.

30. "The successful abbots of the twelfth century were of necessity fiscal administrators rather than saints, like Suger of Saint-Denis, who wrote a book on administration and took charge of the royal government during Louis VII's crusade, or like Samson of Bury St. Edmund's, who inherited an enormous debt upon his accession and spent his reign wiping it out (with the help of a pogrom in the town of Bury, which he controlled)." Little, op. cit., p. 68.

31. John Thomas McNeill, *The Celtic Churches* (Chicago: The University of Chicago Press, 1974), p. 1.

32. Ibid.

33. At Glastonbury, by medieval times the site of the largest and most powerful abbey in England, St. Joseph was alleged to have built a chapel which he dedicated to the Virgin Mary. He also planted his staff, of native Palestinian thorn, on nearby Wirral Hill, where it took root and grew into a great tree that blossomed every year at Christmastime until felled by puritan axes in the seventeenth century.

34. "The organization of the Gallic Church of the fourth century was based on the orderly system of Roman civil administration: bishops had their sees in important provincial centres; ecclesiastical law and administrative took as their models the imperial legal code and civil service procedure." J. F. Webb, *Lives of the Saints* (New York: Penguin Books, 1965), p. 11.

35. For the existence of Irish Deaconesses, see Pere Grossjean, *An. Boll.* LXXIII, 298, 322.

36. Because of its earlier development in Gaul, particularly at the monastic school of Lérins, Tours and Auxerre, while British and Irish monasticism was Egyptian in form, its language and liturgy nevertheless remained Latin. As J. F. Webb explains, "The culture and mentality of the Church in Gaul was thoroughly Roman. Into this order burst the flame of monasticism—austere, passionate, democratic. Its mysticism came from the pagan East, had been christianized by the scholars of the Greek Church, and flowered into the severe ascetical ideals of the Desert Fathers of Egypt and Mesopotamia whose way of life John Cassian of Marseilles describes in his *Institutes* and *Conferences*." Op. cit., p. 11.

37. Cf. W. W. Heist, *Vitae Sanctorum Hiberniae*, Subsidia Hagiographica 28 (Brussels, 1965); the now classic editions by Charles Plummer of the Latin and Irish versions, *Vitae Sanctorum Hiberniae*, 2 vols., (Oxford: Clarendon Press, 1910) (VSH) and *Bethada Náem nÉrenn*,

2 vols., Oxford: Clarendon Press, 1968 (repr. 1922 ed.) (BNE); Sabine Baring-Gould and John Fisher, *The Lives of the British Saints; The Saints of Wales and Cornwall and Such Irish Saints as Have Dedications in Britain*, 4 vols. (London: C. J. Clark, 1907-13); and J. F. Webb, *Lives of the Saints* (New York: Penguin Books, 1965).

38. Cf. Kathleen Hughes, *Early Christian Ireland* (Ithaca, New York: Cornell University Press, 1972), p. 219.

39. Migne, PL, LXXII, cols. 775-90. Cf. Hughes, p. 227.

40. Hughes, pp. 228f. Among the series of tales about St. Brigit and various animals, one at least, "does not seem to belong to a well-recognized folk-pattern," that of the King and the wild fox.

41. *St. Patrick: His Writings and Muirchu's Life*, ed. and trans. by A. B. E. Hood, Arthurian Period Sources, Vol. 9 (London: Phillimore, 1978).

42. trans. by Whitley Stokes, John Strachan and Kuno Meyer, David H. Green, ed., *An Anthology of Irish Literature* (New York: Modern Library, 1954), p. 7.

43. Alice-Boyd Proudfoot, *Patrick: Sixteen Centuries with Ireland's Patron Saint* (New York: Macmillan, 1983), p. 46.

44. Hood, p. 96.

45. Plummer, VSH, I, p. cxli. One of the most fascinating of the hagiographical motifs concerns wolves, which were apparently at least semi-sacred animals to the ancient Celts. In several saints' Lives, hungry wolves approach and are allowed their pick of the herd or flock, often to the discredit of the young saint assigned to watch over them. Plummer continues, "The most curious instance of this is in the life of Molua who is said to have founded an annual feast for the benefit of the wolves. Miracles are wrought on behalf of wolves, and wolves obey the saints' bidding, or execute their vengeance. Ailbe, like Romulus and Remus, was suckled by a she-wolf, and to the end of his life acknowledged this 'kinship by the milk'; Bairre was fostered in the same way. Coman mac Luachain had a standing covenant with wolves." Ibid., p. cxlii. He concludes, somewhat hastily, "All this tends to show that the wolf in pagan Ireland was a sacred animal, and associated with the cult of the sun." Ibid., pp. cxlii-cxliii.

46. Ibid., p. cxlii-iv.

47. "One of the prettiest of these stories tells how Colman mac Duach had a cock, a mouse, and a fly. The cock used to crow when it was time for matins, the mouse would rub his ear to wake him when he had slept the allotted time, and the fly would settle on the line of his Psalter at which he left off reading, to keep his place for him." Ibid., p. cxliv, n. 5.

48. Ibid., p. cxlvi-cxlvii. The reference is to the Life of Cuthbert, c. 21.

49. Cf. VSH, pp. clxvii-cliii.

50. Ibid., pp. cliii-cliv.

51. Ibid., pp. clv-clvii.

52. Ibid., pp. clxxxvff. and passim.
53. Cf. J. E. Caerwyn Williams, *The Poets of the Welsh Princes* (Cardiff: The University of Wales Press, 1978) and Sir Ifor Williams, *The Beginnings of Welsh Poetry*, ed. by Rachel Bromwich (Cardiff: The University of Wales Press, 1980).
54. Meyer's trans. modernized, Greene, p. 18.
55. Jackson, op. cit., p. 63.
56. Eleanor Knott, *Irish Classical Poetry* (Cork: Mercier Press, 1966 ed.), p. 26.
57. 9th cent. Robin Flower's trans., Green, p. 11f. On Sedulius Scottus, see James Carney, "Sedulius Scottus," in *Old Ireland*, Robert McNally, S. J., ed. (New York: Fordham University Press, 1965), pp. 228-250. On Sedulius as the author of *Pangur Ban*, see p. 249.
58. Cf. John J. O'Meara and Ludwig Bieler, eds., *The Mind of Eriugena* (Irish University Press, 1973), p. xiii. One translator observes, "by translating the Ps.-Dionysius he laid the foundations of Western Mysticism,
    . . . his *Periphyseon*, running to more than half a million words, is the most impressive piece of philosophical writing between the ages of St. Augustine and St. Thomas [Aquinas]." Sheldon-Williams in Iohannis Scotti Eriugenae, *Periphyseon (De Divisione Naturae)*, ed. by I. P. Sheldon-Williams and Ludwid Bieler, 3 vols., Dublin: The Dublin Institute for Advanced Studies, 1968., p. vii. Scottus's works are found in Migne PL, Vol. 122, a ponderous collection of commentaries, translations, and original works.
59. O'Meara, loc. cit., p. xiii.
60. O'Meara's paraphrase, p. xii.
61. John the Scot, *Periphyseon: On the Division of Nature*, ed. and trans. by Myra L. Uhlfelder, summaries by Jean A. Potter (Indianapolis: Bobbs-Merrill Co., Inc., 1976), p. xxx. O'Meara notes, "the divine nature, he finally insists, because it is above being, is different from what it creates within itself." p. xii.
62. Potter, p. xxxvii.
63. The tragedy is alluded to in the *Mabinogi* of Branwen. Cf. Rachel Bromwich, ed. trans. and commentary, *Trioedd Ynys Prydein (The Welsh Triads)* (Cardiff: University of Wales Press, 1978), pp. 397-400. For modern versions of the tale, see Gwyn Jones, *Welsh Legends and Folk Tales* (London and New York: Penguin Books, 1979), pp. 225-227 and Elisabeth Sheppard-Jones, *Stories of Wales* (Chicago: Academy Press Ltd., 1978), pp. 131-133. Other stories about submerged cities and kingdoms are frequent in Celtic lore, including that of Ys in Brittany, which is alleged to have sunk in 440.
64. White, art. cit., p. 29.

Chapter Four

CREATION-CENTERED SPIRITUALITY FROM HILDEGARD OF BINGEN TO JULIAN OF NORWICH
300 Years of an Ecological Spirituality in the West

Matthew Fox, O.P.

There can be no respect for our place in the environment and the environment's place in us without a spirituality that teaches us reverence for the cosmos in which we find ourselves. The reigning spirituality of patriarchal culture of the West has not been friendly to the environment; nor has it taught persons to be gentle to themselves, their bodies, their enemies, their imaginations. Subject/object dualisms have characterized the mainstream of spirituality in the West from St. Augustine to Jerry Falwell and points in between. Science historian Michael Polyani has caught the anti-environmental bias of those who preach a fall/redemption religion when he said that St. Augustine "destroyed interest in science all over Europe for a thousand years."[1] An ideology that considers all of nature helplessly fallen does not look kindly on those who spend their lives studying nature, i.e. scientists. To probe the universe is not a salvific act in such a spirituality or religion.

But there is another tradition of spirituality in the West. That tradition, the creation-centered one, considers the environment itself to be a divine womb, holy, worthy of reverence and respect. We are in divinity and the divinity in us according to this tradition—and by "We" is not meant merely the two-legged ones but the entire universe—atoms and galaxies, rain and whales, trees and fishes, dogs and rabbits, and humans too. While little has been heard from this tradition in religious and theological circles in centuries, the fact is that this tradition was alive and well in medieval Europe for a lively period of 300 years. It was the period that gave us Chartres Cathedral, Hildegard's amazing music and mandalas, Francis of Assisi's empassioned and sufi-like lifestyle, Aquinas' *Summa*, Mechtild of Magdeburg's journal and political involvement, Eckhart's mystical-prophetic genius, the rich theology of the *Theologica Germanica* and Julian of Norwich's metaphysics of goodness. The twelfth century renaissance in Europe was in great measure an awakening to the creation-centered tradition which meant first and foremost an awakening to Nature itself.[2] It also welcomed those scientists and mystics who took nature seriously and as a source of divine revelation.

In this article I would like to present a survey of four neglected figures and some key concepts that they cherished and developed during this 300-year span. In particular I will invoke the following champions of an ecological spiritual consciousness: Hildegard of Bingen (1098-1179); Mechtild of Magdeburg (1210-1280); Meister Eckhart (1269-1329); Julian of Norwich (1342-c. 1415). It is evident that I am omitting the two best known creation-centered mystics of this period in the West—Francis of Assisi (1181-1225) and Thomas Aquinas (1225-1274). I am doing so for lack of space but also because these two persons have received considerable attention. In this volume there is a fine article redeeming Francis from his number one enemy, sentimental hagiography[3], and true livers of the spirit of St. Thomas such as M.D. Chenu and Josef Pieper[4] have done superb work in showing us the way to this person's creation theology. The four persons I deal with have been neglected, repressed, forgotten, condemned, misinterpreted, dualistically translated (if at all), and otherwise pushed out of the mainstream of western Christianity's world view. This is the principal reason why the ecological and creation-centered tradition they so richly represent has been all but nonexistent in most Christian theologies in the West (though not the East).

These four persons can rightly be called "Rhineland mystics". Two of them, Hildegard and Eckhart, lived and preached on the Rhine where Bingen is located in Hildegard's case or in Strasbourg and Cologne in the case of the Dominican Meister Eckhart. Mechtild's writings were circulated heavily among the Beguines who were especially numerous on the Rhine[5] and to which movement Mechtild herself belonged. Her Dominican spiritual director, Heinrich of Halle, saw to it that her book was translated immediately into Latin in order to assure its swift dissemination. By 1344 it was translated into the High German that was spoken in the upper Rhine in the thirteenth and fourteenth centuries. From a literal point of view, I am stretching it a bit to call Julian a "Rhineland mystic" since she was a hermitess who, once walled up in her cell in c.1393, never left it to re-enter Norwich, much less the continent. However, from a theological point of view Julian deserves to be called a "Rhineland mystic" for her tradition is radically and richly that of Hildegard and Eckhart as we shall see. She develops the creation-centered theology deeply for she is a theologian of the first order. Furthermore, we know that Eckhart's works were taken into England often under the cover of John Tauler's sermons by Dominicans and others. Dominicans were quite visible in Norwich in Julian's day and in fact occupied a priory right down the street from Julian's cell in a city that sparkled at that time with mystical movements. It is inconceivable that she did not hear Dominicans preach in her church or converse with them and very likely employed them as spiritual directors at the same time that she directed them. Furthermore, Julian's apparent Benedictine roots link her to Hildegard and the rich creation spirituality of the Benedictine tradition.

The six themes that I wish to touch on as basic to an ecological consciousness are the following:

1. The goodness (blessing) of creation.
2. The goodness and blessing that the earth itself is (including human earthiness or bodiliness).
3. Cosmic awareness, cosmic consciousness and a psychology of microcosm, macrocosm.
4. A theology of panentheism as most properly naming our relationship to God.
5. The motherhood of God and the human vocation to co-create the cosmos.
6. Compassion understood as interdependence and justice making.

In dealing with these rich themes that are so essential to an ecological spirituality I will weave and interweave the thought of each of the mystics I have named above.

Three sources that these mystics draw on extensively need to be named. First is the Jewish and Christian Scriptures—as I have indicated elsewhere,[6] the creation tradition is the oldest tradition

in the Scriptures dating back to the 9th century B.C., the Yahwist
(J) source of the Hebrew Bible. It is the tradition of wisdom literature, of the prophets in great measure and of Jesus Christ. The
gospel writers and Paul knew this tradition intimately. A second
source that is often neglected or misunderstood is that of the Celts
who settled in the Rhineland area as Christians in the seventh
century.[7] John the Scot was the first to translate Eastern Christianity's mystical works into Latin, and the Celts depended for their
theology on the Eastern traditions—which never forsook creation
theology—rather than on Jerome and Augustine in the West (who
did indeed forsake creation theology). A keen understanding of
the Celtic contribution to Western culture is evidenced by Paul
Lang when he writes:

> Ireland and Scotland had never experienced antique civilization as
> a reality. The Celts came into contact with Rome, the colonizer,
> much as the East Indians made the acquaintance of modern Eng-
> land. Consequently they did not face the grave conflict between
> ancient learning and Christian faith which caused a sharp reaction
> in the countries within the orbit of classical civilization. They were
> thus eminently suited to bring about a reconciliation of the two
> philosophies and outlooks on life, and communicated their ideas not
> only to their neighbors the Anglo-Saxons, but through their monas-
> tic settlements in the Frankish Empire and northern Italy, to the
> whole of Christian Europe.[8]

It was the Celts who most inspired Francis of Assisi's spirituality,
as Edward Armstrong has demonstrated.[9]

A third source of the mystics we are treating that needs to be
acknowledged is women's experience. Three of these most
neglected mystics are women and the fourth, Meister Eckhart,
was spiritual director to the Beguines or women's movement of his
day. His pre-eminent contribution to creation theology only serves
to underscore how feminism is not a male/female dividing point
but is rather a way of seeing the world that both women and men
are capable of. Feminist thinkers like Rosemary Ruether and Susan
Griffin and Mary Daly and Wendell Berry and Robert Bly in our
time have rightly pointed our that the abusive treatment of nature
and the abusive treatment of women most often go together in our
society. The issue in patriarchy that is most basic is that of dualism.[10] Creation-centered spirituality names dualism as original sin
and offers, as we shall see, a wonderful alternative. For it defines
salvation as holism, as making whole, making one, and therefore
making healthy, holy, and happy.

With this brief introduction we can now begin our exploration of ecological themes in the creation-centered mystics of the Middle Ages.

Ecological Themes in the Creation-Centered Mystics

1. The first theme that this line of creation-centered mystics celebrates that is essential for an ecological spiritual consciousness is that of **the goodness of creation**. Hildegard of Bingen writes: "God is the good. And all things that proceed from God are good."[11] Julian of Norwich, three centuries later, follows up on the same theme. "I know well that heaven and earth and all creation are great, generous and beautiful and good. . . . God's goodness fills all his creatures and all his blessed works full, and endlessly overflows in them." But Julian goes even further. Meister Eckhart's transcendental metaphysics had declared that "isness is God"; Julian borrows from this metaphysics to establish a metaphysics of goodness. She writes: "God is everything which is good, as I see it, and the goodness which everything has is God."[12] To say that "goodness is God" is to re-establish the non-dualistic relationship of Creator and creation. More than that, it is to re-establish a veritable theology of blessing. For "blessing" is the theological word for the goodness that creation is. As professor Mowinckel puts it in his major study on blessing in Israeli theology, "first and foremost, blessing is life, health, and fertility for the people, their cattle, their fields. . . . Blessing is the basic power of life itself."[13] For Julian the blessing that our lives are goes back a very long way. "I saw that God never *began* to love us. For just as we will be in everlasting joy (all God's creation is destined for this), so also we have *always* been in God's foreknowledge, known and loved from without beginning."[14] Julian is celebrating the original blessing that our existences are. Science today can vouch for the accuracy of Julian's theology because she is correct: Had the stars not exploded six billion years ago; had the earth not maintained a certain temperature so that water would flow and life emerge; had the ozone not processed out certain levels of radiation; we humans would not exist. Thus we were indeed loved by the cosmos "from before the beginning."

One reason that a theology of the goodness of creation is so essential for an ecological consciousness is that without it the human race remains greedy and unsatisfied. By truly trusting in the goodness of existence we open ourselves up to more goodness and to less and less elitist understanding of what the good for humankind is and can be. In short, we let go of the sense that more must be better; we learn something of the necessities and of needs. Hildegard of Bingen saw this clearly when she wrote: "God gives, such that nothing that is necessary for life is lacking." And again, "God has gifted creation with everything that is necessary."[15] If humanity can believe that "everything that is necessary" has been given us, then the compulsion for more will give away to a celebration of what is—"isness is God" (Eckhart)—and out of what is, humanity will forge what must be for the earth's survival. Here indeed lies a theology for sustainability, for humanity will not choose to sustain instead of hoard or master until it is at peace with its condition.

Not only is creation radically good and an original blessing; not only is everything that is necessary already here; but also creation for these mystics is itself a source of divine pleasure and divine revelation. Creation radiates delight and beauty and pleasure. Hildegard writes: "There is no creation that does not have a radiance. Be it greenness or seed, blossom or beauty, it could not be creation without it."[16] God is erotically involved, one might say in love with, creation. "Creation, of course, was fashioned to be adorned, to be showered, to be gifted with the love of the Creator. The entire world has been embraced by this kiss."[17] Meister Eckhart teaches that the source of all creation's pleasure is God and that "God finds joy and rapture" in human creation. Furthermore, creation discharges truth as well as pleasure. It is a source of revelation, a Bible in itself. "Every creature is a word of God and a book about God," Eckhart declares.[18] Billions of years before humanity invented books and religions put their teaching to holy writings, God was revealed in the divine and ongoing book that creation is. "If I spent enough time with a caterpillar," Eckhart vowed, "I would never have to prepare a sermon because one caterpillar is so full of God." All of creation is full of the divine—provided we have the eyes and ears to perceive it and the open heart to receive such revelation.

2. A second theme that is essential for a theology of ecology is that of **the goodness and blessing that the earth itself is**. The creation-centered mystics celebrate not only creation in general but the earth in particular. Hildegard writes: "Holy persons draw to themselves all that is earthly."[19] We are a long distance indeed from the dominant symbol of patriarchal spirituality which was that of "climbing Jacob's ladder" precisely to escape the earth! And mother. And matter.[20] Hildegard not only brings together holiness and earthiness but she also relates this embracing of the earth with our celebrating of earth as holy mother. "The earth is at the same time mother, she is mother of all that is natural, mother of all that is human. She is the mother of all, for contained in her are the seeds of all."[21] The earth "is the fleshly material of people, nourishing them with its sap as a mother nurses her sons or daughters."[22] For Hildegard the earth is holy because it is the "source" of humanity. It demands on humanity's part "a right and holy utilization of the earth."[23] Our bodies are "supported in every way through the earth," she declares. And the earth "glorifies the power of God."[24] There is no human chauvinism in Hildegard's appreciation of the earth and humanity's relationship to it. Hildegard celebrates the earth as a living organism, for she sees the air as its soul. "The air is the soul of the earth, moistening it, greening it."[25] Earth is holy and fruitful, a source of blessing, because "all creation comes from it." Yet earth is also divinized a second time because the human body of God's son was fashioned from it. Earth "forms not only the basic raw material for humankind, but also the substance of the incarnation of God's son."[26]

Meister Eckhart, by imaging God as "a great underground river that no one can dam up, no one can stop," is celebrating images of holy mother earth, of the divine power of the earth, of divinity from below and not exclusively from above. If God is an underground river, then the earth is the mediator, the "priest" one might say, between humanity and divinity. It behooves us to embrace and to explore the earth for divinity's sake. Like Hildegard, Eckhart and the other creation-centered mystics celebrate the microcosm of psychic dimension of earthiness. One might call their psychology a geo-psychology. Here is where the awful dualism of body vs. soul that patriarchy champions is healed. Augustine, for example, declared that "the soul makes war with the body." Eckhart in contrast says, "the soul loves the body" and consequently "asceticism is of no great importance."[27] Mechtild of Magdeburg composed a poem to the body that celebrates how gently we can and ought to relate to the physical. She places our relationship to body in the context of realized eschatology and writes:

Do not disdain your body. For the soul is just as safe in
its body as in the Kingdom of Heaven—though not so certain.
It is just as daring—but not so strong.
Just as powerful—but not so constant.
Just as loving—but not so joyful.
Just as gentle—but not so rich.
Just as holy—but not yet so sinless.
Just as content—but not so complete.[28]

A key to healing the patriarchal body/soul split is the letting go of the idea the body is "out there" — which is itself a dualistic mind-set—and to begin embracing the body, the earthiness, "in here." Such an earthiness is everywhere at once. This mind-set is itself non-dualistic and healing or salvific because it celebrates the psychic embracing of earthiness. It redeems earthiness from being an enemy, the dark and repressed shadow of spirituality. Earth too is divine blessing and grace.

Perhaps no one has celebrated the re-union of body and soul, the holiness of matter and earthiness, so richly as has Julian of Norwich. She too sees the issue as one of relationship, as an issue of psychology making room for geology, when she talks about "our sensuality" and God's presence in it. "I understand that our sensuality is grounded in Nature, in Compassion and in grace. I saw that God is in our sensuality. For God is never out of the soul."[29] Sensuality and human earthiness is not something to be feared in this spirituality but something to be embraced since divinity itself operates there. "God is the ground in which our soul stands and God is the means whereby our Substance and our Sensuality are kept together so as to never be apart."[30] What Incarnation means to Julian is the "oneing" of divinity and sensuality, of God and us. If God is the glue or means that keeps substance and sensuality together, then to explore either pole of our makeup is to explore God. In a wonderful poem about both literal and psychic farming, Julian celebrates the struggle that gardening is all about.

> There is a treasure in the earth that is a food tasty and
>   pleasing to the Lord.
> Be a gardener. Dig and ditch, toil and sweat.
> Turn the earth upside down and seek the deepness and water
>   the plants in time.
> Continue this labor and make sweet floods to run and noble
>   and abundant fruits to spring.
> Take this food and drink and carry it to God as your true worship.[31]

Here we have a psychic geology, a healing of matter and spirit, of external and internal farming, a reverence for the holiness and divinity of earth and our origins. Interestingly, Hildegard also offers an image of psychic geology when she writes that people should "look into the field of their soul in order to root out the useless weeds and thorns and briars" that grow there.[32]

Lest we be tempted to sublimate the true implications of her theology on sensuality and sentimentalize it, Julian praises explicitly how going to the bathroom is holy.

> Food is shut in within our bodies as in a well-made purse. When the
> time of our necessity comes, the purse is opened and shut again in
> the most fitting way. And it is God who does this, for I was shown
> that the Goodness of God permeates us even in our humblest
> needs.[33]

The earthiness and the bodily cycles that channel this earthiness
are godly. Eckhart on many occasions celebrates humility as
earthiness, the word coming as it does from the latin word *humus*
or earth. He images the human soul as the "soil" in which the
divine seed and divine word are planted. From this sensual
grounding, God grows. "The seed of God is in us. If the seed had a
good, wise, and industrious cultivator, it would thrive all the more
and grow up to God whose seed it is, and the fruit would be equal
to the nature of God. Now the seed of a pear tree grows into a pear
tree, a hazel seed into a hazel tree, the seed of God into God."[34] As
with Hildegard and Julian, so with Eckhart: Our earthiness is not
an obstacle to divine energy but the very setting for it. Here lies a
truly incarnational theology, one that celebrates the divinizing of
the earth. It is one out of which Teilhard de Chardin grew deep
political implications writing that "the age of nations has passed.
Now, unless we wish to perish we must shake off our old prejudices and build the earth."[35]

3. A third theme that is richly developed in the creation-centered
mystics is that of *cosmic awareness, cosmic consciousness.* The
oldest hymns of the Christian Liturgy, those found in the epistles
to the Ephesians (1.3-23); to the Colossians (1.15-20); to the Philip-
peans (2.6-11) celebrate the cosmic Christ who "fills the whole
creation" and "reconciles all things in heaven and all things on
earth." Yet St. Augustine, whose patriarchal spirituality has
dominated western religion, has no cosmic Christ as scholars have
pointed out.[36] The creation-centered mystics we are speaking of
boast a rich sense of cosmic awareness and of its psychological implications. Hildegard of Bingen writes, for example: "I welcome
every creature of the world with grace." Hers is not a two-legged
chauvinism but an awareness that, as she puts it, "God has arranged all things in the world in consideration of everything
else."[37] The patriarchal religious tradition that begins theology
with sin is committing an act of immense anthropocentrism. For
sin is a human invention in the cosmos and is therefore a late-
comer to the universe—as late as humanity itself. To begin religion
with sin, instead of with the blessing that the cosmos is, trivializes

religion. In fact, the sins that humanity is capable of today are quite cosmic in their scope as we play with military toys that can put an end to twenty billion years of the universe's birthing of this home we call earth.

Mechtild of Magdeburg also celebrates a cosmic awareness and its political/mystical overtones when she writes: "The truly wise person kneels at the feet of all creatures." Like the rich theology of the wisdom literature of the Hebrew Bible, Mechtild deliberately connects cosmic awareness with wisdom itself. "The spirit of the Lord indeed fills the whole world," sings the author of the book of Wisdom (1.7). Hildegard urges us to meditate on the beauties of the universe about us and not to become preoccupied with our introspective selves. "Glance at the sun. See the moon and stars. Gaze at the beauty of earth's greenings. Now think what delight God gives to humankind with all these things. Who gives all these shining, wonderful gifts if not God?"[38] It is for this reason, namely that the creation tradition celebrates cosmic awareness, that it cares deeply not just about knowledge or information but about wisdom. Wisdom and cosmos are co-relative terms as the French philosopher Gabriel Marcel indicates. "The true function of the sage is surely the function of linking together, of bringing into harmony. . .the sage is truly linked with the universe."[39] Mechtild points out the political implications of a world view that considers the cosmos as essential. After saying that "the truly wise person kneels at the feet of all creatures," she adds: "and is not afraid to endure the mockery of others." A cosmic consciousness in a patriarchal and introverted society or religion[40] is sure to bring "the mockery of others" down upon it. An egological and an ecological consciousness cannot co-exist precisely because we are talking about consciousness, that is to say, the human psyche. Cosmos is itself an element of psyche. If it is left out, then quite literally our psyches are damaged and one-sided. Paul Ricoeur writes of this when he says: "To manifest the 'sacred' *on* the 'cosmos' and to manifest it *in* the 'psyche' are the same thing. . . Cosmos and Psyche are the two poles of the same 'expressivity'; I express myself in expressing the world; I explore my own sacrality in deciphering that of the world."[41] Like Mechtild, Marcel also notes the political and moral implications of recovering wisdom and cosmos in our thinking and decision-making.

> The important thing—and I think it is hardly possible to insist on it too much—is that in this outlook the true aim of knowledge and of life is to be integrated in the universal order, and not at all to trans-

form the world by bringing it into subjection to the human will, to man's needs or his desires.[42]

A psychology of microcosm/macrocosm which these medieval mystics offer us is itself radically healing. Hildegard is explicit about the human being a microcosm of the cosmos. "Now God has built the human form into the world structure, indeed even into the cosmos, just as the artist would use a particular pattern in her work."[43] Meister Eckhart too holds a psychology of microcosm/macrocosm. He develops his idea of the "equality of being" in which all creatures are equal at the level of the supreme gift which is that of existence itself or isness. He says: "God loves all creatures equally and fills them with his being. And we should lovingly meet all creatures in the same way."[44] Like Hildegard and Mechtild and Marcel, he draws ethical conclusions from his alertness to cosmic awareness. Eckhart believes that "the first intention" of Nature "is the preservation of the universe." Eckhart insists that creation is thoroughly on-going and the cosmos is being birthed not "out there" but very much within the enlargement of the human psyche. He writes:

> I have often said that God is creating the entire cosmos fully and totally in this present now. Everything God created six thousand years ago—and even previous to that as he made the world—God creates now all at once. Now consider this: God is in everything, but God is nowhere as much as he is in the soul. There, where time never enters, where no image shines in, in the innermost and deepest aspect of the soul God creates the whole cosmos. Everything which God created millions of years ago and everything which will be created by God after millions of years—if the world endures until then—God is creating all that in the innermost and deepest realms of the soul.[45]

It is little wonder that one Eckhartian scholar writes that "Eckhart actually abolishes the methodological distinction between theology, anthropology, and cosmology."[46]

Julian of Norwich also celebrates the Kingdom of God as the cosmos and in the process stretches one's image of soul or psyche. She writes that she saw "the Soul so large as if it were an endless world and a joyful kingdom" with God sitting in the center.[47] Julian offers a meditation on the cosmic Christ when she speaks of Jesus' crucifixion as affecting all of nature. "All creatures of God's creation that can suffer pain suffered with him. The sky and the earth failed at the time of Christ's dying because he too was part of nature."[48] Like the other persons we have considered above, Julian draws ethical implications from a deepened cosmic consciousness. "Those who have universal love for all their fellow Christians in God have love towards everything that exists."[49]

To consider cosmic awareness and cosmic responsibility as essential to spiritual growth is also to welcome the scientist. For who is the scientist if not an explorer of the truths—and hopefully the wisdom—of our universe? There is simply no anti-intellectualism and no fear of science in the creation-centered mystics. Hildegard, for example, sees science as a road to wisdom. "The more one learns about that which one knows nothing of, the more one gains in wisdom. One has, therefore, through science, eyes with which it behooves us to pay attention."[50] She praises the human soul for its "regal rationality"[51] and she calls the human mind "the best treasure, a living intellect."[52] She leaned heavily in her work on the finest scientist of her day, Bernard Sylvester. Hildegard was no mean synthesizer of science in her own right. Her scheme of microcosm/macrocosm, says one scholar, "though complex and difficult, is neither incoherent nor insane, as at first sight it may seem. It is, in fact, a highly systematic and skillful presentment of a cosmic theory which for centuries dominated scientific thought."[53] It has been pointed out that Hildegard herself made scientific contributions as regards the need for purification of water, the discovery of healing medicines and the anticipation of the discovery of vitamins.[54]

4. A fourth ingredient essential to an ecological spirituality is a non-dualistic imaging of God's presence. The creation-centered tradition understands this to be **a theology of panentheism.** For theism is by definition dualistic, implying as it does a person "here" and a God "out there." Carl Jung says there are two ways to lose your soul and one is to worship "a God out there." In the panentheistic theology it is understood that we are in God and God is in us. And by "we" is meant all of creation, all that is, or as Paul puts it (Acts 17.28) God is the one "in whom we live, move and have our being." Mechtild of Magdeburg images God as panentheistic when she writes: "I who am divine am truly in you . . .and you are in Me." Indeed, Mechtild dates her awakening to spiritual maturity to the moment she moved from a theistic to a panentheistic spiritual consciousness. She writes: "The day of my spiritual awakening was the day I saw and I knew I saw all things in God and God in all things."[55] Panentheism, as Mechtild speaks of it, includes a conviction—"I saw and knew I saw"—of the truth of imaging God in a way that is no longer subject/object. Julian of Norwich images our relationship to God in a panentheistic manner as well when she writes that "we have all been enclosed within God." And again, "We are in God and God, whom we do not see, is in us."[56] Hildegard of Bingen, in addition to speaking of the God in us and the Holy Spirit flowing like fire through us, also images God in the following manner: "God hugs you. You are encircled by the arms of the mystery of God."[57] These are panentheistic images of us-in-God as well as God-being-in-us.

Meister Eckhart has developed a mature spirituality of panentheism at great length. He writes that "God created all things in such a way that they are not outside himself, as ignorant people falsely imagine. Everything that God creates or does, he does or creates in himself, sees or knows in himself, loves in himself." Since "God is a being that has in itself all being", it follows that divinity is "round-about us completely enveloping us."[58] Not only are all things in God but God is in all things for Eckhart. "God is in all things. The more he is in things, the more he is outside of things."[59] Inside and outside are not separate. They meld together in a panentheistic theology.

Moving from a theistic ("God out there" or even "God in here") to a panentheistic theology ("all is in God and God is in all") is a requisite for growing up spiritually. Yet, because the creation-centered mystics have been so repressed in the West, it is rare indeed to find anyone—whether theologian or scientist—who has heard of panentheism. Without panentheism there is no authentic ecological consciousness for there is no true sense of the interdependence of all things, of the flowing out and the flowing back that characterizes all authentic living and dying. Justice gets reduced to a good deed and compassion is sentimentalized as feeling sorry for others. The divine Dabhar, that permeating energy that pulsates and quickens all life, is not tapped as the source of divine energy that it is for all peoples and creatures. A theistic imaging of God is essentially adolescent for it is based on an ego mind-set, a zeroing in on how we are separate from God. How many religious believers—and so-called unbelievers!—who may be very adult in their specialized professions have remained adolescents in their imaging of the relationship to God! And how seldom the churches have known enough of their creation-centered mystical traditions of panentheism to instruct people to move beyond this ego stage of development to a mystical stage of adult panentheism.[60]

5. A fifth theme that deserves attention in an ecological spiritu-

ality and which the creation-centered mystics develop is that of **the motherhood of God.** We have already seen how Hildegard praises "mother earth" and how Eckhart celebrates God as "a great underground river" that bubbles up from this hallowed ground. Mechtild of Magdeburg says candidly: "God is not only fatherly. God is also mother who lifts her loved child from the ground to her knee."[61] Mechtild sees the connection between panentheism and maternal images of embracing and surrounding when she writes: "The Trinity is like a mother's cloak wherein the child finds a home and lays its head on the maternal breast."[62] Like Mechtild, Hildegard celebrates the roundness of God—an image that is both panentheistic and suggestive of the maternal in God. She writes of being "surrounded with the roundness of divine compassion."[63] For Hildegard, "Divinity is. . . like a wheel, a circle, a whole, that can neither be understood, nor divided, nor begun, nor ended."[64]

Meister Eckhart frequently images God as mother when he says, "From all eternity God lies on a maternal bed giving birth" and again, "What does God do all day long? God gives birth."[65] For Eckhart a theology of the motherhood of God is so essential because it celebrates all persons' capacities to birth and give birth. Without this side of God being acknowledged, creativity itself is repressed and stifled. Indeed, in patriarchal spiritualities, creativity has not even been a theological category.[66] Whereas in the creation tradition, the *imago dei* or image of God in every person is precisely the imagination or the capacity of each person for creativity. So true is this for Eckhart that he actually declares that "we are meant to be mothers of God." In other words, every time we birth beauty or justice or truth or compassion we are co-creators with God birthing divinity itself.

Hildegard also celebrates human creativity and the human call to co-create with a creative God. "Humankind alone is called to assist God. Humankind is called to co-create," she says.[67] "Divinity is aimed at humanity," she declares, for "God created humankind so that humans might cultivate the earthly and thereby create the heavenly."[68] "God gave to humankind the talent to create with all the world" and for this reason God can say: "I have exalted humankind with the vocation of creation." [69] When Hildegard, as we saw earlier in this study, alludes to how everything that is necessary has been given humanity, she does not mean it is just there for the *taking.* She is sensitive to how much *making* must also take place if the necessities are to be won and justly distributed. In other words, creativity, human imagination and ingenuity are themselves essential ingredients in re-establishing need instead of greed as the basis of an economic and political compassion. A creative person is an orchard, Hildegard insists. "This is how a person becomes a flowering orchard. The person who does good works is indeed this orchard bearing good fruit. And this is just like the earth with its ornamentation of stone and blossoming trees."[70]

No theologian in the West has more thoroughly developed the rich theme of the motherhood of God than has Julian of Norwich. "Just as God is truly our Father," she writes, "so also is God truly our Mother."[71] For her the recovery of God as Mother is also the recovery of divine wisdom—a theme we saw above when treating of cosmic consciousness. For "the deep Wisdom of the Trinity is our Mother. In her we are all enclosed."[72] She connects divine motherhood with panentheism once again in an explicit way when she says that God is "our true Mother in whom we are endlessly carried and out of whom we will never come."[73] Here we have an image of the cosmos as God's womb. Being enclosed is, as we have seen, an essential image of the maternal side of God. Julian says, "as the body is clothed in cloth and the muscles in the skin and the bones in the muscles and the heart in the chest, so are we, body and soul, clothed and enclosed in the Goodness of God."[74] She relates the motherhood of God to a deepening awareness of God as Creator and lover of all of nature. "God is the true Father and Mother of Nature and all natures that are made to flow out of God to work the divine will/will be restored and brought again into God."[75] The motherhood of God is a welcome thing on God's part, Julian assures us. Divinity does not consider motherhood a burden to bear. "God feels great delight to be our Mother."[76] Finally, to recover the motherhood of God is to recover compassion as the operative divine energy. Compassion is more powerful than judgment or law or righteousness. For compassion is grace. "Compassion is a kind and gentle property that belongs to a Motherhood in tender love. Compassion protects, increases our sensitivity, gives life and heals."[77]

Thus we see that the recovery of the theme of the motherhood of God flows naturally from other themes of cosmos, earthiness, blessing or goodness, panentheism. A motherhood of God theology is no mere trifling kudo handed out to keep feminists content: It is a basic issue of letting go of the one-sided God of patriarchy and learning more about the God whose image we are.

Therefore it is also about learning more about ourselves. And about our power for birthing and creativity. Today it is especially urgent that men learn deeply how all persons are motherly as well as fatherly.

6. The sixth and final theme we will consider that is basic to an ecological spirituality is that of **compassion understood as interdependence and justice-making.** Compassion as feeling sorry for others is explicitly rejected in creation theology precisely because in a panentheistic world view there is no other. God is not other and we are not other to one another. Surely this is Jesus' lesson when he told his disciples that to clothe the naked is to clothe him and to feed the hungry is to feed him. Panentheistic thinking requires a consciousness of interdependence. Such a consciousness is a consciousness of compassion. Meister Eckhart captures this sense of interdependence when he says: "Whatever happens to another, whether it be a joy or a sorrow, happens to me." And again he says: "all creatures are interdependent."[78] Hildegard also underscores the interdependence of creation when she writes: "Everything that is in the heavens, on the earth, and under the earth, is penetrated with connectedness, penetrated with relatedness."[79] Eckhart builds on this notion of relatedness everywhere when he says that relation is the essence of everything that exists[80]—not substance, not thingness—but relation. Compassion is about struggling to righten relationships. Hildegard believes that "creation blooms and flourishes when it remains in right relationship and keeps to its assigned tasks."[81]

If compassion is first of all an awareness of the interconnectedness of all things, then it is also about the struggle for justice or for seeing the balance to things restored when it is lost. Meister Eckhart says simply, "compassion means justice."[82] And Mechtild of Magdeburg also links compassion to justice in an explicit fashion.

> If you love the justice of Jesus Christ more than you fear human judgment then you will seek to do compassion. Compassion means that if I see my friend and my enemy in equal need, I shall help both equally. Justice demands that we seek and find the stranger, the broken, the prisoner and comfort them and offer them our help. Here lies the holy compassion of God.[83]

Compassion for all of these creation mystics is the work of the Holy Spirit for, as Eckhart puts it, "the first outburst of whatever God does is always compassion."[84] Compassion then is our origin and our destiny. It is the Holy Spirit at work, as Mechtild says:

Who is the Holy Spirit? The Holy Spirit is a compassionate outpouring of the Creator and the Son. This is why when we on earth
pour out compassion and mercy from the depths of our hearts and
give to the poor and dedicate our bodies to the service of the
broken, to that extent do we resemble the Holy Spirit.[85]

Hildegard also praises the Holy Spirit as "the hope of oneness for
that which is separate," the power that empowers all life. "Holy
Spirit, you make life alive, you move in all things, you are the root
of all created being. . .You awaken and re-awaken every thing that
is."[86] The Holy Spirit, Hildegard says, is "the life of the life of all
creatures."[87] Eckhart also connects the Holy Spirit and justice-
making when he says that the Spirit is the Spirit of transformation,
the "Transformer."[88]

Compassion and justice-making in the creation tradition can in
no way be restricted to relations among the two-legged ones. The
creation mystics are speaking of cosmic relations and cosmic
healings. Sin is laid bare in this tradition as ecological and not
trivial. Hildegard envisions the elements of the earth suffering
from the sins of humankind toward the earth. "I heard a mighty
voice crying from the elements of the world: 'We cannot move and
complete our accustomed rounds as we should do according to the
precepts of our Creator. For humankind, because of its corrup-
tions, spins us about like the sails of a windmill. And so now we
stink from pestilence and from hunger after justice'."[89] She cries
out that "the earth should not be injured! The earth must not be
destroyed!"[90] And she warns humanity that human misery generated at Love Canal or Times Beach is not an invention of the two-
legged ones but a law of cosmic balance and beauty. "As often as
the elements of the world are violated by ill-treatment," she
warns, "God will cleanse them through the sufferings and hard-
ships of humankind. . . All of creation God gives to humankind to
use. But if this privilege is misused, God's justice permits creation
to punish humanity."[91] Thus we see that the creation mystics sum-
marize the deepest spiritual energy of which humanity is capable
in this way: It is the consciousness and work for harmony, justice,
or compassion.

Conclusion

It should be evident from this study that each of the six themes
presented weaves and interweaves into the others. The spiral—not
the ladder—is the basic image of spiritual journeying in the creation tradition. The goodness of creation bursts into the blessing

that earthiness is, which in turn opens one to the whole universe in cosmic awareness, which in turn celebrates the divine grace that all of existence is, bathed in the panentheistic presence of God. The mothering embrace of this same divinity urges us on to our creativity as images of God who are called to return blessing for blessing to the cosmos (Otto Rank defines the artist as "one who wants to leave behind a gift"). Compassionate healing by way of justice-making is the greatest of the gifts we return to creation and the Creator. (In Hebrew, the words for compassion and for womb come from the same word.)

It is evident too from this study that we are indeed dealing with a *tradition* when we speak of creation-centered spirituality. From the first author in the Bible to Hildegard and from Hildegard to Teilhard de Chardin, we are speaking of a deeply felt and richly developed theology. This article has concentrated on only four figures whose lives spanned three centuries of medieval spirituality.[92] I wish to say a word to Protestant Christians as much as to Catholic ones. There was no Protestant/Catholic split, indeed there was plenty of protest and prophetic religion in the medieval church and surely among the four mystics I have presented in this study. In fact, their protesting spirit and their battling for church reform are reasons why they are not well known in the church today. Furthermore, the radical Protestant movement is a direct ancestor of Meister Eckhart's creation theology.[93] And Martin Luther himself, in the first written work he ever published, which was his preface to the very Eckhartian mystical work, *Theologica Germanica*, expresses amazingly high praise for this kind of theology. He writes that "next to the Bible and Saint Augustine no other book has come to my attention from which I have learned—and desired to learn—more concerning God, Christ, man, and what all things are."[94] Luther thus confesses that three influences were key to his theology: the Scriptures, Augustine, and the Rhineland mystics. Yet where is the Protestant seminary today where the study of the Rhineland mystics is given an equal footing with the study of Augustine and the Bible? He praises the "solid tradition" from which the *Theologica Germanica* emanates.[95] It is time that the western churches—Protestant and Catholic alike—embraced Hildegard and Mechtild, Eckhart and Julian, and the tradition they represent with at least as much fervor as Augustine has been embraced. Then our culture might benefit from an ecological consciousness imbued with a power that only spirituality and a spiritual awakening can effect. And only a religious renewal can sustain.[96]

Notes

1. Michael Polanyi, *Personal Knowledge* (Chicago: Univ. of Chicago Press, 1962), p. 141.
2. See M. D. Chenu, *Nature, Man, and Society in the Twelfth Century* (Chicago: Univ. of Chicago Press, 1968), chapter one.
3. See Paul Weigand, "Escape from the Birdbath: A Reinterpretation of Saint Francis of Assisi as a Model of the Ecological Movement", chapter seven above. See also, Matthew Fox, "On Desentimentalizing Spirituality", *Spirituality Today* (March, 1978), pp. 64-76.
4. See M. D. Chenu, "Body and Soul Politic in the Creation Spirituality of Thomas Aquinas", in Matthew Fox, ed., *Western Spirituality: Historical Roots, Ecumenical Routes* (Santa Fe, 1981), pp. 193-214. Josef Pieper, *Guide to Thomas Aquinas* (New York: Pantheon Books, 1962). Also deserving of mention for his creation approach to Aquinas is G. K. Chesterton, *Saint Thomas Aquinas, "The Dumb Ox"* (Garden City, New York, 1956). Of course Dante and Chaucer also deserve to be studied for their creation spirituality but limits of space preclude that happening in this essay.
5. See Ernest W. McDonnell, *The Beguines and Beghards in Medieval Culture* (New Brunswick: Rutgers Univ. Press, 1954).
6. Matthew Fox, *Original Blessing: A Primer in Creation Spirituality* (Santa Fe, 1983).
7. See Matthew Fox, *Breakthrough: Meister Eckhart's Creation Spirituality in New Translation* (Garden City, New York: Doubleday, Image, 1980), pp. 30-35. Subsequent references to this primary translation of Meister Eckhart will be abbreviated: *Breakthrough*.
8. Paul Henry Lang, *Music in Western Civilization* (New York: W. W. Norton, 1941) p. 70.
9. Edward A. Armstrong, *Saint Francis: Nature Mystic* (Berkeley: Univ. of California Press, 1973), pp. 36ff., 52ff., 206ff., passim.
10. See Rosemary Ruether, "Women's Liberation in Historical and Theological Perspective", in Sarah Benteley Doely, ed., *Women's Liberation and the Church* (New York: Association Press, 1970), pp. 26-36.
11. Cited in Matthew Fox, *Original Blessing*, op. cit., p. 42.
12. Brendan Doyle, *Meditations with Julian of Norwich* (Santa Fe, 1983), p. 32. Subsequent references to this reliable translation will be abbreviated: *Julian*. This translation is based on Edmund Colledge and James Walsh, *A Book of Showings to the Anchoress Julian of Norwich* (Toronto: Pontifical Institute of Mediaeval Studies, 1978), Parts One and Two.
13. Cited in Claus Westermann, *Blessing in the Bible and the Life of the Church* (Philadelphia: Fortress Press, 1978), p. 20.
14. *Julian*, p. 88.
15. Gabriele Uhlein, *Meditations with Hildegard of Bingen* (Santa Fe: Bear and Co., 1982), pp. 50f. Subsequent references to this, the only translation ever done of Hildegard into English, will be abbreviated: *Hildegard*.
16. Ibid., p. 24.
17. Ibid., p. 51.

18. Matthew Fox, *Meditations with Meister Eckhart* (Santa Fe: Bear and Co., 1982), pp. 18, 14. Subsequent references to this translation will be abbreviated: *Eckhart*.

19. *Hildegard*, p. 64.

20. See my developed discussion of this key symbol in mysticism in Matthew Fox, *A Spirituality Named Compassion and the Healing of the Global Village* (Minneapolis, Winston, 1979), chapter two, "Sexuality and Compassion: From Climbing Jacob's Ladder to Dancing Sarah's Circle", pp. 36-67.

21. Cited in Matthew Fox, *Original Blessing*, p. 57.

22. Adelgundis Führkötter, ed., *Hildegardis: Scivias* (Turnholti: Brepols, 1978), volume I, p. 116. Subsequent references will be abbreviated: *Scivias*. Translations here and below are mine.

23. *Hildegard*, p. 197.

24. Ibid., p. 50.

25. Ibid., p. 61.

26. Ibid., p. 58.

27. *Eckhart*, p. 58. *Breakthrough*, p. 122.

28. Sue Woodruff, *Meditations with Mechtild of Magdeburg* (Santa Fe: Bear & Co., 1982), p. 43. Subsequent references to this, the only in-print English translation of Mechtild, will be abbreviated: *Mechtild*.

29. *Julian*, p. 92.

30. Ibid., p. 95.

31. Ibid., p. 84.

32. *Scivias*, Volume II, p. 551.

33. *Julian*, p. 28.

34. *Breakthrough*, p. 118.

35. Teilhard de Chardin, *Human Energy* (New York: Harvest/HBJ, 1969), p. 37.

36. Leo Scheffczyk, *Creation and Providence* (New York: Herder, 1970), p. 100.

37. *Hildegard*, p. 65.

38. Ibid., p. 45.

39. Gabriel Marcel, *The Decline of Wisdom* (New York: Philosophical Library, 1955), p. 42.

40. See Krister Stendahl, "The Apostle Paul and the Introspective Conscience of the West", in *Paul Among Jews and Gentiles* (Philadelphia, 1978), pp. 78-96.

41. Paul Ricoeur, *The Symbolism of Evil*, Transl. by Emerson Buchanan (Boston: Beacon, 1969), pp. 12f.

42. Marcel, op. cit., p. 42.

43. *Hildegard*, p. 105.

44. *Breakthrough*, p. 100.

45. *Eckhart* pp. 24f.

46. Reiner Schurmann, *Meister Eckhart: Mystic and Philosopher* (Bloomington: Indiana Univ. Press, 1978) p. 89.

47. *Julian*, p. 114.

48. Ibid., p. 44.

49. Ibid., p. 33.
50. *Hildegard*, p. 66.
51. *Scivias*, volume I, p. 171.
52. Ibid., volume II, p. 557.
53. Charles Joseph Singer, *From Magic to Science; Essays on the Scientific Twilight* (London, 1928 *or* New York: Dover, 1958), p. 215.
54. See Sr. Ethelburg Leuschen, O.S.B., "Hildegard, Saint and Scientist", *Benedictine Review* (Summer, 1958), pp. 48-53. See Hildegard's books, *Naturkunde—'Physica'* (Salzburg, 1959); *Heilkunde— 'Causae et Curae'* (Salzburg, 1957).
55. *Mechtild*, pp. 46, 42.
56. *Julian*, pp. 27, 89.
57. *Hildegard*, p. 90.
58. *Breakthrough*, p. 73.
59. Ibid.
60. So essential is panentheism to the creation-centered mystical tradition that I have found myself writing about it and developing the concept in all my books on spirituality and culture beginning with *On Becoming a Musical, Mystical Bear* (New York, 1972); *Whee! We, Wee All the Way Home* (Santa Fe: Bear and Co., 1982); *A Spirituality Named Compassion*, op. cit.; *Breakthrough*, op. cit.; *Western Spirituality: Historical Roots, Ecumenical Routes*, op. cit.; *Original Blessing*, op. cit.
61. *Mechtild*, p. 109.
62. Ibid.
63. *Scivias*, volume II, p. 565.
64. *Hildegard*, p. 21.
65. *Eckhart*, p. 88. See all of Path III, pp. 65-88 and *Breakthrough*, pp. 293-416, for his immensely rich development of the human as mother, birther and imago dei.
66. For example, the very influential Father Adolphe Tanquerey in his book, *The Spiritual Life: A Treatise on Ascetical and Mystical Theology* (Westminster, Md., 1930), never touches on the topic of creativity in all 750 pages. Asceticism locks creativity out of one's spirituality. The same is true of Jordan Aumann and Antonio Royo's book *The Theology of Christian Perfection* (Dubuque, 1962). In its 692 pages, there is no mention of creativity as a spiritual experience, much less as a form of meditation and centering. Perfectionism also locks creativity out as does patriarchy in all its forms.
67. *Hildegard*, p. 106.
68. Ibid., pp. 89, 88.
69. Ibid., pp. 125, 110.
70. Ibid., p. 54.
71. *Julian*, p. 103.
72. Ibid., p. 90.
73. Ibid., p. 99. Eckhart offers a similar image when he says that all of creation "flows out of God but remains within him/her." (*Breakthrough*, p. 65).

74. *Julian*, p. 29.
75. Ibid., p. 106.
76. Ibid., p. 85.
77. Ibid., p. 81. Space does not allow us to consider how Julian also develops the theme of Jesus as mother based on the gospel passage in Matthew 23:37 and the tradition of Jesus as Wisdom incarnate. See *Julian*, pp. 99, 101, 104f., 110, 132. Hildegard also alludes to this tradition in *Scivias*, volume I, p. 127.
78. *Eckhart*, p. 113.
79. *Hildegard*, p. 41. Consider also her statement: "God has arranged all things in the world in consideration of everything else." (p. 65).
80. *Breakthrough*, p. 198.
81. *Hildegard*, p. 67.
82. *Breakthrough*, p. 435. See Eckhart's entire sermon on "Be Compassionate as Your Creator in Heaven is Compassionate", and my commentary in *Breakthrough*, pp. 417-439.
83. *Mechtild*, p. 116.
84. *Breakthrough*, p. 441.
85. *Mechtild*, p. 117.
86. *Hildegard*, p. 41. "De Spiritu Sancto", in Hildegard von Bingen, *Lieder* (Salzburg: O. Müller, 1969), p. 228, Song Number 15.
87. *Hildegard*, p. 37.
88. Hildegard of Bingen, *Liber Vitae Meritorum*, III, II, "Querela Elementorum", in Heinrich Schipperges, trans., Hildegard von Bingen, *Der Mensch in der Verantwortung* (Salzburg: O. Müller, 1972), p. 133.
90. *Hildegard*, p. 78.
91. Ibid., pp. 79f.
92. For more members of this tradition, see my *Original Blessing*, op. cit., "Appendix A: Toward a Family Tree of Creation-Centered Spirituality", pp. 307-315. Special mention should be made of the Great Nicolas of Cusa (1401-1464), who was scientist and mathematician, church reformer and advocate of church ecumenism, mystic and philosopher, befriender of artist and prophets.
93. Consider Hans Hut, Hans Denck, and Sebastian Franck and their Eckhartian-like "word of God theology" wherein "word" means all creatures and "The Gospel of All Creatures".
94. Martin Luther, "Preface", *The Theological Germanica of Martin Luther*, Bengt Hoffman, trans. (New York: Paulist Press, c 1980), p. 54.
95. Luther also says that in Eckhart's disciple, John Tauler, he found "more solid and pure theology than among all the scholastics". Cited in Bengt Runo Hoffman, *Luther and the Mystics* (Minneapolis: Augsburg, c 1976), p. 154. Hoffman credits Tauler with teaching Luther about realized eschatology. (p. 124).
96. See Robert Bellah, *The Broken Covenant* (New York: Seabury, 1975), p. 162: "No one has changed a great nation without appealing to its soul. . .Culture is the key to revolution; religion is the key to culture."

Chapter Five

FACTORS CONDITIONING THE CHRISTIAN CREATION CONSCIOUSNESS

Claude Y. Stewart, Jr.

"The heavens are telling the glory of God;
and the firmament proclaims his handiwork."
(Psalm 19:1)

"Holy, holy, holy is the Lord of hosts;
the whole earth is full of his glory."
(Isaiah 6:3)

The world is "the theater of God's glory." With this phrase John Calvin echoes the words of the psalmist and the prophet. With the ancient seers the reformer affirms that the splendour and majesty of God are manifested in the things that God has made. The world is the theater of God's glory. Calvin might just as well have said that the world is the theater of divine grace. For all of God's majestic dealings with the world have, in the view of the great reformer, the character of grace: creation is grace, providence is grace, redemption is grace, the final fulfillment is grace. The world as the theater of the divine glory is a world in which the divine goodwill is manifested in God's dealings with, and enjoyment of, that which the divine originator-shaper has made and is making.

For John Calvin nature is a significant part of the worldly theater of the divine glory and grace. The emphasis in Calvin's thinking is upon God and humankind, but nature is not ignored. Humankind is of especial concern to God, but the extra-human dimensions of creation are valued by the creator as well.

Calvin's view is typical—typical of the pre-modern understanding of the world, including nature, in its relationship to God. For Catholic and Protestant alike, the world of nature has been thought to reflect the glory and the grace of God. It is appropriately considered a theater of the divine splendor.

In recent times, however, a new attitude toward the natural world has come to dominance. Some of Calvin's own followers contributed to the emergence and triumph of the new view. We may call it "the modern view." In the modern view nature is understood in ways that do not fit very well with the understanding of nature as a theater within which the divine glory and grace are manifested.

For many modern people, nature has become a machine or tool. This view of nature as a machine is an "invention" of early modern scientists and certain scientifically minded philosophers. It dates back at least to the time of Galileo and was promoted by Descartes, Newton, and Kant. When nature is understood as a machine, God and humankind alike are simply shoved out of the natural world. If nature is a machine, it is something that can run by itself. God is not needed, so God is pushed back from the world. In deism, with its clock-maker image of God, God is placed "out there" as the One who makes the world-machine, sets it to running, and then leaves it alone and does not interfere further— except perhaps for an occasional repair job. In secularism, God is pushed still further away; and the relevancy of the divine to the world-order is simply denied in theory or in practice or in both. If nature is a great machine which runs by itself, then God is not really needed.

Humankind too is excluded from nature by the mechanical model. Human existence is marked by life, by subjectivity, by unpredictability, and by personality. The machine, however, is lifeless, objective—it is "there!"—basically unchanging, and impersonal. Moreover, nature understood as a machine is without value in itself. Machines, tools, are for using. Thus, although humans are pushed out of nature by the mechanistic metaphor, the meaning and value of nature become altogether dependent upon that for which humans use it.

This suggests the second image of nature that is widely presupposed in the modern world: nature is raw material or "resource." Nature is sheer stuff for human manipulation and consumption. It has no rights in itself. It has no life in itself. It has no value in itself. Thus we speak of *our* natural resources of land, water, oil, plants, and animals. All these entities are viewed as commodities or the stuff out of which commodities can be fashioned and traded in the market. This view of nature is an "invention" of businessmen and politicians; it became dominant with the rise of capitalism. And it is buttressed, religiously, by appeal to the mandate given to Adam-Eve to "exercise dominion" over the other creatures.

The third major image for nature that is widely used nowadays is that of the stage. Understood as a stage, nature is the impersonal setting of the personal human drama. The stage, be it noted, is not the entirety of the theater; and the stage can be understood over against both its maker and those who play upon it. With the development (during the past two centuries or so) of the modern "historical consciousness," many theologians have come to view nature this way: as merely the stage or the scenery for the drama of human history. The stage, they say, has no value in itself but only for the actors who play upon it. And God, they suggest, has little or no interest in the setting provided for the human drama; rather, God cares only for the personal and historical dimensions of the drama itself.

Now, I suggest that this is disgraceful! Or, better perhaps, disgracing. It is disgrace*ful* and disgra*cing* to regard nature as a mere machine, mere resource, mere stage. It is significantly disgraceful/disgracing to regard God with respect to nature only as the creator of a world-machine, only as the provider of "resources," only as a shaper of the stage and scenery for human life. This is dis-gracing in at least two major ways. First, this is not a grace-ful view of nature because God has been (in all of these models) pushed back from or excluded from nature in such a way and to such an extent as to make it very difficult to make sense out of claims that God acts in the world of nature. When nature is understood as a machine, resource, and stage, God is understood as positing nature and then letting it go its merry way. The continuing operations of grace in nature are denied—by all these models. Second, the modern view is not a grace-ful view of nature because in it the value of nature is reduced to utilitarian or instrumental considerations alone. Nature as machine, resource, and stage is valuable only as it serves human purposes; it is not valuable in itself. It does not enjoy itself, nor is it enjoyed apart from its utility. Neither God nor humanity takes delight in nature for its own sake. In these two major ways nature is disgraced in the modern period: God is excluded from nature and nature itself is devalued.[1]

The question is "why!" What has happened, or failed to happen, in our history and particularly in our recent history (that is, since the Renaissance) that has led to the "dis-gracing" of nature/creation? What influences have worked to inhibit the development in modern times of a vision of the world as creation that is worthy of the biblical vision and capable of functioning for us with the facility with which that ancient vision functioned for people of ages past? Why has the grand biblical vision of the world as an arena of "glory"—a vision shared by many of the post-biblical precursors of modernity—fallen, for many moderns, into eclipse?

There is to this "why?" no easy or single answer. And in brief compass we can aim only to be suggestive, not exhaustive, in our inquiry. But a perspective can be sought; and a few of the representative, complex, and interrelated factors effecting the "disgracing" of nature/creation in the modern world identified. First, then, an attempt at perspective.

Christianity as Paradigm

The great religious traditions of humankind can, with profit, be viewed as paradigms. A "paradigm," as this term has come to be used in recent discussion both scientific-philosophical and theological, suggests a way of seeing and, in religion, of valuing. It represents a way of being oriented in the world or with respect to some facet of the world. A paradigm consists of a pattern of perceiving and valuing; it is a distinctive pattern of faith. It results from, articulates, and promotes the constitutive, or primary, perceptions and valuations of a community.

Buddhism, Islam, Communism, and the like are all religious paradigms in that they represent historical (hence dynamic) communities defined by peculiar patterns of perceiving and valuing—and ordering life in accordance with the constitutive perceptions and valuations.

Christianity too can be profitably viewed as a paradigm tradition. It is an historical community of faith marked by a particular pattern of perceiving and valuing. Over long ages that pattern has taken shape in, and has been borne by, the history of a people, Israel "old" and "new." The Judeo-Christian pattern of perceiving and valuing has found especially powerful embodiment in certain "examplars"—outstanding personages who at once received the paradigmatic pattern-in-the-making and enriched it. Moses and Isaiah and Paul represent powerful exemplars of the Judeo-Christian paradigm, as do Augustine, Benedict and Francis, Calvin, Teresa, and Martin Luther King. The determinative exemplar of the paradigm that bears the name "Christian" is, of course, Jesus of Nazareth. In his words, deeds, and destiny the peculiarly Christian pattern of perceiving, valuing, and ordering life found: incarnation.

Paradigm traditions find embodiment not only in the lives of historical personages; they give rise to distinctive metaphors and models as well. Metaphors and models are analogical forms which are utilized to explicate the character of the unfamiliar in terms of the character of the familiar. They are selective; they highlight certain features of that with which they deal, and they deemphasize other features. Metaphors and models suggest ways of seeing, that is, they direct and alter perception. They express and evoke attitudes, reflect and shape behavior, interpret experience, and open up fresh possibilities for experience and understanding. Both metaphors and models make claims about the ways things are, but the claims made by models are usually bolder than those made by metaphors. There are other differences; but for the purposes of this inquiry, the two terms are used interchangeably.[2]

The Christian paradigm is rich with metaphors and models for articulating basic Christian perceptions and valuations concerning God, humankind, and otherkind—in their "individuality" and in their togetherness. King and kingdom; citizen; neighbor; bride and husband; parent and child; sister and brother; household; shepherd, pasture, and sheep; wilderness, garden, and city; theater of glory—represent but a few of the more familiar.

Our question, then—What has happened, or failed to happen, in our history and particularly in our recent history that has led to the "disgracing" of nature/creation?—can be resolved into a question concerning metaphors and models. Why has it come to pass in the Christian paradigm tradition that certain metaphors and models have achieved dominance while others—of happier eco-ethical consequences—have played only subordinate roles, if any at all? Why have the images of nature as machine, resource, and stage triumphed in popular culture *and* Christian imagination over the image of creation as the theater of glory? Why has the "re-modeling" necessary for the perpetuation in vital fashion of the biblical vision of the world as an arena of wonders not been more readily forthcoming and more compellingly presented? Why has the modern reenvisioning of the Judeo-Christian creation tradition not been truly worthy of or adequate to the biblical resources? Why have we experienced both a poverty of imagination and a dearth of achievement in regard to Christian reflection upon, and nurturing treatment of, nature/creation?

We shall attempt to give a brief and partial answer to this large and complex question, or series of questions, by trying to identify certain factors or "trajectories" characteristic of our religious and cultural history.[3] Some of the trajectories are of ancient origin;

others, of modern. Some of the ideas marking these paths were set in motion long ago, but the pace of their development accelerated only in the Renaissance and post-Renaissance periods.

The relevant trajectories are of different types. Some are specifically religious. Others are essentially philosophical in character. Still others are scientific and technological, economic and political. Some are distinctively aesthetic. And many of these trajectories—probably most, perhaps all—are complexly interrelated with one another and with others with which we shall not have space to deal.

Several of the factors, or trajectories, of which we shall speak belong to the internal dynamics of the Christian paradigm itself. Some belong more immediately to the dynamics of the cultural contexts within which the Christian pattern of faith has emerged and flowered. Many belong to the dynamics of both Christianity and culture.

Virtually all of the trajectories to which we shall attend have had both salutary and deleterious consequences.

By attending to a few of the trajectories of the Christian paradigm and of Western cultural history, then, we may be able to gain some insight into our contemporary crisis of metaphors and the correlative failure of effective theological reconstruction; this, in turn, may throw light on the factors fueling the environmental crisis.[4] Accordingly, after identifying some of the trajectories (several of them suggested by our initial remarks about modern metaphors) which shape our contemporary sensibilities and thought, we shall return, albeit briefly, to an examination of the question of metaphor formation and theological renewal.

Trajectories within the Christian Paradigm

We turn first to trajectories within the Christian paradigm—factors within Christianity itself which dramatically condition the Christian creation-consciousness. Several suggest themselves: the sense of the priority of the personal, the interpenetration of humans as agents of change, the prevalence of otherworldly aspirations, the passionate concern for social justice, and the tendency to regard God as unchanging and as inappreciative of what goes on in the world.

1. The Priority of the Personal.   One of the most pervasive and persistent trajectories of the Christian paradigm is one which involves the affirmation of the priority of the personal in being.

The consistent witness of the Judeo-Christian tradition is that "the one God who is Being is an 'I,' or like an 'I,' who is faithful as only selves are faithful."[5] Impersonal metaphors for deity are present within the Christian paradigm tradition: ultimate reality, being itself, ground of being, the absolute, power. . . . But a variety of personalistic images have priority. Father (parent), shepherd, husband, judge, redeemer, saviour, spirit, and the like are all utilized to bespeak the personal character of the divine reality. And the image which is most elaborately developed in the Christian tradition is the socio-political metaphor of the great king. The dominance of personalistic imagery for the divine reality suggests that the priority of the personal represents a constitutive perception and valuation of the Christian paradigm.

Related to the affirmation of the personal character of ultimate reality is the conviction that the personal has—a relative—priority within creaturely reality also. In Genesis Adam and Eve stand at the apex of creation, their emergence actualizing the cosmic dreamer's desire to summon into being a creaturely "replica," or "reflection," of the divine. A dream animal, humankind appeared with the capacity for envisioning and deciding and acting and loving. Adam-Eve was in fact a creature "in the image of God" (Genesis 1:27). The awakening of the personal within the world climaxed the initial summoning and shaping activity of the creator and provided the occasion for the divine originator to "rest"—that is, to rejoice in, and celebrate, that which had been wrought.

Although it is ultimately God-centered, Christianity *is*, at a preliminary level, "the most anthropocentric religion the world has seen" (Lynn White) because it affirms with remarkable vigor and consistency the relative priority of the personal in being. But "anthropocentrisms" are of different types. And the rejection of a certain type of anthropocentricity is as pernicious, ecologically and otherwise, as are the historic and common forms of the affirmations of *human*-centeredness.

It is not to be denied that in attempting to state the character and value of humankind, Christians have for two millennia seriously misperceived and misstated the character and value of otherkind. They have, not without notable exceptions such as Saint Francis, focused on God and the human "soul" and the relations between them in such a fashion as to deny a significant inner life and anything but instrumental value to even the most complex of otherkind. They have, in recent times especially, tended to exaggerate the distinction between nature and history, and have, in their theological constructions, tended to reflect almost exclusively upon the personal: God, the self, human culture and history.[6] Christians have pridefully asserted that creation is for "man" alone. They have acquiesced—nay, at times led—in the debasement and exploitation of their extra-personal companions in being, refusing to grant them citizenry in the kingdom of God or to extend a spirit of common neighborliness unto them. Affirmations of the uniqueness and value of the human, in itself and before God, have regularly been made in such a way as to obscure or deny the uniqueness and value of otherkind—in themslves and before God.

Hence, one source of the failure to meet adequately the challenge of (re)envisionment in both the past and present on the part of participants in the Christian paradigm has been the trajectory—ingredient to Christianity as such—toward affirming the relative priority of the personal in being. But the Christian sense of the priority of the personal need not entail only the consequences which have been realized historically. Indeed, the distorted anthropocentricity of the past may be seen as a groping after something important and true, but sensed and expressed only inchoately. It is not simply species, or even Christian, egotism which sees humanity as having a relative "priority" within creation; for it is in Adam and Eve and their family that their creaturely companions find a certain completion not otherwise attainable. In Adam and Eve and their kind, all earthly kind achieve a significant degree of self- and world-consciousness. The failure to appreciate the uniqueness and value of the extra-human dimensions of creation is tragic, and the Christian tradition is appropriately berated by Lynn White and others for this failure. But equally tragic would be the misanthropic attitude which failed to see that all creation finds a certain "summing up" and completion in that sector of creation that has become conscious of itself and its companions. An appreciative concentration upon humanity which is balanced by an appreciative concentration upon nature, both set within the framework of an ultimate concentration upon God as source and center of all, is not to be bemoaned but celebrated. For neither human nor extra-human creatures are, or can be, complete without the other.

Christianity has affirmed a sense of the relative priority of the personal. This, many of us now see, ought to have been done without leaving the other undone. And it has become our challenge, and opportunity, to attempt to affirm the unique grandeur of both otherkind and humankind—in their "individuality" as well as in their togetherness—without disparaging the reality or the value of either.

The sense that there is in being a certain—relative—priority of the personal can, and has frequently, functioned as an inhibitor of the development of a creation theology which deals adequately with the extra-human dimensions of creation. But it need not. And it ought not.

2. Humans as Agents of Change. Another trajectory ingredient to the Christian paradigm, one related to the trajectory we have just examined, is the emphasis upon the activistic character of personal being. God, in biblical perspective, is a "God who acts." The divine primordial musings issue in the positing and shaping of a world which God loves and upholds as a mother cares for her child. Those created "in the image of God" are summoned to exercise a royal stewardship ("dominion"), to nurture by naming and tending their extra-personal companions, and to build loving community among their personal companions in creation ("Be fruitful and multiply. . ."; that is, seek and sustain community). Those created in the image of God are summoned to the opportunity, and charged with the responsibility, of doing in and for creation that which can be done by creaturely agency alone. Those made in the image of God are actors or agents—creaturely creators and lovers.

Homo sapiens, this is to say, is ineluctably *Homo faber*, the tool maker. *Homo fantasia*, the dream animal, is willy-nilly *Homo economicus*, the animal which makes and barters. S/he is also, when true to self, *Homo ludens* and *Homo festivus*, player and celebrator. *Humanitas* is doer, creator of culture and history. This is, in Christian perspective, the human vocation: to be agent. Within the Christian paradigm, humanity is perceived as having been summoned to the twofold vocation of creating and loving.

But the burden of the third chapter of the Book of Beginnings is that humankind has rejected its noble twofold calling in favor of another vocation and that, thereby, the divine project of creation has been disrupted. Faced with the challenge of being human, confronted by the call to actualize the human vocation and thereby to find the joyous fulfillment appropriate to human existence, Adam and Eve have chosen—inexplicably—an alien vocation. In so doing, they have become heir to its correlative destiny, frustration and futility. Instead of promoting the divine project of creation by building human community, humankind has partaken of the unlawful diet of befoulment of community. The twofold voca-

tion of world-nurturing and community-building, and the fulfillment appropriate to it, has been rejected in favor of an alien vocation of world-defiance and community-disruption. And, in rejecting the authentic summons, "humankind" (the term now applies
only very loosely) has rejected the creator. By turning against the
divine project, humankind has turned against the creator and
broken the relation basic to, and inclusive of, all others.

But humanity has not thereby ceased to be agent. Instead,
"man" (the term is appropriate here, for it bespeaks our "fallenness") has turned the mandate to "exercise dominion" into an
excuse to brutalize creation, extra-human and human. He exercises his agency to build monuments to his *in*humanity. The
ancients erect a "tower of Babel" without regard to the environmental and human costs. And moderns, in obedience to the same
"technological imperative," perpetuate the pattern: If you can do
it, do it. The church, all too frequently, reinforces the pattern by
"baptizing" industrial and technological trends without seriously
assessing their potential for human or environmental destructiveness.

Human beings are doers; creaturely creators; and, to the degree
that we are human, lovers. But often our "creating" is unconditioned by our loving. Our character as agents becomes the source
of our aggression toward nature and one another. And, not infre-
quently, our philosophies, our theologies, and our social patterns
encourage our aggression.

The lead motif, "exercise dominion," and the correlative perception of human being as agential, characteristic of the Christian
paradigm tradition, were not mistaken. But the translation and
implementation of the same frequently have been. The sense of
human being as being-in-becoming, constituted by decisions and
actions, can and has functioned as an inhibitor of a really sensitive
way of relating to the world as creation. But it need not. And it
ought not.

3. Otherworldly Aspirations   A third trajectory ingredient to
the Christian way of perceiving and valuing and ordering life has
to do with the sense that personal being, although actualized in
nature and history, has a "super-natural" destiny which lies
beyond earthly history. Decisions and actions taken in history are
perceived as having everlasting consequences. The drama is
heightened by the realization (presented mythologically in Genesis
3) that human beings do not move unerringly toward the fulfill-

ment appropriate to them. Rather, through either pride (aiming at the more-than-human) or apathy (acquiescing in the less-than-human), or through both pride and apathy, humans-in-the-making run the risk of failing to realize a meaningful historical and "final" destiny. Hence, the necessity of redemption.

Whenever the understanding of redemption has been developed in Christian tradition with a sense of the "one flesh" character, not only of Eve and Adam but of humankind and otherkind, the sense of the special destiny of humankind has entailed hope and action directed toward the realization of the historical and ultimate meaning of *all* kind.[7] But whenever the longing for and understanding of redemption has been divorced from the sense that all creatures—great and small, organic and inorganic, human and extra-human—are members one of another and are destined for a common fulfillment, then the Christian sense of a "supernatural" destiny of human being has worked against an envisionment of creation worthy of the biblical resources. That is, whenever redemption has been interpreted not as the "correction" and furtherance of God's project of creation, not as the means of effecting the completion of creation, but as an escape from (the rest of) creation, then the dream of a heavenly destiny for humans has both betrayed the best in the biblical vision and worked against an ecological consciousness and salutary environmental action.

Tragically, the effective divorce of the theology of redemption from the theology of creation has disrupted the lives of many members of the "denominational" families which collectively constitute the Christian paradigm community.[8] This high rate of divorce is conditioned by many factors, at least two of which need to be identified at the moment and discussed at more length below. The one is the tendency to regard relations as external rather than internal to being(s). On this view, individuals can be "saved" apart from their companions. The other factor is the tendency toward the desacralization of nature. On this view, the human or "spiritual" alone is worth "saving" and matter contributes nothing essential to the process of salvation. These factors feed the inclination of Christians to divorce their understanding of redemption from their understanding of creation; but they are not peculiar to the dynamics of the Christian paradigm, however much Christianity may have reflected and reinforced each tendency.

Plainly, the sense of the special, super-natural meaning and destiny of humankind can, and has frequently, functioned as an inhibitor of the development of a really vital vision of the world as creation. But it need not. And it ought not.

4. The Concern for Social Justice.   Those participants in the Christian pattern of perceiving and valuing who have been most sensitive to the *this*-worldly bearing of their faith have usually focused their efforts on the attempt to forge a just social order. Indeed, a trajectory toward the pursuance of social justice represents one of the distinguishing and noblest features of the Christian paradigm. Central to the spirit of prophetic religion has been the commitment to the pursuit of justice.

Oftentimes, however, this perennial concern of members of the Christian community has been experienced as in tension with concern for nature and ecological renewal. Serious engagement with nature has been thought to deflect energy and attention from the church's duty to seek and promote justice within the human family.[9]

The roots of the fear that a vigorous interest in and concern for subhuman beings will sap the energy available for vigorous efforts on behalf of human beings are ancient. The pioneering shapers of the faith of Israel decreed that fidelity to Yahweh—the justice-promoting God—required a complete breaking of all entanglements with Baal, the fertility deity. Preoccupation with the vitalities of nature, sexual and otherwise, was perceived as representing an ensnarement which threatens the capacity to give whole-hearted allegiance to the One who wants justice to "roll down like waters, and righteousness like an ever-flowing stream."

But the people of Israel themselves provided certain imaginative frameworks within which the interests of nature and the interests of humanity could be integrated. One of them is the image which was central to the proclamation of Jesus: the kingdom of God. This powerful image suggests a perceptual and valuational perspective within which humankind and otherkind can be seen as co-citizens, members of a universal commonwealth of being and value.[10] It is an image which enables those who "consider the lilies of the field" and "the birds of the air" to consider also how effectively to feed the hungry and to clothe the naked within the human family. Indeed, participation within the kingdom of God entails a summons to humankind to do everything possible to enhance the general welfare of all kind.

The trajectory, inherent in the Christian paradigm, toward the pursuance of social justice has frequently functioned as an inhibitor of the development of a worthy understanding of and sensitive response to the needs of otherkind. But it need not. And it ought not.

5. God as Unchanging and Inappreciative.   A fifth trajectory ingredient to the Christian paradigm is one which is in prima facie tension with all those considered above. It is the tendency to depict God as the absolute: unconditioned and immutable in character. This understanding of the divine reality is ingrained in the Christian paradigm, including Scripture. The same biblical authors who affirm the priority of the personal in being—and who depict Yahweh as a compassionate God who acts—affirm, or warrant the affirmation, that the divine is—in some sense—absolute, independent, and unchanging.

Now this manner of portraying the divine character has worked much mischief; for this way of understanding divinity has—in the dominant classical tradition—been developed to the detriment of the perception of God as personal and active. Classical thinkers have largely been at a loss to identify a way of integrating the two modes of depicting deity: as personal and active, on the one hand, and as aloof and passive, on the other. They have found it difficult to maintain in intelligible fashion that God is both beyond relations (that is, is absolute) and involved in relations (that is, is creator, sustainer, active lord and lover). They have had to labor to hold together the convictions that God is who God is everlastingly (that is, is unconditioned and immutable) and that God envisions, responds to situations as they become actual, "repents," and rejoices (that is, is conditioned and changing). The amalgamation of the notions of deity as absolute but related, immutable but personal and active, resulted, essentially, in a vision of God as aloof, male, capable of outgoing (creative) love, but incapable of sympathetic responsiveness. God could give, but *he* could not receive. God loves the world with the love (agape) that posits and shapes it to good ends, but God does not love (eros) the world in such a fashion as to allow the divine life itself to be enriched by worldly happenings.

The implications of this dominant way of understanding deity within Western Christianity have proven a disaster in some respects for the attempt to elaborate a compelling vision of the world as creation. The classical articulations of the doctrine of creation tend to self-destruct on the affirmations that God acts without changing and loves without receiving, for to act is to change and to love is to receive as well as to give. The modern mind has found the inherited forms of the "god hypothesis" increasingly unnecessary, and unintelligible.

Yet the classical forms of the doctrine of God have preserved important perceptions and valuations. Such things as the divine preeminence in being, the divine self-identity, the unique adequacy of the divine knowing, and the irreversible commitment of the divine to the project of promoting justice (and rich experience generally) are all maintained by the classical emphasis upon the unconditioned and immutable character of the "absolute." Still, the contradictions and tensions within classical theism are such as to necessitate a reenvisionment of the character and workings of the divine reality. Apart from such reenvisionment—a reenvisionment informed by modern science and culture, as well as by a more sensitive reading of Scripture and certain subdominant currents of Christian history—a really compelling theology of creation cannot be forthcoming.

But the required theological reconstruction is proceeding in a number of quarters. "Process theology" represents one experiment in constructive reenvisionment;[11] "feminist theology," the "theology of hope," and "liberation theology," represent others. Several salutary tendencies characterize these, and other, contemporary forms of theological experimentation. With respect to God, the remedial results include a movement toward recognizing genuine reciprocity between God and the world. This means that God is "responsive love" as well as "creative love." Creation—humankind and otherkind alike—really contributes something to the divine life. God perceives, appreciates, suffers with, and enjoys that of which s/he is source and sponsor. Moreover, the new experiments in theology include a movement toward reconceptualizing the character of the divine action within the world. The male-conditioned model of coercion as the mode of divine power is being supplanted by the recognition that (like a loving parent) God characteristically acts through persuasion, "inviting" worldly actualities to shape themselves in accordance with the divine, and noblest creaturely, intentions. The key to the nature of divine power is found in these new theologies of the Galilean who died crossed, a companion to thieves, but who emerged as the most effective world-changer the Western mind can recall.

As these remarks suggest, various dimensions of Christian theology are being re-formed. The tendency, in brief, is to say that

God is absolute in some respects and relative in others, that God's love and larger intentions for creation are unchanging in their character although they are conditioned in their expressions by situations as they become actual. The pattern of such "dipolar theism" (which affirms that God is both absolute and related, giving and receiving) is informed by the insights of the past but transcends them, building on, among other things, neglected perceptions and valuations inherent in the Christian paradigm.

The vision of God as—in some respects—absolute, unconditioned, and immutable has functioned to inhibit the development of a vision of the world as creation that is both biblically informed and compelling to the modern mind. But, if it be corrected by insights now in process of clarification, it need not. And it ought not.

Trajectories within Western Culture

Thus far we have focused on some fundamental trajectories of the Christian paradigm and tried to suggest something of both their deleterious and their salutary effects upon the Christian envisionment of the world as creation. There are, of course, other trajectories within Christianity that deserve attention; but we must turn now to a brief consideration of a few determinants of Christian vision, most of which are reflected in and conditioned by the historic Christian paradigm but none of which are in themselves part of the constitutive pattern of Christian perceiving and valuing. Among the cultural factors which play an important role in conditioning the Christian creation-consciousness are the following: the bias for atomism, the penchant for dualism, the "cash value" syndrome, the suppression of the feminine, and the eclipse of the sense of the sacred in modern experience.

1. The Bias for Atomism.   A factor which runs through all the themes that we have identified as trajectories ingredient to the Christian paradigm and which has influenced the development of those motifs in regrettable ways is the tendency to regard relations as external rather than internal to beings(s). It is a trajectory which involves viewing entities as independent rather than interdependent, a trajectory expressed imagistically in the early modern philosopher Leibnitz's notion of windowless "monads." This trajectory centers in the understanding of entities as self-contained and self-sufficient. We can call it the "bias for atomism." This bias is the antithesis of the ecologic way of viewing reality, and it is very widespread.

The bias for atomism vitiates our understanding of humanity, God, and nature. In psychology the bias finds expression in some forms of the doctrine of the entitative self: the notion that the self is what it is regardless of the relations in which the self stands. On this view, I am who I am independent of the people I have loved and have been loved by, the animals I have known, the mountains I have enjoyed, the rivers I have canoed, and the cities in which I have lived. In theology the bias finds expression in the doctrine that God is absolute, utterly unconditioned by what the divine has made and is making. In regard to nature the bias finds expression in the view that pollution has no price tag.

The trajectory toward viewing entities as independent entails the conviction that they can be understood and dealt with in their "individuality." It misses the fact that individuality is itself a product, to a signficant degree, of the relations in which an entity stands. Insofar as the non-ecologic preference for "atomism" prevails within the Christian paradigm, it inhibits the worthy re-envisionment of the world as an arena of mutually enriching wonders. To the extent that the bias prevails in the general cultural milieu, it inhibits the realization of the salutary results that should accompany constructive reenvisionment.

2. The Penchant for Dualism. Related to the bias for atomism is another factor which can be called the "penchant for dualism." It, too, involves the tendency to treat diverse types of entities in isolation. And, like the bias toward independency, the penchant for dualism is widespread, especially in modern intellectual history. But the penchant for dualism is even more pernicious than the aforesaid bias, for it represents a trajectory directed toward the denial of significant reality, and hence value, to non-human entities.

In its milder version, the penchant for dualism is reflected in the thought of Galileo and Descartes. The Cartesian philosophy involves a separation of humankind from all else in a fashion more drastic than had ever been done before in Western philosophy. This bifurcation, as the philosopher Whitehead called it, entails the reduction of everything other than mind—the animate and the inanimate alike—to the status of mere bodies marked, above all, by extension in space. But Descartes did grant the non-human world the statʼıs of objective being. It is, he allowed, characterized by a substantiaiity not dependent upon human observation; but its "reality" is of an inferior order and its value limited.

In its harsher versions, the penchant for dualism involves the denial, or near-denial, of significant reality to all that is not human, or "mental." Many recent philosophies such as existentialism and phenomenology tend to affirm, either forthrightly or implicitly, that human beings are essentially alone with themselves.[12]

As these remarks suggest, a widespread negative agreement can be identified as linking several quite diverse schools of modern thought: they all draw back from granting significant reality and/or significant value to "things-in-themselves," especially to the non-human world. They reflect a profound "penchant for dualism." The immediate result is to render the development of an ecological consciousness and attitude impossible. We cannot love what we do not regard as real or genuinely valuable. Thus, the modern temper, insofar as it involves a penchant for dualism as well as a bias toward atomism, seriously undercuts the program of constructive Christian re-envisionment.

3. The "Cash Value" Syndrome.   Another factor, one that has had mixed but, nonetheless, dramatically deleterious results, involves the tendency to affirm that extra-human existents have instrumental or utilitarian value only. For many, the worth of minerals, plants, and animals is a function of their "cash value" alone. This reductionist mode of valuing has ancient roots but has grown rapidly during the era of modern industrialization.[13] It is intimately wedded to the "passion for control" and the conviction that "knowledge is power" that are part of the ethos of technology. The tendency toward reductionistic utilitarianism and the passion for control together constitute a trajectory which has been reinforced by the bias toward atomism and the penchant for dualism. The entire pattern is reflected in the dominant modern ways of imaging nature: as machine, resource, and stage. Nature is depicted by these images as a realm defined by its openness to manipulation and exploitation. And, unless qualified by other modes of valuing, such a pattern of regarding nature seriously inhibits both the wish and the capacity to effect ecological renewal.

3. The Suppression of Women.   The suppression of the feminine represents another trajectory within both the Christian paradigm and Western culture generally which works against the development of a worthy theology of creation. Patriarchy has, doubtless, been pervasive within the Christian tradition; but it is not clear that it represents a trajectory rooted in the *constitutive* perceptions and valuations of the Christian paradigm. Quite the contrary, the trajectory toward the liberation of women, an impetus now accelerating in Western societies, can be seen as inspired by prophetic, universalist, and egalitarian tendencies within Scripture. Hence, patriarchialism is treated here as one of the other factors conditioning our vision, rather than as a trajectory essentially ingredient to the Christian paradigm. Isofar as patriarchy has been wed historically to primary Christian perceptions and valuations, (the expression of) those patterns of perceiving and valuing must be refined in fidelity to the profounder meanings inherent in the Christian paradigm.

Indeed, the depatriarchializing of Christian existence represents an imperative which parallels, or coinheres with, the challenge of converting Christian attitudes toward, and treatment of, nature. For patriarchy has both reflected and inspired the dominant Christian, as well as cultural, patterns of regarding nature. Patriarchy perpetuates a hierarchical ordering of being that is rooted in power rather than in intrinsic value. Patriarchy establishes "worth" by manipulation and domination rather than through appreciation. It attends to degree of power rather than to complexity of organization, capacity for experience, and place in the total nexus of being. Mankind dominates and uses and abuses womankind, as he dominates, uses, and abuses otherkind—and even his own kind—simply because he can. Patriarchy is rooted in, and feeds on, competition and aggression—toward all kind.

The patriarchical vision centers in domination. It perpetuates the bias toward independency, the penchant for dualism, and the tendency to reduce value to worth in the marketplace. It is in principle anti-egalitarian and disharmonious. The patriarchical vision is, thus, the antithesis of the ecological vision. Accordingly, a worthy reenvisionment of the world as creation can proceed only in conjunction with the type of further humanization of wo/man which sensitive feminist thinkers are now pioneering.[14]

5. The Eclipse of the Sacred.   Another factor which we must not fail to note in our list of cultural developments that inhibit the achievement and the influence of Christian reenvisionment is the trajectory toward secularization, or, perhaps more properly, secularism. Secularism represents an exaggerated this-worldliness. It is a cultural mode within which the sense of the sacred and the capacity for wonder and worship are dramatically diminished. Doubtless, much in modern secularity has led to a refinement and enrichment of the Christian pattern of perceiving and valuing.

Indeed, as many have emphasized, secularization is in part a result of trajectories within the Judeo-Christian tradition. And in numerous respects the results of the modern preoccupation with this world of time and space and matter have been salutary. But modernity has produced corrosive acids, also, which tend to weaken our confidence that God has an effective role to play in the dynamics of either nature or history. Moreover, the "disenchantment" of nature—the liberation of humanity from dependency upon, and fear of, the divine and demonic inhabitants of glen and forest—has, for many moderns, been carried over into an eclipse of the sense of the sacramental significance of matter. The modern "desacralization" of nature has completed a divorce between spirit and matter, so that what God has bound together "man" has put asunder.

In a secular world, either everything is sacramental or nothing is. H. Richard Niebuhr said it:

> The counterpart of this secularization . . . is the sanctification of all things. Now every day is the day that the Lord has made; every nation is a holy people called by him into existence in its place and time and to his glory; every person is sacred, made in his image and likeness; every living thing, on earth in the heavens, and in the waters is his creation and points in its existence toward him; the whole earth is filled with his glory; the infinity of space is his temple where all creation is summoned . . . before him.[15]

In a secular world, either everything is sacramental or nothing is. For many modern men and women, nothing is. For them, the world, including nature, is simply "dis-graced." The divine is not present or expressed therein.

Hence, secularization at once contributes to and—with its inherent tendency toward the desacralization of nature and the promotion of one-dimensional world view ("secularism")—inhibits Christian reenvisionment and the power thereof. Consequently, until a post-modern alternative to modern secularity is realized, both intellectually and culturally, many within and without the church will be unable to experience grace in nature or to appreciate that nature rests in grace.

Metaphor Formation and Theological Renewal

This has been an inquiry into religious and cultural determinants of Christian vision. It has involved an attempt to identify a variety of factors conditioning, that is, shaping and limiting, the Christian capacity for envisionment, both classical and contemporary in the area of creation theology. We have examined several, interrelated but distinguishable, factors. We have noted that a number of the factors identified—at least those which represent trajectories inherent in the Christian paradigm—have the potential for salutary as well as deleterious consequences. Part of the contemporary problem of reenvisioning is that of finding ways of preserving the salutary aspects of our heritage, including both religious and cultural determinants of vision, while modifying or eliminating or otherwise transcending the deleterious aspects.

The kinds of factors which we have identified as religious and cultural "trajectories" condition our choice of primary metaphors and basic models. They are reflected in and, in turn, reinforced or weakened by our choice of metaphors and models. We began by reviewing some of the images of nature/creation which have functioned and continue to function importantly in the West. We conclude by rendering implicit the judgment that there are "metaphors of degradation" and (so to speak) "metaphors of glory" and that the required contemporary reenvisionment turns in large part on our capacity to find and/or fashion effective "metaphors of glory."

Metaphors of degradation abound. They are metaphors whose implications for nature and humanity, and even divinity, are largely deleterious. Some of them are good metaphors which have "gone awry," at least in their consequences, because they have not been effectively qualified or balanced by other metaphors with differing implications. The images of nature as machine, resource, and stage are such metaphors/models. Each of them can be construed as affirming something important and true about the nature of nature, about the relationship between humanity and nature, and even about the divine intentions for both the human and the extra-human dimensions of creation. Otherkind does have utility for humankind, for example, as humankind ought to have a caretaking or nurturing utility for otherkind; and the utilitarian value is recognized by these types of images.

But the "intrinsic value" of otherkind is not recognized by them. And, on the whole, the metaphors of machine, resource, stage, and their imagistic kin have promoted the desacralizing of nature, a deepening alienation between humanity and the rest of creation, irresponsible exploitation of otherkind by humankind, unrestrained competition for the benefits provided by natural "resources," and aggression toward all kind. These images have tended to encourage the understanding of God as remote, insensitive, non-responsive, and incapable of being present in or of effectively expressing the divine intentions through nature. The larger bearing of such metaphors is, then, toward the dis-gracing of creation. They are, essentially, metaphors of destruction—degrading to nature, humanity, and to God.

The need, thus, is for other metaphors—grace-ful metaphors, "metaphors of glory." Within the context of the renewed vision such redemptive metaphors could help provide, the more gracious aspects of the degrading metaphors might be recovered.[16]

"Glory" is a term that derives from the heart of the Christian paradigm and bespeaks the deepest meaning of creation. It is a term which specifies the character of the ultimate whence and whither of all participants in the cosmic adventure; hence, it is pertinent, even essential, to the delineation of the meaning of their creaturely careers. All creatures, human and extra-human alike—female, male, neuter; organic and inorganic; fleeting or enduring; extinct, flourishing, or yet to come—are, in Christian perspective, *reflections of* and *reflectors of* "glory." For "glory" specifies the divine character and the divine intentions—*in se* and *ad extra*, that is, in Godself and for creation.

Metaphors of glory are holistic. They articulate the perception that "the trees and birds, the grass and the cattle, the plump vine that gladdens the heart of man are *all bound together in a bundle of grace*."[17] Metaphors of glory affirm the ecology of being: the dynamic interrelatedness and interdependency of all entities. They reflect an appreciation of adversity—in unity. They accent uniqueness and distinctions within being but block atomism and exaggerated dualisms. Metaphors of glory reflect an appreciation of both the personal and the extra-personal dimensions of being. They assert that all existents have their place in the cosmic economy and that the whole is richer than the sum of its parts.

Metaphors of glory are sacramental in bearing. They affirm the coinherence of matter and spirit, nature and grace. They articulate the fact that meaning is mediated through matter and matter finds its full meaning in the emergence and flowering of spirit. They promote the "*re*sacralization" of nature. Metaphors of glory recreate ever anew an awareness of the divine presence perfusing the whole.

Metaphors of glory are covenantal in character. They invoke understanding, tolerance, respect, and even love. They oppose aggression and promote nurturing. They help effect the "gracing" of creation. Metaphors of glory encourage responsible participation in the cosmic adventure. They express a sense of co-crea-turehood between humankind and otherkind and a sense of partnership in creation between humankind and the ultimate source and sponsor of all kind.

Metaphors of glory are life-giving metaphors. Their bearing is toward joy. They point to the Creator's delight in creation and articulate the creatures' delight in the Creator, in one another, and in their own being. As such, metaphors of glory express the spirit of the Christian paradigm, a paradigm which centers on trust in and loyalty to the cosmic adventurer whose cause is the cause of being as such.

Metaphors of glory are dynamic and open. They embody our best insights and sensitivities and invite their extension. They invoke a nisus toward enriched perceptions and enhanced valuations and the reordering of life in accord therewith. They reflect and assist the "reaching out" of being toward greater abundance.

This "reaching out" is reflected in another trajectory characteristic of the Christian paradigm: the trajectory toward self-transcendence. Christianity cannot remain itself without changing, for it expresses the human sense of the reality of, and commitment to, a divine dreamer and agent who everlastingly envisions and fashions the novel subjects of the divine envisionment. The quest, then, for fresh "metaphors of glory" and for theological reconstruction in terms of them represents fidelity both to the Christian paradigm and to the One who wills to make all things new.

Notes

1. The opening paragraphs of this essay represent a modified version of the introductory pages to my volume *Nature in Grace: A Study in the Theology of Nature*, published as part of the Dissertation Series sponsored by the National Association of Baptist Professors of Religion (Macon, GA: Mercer University Press, 1983). These passages are used here by permission of Mercer University Press.

   My characterization of the three modern images of nature is indebted to many sources, most immediately to H. Paul Santmire, *Brother Earth: Nature, God and Ecology in Time of Crisis* (New York: Thomas Nelson, 1970).

2. For a fuller discussion of the concepts of paradigm, metaphors, and models—and of the relationship of myth to these notions—see Ian G. Barbour, *Myths, Models and Paradigms* (New York: Harper & Row, 1974).

3. The space program has given many people today some feel for the meaning of the term "trajectory." The term refers to the path described by a projectile of some type (such as a rocket) in its flight or by a planet in its orbit. The term is used metaphorically in this essay to refer to a pattern of thought or the "path" marked out by certain ideas over a period of time.

The utility of the notion of trajectories for discussing currents within intellectual and cultural history has been demonstrated by James M. Robinson and Helmut Koester, *Trajectories through Early Christianity* (Philadelphia: Fortress Press, 1971) and again by Walter Brueggemann, "Trajectories in Old Testament Literature and the Sociology of Ancient Israel," *Journal of Biblical Literature* 98/2 (1979); 161-185.

My identification of the "trajectories" discussed in this essay is indebted to many people, including Dr. Philip Joranson.

4. In a brief but illuminating essay entitled "Toward a Poetics of Ecology: A Science of Radical Metaphors," Richard A. Underwood suggests that the ecological crisis is a result of "metaphors gone awry." A similar perspective is taken in this essay, although I have no intention of suggesting that the determinants of the environmental crisis can be reduced to metaphoric failures. Underwood's essay is part of a volume entitled *Ecology: Crisis and New Vision*, edited by Richard E. Sherrell (Richmond, VA: John Knox Press, 1971).

5. H. Richard Niebuhr, *Radical Monotheism and Western Culture* (Harper & Row; Torchbook Edition, 1970), p. 45.

6. The tendency for the affirmation of the priority of the personal to find expression in an exaggerated contrast between nature and history is seen in the work of Albrecht Ritschl,Soren Kierkegaard, Reinhold Niebuhr, Carl Michaelson, and a host of others.

7. A sense of the sacramental coinherence of the personal and extrapersonal dimensions of creation seems to be reflected in such biblical passages as Isaiah 11:6-9, Romans 8:21, Colossians 1:15-19, and Revelation 5:13.

8. The tendency to divorce the message of redemption from the theology of creation is manifested at different levels of theological sophistication. In revivalist religion, it is seen in the call for the salvation of the individual "soul" through extrication from worldly involvements. In scholarly circles, it is sometimes seen in an emphasis upon "salvation history" which is neglectful of the larger historical and natural dimensions of the divine project of *World*-making, a project which involves the positing, shaping, and appropriate fulfilling of *all* creatures.

9. The inclination of most modern ecclesiastical spokesmen (spokeswomen have usually known better) has been, until quite recently, decidedly in opposition to what has been perceived to be the romanticizing tendencies of those who attend to nature either in

practice or theory. For a helpful discussion of "nature and the life of the church," see Paul Santmire's chapter by that title in *Brother Earth* (pp. 59-79). Santmire describes the role of nature in neo-orthodox theology (Karl Barth), urban-oriented secular theology (Harvey Cox), and existential theology (Rudolf Bultmann).

10. Paul Santmire has done more than anyone else to explore the implications of the kingdom imagery for the nonhuman participants in creation. He explicitly develops the theme of co-citizenry in *Brother Earth*.

11. "Process theology" represents a school of thought which takes time and relationships very seriously; it affirms that all entities, including God, are dynamic or developing in character and that all entities, including God, receive from and contribute to other entities. For an excellent brief statement of the process perspective on the nature of God, see John B. Cobb, Jr. and David Ray Griffin, *Process Theology: An Introductory Exposition* (Philadelphia: Westminster Press, 1976), chap. 3.

12. For a fuller discussion of the way in which modern philosophy reflects the "penchant for dualism" see John B. Cobb, Jr., *Is It Too Late? A Theology of Ecology* (Beverly Hills: Bruce, 1972), chap. 11.

13. The triumph of the utilitarian imagery and way of regarding nature was furthered by what the sociologist Max Weber called "the Protestant ethic." In accordance with the profoundest bearing of the Christian paradigm, Calvinism has affirmed that the true end of humanity is to serve the glory of God. Moreover, the world exists, in Calvinist perspective, for the glorification of God and for that purpose alone. Humanity becomes the agent for the glorifying of God by actualizing the ancient admonition to "subdue" the earth and to "exercise dominion." But, as Weber pointed out, this motif of glorifying God by worldly activity was coupled in historic Calvinism with the attempt to demonstrate one's election by achieving worldly success. Work became within the Calvinist/Puritan ethos the way of contributing simultaneously to the greater glory of God and to one's own security about the reality of one's election to salvation. The upshot of this complex of attitudes—some exalted and exalting; some more problematical—has been to accent the utilitarian value of nature and to encourage the passion for control. Although the result is in considerable tension with the emphasis on the glory of God, Calvinism has tended historically to promote the reduction of nature to the status of resource and tool for human manipulation.

Weber contended that, from its inception on, the Calvinist ethos was intimately interwoven with that which he called "the spirit of capitalism." The capitalist entrepreneur, like the Calvinist faithful, believed that nature was basically resource and tool. However, the new breed of businessman considered the manipulation of nature to be the means of their own aggrandizement and the enhancement of their own wealth rather than the means of glorifying God and furthering God's cause. In any case, both Calvinist and capitalist—and consistently or not, they have tended to coalesce—adopted an attitude toward nature and humankind's relationship to the natural world that emphasizes the utilitarian character of otherkind. (See Max Weber, *The Protestant Ethic and the Spirit of Capitalism*, trans. Talcott Parsons [New York: Charles Scribner's Sons, 1958].)

14. The literature pointing out that the interconnections between the suppression of women and the maltreatment of nature is voluminous and increasing. See, for example: Carolyn Merchant, *The Death of Nature: Woman, Ecology and the Scientific Revolution* (San Francisco: Harper & Row, 1980); Rosemary Radford Ruether, "Ecology and Human Liberation: A Conflict between the Theology of History and the Theology of Nature?" in *To Change the World* (New York: Crossroad Publishing Company, 1981), chap. 5; an an essay on mythic renewal entitled "The Return of the Goddess" by Everett E. Gendler in Sherrell, *Ecology: Crisis and New Vision*.

15. Niebuhr, *Radical Monotheism and Western Culture*, pp. 52-53.

16. Probably the most obvious place to look for effective "metaphors of glory" is to the Christian tradition itself. Perhaps Calvin's image of creation as the theater of God's Glory could be recovered and newly developed. The kind of imaginative extension of the kingdom of God imagery found in the work of Paul Santmire is promising. The notion of the family of all God's creatures, suggested by Saint Francis, deserves fresh attention.

   Native American and other extra-Christian traditions can also provide resources for the reconstruction that is needed; the image of "mother earth," for example, and the concept of Tao could be appropriated and developed more extensively than has been done heretofore by Christians. Contemporary Western experience suggests such images as spaceship earth, cybernetic systems, and democracy as ways of freshly depicting humankind and otherkind in their individuality and in their togetherness. The notion of creative process, while somewhat abstract, is nonetheless a powerful image capable of bearing a multiplicity of meanings.

   The possibilities for imagistic renewal are many.

17. Joseph Sittler, "A Theology for Earth," *The Christian Scholar* 37/3 (September 1954): 372; emphasis added.

Chapter Six

FEMINIST CONSCIOUSNESS IN CREATION
"Tell Them The World Was Made For Woman, Too"

Marjorie Casebier McCoy

Throughout history, women and the physical environment have suffered similar exploitation under a pattern of male supremacy that has fostered assumptions of dominance/subservience in both the human community and the natural world. Now the oppressed earth and the oppressed females of the earth, in their own ways, are announcing that the abuse they have experienced under patriarchal rule will no longer be tolerated.

The interrelation of woman and nature has deep roots. Traditionally earth has been personified as female and terms like "Mother Nature" and "Mother Earth" are widely used. While these concepts elicit warm feelings about nature as a nurturing process, they also represent images of potential destruction. Thus "virgin land" and "virgin stands of timber" are designations for places men have not yet cultivated and tamed, and "raping the earth" is a description drawn from the violent sexual assault of women.

Given this historical kinship between nature and females it is not surprising that both the ecology movement and the women's movement have arisen at the same time. As we understand their connection perhaps we will be able to hear in woman's voice the voice of the earth that cannot speak for itself. The insights emerging from and in response to woman's suffering can teach us about the suffering of our environment, and guide us in re-shaping our perception of creation to reflect more faithfully the partnership required in that process—man with woman and humanity with earth.

Background

Women have been raised to accept a tradition in which it is assumed that males are superior and females are inferior. They are taught to look at this discrepancy as a fact in the natural order itself, and to believe that men are not only naturally stronger but also more intelligent and capable of initiative and creative imagination than women. Women have been told that biology clearly intends them to be mothers (which means they must first be men's mates) and that motherhood is the most sacred vocation in all creation. Of course their ability to bear children is also their eternal handicap because it is evidence of their weaker, more animal-like nature, making them unfit for public responsibility and most professions. A woman's greatest achievement is, naturally, to be the mother of a great man.

When a woman says she does not feel this way, she is told she is trying to deny her intended nature, destroy the structure of the home and family, and castrate and dominate the males around her. She is advised to accept the male world, which, after all, is the way it is and always has been, as presented to her by the historians, philosophers, scientists, artists, theologians—virtually all male to a man.

Susan Griffin gives voice to this experience of a male-defined world in her book *Woman and Nature: The Roaring Inside Her*.[1] In one particular section Griffin reflects on the way time is divided according to the events of "his history." With vivid poignancy she describes how women must live in a world organized by man around *his* life span, *his* generations, *his* reigns, *his* discoveries, *his* wars, *his* thoughts, *his* creations, *his* story.

If ever we needed to update the creation tradition it is now, and a place to begin is suggested in the sub-title for this chapter. These words are from an address by Frances E. Willard, a mid-nineteenth century woman dedicated to the cause of liberation. Calling for new laws to protect women and children in a time when they had virtually no legal rights, Willard saw such change as necessary for the survival of society. This conviction led her to state quite clearly the nature of their cause:

> We thus represent the human rather than the woman question, and our voices unite to do that which the President of the New York Woman's Club beautifully said in a late letter to the Club of Bombay: "Tell them the world was made for woman, too."[2]

The world was made for woman, too, and if we are to stop the devastation of the earth we need both women and men working together to find a better way to live with each other and with the created order on which we depend.

Feminist Perspectives

Many books and articles being written today by women reveal that life has not always been the way we have been told it is by male researchers who neglected the role and contributions of women. These feminist studies suggest new interpretations of human development based on different assumptions and theories about male/female relationships, and offer a much needed corrective to the one-sided view men have given us in the past.

To illustrate the kind of insight being provided by women, I will briefly review and synthesize selections from their work in the areas of anthropology, history, sociology and theology. These materials will be discussed under the following headings: Earliest Beginnings, The Development of Civilization, The Biblical and Early Church Periods, Rise of Technology and the Scientific Revolution, and The Recent Past and Present.

1. Earliest Beginnings.   This period is explored by Elaine Morgan in her book *The Descent of Woman*.[3] The title is, of course, a variation on Darwin's *The Descent of Man,* and aptly describes the focus of her discussion.

Morgan is keenly aware of the problem we have inherited from those who tried to use the same word to mean both male and the human species. While Darwin believed woman's origins were contemporaneous with man's, other thinkers had their concept of "man" colored by its association with maleness. They constructed their theories in such a way that the mental image of the evolving creature was that of a definitely male figure, whose prowess as a hunter provides all the reasons why we developed the characteristics we have as human beings. Morgan demythologizes this "mighty hunter" concept of evolutionary human development and explores its alternative: a gradual process in which females were prominent. Woman was no more the first ancestor than man was, but no less either. "She was there all along, contributing half the genes to each succeeding generation" (p. 4).

In working out her thesis, Morgan investigates a number of problems that traditional male-centered anthropology has not resolved. Her research leads her to conclude that females played a significant, even central role in the survival of the race. Given the high priority natures places on the propagation of the species, the changes that took place in our hominid ancestors over millions of years would more likely have been to accommodate child-bearers rather than hunters. In protecting and caring for her young, the females would have been pressed to develop skills for providing the necessities of food and shelter and to devise a form of communication.

Analyzing the available evidence, Morgan demonstrates how woman was as much a part of the primitive development of the human species as man. She was not a weak, inferior creature who depended on the male to provide for her, but partner in a process in which survival depended on the mutual activity of both sexes. Thus woman made her own unique contribution to the propagation of the race and to the growth of its primitive cultural world.

2. The Development of Civilization. Evelyn Reed in her work *Woman's Evolution: From Matriarchal Clan to Patriarchal Family*[4] considers the period leading up to the dawn of civilization, that is, up to about 3,000 B.C. As Elaine Morgan questioned the assumption that "Man the Mighty Hunter" determined the evolutional progress of the human species, Evelyn Reed questions the assumption that the "Father Family" model was the basic form of social organization for primitive humans. Her discussion is organized around what are recognized as three great epochs of social evolution: savagery, which rested on a hunting/gathering economy and lasted about a million-odd years (99% of human existence); barbarism, which began about 8,000 years ago with food production through agriculture and stock raising; and civilization, which started about 3,000 years ago and ushered in the practice of commodity production and exchange.

Drawing in detail on the works of various anthropologists and citing many accounts of primitive tribes and their practices, their memories and their traditions, Reed makes a convincing argument that the maternal clan system was the original form of social organization. Tracing the course of matriarchal development she shows the most powerful cause of its downfall and transformation into patriarchy to be the acquisition of private property.

Reed contends, therefore, that the father-family structure, far from being the basic social unit from time immemorial, was a late arrival in history. She does not advocate a return to some lost paradise of matriarchy, but she does hope to reestablish that basic chapter in the story of human evolution so that we can move

ahead in terms of that understanding. Furthermore, she believes
that

> the knowledge that female inferiority today is not biologically
> determined, that it has not been a permanent fixture throughout
> history, and that our sex was once the organizers and leaders of
> social life, should heighten the self-confidence of women who are
> today aspiring for liberation (p. xviii).

From the beginning, Reed points out, the biological advantage
for humanizing the species was clearly on the side of the female.
The maternal functions of women helped them acquire the traits
necessary for collective action, whereas adult males remained in
competition with each other for basic necessities and had to learn
to replace their combativeness with fraternal and social cooperation. Women may have been the ones to take the initiative in
instituting two taboos that were necessary for group survival: a)
against hunting within the clan (so that in a time when it was hard
to separate one's own kind from animals, men could not eat other
members of their own group), and b) against mating within the
clan (thus protecting clan members from the violence that occurs
when males compete for females). It is important to remember
that primitive people did not know how a child was conceived or
what caused menstruation. Women were thought to have mystical
powers by which they gave birth to children.

It is apparent that primitive women were productive in ways
other than procreation. They controlled the food supply,
developed the use of fire in cooking and industry, devised methods
of transportation (heads and backs). They were the medicine
women, the makers of cloth, tanners of leather, the pot makers
and artists, the architects and engineers. But, Reed notes, "The
impressive labor record of women is obscured by the usual
description of it as 'household' work" (p. 124). They also learned
cooperative labor, created communal life, developed their minds,
and, because it was more likely that women would talk while
working together than men would on the hunt, they brought
speech into being.

This matriarchal community described by Reed was not one in
which females ruled over men, a kind of inverted male dominance,
but a clan where the kin of the mother was the primary group—
the mother, her children and her brothers formed a recognizable
blood kin unit. It was the mother's brothers, therefore, who
assumed certain paternal functions for her children. As the social

organization became more complex, there evolved forms of gift reciprocity among clans and, of course, blood revenge when wrongs were done to one kin group by another.

The step toward creating the "father family" was one based not on genitorship of the child, but on ownership. A custom developed whereby a man would give cattle or other gifts to the brothers of the woman to be his mate and then he was entitled to any children she bore. If the marriage ended he kept the children; if she had no children or wanted to keep them, he could ask for his gifts back. Were the gifts not returned (having been used by the brother, perhaps, to get mates for their own sons) a blood feud could result. Eventually the resolution of this kind of impasse was made possible through the determination of a sacrifice, a blood redemption to pay a blood debt.

In the course of time the acceptable sacrifice became a ritual offering of the first-born son—a practice recorded both in history and in myth. As the matrifamily gave way to the one-father family, this blood offering became the price that had to be paid to break through the irreconcilable conflict between the rights of the mother's brothers and the rights of the father. Later in the civilizing process the blood redemption was taken care of by substituting a domesticated animal for the first-born son, a procedure that begins to sound familiar to those who have read the Old Testament story of Abraham ("the first patriarch") and his son Isaac.

The matrifamily had emerged eight thousand years ago at the beginning of barbarism. By the end of the barbarian period some five thousand years later it had been completely replaced by the one-father family. It is midway in that long period of transition that the Judeo-Christian tradition begins to emerge, shaped by the patriarchal character of its time.

With the rise of private property and the patriarchal family, women lost control over their lives, destinies, and bodies and were reduced to economic dependency on their fathers and husbands. At one time girls were prized because their fathers could get property in exchange for them, but eventually even that value was lost and instead of receiving a bride price, fathers had to put up doweries to get their daughters married. After fixing the paternal line of descent by law, the men of that early society then took the next step. They declared that women were only incidental to the childbearing process itself and that the father alone created the child. Thus the "reverse creation" took shape to support the new social structure: Eve was born from Adam's rib, Athena emerged from the forehead of Zeus. The civilized era had begun.

3. The Biblical and Early Church Periods.   A great deal of material about these periods has been written recently from the feminist perspective. One of the most cogent interpreters is Rosemary Radford Ruether, and her book *New Woman/New Earth: Sexist Ideologies and Human Liberation*[5] provides a concise statement of her analysis.

Ruether agrees with other feminist writers that in the patriarchal world view a female is not defined in her own right but in relation to a male-centered understanding of humanity. It is important, therefore, to study the historical development that led to her classification as an inferior part of the human species. Like Reed, Ruether cautions women against thinking they can find their validation in some myth of a primitive matriarchal Eden. Whereas Reed traces the way the matrilineal structure of primitive people became transformed into a patriarchal form that repressed women, Ruether looks at the way the worship of mother-goddess figures was altered to support the power of a ruling male elite.

Belief in a female primordial source of life is not strange, Ruether points out, when we remember that through experience we know it is women who give birth and therefore illustrate the life force upon which both males and females depend. In ancient Babylonian and Canaanite stories there is a genesis myth in which a kind of world egg or womb gestates and differentiates itself into sky (father) and earth (mother). The generations of deities born of these two must struggle against the primal mother who continually threatens to absorb everything back into chaos. The champion is Marduk, the god-king who reestablishes the differentiated chaos. But all of this contention takes place within the matrix of the "Ur-Mother," not outside or above her.

As the myth developed further, the earth goddess represented ordered agricultural nature and, with her fertility goddess daughter, supported the king as he achieved ordered civilization. The generative power was regarded as maternal, but it was put in the hands of the son who reigned as a king. Men in that time saw themselves as dependent on nature but they were beginning to coopt the female into the male power structure.

Ruether then points out a new stage of consciousness that arose about 1,000 B.C. in Hebrew, Greek, and other cultures.

In the classical stage of civilization men entertain the possibility of freeing themselves from dependency on nature altogether. They seek to master nature, not by basing themselves on it and exalting it as an independent divine power, but by subordinating it and linking their essential selves with a transcendent principle beyond nature which is pictured as intellectual and male (p. 13).

In this view the genesis stories show the world not as emerging out of a primal matrix encompassing both heaven and earth, but as a creation brought about by a fiat from above (see Genesis 1:1). Nature no longer embraces all reality but is subjugated into the lower part of a new dualism. Sky and earth are no longer seen as complementary but in a hierarchal relationship. Maleness becomes associated with the transcendent spiritual and intellectual principle of the cosmos, while femaleness is identified with the lower material realm of the natural world.

Ruether gives illustrations of this development in both Greek philosophy and biblical religion. Aristotle regarded women as subordinate to free Greek males and denied her any generative potency (females are simply "defective males"). The Old Testament creation story of the female born from Adam's rib reverses natural experience so that man gives birth to woman with the help of a father God. In Greek literature, the later strata of the Old Testament, and talmudic Judaism evil is attributed to women, with the origins of evil traced to such females as Eve and Pandora (probably debased goddess figures).

There is no indication in Jesus' ministry and teaching that he regarded females in this way. He taught, healed, and worked with women without appearing to assume they were inferior in any way. Nothing in the narrative about Jesus suggests, for instance, that he observed menstrual taboos—a practice used to label women as unclean and segregate them from male privileges. By the early church period, however, the influences of apocalyptic post-Biblical Judaism and the dualistic spiritualism of Hellenism converged to conquer mainstream Christianity and reverse Jesus' pattern of including women equally with men.

Ruether suggests that ascetic spirituality is rooted in a self-alienated experience of the body and the world, with male ideology projecting on females the sexual otherness of its "lower half." Various of the Church Fathers described the body/soul split in terms of female/male differentiation, with female identified with body and therefore with sin. The bodily state, including sexuality and procreation, corresponded to the lower, corrupt realm, and the ascetic virginal state with the high road to salvation. The association of female with carnality meant that a woman seeking higher spirituality beyond sexuality had to repress both her bodily feelings and her female nature—she had to be "transformed into a male." The Virgin Mary became the symbol for idealized spiritual motherhood untainted by actual sexual deeds, while women remained the embodiment of fearful carnal passions. Ruether comments that "the love of the Virgin Mary does not correct but presupposes the hatred of real women" (p. 18).

While the New Testament times showed extensive participation of women in the leadership of the movement, they were gradually excluded from those positions in the church structure. When Constantine made the Christian Church the official religion of the Empire and established the Christian ministry as a social caste with exclusive male privileges, female subordination was institutionalized. Laws of cultic purity from the Old Testament were revived which defined women as unclean and therefore to be excluded from the sanctuary. Professional priesthood was for men only.

The myth of the alien female became the model by which ruling-class males dealt with other subjugated groups, conquered races, and lower classes. Such persons were defined as inferior, lacking in reason and the capacity for autonomy. It wasn't many years ago, Ruether reminds us, that "the Episcopal bishop of California denied women ordination on the grounds that only males possess the capacity for 'initiative' that represents the 'potency' of God" (p. 4).

4. Rise of Technology and the Scientific Revolution.   Carolyn Merchant, a historian of science, focuses on developments in the West during the period between 1500 and 1700 in her book *The Death of Nature: Women, Ecology, and the Scientific Revolution.*[6] It was at this time, she suggests, that the values underlying our present day views of science, technology, and economy began to emerge. Many of our current environmental problems can be understood by examining the shaping of those attitudes, which she describes as "the formation of a world view and a science that, but reconceptualizing reality as a machine rather than a living organism, sanctioned the domination of both nature and women" (p. xvii).

The notion of "nature as a living organism" provided the root metaphor for life in the sixteenth century. This concept, growing out of earlier forms of philosophical thought, expressed the way people experienced their lives in interraction with nature and in relationship to each other. Cosmic and communal life were extensions of the way the parts of the human body worked together in interdependence.

At the heart of this view was the image of nature as female and the earth as a nurturing mother whose purpose in an ordered world was to provide for humanity's needs. After all, even though the female was associated with the lower, carnal elements of body, people still experienced their mothers as warm, loving women, and the earth could be seen as like them. But the earth was also the arena for various forms of natural catastrophe and violence— storms, droughts, earthquakes, eruptions—and if the earth was female, then women must have the same kind of wild and uncontrollable nature that could be unleashed at anytime. Merchant suggests that it was this other image of nature as disorder that evoked the modern idea of power over nature, and mechanization provided the means for that mastery. In the Scientific Revolution the organic world view was replaced by a mechanical and rational vision.

It seems clear that the ecological problems we face today have always existed to some degree, because gradual technological and commercial changes brought environmental deterioration even in the ancient and medieval eras. But the situation started accelerating rapidly with the rise of technological advances. Merchant points out that the notion of the earth as a nurturing mother organism helped check some exploitive tendencies for awhile. For instance, the Roman historian Pliny writing in the early part of the first century had warned that earthquakes might result from violating the earth through mining, because mother earth had obviously concealed metals in the depths of her womb to prevent them from being taken. By the sixteenth and seventeenth centuries there were images directly correlating mining with "digging into the nooks and crannies of a woman's body," an activity judged to be a manifestation of human lust.

The new thinking associated with a mechanistic order provided support for the mandate to have dominion over nature. As nature and earth were personified as female, the images used to describe man's relation to his task were made graphic: nature was a female to be penetrated, explored, dissected through experiment, and, above all, controlled. She was portrayed in statues as a woman taking off her garments and exposing her secrets to science. This identification could not help but affect the attitude of men toward women in general; they too must be mastered and controlled.

One of the horrifying episodes at this time that is described by Merchant (and also by Ruether[7]) is the pattern of witch hunts that extended from the late fifteenth through the seventeenth centuries. All of the disorder in nature that males associated with the dark side of females was focused on women who either dealt most directly with nature (such as midwives and herbalists, most of them widows barely existing) or on young girls who rebelled against male structures. The Christian tradition of misogynism and sexual repression erupted in a craze to persecute and burn such women as "witches" who caused evil, copulated with the devil, and brought havoc against the well-ordered society of men. Figures vary, but Ruether points to evidence estimating as many as a million women put to death as witches during this period. In some villages only one to two women were left out of the entire population of women. This activity may well have been the logical extension of trying to control the mysterious world of nature personified as female.

With the rise of technology the image of the machine replaced that of the organism and brought with it the notion that nature was to be managed. Such assumptions, Merchant suggests, "push us increasingly in the direction of artificial environments, mechanized control over more and more aspects of human life, and a loss of the quality of life itself" (p. 291). It is in this context that she speaks of "the death of nature." Merchant sees the science of ecology as providing the most important example of a holistic approach to this deeply-rooted problem because it attempts to revitalize the sense of the interconnectedness of all things and to rediscover nature as an active, living entity. She also believes that the convergence of the ecological movement with the woman's liberation movement is acting to free both nature and woman from their subjugation.

5. The Recent Past and Present. One other movement that continues to exert influence on women is the romantic myth of feminine purity embodied in the Victorian ideal. Ruether[8] traces the roots of this phenomenon to the time following the French Revolution when the structures of patriarchal society were threatened and the essence of Western civilization questioned. In this period the female, earlier identified with the lower realm of sinfulness and carnality, becomes revered as the delicate, weaker sex whose purity must be preserved. Women were to have nothing to do with the crass, workaday world of males laboring outside the home, but were to create a heaven where their men could return for renewal and refreshment. Needless to say, this was a class ideal indulged in only by ladies of leisure, while working-class women did their own household work and labored long hours in sweat-shops. Nevertheless this attitude became the "ideal," and women were once again coopted into an image projected onto them by men.

Within the Victorian ideal, Ruether observes, the notion of romantic love was merged with the institution of marriage in such a way that the wife was to be a model mother with many children while still remaining sexually innocent and pure. She writes:

> The immaculate conception and virgin birth become everyday miracles. The fact that mother had sexual intercourse with father was the secret scandal of every Victorian household (p. 21).

In spite of the large number of working-class women, the myth persisted that the female was a frail species who could not bear the burden of real work. Even in the early twentieth century doctors were prepared to assert that "women's limited potency was such that any energy drawn to her brain in education could render her sterile" (p. 22). Women were still being controlled by men, but now it was to "protect" them.

One result of the split between the home and world of work was the identification of religion and morality as the domain of woman and the home. "Christian virtue" was regarded essentially as femi-nine virtue. Other kinds of graces such as art, higher culture and the humanities were assigned the same role so that the alienation of woman was extended to include the humanizing elements in society as well—they were concerns of women while men took care of business, government, the waging of war, and other "real world" tasks.

The woman's movement finally did take hold with energy in the nineteenth century, and though it lost momentum in the early part of this century the struggles have been renewed in earnest during the last several decades. Much of the anti-women's liberation sentiment among women may be an attempt to recover and foster that Victorian ideal when women's self-respect was visible through her image as a pure, religious, moral, innocent person. This desire is dangerous, as Ruether points out, because it is yet another male initiated definition of female nature. The myth of spiritual femininity is one that makes woman once more the "other" of man, this time representing his lost goodness rather than his repressed carnality.

This ideal of female purity has implications for the way we look at the world. The beauty and goodness of nature is worshiped as an ideal but the earth is still exploited when the harsh world of "reality" says it is necessary. Thus we express love for the oceans and marine life but we are willing to endanger them by building off-shore drilling rigs; we extol the wonders of our forests and rivers until a hydro-electric dam must be built; we create wildlife refuges and bird sanctuaries until the areas are needed by land developers who will pay high prices; we spend less on research for renewable energy sources because the large oil, gas, and coal companies deny that those resources are being depleted; we praise clean air while continuing to pollute the atmosphere and threaten the ozone layer; we sing of "spaceship earth" as seen from outer space while supporting nuclear development we know is contaminating the environment, endangering the ecosystem, and is capable of destroying the world.

It is not enough to love nature as an ideal because such an abstraction can be replaced quite easily by another one when a change is deemed expedient. The earth exists and has an identity of its own which causes it to act and react in ways we must take into account or bear the consequences.

As women throw off the images that have been projected onto them by males, whether they are of repressed bodily passion or of pure innocent goodness, they can help liberate nature from similar bondage so that we can see it for its own self. Leading the exodus are women who have found their voices and are telling their stories. From them we are learning life has not always been the way men have told us it is and need not be this way in the future. If matrilineal organizations could be changed to patriarchal structures, then it is possible to change again to something new. There are women beginning to respect their bodies and to be able to love their female sexuality for its own sake, without guilt that they have passionate feelings. Biology need not be the primary factor determining their destiny, but can be regarded in a healthy way as one element in the life of a whole person. There are women who are entering vocations of their choice and working in areas previously considered the realm of men—politics, law, economics, ethics, theology, environmental studies. We are learning that women have always played an important part in history and that now their participation in shaping the future will have more visible influence.

The Future

What has been believed about nature has been tied up, consciously and unconsciously, with what has been believed about female nature because both have been defined by male standards of dominance/subservience. The feminist perspective is making it clear that woman is not the "other" of man, but is to be understood uniquely in her own right. So it is with the environment. The world of nature has a dynamic all its own that is to be appreciated and worked with creatively, not controlled and exploited.

How then are we to understand the creation tradition for our time? What images will we find to express and guide our interaction with each other and with the world as we move into a new stage of human development?

For one thing, I think we must consciously seek to eliminate all references to human beings and to the environment that reflect sexual stereotypes of male domination/female subjugation. For those who do not think this is a problem I would offer a recent example. Testifying before the Senate in 1981, unsuccessful Reagan nominee Ernest Lefever quoted a description of the Congo in the 1960's as "that still-female region." When questioned, Lefever explained that " the African continent in the nineteenth century was a female continent, inviting penetration by the colonial powers of western Europe."[9] Such analogies demean not only women and the environment, but men as well, because they perpetuate fictions which do not permit the truly human to emerge in the lives of either men or women.

In moving toward new images, therefore, I would like to stop using feminine pronouns (she, her) for nature and earth. It is too easy to transfer the mysteries of nature's destructive powers to human women. There was a time when hurricanes were all given female names and the change in such labeling is a beginning. I also would like to replace the words "Father God" and "Mother Earth" with "Creator God" and "Parent Earth," thereby emphasizing the functional relationships of deity and environment to human beings in experience. The practice of assuming God has male attributes is a projection of ruling males and fosters a sexually differentiated dualism in which the female will always represent the lower order.

Secondly, we need to stress those elements in the creation tradition that call us to see our interconnectedness within the wholeness of creation, and encourage a sense of mutual respect, compassion, and faithful interaction. As an image to help us here I offer the word "partnership"—with each other and with the earth. This would mean partnership in work and home, in raising children and ministering in the church, in running the government and protecting the environment, in equal work options for females and males.

Partnership, fully informed by the needs of women, could help us rethink our economic system and discover ways to operate so that profits do not have to be made at the expense of nature and of the disadvantaged.

To recognize ourselves as partners with the earth would mean acting responsibly within a process of creation that is still unfolding, which we may help shape but which also shapes us. There are certain qualities we can learn from the earth that belong to the wholeness of our humanity and not to our status as males or females. Among them are: a) patience—new life forms may evolve slowly in nature but alteration does occur; b) flexibility—when life seems settled the storms and the earthquakes come to encourage readjustment; c) nurturing care—the natural elements encourage and enable growth; d) suffering—destruction in the natural world is real as fires and floods take their toll; e) endurance—earth abides through change; f) hope—new life comes from the death of the old; g) interdependence—the ecosystems are intricate and delicate as modification in one area affects another. By closely listening to and looking at our environment, perhaps we can learn how to live faithfully in and with our world.

To put in context what has been said here about empowering feminist consciousness as a source for understanding and re-shaping our view of creation, it seems appropriate to close with this quotation from Frances E. Willard:

> Of all graceless sights this is most graceless: the unseemly word-wrangle of a man against women, or a woman against men. In all that I have said, I would be understood as speaking only of men as they were, and as they doubtless had to be, in times passing and past...But it would ill become me as a woman to forget that if men want the earth, women are enough like them to be content with nothing less than half of this bewitching planet.[10]

Unless we do get together, male and female as equal, interdependent parts of the human species, and recover the sense of this planet as bewitching, full of wonders and possibilities that must be explored in partnership with the world of nature, we may lose it all. The feminist perspective is telling us that the oppressed earth and the oppressed of the earth are once more pressing humanity to change—not in naive romanticism as though returning to some lost Eden, but in responsible anticipation of the new that is yet to come in God's covenant of creation.

Notes

1. Susan Griffin, *Woman and Nature: The Roaring Inside Her* (New York: Harper/Colophon Books, 1978).
2. Anna A. Gordon, *The Beautiful Life of Frances E. Willard* (The Woman's Temperance Association, 1898), p. 11.
3. Elaine Morgan, *The Descent of Woman* (Briarcliff Manor, N.Y.: Stein and Day, 1972; New York: Bantam, 1973).
4. Evelyn Reed, *Woman's Evolution: From Matriarchal Clan to Patriarchal Family* (New York: Pathfinder Press, 1975).
5. Rosemary Radford Ruether, *New Woman: New Earth: Sexist Ideologies and Human Liberation* (New York: The Seabury Press, 1975).
6. Carolyn Merchant, *The Death of Nature: Women, Ecology, and the Scientific Revolution* (New York: Harper and Row, 1980).
7. Ruether, , *op. cit.*, esp. pps. 18, 92, 100-5.
8. *Ibid.*, pps. 19-31.
9. *Ms. Magazine*, September, 1981, p. 36.
10. Frances E. Willard, *Woman in the Pulpit* (Lothrup, 1888), p. 60.

Chapter Seven

ESCAPE FROM THE BIRDBATH
A Reinterpretation of St. Francis
As a Model for the Ecological Movement

Paul Weigand

Probably no other saint in the history of Christianity has been identified with a reverence for nature more than Francis of Assisi. The many popular depictions of St. Francis find their tangible form in the myriad sanctuaries, fountains—even birdbaths—dedicated to the Saint. More recently, he has been proposed to be the patron saint of the ecology movement[1] as it seizes and takes hold of the present generation. To see St. Francis as a link with a more "natural" past, as a model for the present, and as a hope for an environmentally sound future is truly a great honor. Moving in this direction, though, it follows that an investigation into who the Saint was, what he was about and what he eventually did accomplish seems to be in order before we elect him as the model for an age so concerned with proper care of the earth. To do this, I turn to two well-known authors in the faith-environment debate.

In 1967, during the keynote address to the American Association for the Advancement of Science, Lynn White, Jr. made a startling proposal at the end of his scholarly paper. He states: "We must rethink and refeel our nature and destiny. . . I propose Francis as a patron saint for ecologists."[2] Had anyone else but this distinguished historian of science made such a call, it probably would have been dismissed as either very gracious or merely a symbolic gesture. It was nothing of the sort. Professor White elaborates very concisely the development of Occidental technology, and shows that Francis of Assisi appears during a watershed time in the steady crescendo of European technological progress. The problem Francis was dealing with then on a small scale, we now are dealing with on a large scale: technology poses a massive threat to autonomous living and even to survival itself.

White rightly looks to Francis for clues to a modern response to an age-old problem. But Professor White's depiction of Francis poses a problem—it basically is not historically accurate. White depicts Francis as a spiritual "revolutionary" who breaks down the Church's ". . .monarchy over creation and sets up a democracy of all God's creatures."[3] This seems to be an inappropriate implantation of modern liberal political philosophy on a completely different historical context. Francis' motivation was to be more marginal and powerless than White would like to think.[4] White also states that Francis ". . .was so clearly heretical that a General of the Franciscan Order, St. Bonaventure. . . tried to suppress the early accounts of Franciscanism."[5] History again does not bear this out. Francis, knowing his way of life was unique, deliberately traveled to Rome to obtain papal approval of his simple rule— thereby circumventing any charges of heresy that would crop up as his movement unfolded. Any attempts by later writers to rewrite the "facts" were more directed at interpreting the real spirit of the Saint's utterly simple way of life rather than toward suppressing a few embarrassing pecadillos of a benign but naive founder. Francis created an appealing, radically simple lifestyle, and in doing so demonstrated not so much his own revolutionary power as the Church's sinful neglect of the common people and the environment. His simple *option for* the poor made the Church's quest for dominance and imperial power cave in upon itself. There was also an element of humility in the actions of Francis, as White points out. But this humility was overshadowed by a deeper and richer understanding of *respect* for all of creation because it led Francis directly to the Creator of it all. Humility pales in the presence of radical respect because humility is an individual discipline. Respect encompasses an *other*—thereby offering a never- ending, kaleidoscope dialogue with all of creation, humanity as well as the rest of the physical world. Lynn White's identification of Francis as the rich source of transformation of the present order is a good one—but his reasons for doing so need to be rethought.

René Dubos, in reaction to White, rejects Francis and a Franciscan "conservation" for what he chooses as the more appropriate Benedictine "stewardship" model for an ecological stance toward reality. By including Francis with varied ecologists who seem to be saying "don't touch" to all of creation, Dubos has set Francis up as

an otherworldly mystic whose followers all too quickly even abandoned his ways.[6] By picking up on a "passive humility" which
White erroneously attributes to Francis, René Dubos looks for a
more dynamic religious figure on whom he can focus his ecological
stance. He has done well with Benedict of Nursia. The Benedictine
influence in Europe is well documented. Probably no other group
has affected the topography of Europe as much as the Benedictine
foundations throughout the centuries. By setting up avenues for
the cumulative transmission of technological ideas and a brilliant,
systematic approach to agriculture, Benedictines certainly figure
prominently in an ecological history of Europe. But I do not care
to dispute who had a more "hands-on" approach to the environment—whether Benedict or Francis. What I do propose is that
Francis was dealing with a peculiarly relevant idea even for today:
that of bigness or size and how unrestrained growth affects the
satisfaction of basic human needs.

By Francis' day, Benedictine monasteries were very big and
very successful—so successful, that most Church activity, feudal
commerce, land rights, and technical know-how were monopolized
by the Benedictines. One celebrated monastery in northern Italy
was Farfa. It had a direct effect on the social organization of the
towns that Francis was familiar with and served as a model for the
monasteries of the region. Arnaldo Fortini, in his excellent
biography of St. Francis, notes that by reading Farfa's registry
(*regesto*), it ". . . takes us into the presence of one of the most complex and formidable of all feudal organisms, one with a patrimony
that has never been equaled on either side of the Alps."[7] It was, in
short, all-encompassing. No trade, construction, farming, or technology could be carried on without the Benedictine foundation's
approval. It is important to note also that since this was primarily
a "spiritual center," its monopoly went far beyond anything we
have today. Fortini illustrates how atonement for one's sins was
often accomplished by the deeding of one's property (which included serfs) to the Benedictine monastery. By perusing some of
the blood-curdling stories of knightly atrocities of the day, it is
easy to see that there was much "atoning" to be done. Heaven was
being pleased—heaven was being bartered by overwhelming
feudal guilt. And the Benedictines would make any modern
corporate planner choke with envy at the success of their
endeavor.

By Francis' time, though, success had gotten the better of them.
Benedictines could and did offer stewardship of the land, and

mastery of known technology as a reward for penitence and belief. This spirituality's main flaw was that it completely excluded the landless and the poor, who by definition owned nothing. Salvation was reserved almost exclusively for those who had property. Francis upset this marketized spirituality. For him, an attitude of simplicity and of taking only what was needed circumvented the latent "big business" kind of stewardship that Benedictines were noted for and contemporary society is all too keen to copy. René Dubos has overlooked the negative influence of a single major social institution unleashed upon the environment and has preferred to note only its technological contribution. This is at best an historical half-truth. Benedictine spirituality could not and did not satisfy "the folks" of the day. Its highly structured, hierarchical and marketized approach to life parched the spiritual landscape and paved the way for a spiritual wildfire unleashed by Francis of Assisi.

Both White and Dubos are dealing with an historically distorted view of St. Francis. Both impose on Francis a claim that the Saint worshipped nature heretically or at best romantically. This clouds Francis' contribution. Not only did he create a vital and vibrant religious order, but he, by his Rule, laid down some demanding and curiously relevant points for a simple life. Francis broke open the monastic spirituality and freed it for the lay person. He injected the Church back into the world from which it had retreated into the safety of the monasteries of the Dark Ages. In doing so, he stands in the tradition of the great reformers of the Church. He "reincarnated" the Christian message for a new age in a simple, yet demanding openness to life that could respond to basic human need. It is this avenue of thought that will uncover a more penetrating influence of the Saint, and position him squarely in the philosophical and theological range of those who would recover him from the birdbaths and situate him in a contemporary faith/ecology approach to the world.

Possibly the most popular work by the Poor Man of Assisi is his Canticle of Brother Sun (1225).[8] Literally, it is one of the finest examples of pre-classical poetry that was beginning to emerge from the Umbrian culture of the 13th century. Many say this canticle is Francis' finest contribution. It is by far the most often quoted words by St. Francis and surely fits into the picture drawn of him by Lynn White and René Dubos. But a key point generally overlooked in surveying this "hymn to matter" is that the Canticle is a *product* of a long search (20 years) on Francis' part to seek out that which was singularly vital to life: to discover anew the crucified Jesus Christ. In other words, the Canticle occurs at the end of his life, at a point where he gives us a poetic summation of an arduous existence. While there are many insights into the Saint from his spontaneous burst of lyricism, the initial phase of his conversion, what he valued and what he considered worth a life of radical penance is somehow eclipsed. Francis' symbolism is the *result* of his self-denial, radically destitute life, generosity, and care of others (including lepers, who were even ecclesiastically declared "dead"). His "Canticle of Brother Sun" is a *product* of his dynamic spiritual search. It is a reflection of a life dedicated to God. Matter, and all created things, were summed up in this Canticle and offered as a way of praising God *through* creation.[9] Thus, Francis was not advocating a form of pantheism as Lynn White would have it. His search had burst forth in lyrical poetry at the end of his life to celebrate an *attitude* he cultivated in living a simple life.

There is no better place to get the real spirit of the Poor Man of Assisi's understanding of life than in what he wrote in his own Rule.[10] It is within this document that the Saint's inspiration is tested. In all three of its revised forms (1209, 1221, 1223), the Rule is written proof of a readiness to accept persons primarily because of the example of a broken, needy Jesus Christ; Francis starts with the poor and oppressed as the face of Christ, as *the* motivating factor in life. With the double awareness of one's own and others' needs, a single dynamic of selfless love is set up by Francis as the central operating principle of the Church. That this was readily accepted can be documented by the sheer number of friars in Europe just ten years after the beginnings of the Order. By the Chapter of Mats (1221), which was a general meeting of all the friars, 50,000 members crowded the coutryside around Assisi. It was a spiritual wildfire among the populace, blessed and sanctioned by Pope Innocent III. In an unusual move, the Pope gave the Rule of the Order of Friars Minor oral approbation to begin to live a radically simple life based only on the Gospel. Its effect was enormous. From the 13th century onward theological and philosophical systems have tried to understand and integrate Francis' simple witness for each successive generation of believers.

The first ten chapters of his Rule of 1221 reveal how Francis made basic human need the starting point for his way of life. The remaining chapters of the Rule (11-26) focus on the community life of the Friars Minor and the ecclesial organization of the Order. The Saint's understanding of nature and poverty in these few verses gives a rich glimpse into his spirit. By beginning his Rule with scripture quotations from Matthew and Luke, the simple tone and ecological implications are set:

> The Rule and Life of the Friars is to live in obedience, in chastity, and without property, following the teaching and footsteps of our Lord Jesus Christ who says, "If thou wilt be perfect, go, sell what thou hast, and give to the poor, and thou shalt have treasure in heaven; and come, follow me" (Mt. 19:21) and "If anyone wishes to come after me, let him deny himself, and take up his cross and follow me" (Mt. 16:24). Elsewhere he says, "If anyone comes to me and does not hate his father and mother, and wife and children, and brothers and sisters, yes, and even his own life, he cannot be my disciple" (Lk. 14:26). "And everyone who has left house or lands, for my name's sake, shall receive a hundredfold, and shall possess life everlasting" (Mt. 19:29).[11]

From these simple quotes, Francis weaves a life of profound implication for his followers. It is grounded from the first in the words of Jesus. It calls the hearer beyond his/her present, to confront that which is superfluous and opens out into what is a basic spiritual need—to grapple with the call to ". . . come, follow me" (Mt. 19:21).[12] In an all-encompassing hierarchical monastic setting, some of the ecological implications begin to become apparent. Francis undermines the "atonement" system set up by the monasteries, and sets up a spirituality that will also travel with the increasing number of freed serfs that were collecting in cities. Metaphysical ties to land and property are broken. A new path is opened up which is characterized by a focus on the person-in-need above all other considerations.

It is the concept of need that is essential in formulating a new understanding of Francis as the patron of an ecological movement. Francis instinctively sought out only that which was essential. His Rule is not meant to be a harsh reprimand, or an unattainable ideal. Instead, it is a centering on basic physical/spiritual needs of the human person—simple food, adequate clothing, humble dwelling, and shared prayer life; he lays down a foundation for a *radically respectful life* toward others and the created world. It is an invitation and an exhortation to clear away all that is ephemeral in life in order to reach God.

This was an all-embracing paradigm not affected by our modern bifurcations. His effort is not asceticism—a "foregoing" of the world for practice of some "higher" virtue. It was not compartmentalized. The medieval mind saw all of reality as one— stairstepped all the way to the Creator. Thus, when Francis' vision began to spread, it took immediate effect upon the environment. Serfs following his lead no longer bore arms, nobles walked away from teetering estates, monasteries emptied and the countryside teemed with roving preachers spreading the good news of an attainable heaven. And the key to this was always to be ready to respond to another in need, which did not include a preoccupation with personal power. Chapter 2 of the Rule is very clear in this when it exhorts: "But if they are in want, the friars could accept other material goods for their needs, just like the rest of the poor, but not money."[13] Here, his prohibition against money is a logical follow-through in his search for the simple and not, as some would have it, a romanticism. Money, seen as the representation of fluid power, of free-floating access to not only the basic needs for survival but also whim, was anathema to Francis. His repeated admonition to abhor money shows how strongly he was repelled by the ample opportunities to lord it over others, to push one's weight around in society, and to impact nature adversely for private gain.

Chapters 2 and 3 of Francis' Rule embellish his understanding of needs. Francis moves in a masterful style from the internal/individual needs (food, clothing, shelter) to the more external and communal ones. Work is a good case in point. In Francis' time agricultural work affected the environment the most. Cities were only just beginning to flourish and their influence was minimal. Dubos claims that it was the Benedictines who first got dirt under the fingernails of the Church.[14] This may be true, but it was Francis who got the Church *out to* those who *lived by the earth*. His approach is radically different from the Benedictine one: Francis offers an ethic, a way of life for those living in the rural and urban world. His spirituality affected a rapidly changing new society by altering radically the lay person's understanding of his or her self-concept. Now God *emanated from* creation rather than from above it, as the monastic tradition seemed to suggest. The citizen of one of the new nation-states could approach God *through* his work and love for nature without having to go to the monastery to "sacralize" his effort.

Francis' understanding of the importance of work is evident. He did not start a "mendicant" movement (a free-floating group of penitential preachers).[15] By their very nature, mendicants live primarily on the generosity and good will of others. Their nomadic, transient way of life permits little else. But Francis had in mind a perfect marriage of work and the Gospel which would serve as an example to all workers of the time. By working in whatever way the friars could, they integrated themselves and their particular gifts into the world in a way that the monastic orders never could. Only *after* work were the friars to beg. This again is consistent. Work was a part of life; a proper respectful attitude was a way to reach God. Begging was saved for those times when the work was not enough even to meet the basic needs for oneself and those whom one is caring for. Francis' radicalness is shown in his admonition to give away even what little was worked for if another needed it. Begging was appropriate only then. One can see the far-reaching economic implications of this. Radical Franciscan generosity, more than Benedictine stewardship, would affect the notions of accumulation of capital and investment that were beginning to be formed during this era.

From this glimpse of the first ten chapters of his Rule, the central dynamic of Francis' message emerges. He counsels simplicity, acceptance of brokenness, and an openness to the other-in-need. It is a radical *exhortation to humanness* lived out in an environment that did not value the human as greatly as new markets—a situation not unlike our own. Francis' way of life, articulated in his Rule, Life, and Testament, is an invitation to every age to begin again to live fully yet simply and die stretching and reaching for a God who always moves beyond us.

After eight centuries, attempts to live the vision of Francis have undergone many revisions and renewals. Each has been spurred on by the desire to recapture the creativity of the Saint and renew it for the present age. Francis continues to be seen as one of those contradictory forces in the life of the Church and history in general that has tremendous power that emanates from his weakness and simplicity. His life is an example of how to greet change and of how to participate in the reincarnation of Christ again in history. His example still shines, still has the lure of model and patron. It beckons us to change by means of poverty and simplicity, avoiding all pretense, want, and desire to power. It is a plan perfectly suited to an ecological recovery for a world scarred by insatiable "wants." Its value lies not in romantic notions of birds and nature, but of a steeled reverence for life, of taking only what is needed, and letting go of all the rest.

The theological reinterpretation of St. Francis in the light of his response to need will have profound implications for the ecological movement in general and also for any attempt to form particular social policy. With a critical re-reading of the documents, attempts to tag him with pantheism (i.e., White) fail. Also, attempts to relegate him to the naivete of a simplistic conservation movement (i.e., Dubos) are also inadequate. His dynamism resists caricaturization. By proposing him as model and patron of the ecological movement, it could be that ecologists have gotten more than they bargained for. Rather than a sort of devotional "mascot," they have found a powerhouse who draws faith in Christ into direct contact with human need and the natural environment.

Ecological policy, while not the scope of this paper, can be prefigured here. Policy using Francis' stance as a starting point will be characterized by several things, a few of which are ventured before closing. For one, ecological policy will not readily succumb to any smug liberal omniscience—but will have a definite penitential character which Francis manifested so well. Also, international policy might be less myopic—not so much a stingy disbursement of dwindling resources, but rather a simple sharing of essential goods and services, especially when another nation exhibits agonizing, life-threatening need. And finally, attitudes shaped by a Franciscan understanding will be less self-righteous, less cloyingly "benevolent," and far more socially just.

Yes, Francis of Assisi, supposed heretic and romantic, should be a model for an ecological movement. Somehow, though, with the above understanding of human need, the St. Francis of the birdbath will never be the same.

Notes

1. Lynn White, Jr., "The Historical Roots of Our Ecological Crisis." *Science* 155 (10 March 1967): p. 1207.
2. Pope John Paul II announced on April 6, 1980 (Easter Sunday) that he had proclaimed Saint Francis the Patron Saint of Ecology.
3. Lynn White, Jr., op. cit., p. 1207.
4. David Flood and T. Matura, *To Be of the Church*. (Chicago: Franciscan Herald Press, 1975), p. 129.
5. Lynn White, Jr., op. cit., p. 1210.
6. René Dubos, "Franciscan Conservation versus Benedictine Steward-ship," in *A God Within* (New York: Charles Scribner's & Sons, 1972).
7. Arnaldo Fortini, *Francis of Assisi* (New York: Crossroad Publishers, 1981), p. 15.

8. Writings of St. Francis, found in *The Omnibus of Sources*, ed. Marion
    Habig, O.F.M. (Chicago: The Franciscan Herald Press, 1973), p. 130.
9. Ibid., p. 130. For an elaboration and further research on this point, see
    the footnotes given for this cited text.
10. The Writings of St. Francis, *Omnibus of Sources*, p. 31.
11. Ibid., p. 32.
12. Ibid., p. 32.
13. Ibid., p. 32.
14. René Dubos, op. cit., p. 131.
15. David Flood and T. Matura, op. cit., p. 131

Part II

THE NATURAL SCIENCES AS BASIC RESOURCES IN THE TRANSFORMATION OF THE TRADITION

Scientific investigation advances the understanding and appreciation of the created world by focusing on the patterns of its interrelationships, energetic dynamism, and structures. Scientific study is a process that involves observation, experiment, and theory which interprets and generalizes upon its findings.

The philosophy of Descartes, although stripping value from nature (making nature simply material substance), generated a steady stream of scientific inquiry which expanded human understanding of nature. The work of most scientists during the three centuries since Descartes has not been informed by a traditional religious faith, but in recent decades a reconciliation between scientific and religious approaches to understanding the phenomena of the world appears to be growing. On the one hand, without science—a fundamental way for humans to learn about and appreciate the world which has its source in God—the door would be closed upon a religious appreciation and cooperation with natural phenomena and processes. Humankind's understanding of its total creational relatedness, as perceived through the sensitivity and structure of faith, would be much poorer if scientific tools were not available to us. Scientific analysis, then, is highly relevant to the cultivation of creation consciousness. On the other hand, the religious frame of reference aims to evaluate the meaning of scientific data by raising questions about the value of the natural world and humankind's relationship to that world.

In Chapter 8, Robert Russell and Andrew Dufner present their approach, as physicists who are also Christians, to several basic themes in physics that are receiving much attention today. They make one of the most technical presentations of the book; however, even readers who are little acquainted with physics and theology will profit from seeing how the authors approach their subject and from paying particular attention to the opening and final sections of the chapter.

The author of Chapter 9, on "Evolution and Religion," is Led-yard Stebbins, geneticist and world authority in studies of evolution. Following his expert exposition of fundamentals, he identifies his own religious approach as that of a humanist. Then in parallel presentations in Chapters 10 and 11, Philip Hefner and Ralph Burhoe describe the place of evolution in several recent theologies, including Burhoe's "scientific theology."

A third area we have selected for attention is ecology. An integrative discipline, drawing upon the findings of many contributing fields of science, ecology exposes the natural web of patterned interrelatedness in terms of which the many kinds and intensities of environmental abuse and misuse must be understood, evaluated, and overcome. In Chapter 12, Paul Lutz affirms the relationship between religious and ecological thinking.

Chapter Eight

FOUNDATIONS IN PHYSICS FOR REVISING THE CREATION TRADITION

Andrew J. Dufner, S.J., and Robert John Russell

Each of us lives an en-mattered life. We eat the physical stuff of this world, we breathe it, touch it, look at it, work and play in it, and relate through it. Our bodies are made of the dust of the earth, even as the earth itself was made of a long-forgotten star. We meet one another embodied in matter, and relate through flesh, muscles, and bones of atoms dynamically bound with cohesive physical forces. We think with brains of interlocking cells and tell of our feelings, thoughts, and memories with en-mattered signs and oscillations of air. The physical world makes a difference to us, and without real knowledge of it our very lives are imperilled.

So too our faith lives. Christianity is both radically historical and incarnational, enmeshed inextricably in space and time and the earth. Our faith experiences, our reflections on them and our subsequent behavior are matter-bound. Matter matters: to the theologian, to the scientist, to us all.

Since theology necessarily includes the physical world, the natural scientist has something crucial to say towards the truth of conclusions being drawn theologically. For example, though the doctrines of creation, incarnation, and redemption are explicitly bound together theologically, they are implicitly joined to cosmology, cosmogony, causality, materiality. To talk theological sense must minimally imply that one not talk scientific nonsense. (We assert that the converse is also pivotal and nontrivial.)

As we see theology and science set in weave, so also are ethics, technology, and ecology. In terms of energy, entropy, diminishing global resources, and the endangered ecosphere, an understanding of the physical world by the religious communities is prerequisite to relevant theological ethics.

Unfortunately, such an understanding has traditionally been based on common sense views of the natural world. Notions of space, time, matter, energy, cause and effect were much the same whether employed by philosophers, theologians, ethicists, or lay believers. Such terms could be formulated from reflective human experience without the need of elaborate experiments or delicate apparatus to test their adequacy. What is space but a container, or matter but the objects contained? Like landscape painting, our models of the world were based directly on instinct and sense data common to our shared world experience. Yet such an approach to the world leads to knowledge which is both incomplete enough to be fundamentally misleading and, for the most part, wrong.

Small mistakes at the beginnings of large enterprises can result in complete dysfunction as the process unfolds. We hold this to be true for theological and scientific developments as well as for the personal world views of non-specialists. Common sense awareness is simply not enough. It tells us much about our own experience of the world, but very little of both what is actually knowable and of what may really be of critical importance about the world and about us. Common sense will not cure malaria or cancer, nor is it sufficient to resolve the problems of adequate nutrition, shelter, and energy for over three billion people. It is not enough to resolve the contradictions of cynical relativism in our global society. The world is simply too complex and too interconnected to function humanely without the widespread utilization of what has been wrested so arduously from nature by scientific endeavor. This is not the world of Aristotle, nor even of Newton. Neither Plato nor Aquinas knew anything of the laws of thermodynamics, of mass/energy equivalence, of wave/particle duality, nor of their staggering consequences both for what is and what can be done. Indeed, to what extent have even twentieth century theologians integrated into their systems the fundamental discoveries occurring in the very cultures in which they lived and to which they commited their efforts?

Contemporary spirituality and moral theory are both committed to authentic engagement; hence they must now be built on the underlying realities of the world of 20th century experience. Defining the good in a global society requires painfully hard choices, complex risk/benefit analysis and scientifically informed technology assessment. An authentic, contemporary, contemplative quest for a unitive way with God must be pursued realistically in the light of the mutually assured destructive capability now hanging over the lives of all of one's neighbors on earth.

In this paper we shall focus on physics and its impact on the creation tradition in biblical/Christian theology. What can we learn from physics about features or principles of nature which must now be included in the formation of a viable, ongoing and ecologically relevant creation theology? What suggestions can we take from current scientific methodology for theological inquiry? What have we gained from recent physics for numinous spirituality more deeply enmeshed in the body of this world?

The Sweep of Modern Physics

The twentieth century has seen dozens of major developments in the natural sciences. In physics alone, many broad areas have been born and have subsequently undergone tremendous growth and transformation: special relativity, general relativity and cosmology, quantum mechanics, solid state physics, atomic and nuclear physics, quantum field theory and particle physics, to name just a few. In addition, new work in thermodynamics of systems far from equilibrium, and the development of new mathematical approaches to discontinuous changes (such as catastrophe theory), show promise for a deeper synthesis between physics and the life sciences.

Perhaps the most important theories of this century in physics are (special) relativity and quantum mechanics. Beyond doubt, these seem most grounded in experiment and most likely to survive in any further advance of physics. Yet their philosophical implications are complex, contradictory, and often appropriated only partially and inaccurately into the theological arena.

Special Relativity.   The problem of motion, and hence of space and time, forms a central feature of philosophy, science, and theology. From Aristotle through Kepler, it was motion as such which needed accounting for. It was not until Newton that uniform relative motion in three-dimensions was taken as natural, leaving only changes in velocity (accelerations) in need of explanation. It is really at the second level of abstraction, where acceleration comes into being as the change in the change in position with respect to time, that one finds modern physics.

Newtonian mechanics pictured the world as an infinite 3-dimensional, flat, Euclidean manifold in which particles of matter moved freely either in straight lines, or in curved trajectories whose shape was determined by imposed forces. Time was merely a parameter whose passage was uniform everywhere and, like space, unaffected by the motion of matter. In Newton's scheme, all observers moving at uniform and constant velocities relative to each other formed a class of equivalent, so-called inertial observers. According to Newtonian/Galilean relativity, no special status could be defined operationally for any individual observer in such an equivalence class. All would construct the same form of the laws of mechanics (e.g., F=ma), though their individual measurements (of forces F and accelerations a) could differ numerically.

Three key observations follow from this principle of relativity: 1) Absolute rest could no longer be given physical significance. 2) Strict simultaneity held amongst all observers: what constitutes the present state affairs for any one observer would constitute the identical state of affairs for any other observer. The 'present' was global, unique, well-defined. Because of these two points, one could imagine the past or the future as an infinite set of such presents unambiguously generated from a given moment by the total set of forces at work. Hence classical mechanics could view the universe as fully determined by its initial conditions. 3) Any event in the present could in principle influence (or cause) any event in the future, since no fundamental limit was placed on the velocity of causal transmission.

Einstein continued the program of relativity that Newton began: to manifest the equivalence of all inertial observers by the requirement that the laws of physics they each construct must take the same form. Strikingly, though, he insisted on the full weight of this principle, because for him even the constants of the equations must retain their exact numerical value.

One such constant is c, the speed of light. That the speed of light should be invariant when measured by relatively moving observers seems a shock to one's instincts. (If you were to pass someone going in your direction at 45mph on the freeway, you would hardly expect your own speedometer to read 45mph too!) Yet the results of the Michelson-Morely experiment (1887) indicated just such a perplexing result might be at work in the heart of nature.

Einsteinian invariance entails a strict, new requirement on the transformation of the space and time (x,t) coordinates from one observer to the next, moving at relative velocity v. Specifically the values (x,t) must transform 'covariantly' into the values (x',t'), according to the Lorentz transformations. Only this covariant transformation will preserve both the form and the constants of the laws of physics: the space and time coordinates vary in just such a way that the form of the descriptions of physical phenomena do not change.

The Lorentz transformations, however, imply radically new definitions for space and time, challenging our common sense experience and our instincts for how the world works. Of paramount importance is the coupling of (3-dimensional) space and time into a (4-dimensional) 'spacetime' manifold. Consequently, two events which are simultaneous for the (x,t) observer will not appear simultaneous viewed by the (x', t') observer. Even the measurements of the lengths of meter sticks will depend on which observer measures them, as underscored by the famous 'Lorentz contraction' and 'time dilation' effects. Indeed, space or time measurements alone, such as the size of a room or the rate a clock ticks as it moves past me, are more like mere pieces of a deeper spacetime whole. Like the shadow of a rotating ruler, they seem to contract and expand, though the ruler itself does not. Coming out of these same transformations is the prediction of the equivalence of mass and energy, two properties of matter which in classical physics are unrelated. All of these strange predictions of the special theory of relativity have been abundantly confirmed by experiments ranging from cosmic rays to lasers, from particle accelerators to supernovas, and from a makeshift lab in the stadium of the University of Chicago to the tragedy of Hiroshima and Nagasaki.

Central to this theory, however, is the existence of spacetime quantities and forms which are invariant, and in this sense absolute. These would be measured to be the same by all inertial observers. As such they describe "what happened" in any event without specific reference to any single observer. Using the Lorentz transformations, relativity theory allows us to move from one picture of this event to any other picture constructed by an observer in uniform relative motion with respect to us. Hence there is not just one "correct" view of the world, but an infinite set of such views. Yet if another's description cannot be reached via a Lorentz transformation, it must either be a description of some entirely different physical event, or else be inherently faulty.

These Lorentz transformations therefore act as equivalency generators of mutually consistent views of the world, sorting out which views fall within the equivalent set and which are to be thrown out as unphysical or unrelated. Whereas in the Newtonian world all views of inertial observers were manifestly identical, now physical equivalence is hidden at a deeper level in the spacetime arena.

General Relativity.   Einstein's special relativity included the metaphysical notion of an absolute spacetime. Physically this meant that the set of all inertial observers could still be thought of as constituting a special class of observers, those which were not "accelerating". But the question is: accelerating with respect to what? Einstein's dissatisfaction with answers to this question was a key factor in his construction of the general theory of relativity.

Einstein resolved the paradox of relative acceleration by viewing each observer as a "local" inertial observer. In a limited domain of spacetime, each could reconstruct the laws of physics according to special relativity. Each local inertial frame can be thought of as a small piece of flat spacetime. Neighboring pieces must be sewn together at slight "angles" such that their integrated surface is "curved," like the small mirrors attached to a reflecting ball at a disco. With the achievement of this new approach, Einstein could maintain the principle of local special relativity while undertaking an explanation of gravitation on a global scale.

For Newton gravity was a force exerted between massive bodies in absolute Euclidian space. For Einstein massive bodies bend the space they are in, and this bent space in turn determines matter's motion. The dialectic of action and reaction was now extended to embrace geometry and mass/energy, and was embodied mathematically in the non-linear geometrodynamical equations of Einstein's gravitational theory, the general theory of relativity.

Suppose we consider a model universe of "dust"—isolated pieces of structureless matter, distributed isotropically and homogeneously. If we solve Einstein's field equation for this uniform distribution of matter, we obtain two types of model universes: "closed" corresponding to the 3-sphere (a finite 3-dimensional hypersurface of positive constant curvature) or "open" corresponding to the 3-saddle (an infinite 3-dimensional hypersurface of constant negative curvature). In both of these models, the radius expands in time.

Is the universe actually expanding? Astronomical observations show that we must consider distributions of matter on the scale of galactic clusters before matter is in fact distributed homogeneously and isotropically. Hence the "dust" particles in our our cosmological models must be thought of as representing clusters of galaxies, each containing on the average 100 million million stars! That such an overwhelming amount of matter is distributed evenly throughout spacetime is surely one of the most impressive features of the universe. In 1926, Edwin Hubble announced that these galactic clusters had been found to be receding from us and from each other. Both the expansion and evolution of the universe itself had therefore been discovered!

According to standard big bang models, the universe is thought to be roughly 15-20 billion years old since the start of its present expansion. Further observations have shown that this expansion is not constant in time, but is in fact slowing down. Both the open and closed models predict such an effect, but they differ radically in their scenarios for the final stages of the universe. In the closed model, the universe will slow down till it reaches a maximum size, after which contraction will begin, returning the universe to an arbitrarily small size in the finite future, probably 50 - 100 billion years from now. If however, the universe is open, it will continue expanding forever, growing steadily colder and more dilute. Death by white-hot incandescence, or death by frozen dissolution: neither scenario seems apt for human hope.

Quantum mechanics.   By the mid-1920's, a wealth of experiments showed that the classical division between waves and particles was inadequate for an accurate description of matter at the microscopic level. The duality of wavelike and particlelike properties of light and of electrons had become incontrovertible. The formulations of quantum theory by Heisenberg and Schroedinger in 1926 reflect this duality in different ways. For Schroedinger, the wave model was central, typified by the wave function psi, while for Heisenberg, nature displayed an irremovable indeterminacy at its microscopic level, characterized by the uncertainty relations in such conjugate variables as position and momentum, time and energy.

Niels Bohr tied these two approaches together in his famous principle of complementarity. Here the wave-particle duality and the probabilistic nature of quantum systems were nested into a deeper insight into an underlying view of nature. Bohr argued that a precise description of natural processes as occurring in space and time and a description of such processes as evolving under the influence of determinable causes are mutually inconsistent and incompatible. For Bohr, any experiment to determine the causes of a process in nature, such as incandescence or diffraction, precludes the possibility of describing those causes operating in space and time. Alternatively, if one tries to describe the spacetime trajectories of fundamental processes, such as the curved path of an electron, one cannot fully specify the set of causes which are operative in spacetime on the electron. Nevertheless, a complete description of nature involves both spacetime and causal descriptions. The stipulation of their joint necessity in view of their experimental incommensurability constitutes the complementarity interpretation of quantum physics.

Bohr argued that complementarity is displayed in any conceivable experiment one does on elementary processes. Yet this need not be so only because of uncertainties induced at the microscopic level by the experimental process itself. Rather, in any experiment, one must choose equipment which can in principle only measure either momentum or position with arbitrary accuracy. For example, if one measured momentum by the recoil of the capturing apparatus, one loses information as to where the collision actually occurred between the incoming particle and the apparatus. No experiment can be conceived of in which both variables can be measured with complete precision. In this sense, Bohr suggests that the observer of nature is inextricably coupled to microscopic processes themselves.

Several alternate interpretations of quantum mechanics have also been advanced. Einstein, de Broglie, and, more recently, David Bohm, have suggested that statistical behavior found at the microscopic level arises from deterministic regularities at an even deeper level. Such a "hidden variables" theory is consistent with a realist interpretation of quantum mechanics.

More recently, Bohm has developed a new paradigm for understanding physical phenomena: the implicate order. Here a subject/object dichotomy is treated as an abstraction, and nature is seen as fundamentally holistic, in broad consistency with a Whiteheadian perspective.

Other approaches to the paradox of quantum phenomena involve the possibility, advanced by von Neumann and others, that consciousness itself is inextricably linked to the chain of interactions from the microscopic to the macroscopic worlds which bring about concrete results in the measurement process. This interpretation seriously challenges the Cartesian separation of "mind" and "matter." Other researchers have questioned the necessity of two-valued logic, turning instead to multivalued logic or non-distributive logic. Still others argue that the statistical interpretation of quantum mechanics offers the most promise to the issues at stake in quantum epistemology and ontology. In any case, it seems clear that the variety and intensity of research along these fronts indicate the illusive subtlety and importance of quantum phenomena both to a valid understanding of nature as well as to the inclusion and appraisal of that understanding by theology.

Conservation laws, energy, and thermodynamics.   Though change and impermanence are central features of quantum physics, permanence and changelessness seem equally fundamental to other perspectives on quantum phenomena. Fundamental symmetries seem to govern all elementary processes in nature. They imply that certain properties of matter (such as change, parity, spin, and so on) are conserved in the various interactions which matter continually undergoes. Nature is constrained in inviolate ways, and the dialectics between change and changelessness, flux and permanence, like that between space, time, and spacetime, typify the frontier of elementary particle physics.

Some properties, like electric charge, are strictly conserved in all of the four fundamental interactions (gravitational, weak, electromagnetic, and strong); hence, in all known processes, the sum of the electric charges of the interacting particles is the same before and after the event. Similarly the total number of heavy nuclear particles (baryons) and the total number of lightweight particles (leptons) are each conserved no matter what else might happen. Conservation of energy, of linear and spin angular momentum, hold for all interactions, and have served historically to trigger the search for and discovery of new elementary particles (e.g., the neutrino). Other properties, however, are only selectively conserved in various interactions, while still others are not conserved at all.

Like the illustrations given above in the discussions of the implications of relativity, the conservation laws of physics are ways by which we can distinguish classes of physically possible events from classes of events which nature does not allow. Such laws are fundamental to our comprehension of the way creation manifests itself to us.

Corresponding to each conserved quantity there exists an underlying symmetry in the structure of matter, reflected in the symmetrical structure of the governing equations. For example, when interactions are symmetric in time, their descriptions are independent of when the clocks measuring the interaction are started; mathematically this corresponds to the conservation of energy. When interactions are symmetric in space, i.e., independent of translations of the spacial coordinate system, (linear) momentum is conserved.

At a broader and deeper level, physicists are now probing for ways to unify the strong interactions with the (already unified) electro-weak forces such that, at earlier stages of the universe, all of these phenomena were manifested by one underlying interaction. Such "grand unification theories" would display the symmetry of physical reality in elegant and universal fashion; present differences of the strengths of interactions and the masses of particles would presumably arise through a spontaneous symmetry breaking associated with the cooling and aging of the universe. In addition, the proton, long thought to be stable against all decay processes, would eventually decay, leaving only the lightest leptons and massless bosons in the final stages of the universe. Other theories invoking a principle of "supersymmetry" aim at including gravitation, as spacetime curvature, along with the other interactions of a single unified theory of nature.

Some macroscopic laws come into play only when collections of microscopic events are examined in bulk. A well-known example are the laws of thermodynamics. Although energy is universally conserved (according to the first law of thermodynamics), energy available to do useful work is continually decreasing globally. Entropy can be defined as a variable whose increase signifies this loss of available energy. Hence in every kind of process that takes place in our observed world, whether on earth or in a distant galaxy, the amount of energy available to do work is less after the process than before. How life arises out of the less complex stages of planetary environments represents a question tying physics to the microbiological arena, and entropy as a measure of disorder plays a central role in such discussions.

Implications for the Christian Creation Traditon

The Christian creation tradition centers in Christ (John 1:1-14, Col. 1:15-17), in whom God the Creator is known and encountered. In historical Christianity, we often find the creative power and presence of God explicated through two themes: creatio ex nihilo and creatio continua. The former is meant to assert the absolute freedom of God in creating the world, and the creatureliness of all that is. No principle or substance is held to have autonomous existence or power apart from God. The older theme of *creatio continua* reflects the continued creative participation of God through the openness of creation. The cosmos is not yet complete or fulfilled, and history is given a direction and a hope, freed from cyclic repeatability and meaninglessness. In addition, the "new creation," normatively manifest in Jesus the Christ, signals a radical appearance in history of the redemptive, healing activity of God, overcoming the brokenness and fallenness of actual creation. In recent process thought, we find stressed the participation of God in the evolution of the world as a persuasive immanence, embracing and experiencing creation, and a deep vision of the openness and organic unity of creation. Can these various creation themes be put into resonance with modern physics?

Special relativity.   We have seen that special relativity theory is, in an important sense, a search for what is invariant, for what is the same from everyone's point of view, in the multiplicity of descriptions of an interaction. It tells us that "what happened" is the common content of all observations of the world. At the same time it tells us what in each different but equivalent description is relative to our own particular point of view. It provides a method for moving from our own description of an interaction to another observer's viewpoint, thereby clarifying through the common underlying reality both the differences and the deeper equivalency of each separate or relative perspective. And though this method can be used to display the infinite multiplicity of equivalent legitimate reconstructions of a common experience, it still leads to the exclusion of an infinite number of reconstructions which are physically inconsistent with that experience.

What can we gain from this new awareness for our religious vision of the creation and for theological methodology? Pluralism stands for the legitimacy of radically differing world views of nature, history, humanity, and God, and competing moral or ethical systems by which we might approach global problems in ecology, human need, and finite resources with their attendant political issues. With a pluralistic approach, one can maintain the right of each world view to form its own representation of what counts as ultimate, though acknowledging that all such representations are partial, abstract, incomplete, and in need of dialogue with other views. On the other hand, extreme relativism seeks to deny the possibility of any form of ultimacy precisely because of the existing multiplicity of systems; while literalistic fundamentalism, in its many ideological forms, attacks the multiplicity of pluralism as illusory, thereby polarizing the choices into "either/or" formulations. Must we choose between the attitude that there is only one true version and the attitude that no version is true since everything is 'relative'? Can there be many truths and yet genuine falsehood? Perhaps the balance between particularity and universality, discovered in the physical arena of special relativity, can support pluralism in its balance against the exclusiveness of fundamentalism and the cynicism of radical relativism.

One analogy in theological methodology would point toward a search for the invariants of faith experiences and toward attempts to find "covariant theological transformations" which would help to demonstrate ecumenical and interreligious equivalence classes in the representations of these same invariants. Current, paradoxically juxtaposed, theological world views are scarcely more problematic than some of the apparent contradictions of special relativity which have since been resolved by careful efforts. If they were taken seriously, we would have a renewed hermeneutic of interpretation for both being and becoming in the whole of human experience including our experiencing of nature. Moreover, though spacetime is still an absolute feature of this theory, the infinite multiplicity of viewpoints enfolded within it suggests the inexhaustibility of nature.

Relativity can be interpreted as a (critical) realist view of nature in which there exists a core of reality knowable by each observer that is the same for all observers, though the descriptions of it may differ enormously, reflecting the differences in the spacetime 'perspective' of each observer. Relativity theory also provides a method for deriving the core reality (characterized by the spacetime invariants) through the covariance of the "language contract," the covariant transformations between physically equivalent, though apparently contradictory, descriptions of the core reality from multiple points of view.

Can we find an analogy between the spacetime invariants in relativity theory and various normative theological principles which serve to coordinate our religious experience and histories? Perhaps our ecumenical task is not so much to construct a unique history but rather a uniquely consistent, enfolded atlas of histories. Spacetime structures seem inexhaustibly rich. Similarly, the multiplicities of history and tradition may be inherent and necessary if the atlas of histories is to more closely replicate the transcendent history of our faith while preserving the irreducible and differentiated reconstructions which manifest the uniqueness and unrepeatability of particular community experiences. We may be more fully "one in the Spirit" when we view this unity as a dynamically interlaced fabric of traditions joined in a "hyper-covenant" of covenants.

What would constitute a theological symbol of the means for such an enfolding? Within Christianity, the "Christ-norm" might serve as a symbol by which the infinite set of religious experiences can be recognized and correlated within the ambiguity of fragmented existence. Special relativity stands in physics for a balance between conflict and deeper unity. Might this be a motif for theological accord, and spiritual unity, and for a new harmony between human and non-human nature? Such a physical/theological vision of the whole of creation would affirm its infinite diversity, its inexhaustible vitality and countless self-referentiality laced together into a dynamic and unique whole, resplendent in creatureliness and surpassing the experiences of any finite subset of our lives.

General relativity.   With general relativity we have more than the kinematic surprise of special relativity altering our common language and descriptions of experience. General relativity gives us a new dynamics, the dynamics of geometry. Now on the cosmic scale we meet inexorable interdependent connectivity. Massive materiality shapes geometry which then dictates how matter moves. Out of this, general relativity gives us an evolving universe, enormously increasing the scope of "evolution" given us in geology and biology. Yet while its 3-surfaces ("now" 's) evolve with infinite multiplicity, in 4-spacetime there is form, wholeness, completeness, fulfillment, statis and symmetry. Form and dynamics, motion and permanence, matter and geometry: these majestic themes still embrace the current world physics. . .and of the theological creation tradition. . .with roots over two thousand years old.

In general relativity, all that is participates in all that is. Even the shape and structure of the universe as a whole is dynamic, interactive, and reflective of the material world, and the properties of the parts (like the mass of individual objects) are partially determined by those of the whole (the distribution of the rest of the mass of the universe). For Newton, 3-dimensional space was flat and infinite, absolute and independent of the activity of matter within it. It thus could serve as the sensorium of God, as articulated by the deists. With Einstein, one no longer thinks of geometry as ontologically prior to matter. Of course we recognize that space, time, and causality can be considered as interpretative categories brought to the process of perception. Nevertheless, Einstein's treatment of spacetime as a physically dynamic aspect of nature brings a new challenge to the epistemological and ontological questions involved in matter and geometry. In a sense, the geometry vanishes and only its effects on the material world remain, precisely as effects which themselves can be affected by the world. The universe of Einstein is radically self-referential!

What should we make of the significance for theology of the initial singularity and finite age of the universe as suggested by current physical cosmology? Physics itself provides rather neutral, agnostic grounds for any aggressive interpretation of the singularity. Its equations cannot probe it, and little can be said of the existence of matter before it. Yet to many physicists, the most shocking thing about modern cosmology is its inability to 'eternalize' matter. All that is seems contingent on an initial starting point, which itself is without physical precedent or cause. One must be very cautious here. Some theologians have been eager to find evidence for a traditional understanding of creation in this account, stressing the theological importance of a finite universe (both in age and size). It may well be, however, that any physical cosmology which science generates, including one without an initial singularity or a finite age, is equally compatible with the broad sweep of the Christian creation tradition, in which the acceptability of an infinitely old, infinitely large universe has also occurred in historical Christianity.

Several methodological analogues for theology may be gleaned from the methodological issues modern cosmology. The latter grew out of the dialectic of spacetime and matter. These two are active, co-determining principles, and neither is given ontological priority before the other.

Throughout the history of Christianity one finds dialectic tensions within both theology and religious experience. One need only think of problems such as free will and grace, personal sin and communal responsibility, faith and praxis, contemplation and action, and especially for the creation tradition, between human and non-human nature. Can these polar concepts be compared to the dialectic of matter and geometry?

A fundamental feature of this dialectic in physics is the existence of essential (irremovable) singularities in solutions to Einstein's field equations. The occurrence of singularities in physical theory suggests that they may occur in theology as well. Put into theological language, we expect that where we find dynamic interplay between contending theses, we should also find inexpressible, singular features of the dialectic experience. Not only should well-ordered theological processes occur, but cataclysm, discontinuity, abandonment, and mystery. In the dialectic of religious experience will occur essential, irremovable singularities of religious mystery: inexhaustible, self-disclosive, compelling. Put into the language of Polanyi, such singularities contain more than they can disclose. No conceptual transformation, no alteration of language or culture, can fully articulate nor remove the essential mysteries of the faith. With special relativity we found that only the unfolding of infinitely many recollections of the central experiences of religious mystery can approach the structures and secrets hidden therein. With general relativity we may find in addition that only with the integrated experience and final recollection of the entire salvation history of the Church can a vision of the people of God be discovered which both transcends the perspectives of each age is articulated through the realizations of these ages in the faith and life of its people. The mysteries of these transhistorical phenomena stand as inexhaustible singularities to each age: compelling, healing, beckoning. At the heart of the creation tradition such singularities punctuate our vision of human and non-human nature.

Quantum mechanics. Quantum mechanics brings both ontological and epistemological insights to the creation tradition. Wave/particle duality suggests that nature manifests itself in mutually contradictory forms: at one time discrete like a particle, and at another time continuous, like a wave. For completeness both qualities are required, and with both, no more are needed. Consistent, unified picturability vanishes, and nature becomes quixotic: not arbitrarily, but consistently so. In one kind of circumstance it appears as one kind of reality and in another as the other. Classical simplicity does not fit the world we now know.

Quantum theory presents a strong epistemological restriction on our knowledge of the world. Precise causal descriptions (the effects of so much energy or momentum transfer) and precise spacetime descriptions of an event are now seen as incompatible, as measured by the Heisenberg uncertainty relations. Again we encounter a previously unsuspected interconnectivity. This time it is not in terms of forces, particular properties, geometry or the like, but rather in terms of knowability. Nowhere prior to this

century had we suspected that the knowability of energy and
time, of momentum and position, were mutually limiting. But is this
complementarity purely epistemological? It may turn out that not
only our knowledge of nature but nature itself possesses these uncertainties at the ontological level. A measure of freedom may
reside in some of the basic physical properties of all creation. The
continually creative activity of both God and human beings in the
natural world would have both access and limitations heretofore
unrealized.

The full ramifications of such duality are manifested in nature's
interactions. Many of the ways matter effects changes in matter
are discrete, not continuous. Changes come in jumps. Causality
does not smoothly effect its results, but only in packets of cause for
packets of effects.

Fundamental matter is also found to be thoroughly 'organic'.
When parts are bound in one of nature's forms, even at the level of
protons in the nuclei and electrons in atomic shells and even for
short periods of time, some properties of the whole are not predictable from the properties of the parts, while properties of the
parts depend in a signficant way on the complexion of the whole.
If the whole extends macroscopically, consciousness itself may
have a more direct physical basis and significance than was previously appreciated. If the whole extends cosmologically, the prediction of an initial singularity from general relativity takes on deep
new significance. Nature may as a whole be much more self-referential than we have typically understood either from biological/
ecological models or from the natural theology currently being
constructed by some authors.

World views consistent with this new knowledge of creation will
look for genuine novelty, dynamic interactivity, cosmological synthesis, and a new harmony between human and non-human
nature, in which the delicacy and dignity of the whole transcends
final or exhaustive analysis.

Conservation laws and entropy.   In light of the fact of increasing entropy, one also expects new dimensions of morality reflecting the interests of the community. Conservation becomes
fundamental, as responsive to the most basic needs for survival.
Stewardship is the corresponding virtue, and reverence the
dominant motif of spirituality. Concern is no longer focussed exclusively on people and things but on all of creation, and each

separate, interrelated part is respected for the mystery that lies at its core: the gift of God's presence, given for us all.

Conclusion

We have touched on several of the wealth of themes in current physics which bear upon the Christian creation tradition as it flourishes and evolves in modern religious thought. We have stressed such themes as novelty, complexity, interconnectivity, openness, uncertainty, symmetry, and beauty as pivotal to the over-all view of creation arising from modern physics. Much has, of course, been left unsaid, but the central conviction of the positive impact of science for our faith and praxis has, hopefully, shown through in some measure.

From special relativity we gained new appreciation for the complexity and plurality of our experiences of nature, and the interplay between dynamics in temporal processes and form in the spacetime patterns. Methodologically, our procedure for constructing physical theory must respect this interplay between diversity and underlying unity through the principle of Einsteinian covariance. We suggested that this principle supports religious ecumenism in general, and that in particular the norm of Christ can serve as an invariant among the Christian creation traditions and atlas of histories.

From general relativity we took a deeper appreciation for the dynamic interdependence of the cosmos, in which infinite sets of local spacetimes ('world views') are nested together in a seamless manifold characterized by at least a past essential singularity. In Einstein's field equations we found a mathematical expression of the dialectics of matter and geometry, form and dynamics, self-determining and self-contingent features of the universe. From the principle that "all that is participates in all that is," we traced the loss of classical objectivity and 'spectator' language and the central role of singularities in 'participator' physics. Theological mystery, an essential ingredient of the creation tradition in all its forms, mirrors the role of singularities in physical theory and its inevitable presence marks the complexity rather than the irrationality of Christian faith.

Quantum theory brought with it the notions of complementarity of spacetime and causal descriptions of natural processes, the inevitable occurrence of discontinuity and of wholeness which challenges our macroscopic intuition. It challenges us to construct the creation tradition such that humankind is inextricably bound to the whole of nature in deeper and more interdependent ways, and such that the discontinuities of our evolutionary past, as well as the smooth continuities, allow for emergence and novelty, openness and indeterminacy, along with predictability and continuity, integration and unity.

Finally, from the functioning of symmetry in physics, we gained new appreciation for the beauty and simplicity of nature underlying and supporting her complexity and contingency. The conservation of energy serves as a strong criterion of our global management of finite resources, while the exacting cost of increasing entropy focuses our assessment of global solutions to human and environmental needs, both for present and future generations. Such questions are seen by the authors as central to the relevancy and worth of any revised creation tradition.

Chapter Nine

EVOLUTION AND RELIGION

G. Ledyard Stebbins

Evolution is a fact. This statement is now generally accepted by scientists who are familiar with the relevant discoveries, observations, and experiments that have been made in geology, paleontology, biology, and biochemistry during the twentieth century. The following statements, that support the primary one just made, are equally valid as facts. The earth is more than four thousand million (four billion) years old. It originated contemporaneously with the solar system, which occupies a minute part of our celestial galaxy. The galaxy itself is a cluster of stars that is enormously vast compared to the size of the solar system, but minute compared to the extent of the universe. The origins of the universe, the solar system, and the earth are a small part of cosmic evolution, and are not discussed in this article.

Biochemical evolution, that brought into being the first living organisms, began as soon as temperatures on the earth's surface became cool enough so that organic chemical reactions, leading to the formation of complex molecules containing carbon, hydrogen, oxygen, nitrogen, and several other chemical elements, could be formed. A reasonable estimate of this time is about four billion years ago. Its first stage was the formation of small carbon-containing molecules (nucleotides, amino acids). These served as building blocks from which were constructed the large molecules (nucleic acids, proteins), of which living systems chiefly consist. This stage probably took place quickly. It has been repeated several times on a small scale, under conditions that simulate the environment that is believed to have prevailed on earth four billion years ago. The second stage, the formation of functional nucleic acids and proteins, must have required much more time. It could not begin until many pools of water or shallow seas were filled with an "organic soup" consisting of millions or billions of building block molecules. At first, functional relationships between larger, aggregate molecules, the ancestors of nucleic acids and proteins, must have been weak and inefficient. The modern efficiency of large molecules that contain informational messages coded in the order of their units, as described in a later section of this article, could not have appeared all at once in its perfect form. It was probably the outcome of spontaneous chemical changes, accompanied by natural selection of prebiotic molecular systems that could replicate themselves more quickly and efficiently than their neighbors. The length of time required for prebiological chemical evolution is not known, but a reasonable guess is between a hundred million and four hundred million years, possibly shorter.

Biological evolution began about 3.5 billion years ago, the age of the oldest known fossils of living cells. For more than two billion years, the earth's oceans and lakes were filled only with microscopic, structurally simple forms of life, similar to modern bacteria. For six hundred to seven hundred million years more, relatively elaborate, but still microscopically small forms of life prevailed. The first animals (sponges, jellyfishes, and worms) and plants (seaweeds) large enough to be visible to the naked eye evolved between 900 million and 700 million years ago. Then, over a period of about seventy million years, the major subdivisions (Phyla) of the animal kingdom came into being. The phyla of land plants (mosses, ferns and their relatives, seed plants) evolved one hundred to two hundred million years later. The entire time span during which relatively large organisms evolved is only the latest 1/7 to 1/5 of the total time span of biological evolution.

Hundreds of fossils are known of animals intermediate between major groups (classes) of the animal kingdom. By no means all such transitions are represented, but between some of them, such as reptiles and mammals, a succession of fossils is known that covers a time span of more than 100 million years. Because many kinds of organisms are rarely preserved, and many older strata that formerly existed have been lost by erosion, the fossil record is incomplete, and many gaps exist. Nevertheless, the number of gaps between successive dates of fossils belonging to the same species or genus (kind) of animal is as great as the number of gaps that separate different kinds. For instance, an archaic kind of fish (Coelacanth) was once believed to have become extinct a hundred million years ago. About twenty years ago, a Coelacanth was caught as a contemporaneous animal, living in the deep ocean off the east coast of Africa. A gap of about 100 million years separates the most recent fossils from the contemporary individuals of this kind of fish. Similar gaps exist in the fossil record of the Tuatara "lizard" (*Sphenodon*), lungfish, tree shrews, opossums, and many other kinds of animals. The presence of this kind of gap supports the belief that gaps between major classes and phyla are due to imperfections of fossil records. They do not mean that new kinds were created separately or arose in a single step or saltation.

Contrary to the claims of many authors, evolution does not violate the second law of thermodynamics. As set forth by physicists and chemists, this law states that energy always flows from a source to a sink. When this happens in a closed system that neither receives nor gives out energy, the order of the system is reduced; its entropy increases. The earth's film of living organisms is not a closed system. It is constantly receiving energy from the sun and from the earth's internal heat; and is releasing energy to the depths of outer space. With respect to energy flow, individual organisms are no more than highly complex eddies in the constant flow of energy from the solar and terrestrial sources to the external sink. Each individual, moreover, follows the second law during most of its lifetime. A plant converts solar energy into its own organized body, but the latter decays and becomes disorganized. An animal takes in and consumes organized plant material, and discharges unorganized waste. Eventually, its body decays and becomes disorganized, that is, increases its entropy. Before this happens, a tiny portion of the body's ordered system, eggs and sperm, are released and carry information for building up a new but still temporary ordered system. Evolution consists of adding to, subtracting from, or rearranging a small part of this tiny fraction of transmitted order in a succession of open systems. The mechanism of replication depends upon physico-chemical properties always present in certain kinds of molecules whether or not they belong to an ordered system. Consequently, evolution acts at levels several times removed from the closed systems to which physicists and chemists apply the second law of thermodynamics.

The Causes of Evolution

Although the web of knowledge about the causes of evolution still contains many gaps, its basic framework is accepted by most scientists who have studied the problem at first hand. This framework is built around the following theme: major evolutionary changes, leading to the origin of new kinds of organisms, result from the successful response of populations of animals, plants, and microorganisms to challenges posed by major changes in the environment. Success depends upon the presence of a preadapted gene pool, containing genetic variability sufficient in amount and of the right kind to make the new adaptation possible by means of a moderate amount of change in the genetic or hereditary makeup of the population. The actual mechanism of change is Darwinian natural selection. It is based upon a higher rate of survival and reproduction on the part of those individuals that are better adapted to the new conditions. The environment of some organisms, such as free living bacteria and small, simple plants, consists chiefly of physical factors, such as temperature, moisture, and the mineral content of the soil. For most higher animals and plants, however, biotic factors such as food, predators, diseases, and beneficial relationships with other kinds of organisms overshadow in importance the effects of physical factors.

The components of the evolutionary process are, therefore: (1) hereditary variation in populations; (2) the particulate nature and faithful transmission of this variation; (3) differential survival and reproductive rate of better adapted individuals; (4) occasional mutations, that enrich the gene pool.

During the past fifty years, evolutionists have devoted most of their efforts to exploring the nature of these four components. A fifth component, reproductive isolation, has received an equal amount of attention since it accounts for the fact that different but related evolutionary lines can exist simultaneously in the same habitat and exploit this habitat in different ways. Reproductive isolation comes about via particular kinds of interactions between hereditary variation, mutation, and natural selection. It is exemplified by the mule, a sterile hybrid between horse and donkey. A brief summary of the results of this research follows.

Experiments under controlled conditions have shown that most populations of organisms contain a vast store of genetic variability. Recently, these amounts have been measured precisely by direct studies of protein molecules, that are the immediate products of gene activity. Calculations based upon these experiments show that the number of combinations of hereditary units or genes that could be formed in most populations is many times greater than the number of individuals in the population. Since the transmission of gene combinations from one generation to the next is much like the shuffling and dealing of playing cards in a game like bridge or whist, a good analogy is between the combination of cards in a hand and of genes in an individual. A commonplace observation is that even the most inveterate bridge player is almost never dealt exactly the same hand twice in his or her lifetime. Since most populations contain hundreds of different kinds of genes, as compared to the 52 kinds of cards in a deck, the excess of combinations that are possible over those that are realized is far greater in heredity than in card games. The amount of possible hereditary variation in most populations is infinite compared to the number of individuals that it contains. What counts is not the amount but the kind of variation.

A large number of experiments have explored the way in which hereditary units or genes are transmitted. Transmission is based upon the special properties of nucleic acids, DNA (deoxyribose nucleic acid) and RNA (ribose nucleic acid). Each molecule is an enormously long "tape," containing hundreds or thousands of units, of four different kinds. The ordered sequence is copied in a way similar to copying a telegraphic tape in a copying machine. When RNA takes part in constructing proteins, complex molecules that perform the work needed to keep a cell or body alive, the nucleic acid code is translated into another code, represented by the orderly linear sequence of amino acid units in the protein molecule. Since this sequence consists of hundreds or thousands of amino acid units of twenty different kinds, their information resembles that contained in a written sentence, containing the 26 letters of the alphabet, arranged in a particular sequence. Protein molecules exist for only a short time, and cannot be directly copied. Only DNA and RNA can transmit hereditary information.

Natural selection, therefore, acts upon a vast store of hereditary variation already present in populations. Numerous experiments with artificial and semi-artificial selection (controlled alteration of the environment without actual selection of desired individuals) have shown that the gene pool can be altered in any of several different ways, given the right kind of selection. Drosophila flies, for instance, can be selected for increased or decreased body size, higher or lower number of bristles on the abdomen, longer or shorter wings, attraction toward or avoidance of light, and many other properties. Comparable experiments with mice have revealed an almost equal amount of versatility. Populations can become adapted to many new kinds of environments by means of complex changes in the frequencies of the genes that they already contain, without adding any new kinds of genes via mutation. Other observations and experiments have reproduced changes in adaptation that have been recorded in natural populations during recent history. This research has shown that natural selection can either promote evolution or retard it, depending upon whether interactions between populations and their environment are changing or remaining constant.

Of course, human artificial selection has not yet produced entirely new kinds of organisms that can survive in a natural environment. Inferences based upon the fossil record and upon the geographic and spatial distribution of modern organisms have shown that such changes can be completed only during tens or hundreds of thousands of years. Hence an experimenter can produce new adaptive systems within his lifetime only by increasing the rate of evolution a thousand-fold. As their knowledge of evolution increases and becomes more definite, evolutionists may soon be able to speed up the process to such a degree. The ultimate aim of experimental evolution, producing an entirely new kind of adaptive system that persists even in the absence of human guidance, may be achieved during the lifetime of contemporary investigators.

My optimism on this score is based upon what I know about the transformation of domestic animals by means of artificial selection. Over a hundred years ago, Darwin recognized that artificial selection could give rise to fancy breeds of pigeons that possessed a higher number of tail feathers than found in any wild species belonging to the family of pigeons and doves. Among plants, an ear of corn with its silks and husks is as much a novel or qualitatively different structure as any that exists throughout the plant kingdom. Yet evidence from fossil corn, from comparisons between modern corn and its nearest relatives, and from many genetic experiments, shows that the ear of corn has evolved gradually from a structure much like a corn tassel, that contained seeds.

Was Darwin mistaken when he relied upon artificial selection to support his theory of natural selection? I believe that he was correct. Animal and plant breeders do exactly what natural selection is supposed to do, only much more intensively. They encourage the reproduction of certain individuals, that possess adaptations suited to human needs, and discourage or prevent the reproduction of others that are less well adapted. Differential reproduction is the keystone of both artificial and natural selection. Furthermore, both kinds of selection have similar limits. A breeder would never try to convert a breed of cattle into one of sheep or swine; similarly no evolutionary change of this nature has been recorded in the evolutionary history of wild animals. Cattle, sheep and swine have all evolved from a common ancestor that looked very different from any modern animal. Logically, therefore, we can expect natural selection to bring about changes as great as any that artificial selection has produced, provided that these changes fit the population to a habitat that is available to it.

Chance and Purpose in Evolution

One might ask at this point: does this theory about the mechanisms of evolution imply that all of the myriads of animals and plants on the earth have evolved by pure chance? Is evolution completely lacking in direction and purpose? The answers to this question are a combination of "yes" and "no." Direction is imposed by limitations upon the scope of natural selection, particularly in complex animals and plants. Some kinds of mutations can never be favored by natural selection, because they interfere with the harmonious development and functioning of the body. The more specialized are the animals belonging to a particular evolutionary line, the fewer are the options open to them. Primitive lizards could evolve into snakes by losing their legs and changing their bodies in several different ways, but once snakes had first evolved, they could give rise only to other snakes of different kinds. Whatever direction is imposed upon an evolutionary line is based upon previous direction of change. Biological evolution has never progressed toward a predetermined goal. The only exception to this principle is human evolution.

Distinctive Features of Human Evolution

What is distinctive about human evolution? What sets us apart from all other members of the animal kingdom? Has human evolution acquired purpose, foresight, and direction that is absent from the evolution of animals and plants? If so, how has this come about?

Before answering these questions, we must be aware of the ways in which we humans resemble and differ from our cousins, the great apes. Recent research has shown that in most characteristics humans and apes are much more alike than was previously supposed. The observations of Darwin and his contemporaries, that chimpanzees resemble humans in their anatomy more than they resemble tailed monkeys or any other animal, is fully supported by modern research. Moreover, biochemical investigations have shown that apes possess all of the enzymes and hormones present in the human body, and that with respect to many kinds of proteins, such as hemoglobin and other components of blood, their molecules resemble ours more closely than do their bones and other anatomical structures. Moreover, they can be taught the rudiments of language and can learn to recognize their own image when looking into a mirror. Apes, like humans, differ from most other animals in possessing the capacity for self recognition.

Moreover, the social life of chimpanzees, gorillas, and many kinds of monkeys has much in common with that of humans. They recognize and submit to the authority of a leader, but under certain circumstances may overthrow and replace him. Mothers love not only their own babies but often show affection for the offspring of other mothers. Among different kinds of apes and monkeys, we can find all of the associations between males and females that exist in human societies. These include lifetime or temporary bonds formed by individual couples; harems controlled by a single dominant male; and roving males who consort with females only for the purpose of mating.

Still another characteristic, formerly believed to be distinctive of humans but now recognized in a rudimentary form in chimpanzees, is fashioning and using tools. These animals make sharp pointed sticks and use them to poke into termite nests, extracting grubs that chimpanzees regard as a delicacy. From all of this evidence, human evolutionists have concluded that the common ancestor of apes and humans had already evolved a long way toward our species with respect to anatomy, bodily chemistry, and social structure. Moreover, this common ancestor must have possessed the rudimentary capacity for such distinctively human traits as language, self realization, and the fashioning and use of tools. Evolution of humans from apes was in most ways a continuation of directions that had already been established in the evolution of apes from tailed monkeys and more primitive primates. Anatomically, the human direction involved a shift to erect posture, freeing the hands for continuous fashioning and using of tools. In addition, humans became larger in all respects, but particularly with respect to the size and conformation of their brains. Those parts of the brain that are responsible for language, memory, and thought increased at a disproportionate rate. Natural selection promoted all of these changes via interactions between ancestral human or hominid populations and their environment of the open savanna, in which finding food and escaping predators became much more vital to their existence than it had been in the former benign environment of tropical forests. Adaptation based upon dependence upon and improved manufacture of tools was a direction of evolution that must have begun when our ape-like ancestors first came down from the trees and began permanent life in savannas.

With respect to the nature and functioning of our brains—particularly the fully developed ability to talk, store information in a memory bank, and think abstract thoughts—humans are truly distinctive. Contrary to all other characteristics except posture, the mental gap between apes and humans is greater than the mental gap between apes and tailed monkeys or any other kind of animal. This single distinctive difference is of overriding importance. It has paved the way to the evolution of three transcendent human traits: artisanship, conscious time binding, and imaginal thinking.

Artisanship is more than merely the use of and dependence upon tools, acquired by hominids (*Homo habilis*) about 1.5 million years ago. Humans became artisans only when they learned how to make tools according to a definite, preconceived design that is passed down from one generation to another either in the form of a precise mental image that can be learned and memorized, or by a specially prepared template such as a blueprint. Only after tool making had evolved into artisanship could humans evolve toward culture and civilization. This revolution consisted of the shift from stones chipped in an irregular fashion via tools having a fixed though crude pattern to the finely fashioned spearheads, arrowheads, needles, and fishhooks used by Cromagnon men. The pyramids of Egypt, the Parthenon, Roman palaces, medieval cathedrals and modern skyscrapers, as well as wheeled carts, chariots, carriages, railroad trains, automobiles, and airplanes are all elaborations of the artisanship that was already well developed 15,000 years ago.

Conscious time binding means planning for the future by recalling past experiences. Anthropologists cannot tell when this distinctly human trait first appeared, although its earliest indications are evident from the use of fire and the presence of hearths 400,000 years ago. The use of fire and more exacting forms of conscious time binding became particularly important for human societies when they left the benign climate of tropical Africa and became adapted to the seasonal climates that prevailed throughout the temperate zone during the Ice Age. The first calendars, consisting of systems of nicks carved into bone, recorded the waxing and waning of the moon for humans living 15,000 years ago. After the ice age, when humans began to till the soil and build cities, they could survive only because they could predict the future on the basis of past experience.

The evolution of artisanship is stimulated largely by *deductive thinking*, that solves problems connected with fashioning tools and designing buildings, vehicles, and numerous other technological devices. Conscious time binding required anticipatory or *prophetic thinking*, that brings forth predictions about what is most likely to happen in the future. A third kind of thinking is *imaginal thinking*, that is the most characteristically human of all traits. It consists of imagining events, structures, or conditions that have never existed before. It already existed about 70,000 years ago, as is evident from remains found in Shanidar Cave, in the hills of Kurdistan, Mesopotamia. There, anthropologist Ralph Solecki found a skeleton carefully laid in a particular position, surrounded by the tools that he needed during his lifetime. From the dust surrounding the grave, botanists isolated pollen belonging to the most beautiful flowers that still grow in the vicinity: bachelor's buttons, hollyhocks, and ragwort. The inhabitants of that cave must have thought about an afterlife and have prepared their chief to enter into it. Imaginal thinking is evident from cave paintings made 15,000 to 20,000 years ago in Europe that depict animals which have never existed as well as masked humans who look like sorcerers. Imaginal thinking is the basis not only of complex progress in artisanship, such as the invention of the arch, of steam engines, telegraph, radio, television, airplanes, and computers, but also of literature, art, music, science, and religion. The progress of civilization is synonymous with the purely cultural revolution of imaginal thinking and the inventions that it makes possible.

Biological and Cultural Evolution

The most distinctive feature of human evolution is that humans have met the challenges of a rapidly changing environment in a way completely different from that which has prevailed in most evolutionary lines of animals. Instead of changing their biological nature they have supplemented it with a massive superstructure of traits and attitudes that are transmitted from one generation to the next, not by biological means but by teaching and learning.

The transmission and modification of old cultural traits and particularly the acquisition of new ones is called cultural evolution. It and biological evolution have existed side by side during the ancestry of humans for millions of years. Societies even of Old World Monkeys can acquire new cultural traits. Macaque monkeys native to Japan, placed by humans in new environments and fed by them, learned to wash the potatoes that they were offered before eating them. Recent experiments with domesticated chimpanzees and gorillas have shown that these apes can learn complex skills even better than can monkeys and other animals.

Cultural evolution resembles biological evolution in several different ways. Human populations are able to evolve culturally because they possess a store of ideas, customs, and traditions that can be compared with the gene pools of animal populations and transmitted faithfully from one generation to the next by imitation, teaching, and learning. Human societies meet challenges posed by changing environments, including those imposed by culture itself, by drawing upon this cultural pool. From time to time, the cultural pool becomes enriched by new ideas and inventions. The composition of the cultural pool changes by means of cultural selection, that resembles natural selection of hereditary biological traits.

Nevertheless, cultural evolution differs from biological evolution in three important respects: vastly wider scope of adaptation; far greater speed; and the capacity to progress toward an intended goal.

By means of our cultural evolution, we humans have become able to adapt ourselves to a far wider range of environments than is possible for any animal species. This is because we have reversed the method of adaptation. As was first pointed out by evolutionist Alfred Russell Wallace during the 19th century, animals become adapted to new environments by changing their hereditary nature; humans by altering their environment to fit their needs, and by supplementing their physical powers with the products of artisanship. Alone, naked, homeless, and without tools, a human being is one of the most helpless creatures in the entire animal kingdom. Allied with our fellow men; clad in garments that suit the environment that we are occupying; housed in buildings appropriate to our needs; equipped with tools for construction, lethal instruments of destruction, vehicles for transport at breakneck speed over land, sea and air; and above all possessed with the ability to plan ahead and work together to achieve our goals; we humans can cope with any environment that exists on this planet, or that may exist for millions of years in the future.

Because of our cultural evolution, combined with our ability to teach and learn, we humans have greatly increased the speed with which we can respond to challenges posed by new and changing environments. A wealth of experimental evidence, supported by the facts of molecular biology, has shown that biological or physiological adaptations acquired during an animal's lifetime cannot be transmitted by genetic heredity. The gene pool can be altered only by the action of natural selection over many generations; in humans, this amounts to hundreds of years. By contrast, new cultural traits can spread throughout the world in a decade or less, as is evident from the radical transformations of many human cultures that have taken place during the past half century. Because of this difference, adaptation via genetic change is as absolute for humans as is long distance transport on foot via forced marches. Moreover, no environmental change can arise so suddenly that society cannot become adjusted to it, given full use of our capacity for planning ahead and cooperating to realize established goals.

Because humans can formulate goals and strive to achieve them, human evolution, in which biological and cultural evolution go hand in hand, has a time binding dimension entirely different from the biological evolution of animals and plants. The direction of biological evolution is determined entirely by contemporaneous and past events. Only human evolution has the capacity to progress toward a predetermined goal. Once our ancestors had become able to look ahead to the future in the light of past experience, they could plan ahead and think about life for their offspring and for future generations. When they had also developed fully the ability to imagine, talk about, and illustrate situations that had never before existed, they could endow human evolution with plan and purpose. Little did it matter that most plans went astray and were never carried out. In biological evolution, natural selection has dictated that the great majority of genetic mutations do not increase the capacity of a population to evolve in response to environmental challenges; instead, they sooner or later disappear from the population. What matters is that among the thousands of mutations that are always taking place, a few of them, in a small proportion of existing populations, can enable their fortunate possessors to evolve further, while other populations either stagnate or become extinct. Similarly, we can expect that the great majority of ideas and inventions conjured up by individual humans or societies will be discarded and perish without contributing to a "better" life for future generations. Most important for the future evolution of humanity is the preservation of a sufficiently large store of inventions, ideas, and plans for the organization of future societies so that present and future generations can meet challenges presented by rapidly changing environments. Since humanity now exerts a controlling influence over many factors of the environment, both inanimate and biological, the plan and purpose that people must acquire in the future will have to be directed toward controlling the individual and collective actions of our own species to a much greater extent than in the past. Controls must be based either upon coercion by force or upon education and persuasion. In the atomic age forceful coercion, extended to its ultimate limits, could destroy utterly either our species or our culture. Consequently, education and persuasion have become more valuable than ever before.

Moreover, history has shown clearly that humans are creatures of emotion, to whom reason and logic have little persuasive force, compared to the dynamism of a demogogue, a preacher, or anyone else who knows how to arouse our gut reactions. The emotional impact of religion has played a dominant role in guiding human culture throughout history. Whatever increase in social harmony and the functional efficiency of society that we may have acquired is due as much to emotional religion as to reason and logic. In our present time of crisis, neither religion nor its persuasive function can be discarded; we need them more than ever before. To what extent can religion help us to achieve our desired goals?

Science and Religion

Since I am neither a prophet nor a theologian, I shall not try to answer the question posed in the last paragraph. I shall, however, offer a few suggestions, based not only upon my thoughts as a scientist, but also the experiences of my childhood and youth as a baptized and confirmed Episcopalian, and my later experience as a Unitarian. I have supplemented this experience by reading both recent and somewhat older histories and commentaries on religion: *Introduction to the History of Religions* by C. H. Toy (1913); *Religion in Science and Civilization* by Sir Richard Gregory (1940); *Man and His Gods* by Homer Smith (1952); *Life and Thought in the Ancient World* by C. C. Eastwood (1964); and several recent articles by R. W. Burhoe.

My first suggestion is that a religion suitable for modern times must discard all explanations of the nature of the cosmos, of our planet, or of life that depend on the intervention of a supernatural force. I cannot believe in a deity that can perform miracles, up-setting from time to time the normal course of events, or in a master planner having a supermind that is able to direct the course of evolutionary change. I find equal difficulty in believing that a supernatural deity created the universe, and endowed non-living atoms and molecules with the properties that made life and biological evolution possible. These elements of religion are descended from the animism that induced all primitive societies to endow animals, plants, and even certain rocks or stones with spirits that could affect human lives. They are based upon human inquisitiveness, which makes us prefer any answer, however far-fetched it may be, to the debasing but sometimes necessary admis-sion: "We just don't know." Consequently, some members of every society have been able to improve their standing among men by providing supposed answers and surrounding them with mysti-cism and emotional appeal. As priests or oracles, they could pose as "servants" of the "gods" that according to them control natural phenomena. Little has it mattered that, one by one, supernatural explanations of natural phenomena have given way to purely naturalistic explanations based upon reason and logic. Once a priestly caste had arisen and become allied with secular leaders who used force to control their people, it could not be displaced. Throughout history, priests of various religious faiths have obstructed the spread of ideas opposed to their own. During the Christian era, the great social progress expressed in the teachings of Jesus was retarded by emphasis on doctrines maintained because of their advantage to members of the clerical hierarchy. Examples are the conflicts that raged during the 4th and 5th centuries over the bodily nature of Jesus; the militant missionary impulse that during the crusades caused western Christians to defile, in Constantinople, the sanctuaries of eastern Christians; the horrors of the Spanish Inquisition; the suppression during the 17th century of Galileo's science; and in modern times, the funda-mentalist opposition to Darwin and evolution.

My second suggestion is that the concept, "religion and politics don't mix," which is accepted by most Americans, needs to become much more widespread and generally practiced. This is a relatively new concept. Most western and middle eastern coun-tries, both Christian and Islamic, have at least nominal state reli-gions, and in some of them, such as Spain, Italy and currently Iran, the church continues to wield great political power. The conflict is not between religion and politics per se, but between an autocratic religious hierarchy or, in the United States, a highly vocal and well financed religious minority, and a democratic political structure. True democracy, in which majority opinions prevail, cannot be achieved until policies based upon religious prejudices are subordinated to secular control based upon the will of the people and their elected representatives.

My other suggestions are more positive in character. They are based upon problems posed in the last section: (1) How can we set goals that are both practical and adequate; and (2) How can we cooperate to achieve them? The experiences of the supposedly rational philosophy of the French revolution, followed by atheistic communism and national socialism have shown that pure reason generates too rigid a framework for social goals. I believe that religious faith, divested of the belief in supernatural miracles and supported by rational deduction, can provide a better alternative.

This kind of faith cannot be imposed from above. If people are to be encouraged to combine faith with reason, they must be allowed to express themselves and to have their opinions heeded and evaluated by others. Blind faith in the inviolate authority of a supreme being, as it is interpreted by a religious hierarchy, must give way to a reasoned faith in the wisdom, idealism, and honesty of our fellow human beings. If we consider others unworthy of our esteem, we should not turn away from them, but rather seek to understand them better, and cooperate with them in educating the coming generation. In an age of comparative enlightenment and educational opportunity, democracy among religious faiths is becoming as important as it is in politics.

New religions, however, cannot neglect the emotional needs of individuals. Most people have problems that they cannot solve by means of reason and logic, and so need some kind of sympathy and psychological help. The "downy couch" of the pyschiatrist has for some people been an effective substitute for religion, but for others has failed completely. In particular, it has done little for those who are economically and socially disadvantaged. For them, the charity that has traditionally been provided by members of orthodox sects, particularly parish priests, monks, nuns, and others having low rank in the ecclesiastical hierarchy, still does much to relieve misery and suffering. Whatever may be their other benefits, changes in religious forms or practices will be successful only if they provide solace in times of trouble.

Finally, and most importantly, religions of the future must place far more emphasis upon the brotherhood and sisterhood of all humanity than any religion, even Christianity, has placed in the past. The very meaning of the word religion connotes a binding together, a partial sacrifice of free will and personal license in the interest of one's fellow men. In democratic nations, this binding together and sacrifice cannot be imposed from above; it must come about voluntarily, from the grass roots. Traditionally religion maintains that we are bound together for our mutual good by the omniscient influence of an all-powerful God, Who is constantly watching over us. This God is believed to have existed since the beginning of time, even though God's existence was not recognized by the majority of people, the "heathens," until the missionary activities of the Christian and Islamic churches revealed God to unbelievers. Most modern anthropologists, on the other hand, believe that the concept of a universal, all-powerful God is a relatively recent invention of civilized humans.

Science can in no way provide a basis for deciding between these two or any other alternatives. We can neither perform experiments nor make observations concerning the existence or nonexistence of an impersonal spiritual God Who lives not in a physical heaven but in the minds and hearts of human beings. But does this really matter? Concepts of God have lifted up the spirits of millions of people during more than three thousand years of human history. The concept of a powerful and lasting influence for good is vastly and inconceivably greater than the will, desire, or spirit of any individual human being. Humanity needs it. If this were not so, God would have died long ago.

I believe that we should not waste or time arguing about the physical nature of God,   or about whether or not God can perform supernatural miracles. Personally, I find the greatest meaning in my life to be based upon the following paraphrase of a familiar New Testament exhortation: "Let your light so shine before men that they may see your good works and glorify the Spirit that made them possible." If we can all carry out this extremely difficult exhortation, why should we worry about earthly events that are beyond our control, such as the possible extinction of civilization or humanity two hundred years from now, or the eventual extinction of life on the planet earth caused by the exhaustion of energy derived from the sun?

If this sounds like the philosophy of a humanist, the message is truly received. My ideal is to become a respectful lover of all humanity. I sincerely hope that similar ideals may govern the spirits of more of us, and that we who share them become more closely tied together by bonds of mutual respect.

Suggested Reading

The following books are relatively non-technical and provide supplementary information.

Scientific American, vol. 239, no. 3, September 1978. A collection of articles by various scientists on the most significant topics.

Bonner, J. T. *The Evolution of Culture in Animals.* (Princeton, N.J.: Princeton University Press, 1980).

Cloud, P. *Cosmos, Earth and Man.* (New Haven: Yale University Press, 1977).

Stebbins, G. L. *Processes of Organic Evolution.* (Englewood Cliffs, N.J.: Prentice Hall, 3rd edition, 1977).

Stebbins, G. L. *Darwin to DNA: Molecules to Humanity.* (San Francisco: W. H. Freeman Co., 1983).

Lancaster, J. *Primate Behavior and the Emergence of Culture.* (New York: Holt, Rinehart and Winston, 1975).

Smith, H. *Kamongo, or the Lungfish and the Padre.* (New York: Viking Press, 1949).

Dubos, R. *Beast or Angel? Choices That Makes Us Human.* (New York: Scribners, 1974).

Goodall, J. *In the Shadow of Man.* (Glasgow: Fortuna/Collins, 1972). An account of life among chimpanzees.

Leakey, R. and Lewin, R. *Origins.* (New York: Dutton, 1977).

Poirier, E. *In Search of Ourselves. An Introduction to Physical Anthropology.* (Minneapolis: Burgess, 1977).

Schaller, G. *The Year of the Gorilla.* (Chicago: Univ. of Chicago Press, 1964).

Washburn, S. and Moore, R. *Ape into Man: A Study of Human Evolution.* (Boston: Little, Brown, 1974).

Chapter Ten

CREATION: VIEWED BY SCIENCE, AFFIRMED BY FAITH

Philip Hefner

This essay attempts to tackle the theme of this volume by setting forth in a brief compass what an entire doctrinal treatment of creation would look like within the framework of the scientific understanding of the world. At the foundational level, our attitude and action toward the environment depends upon the theological view we have of the world. This theological view of the world is equivalent to what we traditionally call a doctrine of creation. Underlying this approach is the definition of theology that is proposed by St. Thomas in his *Summa Theologica*. Thomas argued that theology treats of many things, including both God and creatures, but of the creatures insofar as they are "referable to God as their beginning or end,"[1] or as they are considered to be God's "effects."[2]

> Some, however, looking to what is treated in this science, and not to the aspect under which it is treated, have asserted the subject-matter of this science to be something other than God—That is, either things and signs, or the works of salvation, or the whole Christ, that is the head and members. *Of these things, in truth, we treat in this science, but so far as they are ordered to God.*[3]

Within the framework of this understanding of theology, we recognize both the task of the doctrine of creation and also the widespread failure of the doctrine. The task is to perceive how the world ("things and signs") is referable to God as to its beginning and end. Since the scientific understanding of the world is one of the chief ways in which we encounter this world and know it, the task is to discern how the world scientifically perceived is referable to God and how it can be the *effect* of God. The widespread failure of the doctrine is precisely this, that theologians have been unable or unwilling to order the current scientific understanding of the world to God. Both religious folk and thoroughly secularized persons act toward the world, toward our environment, in ways that are influenced by their sense of how that world is related to God—or by the total absence of either a belief in God or of a perceived relationship of the world to that God.

As we approach a genuinely theological understanding of the world, we will consider two sets of presuppositions that must be incorporated and synthesized in that understanding. The one set of presuppositions comes from our theological tradition. Each theologian will retrieve these traditional elements from a different perspective and give them a distinctive interpretation. They constitute our Christian identity as we approach our theme, and even when we revise or reject traditional components, they must be acknowledged in their identity-bestowing role. The other set of presuppositions comes from the scientific pictures that govern our coming to knowledge of the world and of ourselves in it. The traditional theological presuppositions remind us how earlier generations of Christians have referred the world to God, whereas the scientific presuppositions clarify just what understanding we today have of the world that is to be viewed by our own generation theologically in its relation to God.

I. Presuppositions from the Christian Tradition

What is the status of the world before God? That question can be answered in one word: *Creation*. To say that the world is creation is to utter an item of faith, not a fact of observation. It means that Christian faith (and at this point, Jewish faith is one with Christians) sees the world as the creature of God's own making, which is finally dependent upon its Maker and none other for its being, and which is in every moment dependent; further, the world is bearer in itself of a special relationship with its Maker. Let us unpack this summary statement with the resources of classical Christian doctrine and belief.

Creation out of Nothing.   The fundamental building block in the Jewish and the Christian view of the world as creation is the classical *creatio ex nihilo*, "creation out of nothing." In some theological circles this doctrine is rejected on the grounds that it is simply ancient philosophy or speculation about the chronology of pre-existent times because it speaks of the "beginning" of the world in a way that science renders impossible. Against these critics, I argue that the doctrine is an affirmation that has been held tenaciously down through the centuries, because it enshrines a fundamental Christian belief about God. If God is truly the God that Jews and Christians have believed in, that God is the source of all that is, and continues to be the creative source of power and health. This classical doctrine has persisted in the Christian theological tradition, not because of specific literal biblical support, but rather because the Christian picture of God requires the "out of nothing" dimension. The nub of the creation-out-of-nothing affirmation is this, that the only relationship between world and God that is consistent with what Christians and Jews believe about God is one in which the planet is totally dependent upon God for its origin and perseverance.[4] We are most familiar with this affirmation from its Godward side, that after all God is the powerful Creator-God on whom all is dependent for its being. The other side of this affirmation is more startling for us today, namely the worldward side. From this side, we are asked to behold this planet of ours and observe that it came from God as far as its origin is concerned, and from none other. The planet is God-conceived and made. This is an important aspect of the world's status, and this is one basic element of what it means to call it "creation." The creation-out-of-nothing doctrine reminds us that if we cannot say this about the world, then it is not only our doctrine of the world that is called into question, but even more it is the doctrine of God that is challenged.

Continuing Creation.   Creation is not simply protology, what happened at the beginning, before time was created. Creation also refers to God's ongoing sustaining of the world. No one emphasized this more strongly than Luther, who professed that he had difficulty accepting the miracle stories of the New Testament, because every moment of the world's existence is a miracle, depending on the ongoing grace of God. In his catechisms, Luther spoke of creation almost exclusively in terms of human creation, but the principle is there: "I hold and believe that I am a creature of God; that is, that he has given and constantly sustains my body, soul, and life. . . he makes all creation help provide the comforts and necessities of life—sun, moon, and stars in the heavens, day and night, air, fire, water, the earth and all that it brings forth, birds and fish, beasts, grain and all kinds of produce." (*Large Catechism*, explanation of the First Article of the Creed).

Traditionally, this belief in the continuing creation (*creatio continua*) has been augmented with a discussion of *secondary causes*. God is the immediate source of primary causes, but assigns to those first causes the creative and ordering power to reproduce and to maintain their own subordinate causality. Both sets of causes hark back finally to God the ultimate Creator. Deism is ruled out. Correlated to primary and secondary causes is primary and secondary matter (*materia prima* and *materia secunda*). Primary matter is what God created *ex nihilo*, at the very beginning, whereas secondary matter is that which is produced according to the laws of nature, from the primary stuff.

This assertion of continuing creation, when coupled with the creation out of nothing, makes a powerful statement about the non-human creation as a trustworthy environment for the human. It asserts that the world about us is not antithetical to our human destiny and God's will, but that it is a fundamentally friendly home for us. It cannot be otherwise if it has proceeded originally from God's creative intention and continues to be sustained by the will of the God who has expressed a fulfilling, redemptive will toward us. This statement about the reliability and benevolence of the ecosystem under God is one of the most striking faith-statements in the Christian system of belief.[5] It takes on more vivid meaning when it is juxtaposed to what we shall say about the destiny of the planet and its processes.

Continuing creation amplifies our understanding of the world's status. It is not only dependent upon God as its source, but also as the ground of its ongoing operation. Every moment, it is firmly in God's hands. This is another aspect of what it means to say that the world is creation.

Imago dei.   There is a third building block in theology's understanding of the world's status: the teaching concerning the *imago dei*, the image of God. This category is applied in the theological tradition exclusively to human beings. Although the term has a long history and is almost universally attested in the theological tradition, there is not agreement on its exact meaning. Some scholars have noted two different kinds of meaning ascribed to the *imago dei*.[6] The one tradition of meaning equates the term with specific human characteristics that are God's image in humans— love, uprightness, the capacity for dominion over animals, to name a few. The other kind of meaning refers to the basic structure of human being that enables communication between humans and God. Augustine was one of the most important representatives of this second strand, and he put it in his famous prayer: "O God Thou has created me for Thyself, and my heart is restless until it finds its peace in Thee." In light of the variety of meanings given to this term, even among biblical exegetes, I suggest that we be content to say that *imago dei* refers to some kind of special relationship between human beings and God.

Even though the image of God concept is applied only to human beings, it is important for our theological understanding of the world's status before God, for at least two reasons. First, since the human is made up of the basic stuff of the planet, the image of God in that human being indicates that the world is itself capable of being a vessel of that special relationship to which the *imago dei* points. Second, the world, whatever else it is, is also from a theological point of view the nest of that creature who carries the image of God. "Nest" is too weak a word. The planetary ecosystem is a support system that stands in so intimate a relationship to *Homo sapiens* that we are fully dependent upon it. Furthermore the evolutionary processes that produced that ecosystem are the same processes that produced humans. That the special relationship to God that we call *imago dei* is intertwined with this ecosystem and the processes of evolution is an important indicator to the theologian of the world's status before God.

What is the status of the planet before God? Our theological tradition asserts that the planet was the object of God's creative action at the beginning, and that God alone is the source from which the planet came into being. Furthermore, the planet continues to be the object of God's creative sustaining concern and activity, a sustaining activity that renders the processes of the planet reliable for us. Finally, God did not leave the creation without a witness to its divine ambience, since God's creative activity includes a creature right at the heart of the planetary processes that bears the image of God. All of this we sum up theologically in the term, Creation; the planet *is* creation.

The Destiny of the Planet in God's Hands—Consummation. The question of destiny is central to the assessment of the world, because destiny suggests that there is a basic purpose or meaning inherent in the existence of the world. If this be so, then the condition of the world at any moment will be judged by comparing its trajectory with its destiny.

What is the intention of God's activity toward the world? I believe that the tradition of Christian faith and theology is clear, if not unequivocal, in its assertion that God intends to perfect or fulfill the creation.

The biblical records give ample testimony to the belief that God cares for the creation according to a plan for its fulfillment. The evidence ranges from the orderly plan of creation itself in Genesis, chapter 1, to visions of the earth being made perfect at the last day, as a fit environment for the People of God in their final glory. The prophet Isaiah, for example, writes: "I create new heavens and a new earth;/ I create Jerusalem a rejoicing, and her people a joy./ They shall build houses and inhabit them;/ they shall plant vineyards and eat their fruit./ They shall not build and another inhabit;/ they shall not plant and another eat. The wolf and the lamb shall feed together,/ the lion shall eat straw like the ox;/ and dust shall be the serpent's food./ Sharon shall become a pasture for flocks;/ and the Valley of Achor a place for herds to lie down." (Chap. 65).

The New Testament speaks of God as one who notes every event, even that of sparrows dying, so that care may be taken for the earth. Paul speaks of the entire creation being liberated with the redemption of humans. The Book of Revelation closes with a vision of a new heaven and a new earth, which is expressed in the imagery of the earthly Jerusalem made perfect beyond our fondest dreams.

More important than the multitude of biblical texts that could be adduced is the inherent theological rationale for the concept of the world's consummation. The most powerfully expressed attribute of God in our tradition, including biblical traditions, is God's *faithfulness*. God is not a deceiver. God does not make promises or raise hopes and then betray them. Time and again this has been asserted in the Jewish and Christian interpretation of historical events. It is equally applicable to the history of nature, to cosmic history. Indeed, with our knowledge now that humans are a part of the ecosystem and its evolution and not separate from it, if God is faithful in any portion of the world, in human affairs, then God must be faithful in the whole, since the world is one seamless robe.

Consummation is the best word to describe what God is about in the creation and hence what the destiny of the world is. Consummation is not termination, it is not destruction, but rather it is bringing all things together in the whole that God intends. Consummation is, of course, fully under God's dominion. God even defines what consummation is. We do not know what the fulfillment will look like; we are not promised that it will fit our personal agenda. What we are promised is that the consummation, whatever form it takes, will be consistent with God's redemptive, benevolent intention, and in this sense it will be the perfection and fulfillment of the entire planetary creation.

II. Interpreting the Tradition within the Scientific Understanding of the World

Materialist Modes of Explanation.   Materialism has been a pejorative term for theology for much of its history, particularly in the modern period. In order to understand why this is so, we might do well to recall R. G. Collingwood's sketch of the history of the concept of nature or matter in western civilization.[7] The ancient period viewed nature as analogous to the living organism. The Renaissance and Enlightenment view of nature was based on the analogy of the machine. In this Renaissance understanding, nature was devoid of life and of intelligence. Nature, as body, is alien to the mind, but at the same time, nature is the product of mind, the divine mind, just as machines are the product of human minds. The modern view of nature or matter[8] is decisively influenced by the work of the physicists at the end of the 19th century and the beginning of the 20th, as well as by Darwin. This view understands that nature includes process and change. Its analogy for understanding nature is that of historical process.

Even though we are well into the modern, or even the postmodern, period, the prevailing view of nature in our time is still that of the machine. For us and our predecessors, the machine view of nature makes it impossible to relate God or our own humanity to nature in an intimate manner that might pertain to the essential character of either. We know what machines are, we know their character, and we know that God is, in essence, nothing like a machine. Therefore, it is necessary to distance God from nature/matter as far as possible, and this is done by constructing impressive theories of transcendence. It is a question whether classical, medieval, and modern concepts of transcendence were required more by our understanding of God or by our concept of nature/matter.

Similarly, this mechanical view of nature/matter requires that we separate ourselves from it. We know that our own essential character as persons, our personhood, which is the most precious thing about us and God's greatest gift to us, cannot be subsumed under the image of the machine.

Science deals primarily with explanations of the world in material terms. Matter or nature provides the framework in which science explains the world to us, whether in cosmic scope from the Big Bang to the entropic cold storage death that is often posited as the end of the universe in which we live, or in terrestrial terms of the development of planet earth and its life. It is clear that if we are operating with the view of nature as machine, then natural or materialistic scientific explanations are in a sense abhorrent to our theologically centered vision. Such explanations are not only impotent for explaining what pertains to God or to us as humans, those explanations must in addition be decisively distanced from the realm of the divine and the essentially human.

A more adequate image of nature/matter as historical process opens up a different vista for us, however. Let us consider the broadest possible view of nature as historical process. Nature/matter is the energy related by the Big Bang, which in turn formed the hydrogen atoms that evolved finally into what we know as the universe today. The celestial phenomena, the solar system that is our own, the evolution of life on planet earth—all of this, too, is part of that process of nature/matter that originated with the Big Bang. Matter is also the emerging DNA, that key to life, which arose from the primeval soup, and which finally became human being.

If this is a more adequate view of matter, must it be distanced from God in the same manner as the machine-like nature? If matter can itself be viewed as a self-transcending process that can be the release of primal energy and also the DNA that makes life what it is, then what relation can that have to God's transcendence? If the outcome of that material process is the human brain, which is the physiological seat of those most precious characteristics of my selfhood—the capacity for music, poetry, social organization, and the view of myself as a child of God—then what is the relationship of nature/matter to my essential personhood as a human? Is God's transcendence to be conceived as distance from nature/matter? As an "up there" or an "out there"? Or is that transcendence an "in there" that is conceptually more credible, even though it remains a mystery, in the face of our probing? What must we say, then, of materialist modes of explanation? Is materialism what earlier generations considered it to be if our basic image of matter/nature is different? Is this materialist explanation reductionistic in the old sense? Is it so inimical to God and to human being? These questions are important in themselves, and it is essential that we understand that "materialism," "matter," and "nature" are dynamic terms that are decisively changing their meanings. If our theories of how God is or is not related to the world are dependent upon concepts of the matter/nature realm that are obsolete and superseded, our theology of the world and doctrine of creation will be abortive. Further, we must bend every effort to understand the material realm in the most dynamic manner possible, since this realm is fully incorporated within any doctrine of creation. Our initial definition of theology as the reflection that relates everything to God comes into force here. The doctrine insists that the material realm is created by God *ex nihilo* and that it is fully dependent upon God not only for its origin but also for its continuing life and consummation. Thus, all of the processes of matter/nature that are discovered by science must somehow be related to God, even though that relationship is difficult to conceptualize. Since all of what we term "environment" is in this realm of matter/nature (perhaps "environment" is a synonym for that realm), a concern for the environment will be heavily dependent on how that realm is related to God.

Evolutionary Processes and Mechanisms.   The processes of the material realm are *an evolution*. Evolution is used to apply to several of the world's domains. It is applied to (1) cosmic processes, from the so-called Big Bang to the Big Burnout;[9] (2) terrestrial processes, including the emergence of life, DNA, and the appearance of *Homo sapiens;* (3) ontogeny, the development of the individual from conception through birth and maturity, including the development of the brain; and (4) the psychosocial realm that we also call culture. The various sciences are not yet to the point where they would bring these four different domains under one concept of unitary evolution.[10] It is clear that the specific processes by which evolution proceeds are not the same in the four domains. However, the unity of the process is surely the direction in which a materialist mode of explanation would tend, since from Big Bang to the formation of culture there is but one source and unfolding energy. Christian faith would find it difficult to ascribe these various aspects of evolutionary process to any final cause other than the one God. The essays by Stebbins and Burhoe in this volume point in this direction.

    An evolutionary mode of interpretation poses some challenge to our theological understanding of the world. On the one hand, it forces us to attend carefully to the basic manner in which phenomena are produced in nature, whether living or non-living—namely, as possibilities or extensions of what exists at any given moment. New things are continually engendered, but only as possibilities inherent in the cards that have at any moment been dealt out by the exigencies of nature. Ultimately, this means that everything that exists at present has developed as a possibility of the energy released at the Big Bang (or its equivalent). In the approximately 16 billion years since that singular event, evolution has proceeded in the way of accretions that are possible if the interaction between what exists at any moment and its environment can accomplish a stretching of what is given into something new. If we may apply the term "spirit" to the distinctive characteristics of human beings, then we may say that evolutionary modes of interpretation challenge us to ask about the physical antecedents of spirit. This is a challenge that is embodied by sociobiology. We can hardly overestimate the impact that would be made on our attitude toward the environment if we genuinely perceived that we ourselves have emerged as one of the environment's possibilities.

Sociobiology and its predecessor disciplines (like ethology) have opened up large and somewhat disturbing horizons on this point. In his masterwork, E. O. Wilson announced early on that altruism was the "central theoretical problem of sociobiology"[11] — a startling comment for a religious community that places an act of altruism at the center of its faith in the Cross of Jesus.[12] Besides altruism, work has been done to show the biogenetic bases of such characteristics as mother love, ritual, honesty, truth-telling, common sense, humor.[13] More recent researches just now are focusing also on such sweeping questions as the biogenetic foundations of Jung's archetypes.[14]

The upshot of this challenge is that what we call spiritual attributes of the human being are written into the prior physical processes of evolution. Even the exalted notion of vicarious sacrifice may fall into this category. To say that these characteristics are rooted in the evolutionary process is to say as well that they have emerged in the process of natural selection, that they have somehow been related to the processes of survival and genetic transmission. The theological vista here is almost staggering. It calls us to acknowledge the materiality of God's working, and it also enlarges considerably the sense in which the spiritual is the key to understanding all of reality.

Another challenge posed by the evolutionary mode of explanation is that of functionalism and reductionism. Within the evolutionary model as it pertains to the emergence of life in the terrestrial sphere, the mechanisms of natural selection are operative. This implies that organisms negotiate their survival vis-a-vis the environment through adaptation and differential reproduction rates. When human beings are placed within this framework, then the question arises, what function related to adaptation do they serve? Even their distinctive "spiritual" characteristics are questioned in this way. This type of reductionism has always been repugnant to theology. The added nuance, that life-forms aim at survival, is equally unwelcome to theology, since it seems to deepen the reductionism and somehow trivializes the spiritual quest.

Nevertheless, precisely because the Christian Faith is also a form of determinist philosophy, arguing that God is the primary source and that the divine providential will governs creation, we cannot take a simplistically negative stance toward functionalism. We may be wary, but we must be open to the possibility that Christian Faith rather broadens functionalism than rejects it and this broadening receives its character from the fact that the Faith does not reject determinism, but rather places it in the realm of primary cause, rather than in the realm of secondary causes. Christians affirm that this life is part of something larger than itself, and that it is not an end in itself. That affirmation is after all what functionalism is also after, as are the sociobiologists—for them life takes place within the process of evolution and serves the purposes and processes of evolution.

The Christian would want to paint the evolutionary context in very large strokes indeed, and suggest that perhaps there is a transcendent functionalism at work in the process of evolution, namely, the will of God and the divine ways. The purpose of humans, as the Westminster Catechism puts it, "is to enjoy God and glorify God forever." Or, we may speak of God's Kingdom encompassing all evolutionary processes. Such is the essential task of theology as we have defined it, and such suggestions in turn recast the terms "survival," as well as "evolution," "adaptation," and "natural selection." It is said that survival is not enough. For the Christian that depends on how survival is defined. Survival of a creature that consists of nothing (to borrow Donald Campbell's phrase) but biophiliac skin surface hedonism is surely not enough. Nor is the survival of a sky-scraper-erecting, missile-throwing creature enough. But the survival of a creation that embodies God's will is something else. The non-theistic humanist senses this about Christians immediately. He is more likely to see us as kin with the scientist's functionalism, and since he does not understand it, he will be suspicious.

We are challenged by the evolutionary explanation to clarify the function of life and its rationale for survival in deeper, ultimately more adequate terms. E. O. Wilson writes, "no species, ours included, possesses a purpose (or function) beyond the imperatives created by its genetic history."[15] Faith searches ceaselessly to understand just what those intrinsic purposes are and how they are referable to God.

The Appearance of Homo sapiens. The question of the direction and purpose of evolution is a natural one that has always been asked. To relate evolution to God, perhaps in Newman Smyth's words, "as God's way of doing things," is to put the question of direction in the forefront. In my judgment, the most persuasive commentators on the direction of evolution have been thinkers like Teilhard de Chardin, Alfred North Whitehead, Theodosius Dobzhansky, and Ralph Wendell Burhoe. They speak of a unitary evolutionary process that moves from origins through the appearance of *Home sapiens*. They speak also of a developing increase of complexity that up to this point is most highly developed in the neocortex of the central nervous system of individual human beings and in the accumulated mass of brains that is human culture and its products. In Teilhard's terminology, this is the evolution from geosphere to noosphere; Burhoe points to a similar development from cosmotype through genotype to culturetype. The earliest stages of this evolution point us to the Big Bang and the development of hydrogen into the beginnings of the planet. The later stages point us to the global human culture that has emerged from the planetary stuff which is thus to be considered the most recent development of the planet itself. Teilhard spoke of this global human phase as evolution becoming aware of itself.[16] Others have said that it is the *universe* become aware of itself.[17]

Within this scheme, the thread of evolution is toward the development of consciousness, individuality within community, self-consciousness, the ability to make decisions on the basis of self-consciousness, action on the basis of that decision, the reception and assessment of feedback, correction, and renewed action on the basis of correction. Such an interpretation does, of course, put *Homo sapiens* at the center, because it assesses the entire planetary process of evolution against the background of the human. On the other hand, we argue that the human is a phase of the planet itself (Teilhard called it the "thinking envelope" of the planet), and the human has emerged from no other womb than that of the planet itself.

Even today, an image that is often used to picture the human species on the planet is that of a house with tenants. The planet is our house, and we are responsible to act accordingly. I am suggesting a different image that is more accurate. The tenants are a part of the house, comparable to windows and doors. The house evolves, and one of the sectors in which its evolution is discernible is the sector called "tenants." Indeed, the most significant sector of the house's evolution is the tenants, if by "most significant" we mean the most advanced decisive sector of the house.

If the foregoing speculations make sense, we are ready to ask what the role of *Homo sapiens* is within the planetary ecosystem, in the position of leading edge of the whole of terrestrial evolution. I find at this point that the concept of "Defined and Self-Defining" is useful. The human species comes upon the scene very largely already defined. The entire evolutionary process prior to *Homo sapiens* has defined the creature in ways so massive that no elaboration is needed here. This definition is so substantial that we can say that the human is the evolutionary process become aware, rather than setting the human self-awareness over against that evolutionary process as something alien.

Homo sapiens' identity is not fully described, however, in the insight that the species is already largely defined when it comes upon the scene. Indeed, the proprium, the distinctive element, in the identity of the species is that it engages in self-definition. Humans define their own niche in a way that no other species does. Perhaps it is better to say that the niche is an item to be defined for *Homo sapiens* in a way that it is for no other creatures.

In a very decisive way, however, the human species defines the rest of the ecosystem of the planet when it defines itself. "Decisive" is the key word here. The human species is decisive in a way that no other species or element of the ecosystem is. Other creatures and elements of the ecosystem are decisive, in the sense that if they disappear or run amok the whole ecosystem will be affected. The distinctiveness of the human species, however, is that it self-consciously makes decisions about itself which bestow a definition on other parts of the ecosystem.

One of the elements within this self-defining process that must be given special attention is the element of freedom. There is one sense in which the process of self-definition is comprised of almost total freedom. The process is free in that the human species is allowed to act in whatever way the prior definitions of the evolutionary process permit, and it must bear the total responsibility for its decisions of self-definition. No power intervenes to inhibit a defining decision except for the powers inherent within the ecosystem, and no power moves in to pick up the pieces after a decision is made except those same inherent powers, including the power of the self-defining human species that made the decision in the first place. The ecosystem is bathed in freedom in the sense that it is genuinely and fully vulnerable to the decisions and actions made by its own cutting edge of development, the self-defining *Homo sapiens.*

The view of the planet and *Homo sapiens* that I have been ela-aborating might appear to some to be excessively anthropocentric, even arrogant in its ascribing self-defining powers to the human. On the other side, we remind ourselves that *Homo sapiens,* as active and aggressive as the species is in carrying out its distinctive activities, is thoroughly passive with respect to the role it has been given. From a purely materialistic perspective, *Homo sapiens* was produced by the blind and impersonal processes of evolution. The species did not play any role in achieving its role or in steering the process to favor its emergence. Rather, there is something about the evolutionary system that predisposed itself toward the adaptive success of the human species. For a religious person, it is God who has created *Homo sapiens* and not the species itself. Of the defining factors that have made the species what it is, the will and action of God must be counted as preeminent.

The nature of God's will in this realm is worth reflecting upon. What does it mean that God willed the emergence of a self-defining creature, to whom the whole of the planetary creation is vulnerable? What does this imply for our conceptualizing the meaning of being human? And what does it mean that God has left the correction of the self-defining creature's errors solely to the powers inherent in the physical creation? Does it mean that there is something about God that loves freedom and responsibility? That God's own free decision is creation cannot be brought to consummation except through the agency of that creation's own self-awareness, self-defining, and freedom? Could it be that this is a clue to the meaning of that elusive concept, "image of God"? Is it the case that the self-defining, free, and responsible character of *Homo sapiens* is integral to that image?

These questions merit our reflection. Such questions bring us to the boundary of deep spiritual reflection, even mystical reflection, just as they bring us to the edge of very hard intellectual reflection. Such reflection has suggested to me that *Homo sapiens* might be considered to be, at its very essence, a *created co-creator.*

"Created" in that *Homo sapiens* was defined prior to its actually assuming its role in the evolutionary process, created by God through the process of evolution itself. "Co-creator" in that God has in significant manner rendered the entire divine work of creation (at least on planet earth) vulnerable to the creating work of the human species.

This sketch of *Homo sapiens* preserves what is essential in the traditional presuppositions of Christian faith. It corrects those presuppositions at several points, including two that we mention here. First, we must revise drastically the notion that the non-human world was created as a habitat for the human and that it exists for human exploitation. Gregory of Nyssa in the fourth century put this in classic form when he wrote that

> the Maker of all had prepared beforehand, as it were, a royal lodging for the future king. . . .and when all kinds of wealth had been stored in this palace. . . .he thus manifests man in the world. . . .For this reason man was brought into the world last after the creation, as one whom it behoved to be king over his subjects at his very birth.[18]

Our discussion has insisted, rather, that it is more adequate to refer *Homo sapiens* to God by viewing the human species as the most recent dynamic zone of the world's evolution within the purposes of God.

The tradition also pictures human development as a vast decline, due to the Fall and original sin, from the bliss of Eden. This view of evolution as decline must be rejected. The traditional concern for sin and evil can be reinterpreted so as not to lose certain perennial concerns (although space does not allow us to discuss that matter here). Robert Francoeur[19] and Paul Tillich[20] are examples of theologians who have been able to incorporate the scientific insight that evolution proceeds by way of advancement, not decline, without subscribing to the false wisdom that advancement is the same as moral improvement.

The Significance of Our Era.   Our epoch seems to be the era when we are first becoming aware, on a planetary scale, that our decisions as the cutting edge of evolution *do* make a powerful difference and the time when we are glimpsing, again on a global scale, the size and number of the pieces that will have to be picked up if we make serious errors in our self-defining judgments. This may be the first era in which we are aware (or becoming aware) that we can no longer follow the momentum of the past in an unreflective manner. Growth for its own sake, aggressive militarism for its own sake, thoughtless use of non-renewable fuels—these are just a few of the trajectories pushed upon us from the past that must be questioned and responded to in a reflective manner. Further, we are becoming aware that we do not have the answers to the many questions that arise about what direction our self-defining should take. We are becoming aware that the planetary human community has many divisions and that the self-interests of the many groups in that community do not automatically mesh. In other words, in our epoch we are barely glimpsing that we are indeed the self-defining leading edge of the planet's evolution; we are co-creators, but we have not yet clarified the values and directions in which we should guide our self-defining powers. If we are to properly discern the condition of the planet, we must be very clear about the threshold on which we stand at this moment in history. This moment is a very precarious one, because *Homo sapiens* not only does not have full knowledge about itself and its role in the evolutionary process, it also has not developed the psychic and spiritual strength inwardly to cope with the self-knowledge that is breaking in upon us. Further, it does not have the answers about values and strategies that it needs. The species is beset by extremists—those on the one hand who have already lost heart and preach a self-destructive pessimism and despair, and those on the other side who refuse to open their eyes and see the new situation in which we and the planet exist today. Surely, no period in history has been more precarious. We are like the adolescent who does not yet understand itself or its situation, but who is challenged to expend its almost-adult strength and wisdom to the utmost for survival.

Assessing science and technology. Science and technology are part of the process of evolutionary development. They are products of culture, the sort of products that only the human community of brains could imagine and bring into reality. They are agents of self-definition that give such great power to *Homo sapiens*. As such they must be brought under the reflective and intentional self-awareness of *Homo sapiens*. This is not a simple matter, partly because humans have been so unreflective about what is involved in the emergence of science and technology. Only the gravest consequences can be expected if these agents are not brought to heel, so that they serve the best purposes that *Homo sapiens* can conceive.

The Final Theological Judgment. Our theological interpretation of the world has focused on how the world may be related to God as its source (*ex nihilo*), sustaining force (*creatio continua*, which involves determinism and functionalism), and perfecter (*consummatio*). The most basic theological question has not been posed, however—the question "What is the significance of the world for God?" The answer to this question gives content to questions regarding the purpose and direction of evolution, the content of God's providential will. Traditionally, theologians have answered this final question by depicting the creation of the world as a divine charitable act, a deed of graciousness for which we must be grateful. Our discussion, particularly at the point of reflecting upon freedom and self-definition, leads in a different direction. Ultimately, it seems most adequate to say that the creation of the world is a function of God's being (or becoming fully) God. It seems unavoidable that we must speculate that God created this world, and the world unfolds because it is essential to God's goodness to do so. *Why* this is so, we cannot fathom, but *that* it is so is the most adequate perception we are allowed at present. Although traditional theology has not suggested this, more modern systems of theological thought, such as Hegelian and process theologies have made this point strongly.

The condition of the planet and our stance toward the environment must be measured by the purposes which ought to govern the self-defining edge of human activity. These purposes, in turn, are decisively conditioned by the ultimate theological judgment, what we discern as the world's significance for God. Theologically perceived, the goal of human activity (as self-defining edge of evolution) is to participate creatively, as God has given us the opportunity as co-creators, in God's own work of consummating the creation. If that work of consummating is in turn a substantial aspect of God's being God, the relationship between our understanding of God's nature and the goal of evolutionary processes, especially human activity, becomes even clearer. The nature of God for Christians has been set forth in Jesus Christ. We may state the meaning of God as revealed in Christ to be *the way of self-giving love aiming at the eschatological perfection of that love.* Humans are to act so as to be in accord with the love which God is working out as the perfection of the creation. Do we want to preserve the ecosystem? Do we want to practice ecological responsibility? In what direction? Should snail darters be preserved? Should fossil fuels be preserved? Should auto emissions and steel plant pollution standards be relaxed? From a theological point of view, these questions do not permit a simple knee-jerk reaction, in either a so-called liberal or conservative direction. The answers must be consistent with what we think God's being is all about and with what we think the consummation contributes to that being. It may well be that the consummation is consistent with our action to bequeath to the next generation enough fuel (whether fossil or synthetic) to sustain a high civilization. Does God's being and consummation require that humans leave every terrain in exactly the same condition in which they first found it? Development and technological exploitation of the planet are not necessarily bad. Good or bad is determined by the purposes and strategies with which the planet is developed and exploited. Environmental questions are inseparable in this purview from justice questions. It is precisely the value-system and the strategies for dealing with ecological and justice questions that we lack today. The theologian will want to insist that we develop values and strategies that are consistent with what we believe about God and about God's being as it is revealed in the world's unfolding. Four questions must be pressed: Are we acting as if the planet is God's creation? Are we acting as if the planet were on its way to the consummation that God desires? Are we acting in full recognition of the role and purposes of *Homo sapiens* as self-defining co-creator, created as such by God? Do we acknowledge that the being of God is the final arbiter of our actions and their correctness or error? Ultimately, God's own being God is served, by a creation that freely acts according to the mandate of self-giving love. The content of our action is that love. The mode of our action aims finally to be undertaken freely as an outpouring of ourselves for the world.

Notes

1. St. Thomas Aquinas, *Summa Theologica*, Q. 1, Art. 7.
2. Ibid.
3. Ibid.
4. Those positions that reject creatio *ex nihilo* tend to speak of reality that is co-eternal with God, which God does not create, which is not dependent upon God. Evil is often assumed to have its origins in this pre-existent reality. See the discussion by Philip Hefner, "The Creation," in Carl Braaten and Robert Jenson (eds.), *Christian Dogmatics*, vol. 1 (Philadelphia: Fortress, 1984). For a forceful opposing view by one who rejects the doctrine, see David Griffin, *God, Power, and Evil* (Philadelphia: Westminster, 1976).

5. Gustaf Aulen has made the point that the principle of creation must be identical to the principle of redemption, if the unity of God and the divine purpose are to be maintained. See his book, *The Faith of the Christian Church* (2nd English Edition; Philadelphia: Fortress, 1960), pp. 162-67.

6. See the extensive summary of the historical tradition of interpreting Genesis 1:27 in Claus Westermann, *Genesis*, vol. 1 Biblischer Kommentar, Altes Testament (Neukirchen: Neukirchener Verlag, 1980), pp. 204-14.

7. R. G. Collingwood, *The Idea of Nature* (New York: Oxford University Press, 1945).

8. The terms "nature" and "matter" are difficult to use with precision, partly because they are dynamic and changing in meaning, as Collingwood explains. Physics today would make matter synonymous with energy or energy-event. I use the term matter/nature to indicate that the two words are linked in one concept that includes both subatomic reality as it appears to the physicist ("matter") and also the environing world that we commonly refer to as "nature."

9. "Big Bang" refers to the cosmic singularity in which our universe had its beginning. This theory seems to be accepted by the vast majority of cosmologists, although there are a number of versions of it. Big Burnout refers to the apparent impending demise of planet earth in about 2.5 billion years when, in its own natural evolution, our sun will expand dramatically to many times its present size, becoming a "red giant," and thereby consuming the earth. See James S. Trefil, *The Moment of Creation* (New York: Charles Scribner's Sons, 1983).

10. For some useful suggestions on how this unitary theory might take shape, see Victor Turner, "Body, Brain, and Culture," *Zygon*, 18 (September 1983), pp. 221-246; Ralph W. Burhoe, "Religion's Role in Human Evolution: The Missing Link between Ape-man's Selfish Genes and Civilized Altruism," *Zygon*, 14 (June 1979), pp. 135-162; and Burhoe, "The Source of Civilization in the Natural Selection of Coadapted Information in Genes and Culture," *Zygon*, 11 (September 1976), pp. 263-303.

11. Edward O. Wilson, *Sociobiology: The New Synthesis* (Cambridge, Mass.: Harvard University Press, 1975), p. 3.

12. For a discussion of pertinent issues on this point, see Philip Hefner, "The Cultural Significance of Jesus' Death as Sacrifice," *The Journal of Religion* 60 (October 1980), pp. 411-439.

13. See George Pugh, *The Biological Origin of Human Values* (New York: Basic Books, 1977).

14. See Anthony Stevens, *Archetypes, a Natural History of the Self* (New York: Wm. Morrow, 1983).

15. Edward O. Wilson, *On Human Nature* (Cambridge, Mass.: Harvard Univ. Press, 1978), p. 2.

16. See Teilhard de Chardin, *The Phenomenon of Man* (revised ed.; New York: Harper, 1965), esp. pp. 254-311.
17. This variation on Teilhard is Nicholas J. Yonker's. See his *God, Man, and the Planetary Age* (Corvallis, Ore.: Oregon State Univ. Press, 1978), p. 1.
18. Gregory of Nyssa, *On the Making of Man*, i. 5, *Nicene and Post-Nicene Fathers*, vol. 5 (Grand Rapids: Wm. Eerdmanns, 1954), pp. 389-90.
19. Robert Fancoeur, *Evolving World, Converging Man* (New York: Holt, Rinehart, and Winston, 1970).
20. Paul Tillich, *Systematic Theology*, vol. 2 (Chicago: Univ. of Chicago Press, 1957), pp. 29-43.

Chapter Eleven

COSMIC EVOLUTIONARY CREATION AND CHRISTIAN GOD

Ralph Wendell Burhoe

I understand this group of essays is to search for some better relation between the Christian faith and the environmental crisis. My role in this is to clarify a new synthesis of the concepts underlying *evolutionary creation* with *traditional concepts of God*, the creator of heaven and earth. This chapter is intended to intermediate, particularly between two chapters in this book: that of a highly competent scientist, Ledyard Stebbins, and a highly competent theologian, Philip Hefner, with each of whom I seek a better union of science and human values and closely share his ideas in his own field. But better to fit the facts of both religion and science jointly, I submit a view seeking to make a more complete union at the rational level, hopefully helpful in and beyond this book.

So far as the environmental crisis is concerned, there is little doubt that modern scientific pictures have predicted and revealed the problems. So far as Christian faith is concerned, it has been charged with desacralizing nature and making Christendom indifferent to, if not a despoiler of, our ecosystem.[1a]

My thesis is that the present environmental crisis, like many other human crises, stems primarily from the failure to communicate our religious tradition's concept of our creator credibly to a scientific-technological world; that the necessary revitalization of the essence of our traditional creation story now can be corrected with the vital help of the new and richer understandings of religious questions achieved by the sciences; and, if corrected, could save us from environmental and other crises.

The heritages of cultural *information*[1b] (which help shape the structures and behavior patterns of all religions, as well as of languages, technologies, etc.) have evolved under generation and selection by the same system of powers that also provides the information in our genetic heritages (which shape basal levels of all our structures and behaviors of body and mind). Indeed the evidence is high for the view that the same system (nature and its laws) selects the structures and behaviors of all events in the evolution of the cosmos. What the scientists now call nature turns out on careful inspection to do essentially the same kinds of things our ancestors ascribed to God, the Creator.

In the past few decades there has been growing evidence and hence conviction among scientists that biological evolution is a special segment of cosmic, chemical, and other evolutionary processes, all of which interact in a hierarchy of stages (including subatomic, galactic, atomic, chemical, genetic, neurological, cultural, conscious, and rational) under a single, cosmically uniform system of law.[2ab] Insofar as this is valid, the gap between the recent concepts of cosmic evolutionary creation and traditional concepts of the Christian Creator God may be not only very much less than that implied in C. P. Snow's *Two Cultures*, but may be even less than the diminished gaps reflected by A. R. Peacocke's *Creation and the World of Science*.

Moreover, if religions, like languages and genes, have been selected as universally characteristic and essential for our lives— selected by the total system of forces that for thousands of years have been shaping human evolution—then traditional religions, on scientific grounds, can be presumed to be laden with wisdom and motivation for optimal human adaptation to the sovereign reality upon which life depends. Religious wisdom may thus become as respected among scientists as has the wisdom of the genes or of primitive cultural technologies.[3a-c]

This, of course, does not at all mean that the Hellenistic and Medieval world views of most Christian theological interpretations would be acceptable to scientists as contemporary conveyors of "what is really true," even though they might concur that the scientific world view might confirm traditional programs for human duty, hope, behavior, and ultimate destiny.[4]

My thesis states, furthermore, that religions in general have been the primary integrating links between sociocultural systems, their gene pools, and their environments. Cultures and gene pools are required to be highly coadapted to one another as well as to their common environment.

Coadaptation is another important concept for understanding the scientific grounds of this paper. The term comes from biogenetic pioneers who sought to explain the compatibility of any gene with the others in the total recipe for producing an integrated cell or organism. This internal compatibility of a multitude of symbols of DNA molecules, which instruct the developing structures and behaviors of each organism, is the first and fundamental meaning of my use of the term coadaptation. To produce adaptation of the whole organism to the external world there must first be a coadaptation of the organism's various internal structures and functions. Natural selection is involved in both levels, weeding out all information bits or pieces which are incompatible internally and all whose collective impact is to produce an organism not able to survive to reproduce in the context of its habitat.

Secondly, *coadaptation* refers to the compatibility of whatever collectivity of organisms are dependent upon their relationship one to another in a shared habitat. The genes of a lion are co-adapted with those of the deer which it must catch in order to eat, and vice versa for the running speed and other strategies of the deer who are to survive. This coadaptation in the ecosystem is not limited to predator-prey relationships but also involves mutual cooperation among species, such as bees who provide flowering plants with a useful means for genetic variability and the flowering plants who provide the bees with needed food. Thus coadaptation can involve mutual adaptations of several millions or billions of genes that may be required for programming the structures and behaviors (phenotypes) from individual cells to total ecosystems.[5a(1)-(3)]

In a 1976 paper I used *coadaptation* in a third and new sense to characterize the relation between two very different kinds (*species*) of information which structure human nature—the genetic and the cultural—to account for the not-genetically-programmable altruism of human populations beyond close kin.[5b-d]

I gave a new picture of the coevolution of the elements that make up humanity, pointing out that the information pool in the culture of a sociocultural system was selected differently and independently from the pool of genotypes that also shape the structures and behaviors of the same population. I also pointed out that the religious core of culture emerged as the source of the most effective perduring memories and transmitters of values (goals of action) of a sociocultural system—much longer-lasting than those of individual organisms, much more needed (sacred) for viability than other elements of culture. I showed why the information transmitted by primitive religious culture was so essential for viable human societies that selection pressures within each competing society would closely coadapt its religious and gene pool's information heritages to accelerate the mutually beneficial symbiosis between the societal culture and gene pool. Religion, with roots in genes and culture, is a central agency of the symbiosis. The selection of the sociocultural phenotypes, jointly programmed by their symbiotic genetic and cultural information, would modify the information patterns in both the genes and cultures so that the joint programming provided a more viable sociocultural phenotype. A more viable sociocultural phenotype means, of course, more adapted or more viable simultaneously in terms of either genes or societies.[6a]

One evidence for this is that the genetic programming of the brain highly resonates with religion's need to generate effective motivation. The overwhelmingly genetically programmed lower-brain structures provide religion with its capacity to motivate two vital functions of religion: (1) the otherwise impossible altruistic service the average individual renders to other individuals of the sociocultural system (most of whom are not close kin and hence service to whom, as programmed by genes alone without religion, is negative); and (2) adaptation to the will of the gods (the more than human powers, tantamount to what we now call natural selection) that usually reward us for serving their many requirements, including the social patterns they favor. The coadaptation that effects the altruism to non-kin conspecifics is possible because religion "guarantees" the reciprocity of altruism within each religious community, and hence guarantees a superior habitat for genetic success of that gene pool. The coadaptation that motivates the worship of or adaptation to the ultimate powers (the forces by which nature or the reality system selects one pattern over another) is clearly the adaptation of the core values of the culturetype to the ultimate reality to which all living systems must be adapted.[6b(1)-(3)]

The outer cortices of the brain, where sociocultural inputs of ritual, body-language, linguistic, and other information are handled, are so connected with the lower, motivational centers of the brain that an enculturated religion, if indeed it is suitably coadapted to the genetically programmed basic motivational system, may so modify the expression of genetic information as to provide an enlightened devotion to the requirements of its gods, including altruistically devoted service to a society.

This mutual adaptation of the enduring sacred cores of both a culture and its gene pool to their common ecological niche made religions and genes mutually beneficent symbionts. Selection came whenever one of their jointly programmed phenotypes became a more viable pattern than others.

Without a suitably evolved religion, with its close coadaptation to basic genetic as well as cultural and ecological requirements, there is little chance to generate individuals who internally (noncoercively) choose to serve altruistically a non-kin society; or who internally prefer to do with respect to the ecosystem whatever is vital or sacred for the long-term viability of the life program created on earth. (N.B.: We can never escape the cosmic ecosystem.)

Since *coercive* societal control of individual or collective behavior is inherently unstable and inadequate for significant long-term viability of any system—especially for the cultural symbiont which can only exist at the pleasure of the gene pool with which it is symbiotic (some say: upon which it is parasitic)— a revitalization of a sound religious faith with respect to what is simultaneously sacred for the individual, the gene pool, the society, and the ecosystem is essential to the resolution of not only our ecologic crises but also of our sociocultural and personal crises.[6c-d]

Evidence for my thesis comes from both historical and scientific sources. I have had cooperation and scrutiny during more than three decades from many leaders in religious studies as well as in the sciences. The thesis originated among scientists concerned primarily with evolutionary theory but also with human destiny. It may be our best hope for resolving the problem of this volume and many other human problems.

Religion in Evolution

Following the three symposia in 1960 of the American Academy of Arts and Sciences on the relation of cultural to genetic evolution,[7] it became clear to me that there were hierarchical stages or levels in the information that shapes our structure and behavior, including the two very different levels of genetic and cultural information and sublevels within each of them. It was also clear that the earlier levels of cultural evolution (including religion) were not and are not fashioned basically by human reason but, like information selected in the gene pool, may and largely do come from selection of partially random variations and yet, under careful scientific examination, may be found to be highly ordered systems.[8] This permitted scientists, for instance, to provide evidence, not hitherto known by theologians, for a deeper understanding and appreciation of the nature and importance of religious ritual.[9] We find this new scientific appreciation also true for the most advanced levels or stages of religion, even in the several levels of traditional theological efforts at rational interpretation.[10]

Several of us concluded that there has been so much wisdom evolved in religious and theological tradition for shaping good or right human behavior that no civilization, especially a high scientific-technological one, can get along without a powerfully internalized religious sense of what is sacred for us. We felt science confirmed ancient religious views of the sacred, that awareness of sacrality results in part from our ultimate hopes and fears concerning the system of power upon which our destiny is utterly dependent. Without this sense of sacrality, humans seem not to be motivated to a proper respect for, or necessary self-restraints on behalf of, their environing ecosystem, which, by the way, includes their societal system.

For an effective and stable social order in harmony with its ecosystem, it seems necessary that a sufficient percentage of the goals and actions of all its individuals be bound into (*religandi sunt*) a culturally (non-genetically) transmitted system of shared values. This can happen when the average individual is non-coercively persuaded that its true, unique, and ultimate self will be more greatly rewarded, by the ultimate system of power, for adopting those values.

That self is the collectivity of expressions of variations on the themes or patterns of a complex and enduring information system (including coadapted genetic, cultural, and habitat patterns), which comes close to one of the earlier meanings of "soul."[11]

Primitive religions notably have established relatively harmonious genetic, societal, and ecosystemic goals for tribal populations under a selection pressure for viability that must coadapt the current rituals and beliefs of their cultures to requirements of gene pool and environment. A similar selection operated on the later, great religions. But today most faiths are not adapted credibly to our new scientific-technological context.

For me, the solution of the ecologic crisis becomes clear when we recognize that we can and we must credibly reinterpret within the context of the modern, scientific world view the primary elements of the traditional religion within which modern science arose: Christendom. Science and its technology arose in Christendom. But when Christian interpretation separated itself from its scientific infant, it left in the wilderness an unsanctified child that grew to be an overwhelming giant, which seduced a religiously and morally unprepared world. Christian faith eroded and dissipated as it failed to be interpreted credibly in the context of the rapidly expanding scientific enlightenment.

I shall seek to show that this ancient, sacred, religious wisdom — which very early had advanced by means of rational interpretations (theologies that sought to be in tune with the sciences of their times) to be quite credible in the context of a foundational stage of modern science in the Hellenistic world — may become again, through new interpretations in the light of the modern sciences, the sacred center of our civilization and central for resolving not only our environmental crises but also our many other crises — inter-faith, international, interpersonal, and personal.[12a-b]

Religion is not obsolete, but only its current interpretation in a scientific culture is inadequate for those enculturated in the scientific world view. The revitalization of its sacred function is more essential for the future of the race than other culturally transmitted technologies, including medicine, politics, or even secular education and language. Because of its sacred function to unite non-coercively (voluntarily) the diversely programmed (genetically, non-kindred) individuals into proper social attitudes and behaviors toward others in a sociocultural system, and its function to orient their social collectivity into proper attitudes and behaviors relative to the ecosystem, the viability of a human ecological niche requires a reinterpreted and revitalized religion. The Lord of history's selections processes seem to favor this eventuality.

A key model for my vision of human nature and its dependence on a larger and higher-powered system of nature is the picture of evolution presented by contemporary sciences. I have been nourished in accounts of evolution that overlap very closely with Ledyard Stebbins' account in his essay for this book: "Evolution and Religion." I deem his chapter to be about as good a scientific story of creation as anyone now can tell, and more comprehensive and valid than most, especially for the task of this book.

But for my purposes I shall utilize some newer, not yet widely tested or demonstrated elements of evolutionary theory, particularly concerning culture and religion. A closer examination of religion in the light of the sciences is needed, especially in scientifically informed communities, for appreciation of the very essential role of religion in human origins, evolution thus far, and continuation in the future. I suggest that it might be lethal if we dropped the functions and wisdom of traditional religion simply because religion's superficial ideological clothing was found unscientific and hence obsolete. Religion's alleged obsoleteness resulted from understandable but nevertheless erroneous perceptions by both theologians and scientists who had not yet seen religion scientifically, and this must be corrected.[12c]

The students of comparative and historical religion in the past century have already noted that religion itself evolves, changes in time. Even within the biblical record of the Judeo-Christian tradition itself, the careful reader may be impressed with the changes in perceptions of religion from the older elements of the Old Testament text to the later ones of the New Testament. Almost every Christian has noted the impressive words: "It was said of old that . . . but I say unto you." Such biblical proclamations of changes and improvements of religion in the course of time are themselves a witness to the fact that it is an evolving system.

In my decades of work to understand religion scientifically, I have discovered that all religions and theologies may be seen to be evolving, like the patterns of the earth and the life upon it as portrayed in the sciences, under selection or judgment by an objective, super-human system of powers. Although religions are as different as different animal species, they all carry the same general message, as does the DNA of the different animal species. This message tells what to do in order to have optimal life. The common theme of what religions recommend for this purpose is that individuals and societies must conform to what the system of sovereign spirits, gods, God, or ultimate reality requires, if humans want any future.

At the same time I have come to understand that the scientific picture of our creation—under a system of largely hidden forces operating in nature over time to create and select the viable patterns—gives the same message: all individuals and societies, even human ones with the most powerful scientific technologies, to have any future must conform to the requirements of the sovereign powers. If we do not adapt to meet the requirements for fitness in a possible ecological niche, we have no future. Because of the selection pressures made by such requirements, they thereby come to be held by us as sacred. The cosmic ecosystem, which is our matrix, seems to have many of the attributes of the religious creator God. The cosmic hierarchies of stages and laws from atoms to human sociocultural systems are reflected or imaged in the insides of our being as well as constitute the potentialities of the habitat with whose future kingdom our nature must fit or perish.[13]

I conclude this section with a brief synopsis of how, in the light of the sciences, I conceive of religion and its evolution. I define religion as "whatever it is" that generates the motivations or the internal wills that lead people to love, trust, and heed, above all, the gifts and requirements for their lives made by the transhuman, transcendent, or "ultimate" system of powers that created them and determines their destiny. It turns out that a by-product of this devotion to the "ultimate" is the only source of motivation to love, trust, and heed the gifts and requirements of the sociocultural system, into units of which the very nature of each individual has been inseparably extended by the "ultimate" system of power. In traditional religious language the "ultimate" system of power has been called the gods, or God, or the Ultimate, etc. In scientific language it is called nature, whose process of creation is called evolution. The scientific perspective is becoming a clarification and extension of earlier evolved perspectives.

In scientific language, the evolution of religion proceeds under natural or real selection by the relative fitness of the expression of variant culturetypic patterns of religion in variant phenotypes of biosocial organisms. Each such phenotype is constituted by a mutualistic, symbiotic union of coadapted genetic and cultural packages of information in a population of individuals sharing a common culturetype. Cultural information is not transmitted by genes but only from brain to brain. The religious sector of the culturetype is that in which exists the encoded memory required for generating the most sacred or critically significant values that are transmitted by the culture.

Genetic and cultural heritage are intertwined in each brain so that they are jointly involved in programming a human's response to its ecosystem and thus define its ecological niche. A dominant element of a human's ecosystem is its biosocial organism, the information and behavior characterizing a larger-than-kin-group population. The individuals within such a population are bound together (*religata*) by the religion since it carries the coadapted primal goals or values of both the genetic and cultural symbionts. This mutualistic bond provided between their varied genotypes and their common religious culturetype is what enabled the extension of kin altruism to a non-kin biosocial organism and made it for the first time a unit for group selection.

Religions are selected, like all other systems in nature, whenever a variant form of a biosocial religious community turns out to be more viable than other forms. Whatever genetic and culturetypic elements characterize the symbionts constituting a surviving biosocial phenotype are thereby selected.

Because cultures can change and evolve thousands of times faster than gene pools, biosocial evolution is much faster than genetic evolution. The differential rate of evolution produces unstable situations when the timing of the mutual coadaptations are out of phase, a phenomenon that produces cycles in human evolution. The coadaptation of religion to the phases of the gene pool characteristics of its population is critical. More often critical are the phase lags in coadaptation with religion of the other elements of the sociolcultural system that historical changes bring to pass. When a religious reformulation to meet the new requirements is not possible, the sociocultural system tends to deteriorate and either its religion is reformed or the society becomes inviable.

The Rise of Science
and the Decline of Religion

In the twentieth century every religion is sadly out of phase with the rapid changes in the sociocultural organism of the world produced by modern science and its technologies. Among other causes, the phase lags are produced by the cognitive incompatibility of all religions with modern sciences and by technology's rather abrupt transposition of all sociocultural organisms of the world with their separate and unintegrated religions (a situation which produces hostility and war) into a single interdependent city.

In Christendom, the phase lag has debilitated faith in its creator God, even though I have suggested there is a similarity between its traditional *God* and the new scientific understanding of *nature*. The similarity has not been recognized very widely for many reasons.

One reason is that the scientific pictures of our creation have only recently become clear.

Another is that we have only just begun to have sufficient theoretical evidence and coherence in our theories of the common and coadapted selection of genes and cultures. Selection for viable brain behaviors selects genetic and cultural heritages for their joint effect. This has to include religion.[14a-b]

Another is that only very recently have there arisen credible theories of how genetic and cultural information are combined to produce the patterns of individual development (behavior) and of "inner" or "subjective" human values (feelings, perceptions, motivations, hopes, fears, etc., including religious experience).[15]

Because of the overwhelming power of new scientific technology to satisfy human wishes as if by magic, most evaluators of new scientifically informed and seemingly beneficial applications in agriculture, banking, business, communications, engineering, manufacturing, medicine, religion, and, in fact, most other human accomplishments, naturally but somewhat naively suppose that this is human choice creating ultimate good. First they overlook the fact that many "improvements" are sooner or later found to have "side effects" that result in a situation that is worse than before the "improvement," unless a number of corrections are made (coadaptation), and sometimes even that is not possible. Secondly, they overlook the primary fact that by grace we have been endowed with a preselected wisdom that has been devised not by us but by the circumstances that selected our genetic and cultural heritages, such that they already largely conform to the bulk of the requirements of our environment. And thirdly, they overlook the fact that no new variant of our inherited wisdom is going to be viable unless we have successfully found and met the requirements for viability that will be imposed by the forces of our real circumstances. Except the Lord build the city, they labor in vain who build it. However, a number of more sophisticated analysts in various fields have properly noted the evolution of human arts under selection by factors beyond the authors' control.[16a]

This growing scientific understanding of human destiny—as being judged and selected by the operations of its total ecological niche (according to cosmically valid rules)—is all so recent and scattered in different disciplines that few are yet aware that the scientists' system of sovereign powers (they call it nature) is equally sovereign over human social and psychological or mental behaviors and experiences as over lower species of life or over the structures and behaviors of astronomical and geophysical events.

Another set of reasons for not recognizing modern science as a significant additional revelation of the nature and requirements of the determiner of human destiny is the cumulation of ecclesiastic, philosophic, and other anathemas against scientists' meddling with the understanding or interpretation of religion or human values, beginning as far back as Galileo. The anathemas arose from those who had some reason to fear that the seemingly negative implications of scientific findings for the effectiveness of their view of sacred truth might tend to destroy the effectiveness of religious faith and human hope and morals.

During the 18th-century Enlightenment and 19th-century Romantic periods, the ban on adverse scientific implications for religion continued but changed its strategy. In the centuries since philosopher Immanuel Kant—when the validity of scientific findings and their seemingly negative effect on contemporary modes of transmitting religious faith could no longer be denied—the defenders of the faith gave up the earlier attempts to suppress the seemingly negative implications of the sciences for religion and tended to follow Kant's lead in asserting a realm of thought for values, quite separate from that for the sciences. With such a separation, neither science nor religion was presumed qualified to speak meaningfully except in its own sphere.

Many of the educated (even scientists as well as those in the humanities) apparently found it easier to follow, at least publically, the philosophical and religious apologists in concurring that the sciences were irrelevant for religion and morals. The net result was a rise in enthusiasm for science because its truths made possible so many marvelous and desired benefits, and a slow but inevitable decrease in enthusiasm for their faith in traditional religious beliefs and practices.

During the 19th century and even today, there have been some of the educated and half-educated whose brains could not dichotomize their world so easily; and they continued the battles of the books (and educational policies), seeking to demolish the claims of official religion—which they often decried as primitive superstitions. In Western civilization, religious apologists fought a losing battle as scientific knowledge grew and spread because of its wonderful usefulness in all technological arts, including arts close to religion, such as medicine.

The impacts of both the general waning of strong religious convictions and the direct intellectual attacks upon traditional religion left the general public with less and less enculturation to guide their behavior to long-term values. Increasingly the general faith tended towards a hedonistic—"do what ya wanna do"—grounds for behavior, with diminishing respect for the religious tradition, the state (which ultimately depends upon a sacred undergirding), the public weal, or the ecosystem. As a result, the applications of scientific technology increasingly have been made on hedonistic grounds unrefined by religion.[16b] Toward the end of the 20th century it is increasingly being recognized by thoughtful intellectuals that this is leading the world toward disaster. The less educated are tending in greater numbers to rally towards traditional or novel cults of religious salvation, which by their fit to the coadapted genetic programming of our brains are appealing but which by their intellectual nature are not able to adapt to rational or scientific world views. The picture is akin to Robert Heilbroner's gloomy portrait of the *Human Prospect.*[16c]

The above-described historical response patterns were natural strategies prior to a few decades ago, before the sciences began to investigate human nature in new depths and to find that their investigations included the nature and source of human values and religions. The sciences of the late 20th century are quite different from those of the late 18th, and increasingly have become recognized as revealing much about religion and human values in the context of the scheme of things. Surprising to many, what they find provides a new appreciation for the wisdom of religious traditions.[16d-e]

The evolutionary theory—and several contributing sciences such as genetics, neurophysiology, sociobiology, anthropology, psychology, and many others—has begun to build up fairly objective understandings of the nature, importance, and sources of subjective feelings, meaning, fears, and hopes, including the importance of traditional religious experiences, practices, beliefs, and institutions for personal and public welfare. In fact, many recent studies provide a new kind of scientifically grounded— even though often begrudging and not fully confident—respect for traditional religion's virtues.[17]

Curiously, in this same period religion has lost face from the work of its presumed friends in philosophy, biblical, and historical studies, as well as in sociology and psychology. These and related studies increasingly have suggested that the scriptures were not so much sacred revelations direct from the gods as human writings edited to sell one or another sociopolitical pattern. They showed God or the gods not so much as objective realities but as humanly generated symbols for social control or the byproducts of psychoneurotic imaginings. Many view these studies as discrediting faith in religion far more than had the earlier seemingly negative implications from the natural sciences.

Also, since the 18th century, more and more people in Western civilization have come to understand the post-Enlightenment, critical, humanities studies to be our most authoritative descriptions of what is really true about our values and destiny. Curiously these humanistic fields have distanced themselves from theology more than have natural scientists. Theology came to be regarded by many as a no-longer-significant discipline of learning. During the past few centuries, by increasingly cutting themselves clear from any relevance to meaningful statements from science, the sociocultural institutions of religion, theology, and morals cut themselves off from what many today feel are the best instruments for making credible any pictures of human reality and destiny.

The movement to disjoin sacred values from scientific facts, which was mounted in the 18th century, accomplished the reverse of what was intended: It has diminished the possibility, within a world that has faith in science, of faith in a more-than-human system of power, which more successfully had flourished in the context of earlier views of reality.

As a result, Christian religion, especially its once masterful intellectual adaptations in theological interpretation to fit the reigning cognitive schemes of Hellenistic and Medieval culture, has greatly faded. In spite of their strong emotional and moral needs for help, people increasingly find religion's alleged system of reality to be less and less real or significant.

Religion's Necessity and the Rise of Inadequate Religions

Lately, as the sciences are more and more confirming the virtues of religion and view it as evolved and selected by the same creative and omnipotent system, which many recent scientists have come to view as the nature that is indeed our creator, that which has generated and rules everything we know about in the world (including the structures of human thought and feeling as well as the physical world)—it has become clear to many scientists that humans cannot live by bread alone. Translated, this means that genetic wisdom and a plenteous supply of food alone—without a symbiotic injection into the central nervous system of a completely non-genetic but relatively stable body of cultural information laden with suitable sacred values—cannot make a human. To become human we must be suckled and constantly fed thereafter on sacred information from our sociocultural system.[18a-c]

During the 19th century, the desperately needed functions of religion became so weakened that there emerged a number of new salvation programs which came to play a large role for human hopes in Western Civilization. Among these were Marxism and Freudianism. These salvation programs, which tended to spread to the non-Christian cultures as the scientific-technical world view infected and weakened their traditional religious cultures, generally sought to accredit their own validity by claiming coherence with the 19th-century scientific or Enlightenment views existing in the minds of their founders. To make this clear they tended to debunk traditional Christianity as an outmoded if not debilitating myth and superstition, and they sometimes accused it of suppressing the socioeconomic rights of the poor or of suppressing the rights of individuals to do what they want to do. There were numerous other salvation programs, including the philosophical and political humanisms, Fascism, Nazism, as well as various allegedly religious cults.

Moreover, Marxists, Freudians, and other psychosocial ideologists have perhaps been even more unable to welcome the recent findings by the natural sciences (such as evidence for the superior virtues of traditional religion for psychosocial therapy or the more objective validity of some of the symbolic communications) than has the theological community.[19a-c]

In general these newer salvation missions (which at a superficial intellectual level may at first seem more attractive and, in the context of our new scientific culture, equally credible with what many Christian theologians have offered) are often disastrous because they usually have lacked both the new wisdom of modern science and the traditional wisdom of religion, both now necessary to bind together the dual systems of sociocultural and genetic information so as to provide a superior symbiotic wisdom that fits the foundation that has been selected for during thousands of years. Many new *isms* are lethal and soon die.

One of the bad side effects of these superficial or simplistic new salvation programs was that they could not motivate very well a collective altruism and usually had to turn to turn politically totalitarian and coercive police-state control, which means an unstable and sooner or later non-viable system. Likewise, the Freudian and related salvation programs, which were aimed at freeing individuals from control by religion or state, tended to weaken social responsibilities and hence to undermine their sociocultural foundation.

To fill the same void of religion and values, there has arisen a parallel group of salvation movements: new sects or cults, often purporting to relate to some existing religion. Many of these also have been superficial, initially plausible only to the less sophisticated, and not very viable. Inadequate in their own structures, in their coadaptation to either the gene pool or larger sociocultural system, and rather hopeless in their adaptation to life in the context of modern science, they also often fall to coercive ways and fail to endure.

Religion Seen by Science; Eliade's Sacrality; Our Problem

My picture of religion in the light of the sciences finds it a phenomenon that was creatively central in the emergence of humans from ape-men in a long-selected and complex history—involving the many interacting stages of phenotypic products that have been programmed jointly by genes and cultures. Religion is the central value-generating agency of a huge network of information that establishes and regulates human nature in relations to itself internally, to its sociocultural system, and to its environment. The scientific picture indicates that very little of this information, today as in the past, reaches conscious, cognitive, or scientific attention. Even about our communication in language, most of us do it readily enough, but few have more than a most superficial capacity to explain how it works or it came to be.

This helps explain why most of the critics and reformers (including Kant)—beginning in the Enlightenment and still today, with only the freshman or sophomore level of present scientific information available to them about human nature, culture, and religion—focussed their attention primarily on the superficial, cognitive dissonances between science and religion, and hence failed to redeem the obvious weaknesses in Western civilization. Of course, the Medieval, Hellenistic, and even more primitive cognitive structures (in which Christian belief remains embedded) do not fit with those of modern science. Of course, the new scientific pictures of the nature of humans and religion were not available until recently, and hence religion was only superficially understood in terms of its cognitive clothing. These inadequate tools for analysis explain why many philosophers and historical critics (e.g.: H. G. Wells) have been notorious for their failures in predictions of religion's end. The evolutionary picture of continually new emergents in human cognition and science makes it clear how true it is that "now we see only dimly, as in a poor mirror."

Aside from pointing out that we see, in this selection of coadapted genetic and cultural information packages, a richer picture of human nature, including humanity's distinctive transcendence of the animal kingdom and a new insight into religion's role in the coadaption of genes and culture, I shall have to leave to your reading of other papers your fuller appreciation of the capacity of scientific investigation to understand ever more detailed aspects of human nature, from inner feelings and experiences (including religious) to the total reality in which we live and move and have our being. But now, we should examine our recently discovered confirmations by the sciences of some of the the functional virtue of the wisdom already selected in traditional religion and traditional religious concepts, and the resulting promise for resolving our ecological crisis.

I trust the argument thus far indicates that the problem of compatibility of science with religion or theology seems to reside, not so much in whether there is a system of power transcendent to humans that is their creator, but rather in how far there can be a genuine compatibility of attributes between what the scientist calls the reality of nature's evolutionary creation, as far we know that, and what the religions call the ultimate reality or Christianity's sovereign God the creator of heaven and earth, as far as we know that. Some outstanding scientists who have looked at religion scientifically presume they can authentically translate back and forth between the religious and scientific symbol systems designating ulterior sources or powers, just as readily as they can translate back and forth between primitive cultural traditions and scientific findings on nourishment and the primitive rituals and myths shaping diet. They have found substantial confirmation of non-cognitively selected basic wisdom in primitive cultures.[20] The evidence of history suggests that the credibility, within a scientifically informed population, of the wisdom of a religion's symbol system depends on whether it can be translated into symbols credible to scientifically informed minds. But the virtue of the wisdom does not stem from the level of the scientific or prescientific symbol system in which it originated or currently is expressed.

I have sought to provide a summary view of why I and a number of exploring scientists and scholars believe that a revitalization of a strong and moving religious faith for the world population indeed could be accomplished today in the full light of the sciences and that such a revitalization is necessary for human salvation in an age of science and technology, with its crises not only with respect to the environment but also with respect to intra-human behavior in the presence of nuclear weapons, loss of meaning and hope, and simultaneously new sicknesses of souls and civilizations.[21]

In such a brief review I have given primary focus to showing why the philosophical-theological separation of human values and religion from science, instead of saving values and religion, was an error that is gravely disrupting them. I have also sought to give reasons why this separation is no longer necessary but has become potentially lethal.

I have not been able to mention most of many other problems that philosophers and theologians raise, such as the paradoxes of freedom versus determinism; mind and soul versus matter; God as a kind of personal and gracious father versus God as inexorable mechanical destiny; the relation of the "mighty acts of the Lord of History" to those of natural selection; prayer in a scientific world view; Christianity and the non-Christian world; etc. Our failure to deal with all these questions is not because we haven't wrestled with them and got some useful findings, but just because it can't be done in a short space. I refer you to some of our efforts on these matters.[22a-d]

I suggest it will now be more profitable for the purposes of this paper and book if you will ask yourself: Well, what if the claims of this new interpretation of religion and theology in the light of the sciences turns out to be true? What difference would that make for a synthesis of the Christian "God" and the scientific "nature" and how would that resolve our ecological crisis and perhaps some of our other problems?

In the first place, since the scientists heartily believe in their hypotheses about "reality" which they call "nature" (meaning the nature of reality as far as humans can understand it), a nature which they and their colleagues have so carefully tested, then a high correlation with the God concept would allow, might even logically impel, them and the rest of the secular world that has faith in the scientific world view, to appreciate more fully the sovereignty and grace of the ultimate system of power.

Strong logical convictions about important matters can generate feelings and behaviors, which could come close to those of Christians in the past, when many of them seriously considered their God indeed to be the source of all creation and to be the almighty and ultimate power that presides over the destiny of humans as well as the rest of the cosmos.

While not many high-ranking scientists have yet been led to a scientific-religious appreciation of the Christian concept of God (not many have been associated in the breakthroughs in understanding religion), a few have. A number of them, from a largely agnostic background have felt the scientific pictures imply that we are indeed beholden to the cosmic scheme and are on earth its favored children.[23]

This could conceivably reintroduce the sense of sacrality about our world, which sacrality, Mircea Eliade has noted, means "in the perspective of religious man of the archaic societies. . .that the world exists because it was created by the gods, and that the existence of the world itself 'means' something, 'wants to say' something, that our world is neither mute nor opaque, that it is not an inert thing, without purpose or significance. For religious man, the cosmos 'lives' and 'speaks.'The mere life of the cosmos is proof of its sanctity, since the cosmos was created by the gods and the gods show themselves to men through cosmic life."[24]

He contrasts this with the present situation: "In a summary formula we might say that for the nonreligious men of the modern age, the cosmos has become opaque, inert, mute; it transmits no message, it holds no cipher. . . . As for the Christianity of the industrial societies and especially the Christianity of intellectuals, it has long since lost the cosmic values that it still possessed in the Middle Ages. . . .The religious sense of urban populations is gravely impoverished."[25]

Perhaps Christian theology was so saturated with the Hellenistic, urban philosophies and was otherwise struggling to emphasize important new understandings of the individual's relation to other humans, under a gracious as well as sovereign heavenly father, that it fell short in proclaiming its fundamental belief (clear enough in Genesis and Psalms of its Old Testament canon) that the observable phenomena of the non-human world (which seems to be a prominent pre-modern-science meaning of "nature") were, like us, also the creation of the ultimate God and hence sacred witnesses of God's nature and power. In the New Testament the same God was also recognized through the witness of Jesus as our beloved father. I have already described in the section on "The Rise of Science. . .", above, how the defenders of faith and morals, especially since the 18th century, built a moat to isolate their realm from interpretation by the scientific revelations concerning nature. But since then science's nature has expanded from the non-human environment to the total system of reality, including human nature (body, mind, and perhaps soul) and its relation to and destiny in the larger total reality. Science's nature lies in mystery beyond the little of which we have some clear understanding. But this new scientific revelation of an immanent and transcendent reality now opens hope for bridging the moat and for a vast enrichment of theological interpretation of our highest concerns that will enable proper resolution of the present ecological crises and the obstacle that prevented historian Lynn White from finding a satisfactory solution.

Lynn White on Christianity and the Ecologic Crises

White's famous 1966 address on "The Historical Roots of Our Ecologic Crisis" to the American Association for the Advancement of Science[26] I think properly claimed that "what people do about their ecology depends on what they think about themselves in relation to things around them. Human ecology is deeply conditioned by beliefs about our nature and destiny—that is, by religion...Our daily habits of action, for example, are dominated by an implicit faith in perpetual progress which was unknown either to Greco-Roman antiquity or to the Orient. It is rooted in, and indefensible apart from, Judeo-Christian teleology"—except, I would add, a new defensibility is at hand in scientific evolutionary theory that has made it quite clear that there has been a several-billion-year history of progress toward ever more complexity in life systems, ever more widely adapted in their solar-system habitat, progressing now ever more rapidly forward within the new super-animal kingdom of human cultures.

White went on to say that "by destroying pagan animism, Christianity made it possible to exploit nature in a mood of indifference to the feelings of natural objects.... Man's effective monopoly on spirit in this world was confirmed, and the old inhibitions to the exploitation of nature crumbled."

After presenting good evidence that, "modern Western science was cast in a matrix of Christian theology," he noted that "some may be happy at the notions, first, that, viewed historically, modern science is an extrapolation of natural theology and, second, that modern technology is at least partly to be explained as an Occidental, voluntarist realization of the Christian dogma of man's transcendence of, and rightful mastery over, nature. But, as we now recognize, somewhat over a century ago science and technology—hitherto quite separate activities—joined to give mankind powers which, to judge by many of the ecologic effects, are out of control. If so, Christianity bears a huge burden of guilt."

The evidence presented in his paper tends to convince one that he is probably right in saying: "What we do about ecology depends on our ideas of the man-nature relationship. More science and more technology are not going to get us out of the present ecologic crisis until we find a new religion, or rethink the old one."

He concluded that "No new set of basic values has been accepted in our society to displace those of Christianity. Hence we shall continue to have a worsening ecologic crisis until we reject the Christian axiom that nature has no reason for existence save to serve man."

To resolve the problem, White suggested that "The greatest spiritual revolutionary in Western history, Saint Francis, proposed what he thought was an alternative Christian view of nature and man's relation to it: he tried to substitute the idea of the equality of all creatures, including man, for the idea of man's limitless rule of creation. He failed.... Since the roots of our trouble are so largely religious, the remedy must also be essentially religious, whether we call it that or not. We must rethink and refeel our nature and destiny. The profoundly religious, but heretical sense of the primitive Franciscans for the spiritual autonomy of all parts of nature may point a direction. I propose Francis as a patron saint for ecologists."

Conclusion

My proposed resolution is not to lean on White's Franciscan proposal "to depose man from his monarchy over creation and set up a democracy of all God's creatures." Evolutionary as well as Christian teachings say that man's monarchy is erroneous and his implied equality with other creatures impossible.

Soil is not equal to grass, nor grass to deer, nor deer to wolves, nor wolves to humans, nor humans to God. To be sure, at the level of God—as the symbol for what creates and determines the course of the total system or ecology of the cosmos—we properly may conceive that all elements are equally a part of God. (We here presume that what little we may know of God may include any "realities" science finds to lie behind any phenomena.) But, at the level of action of humans or lesser beings, our differences and unique statuses are of the essence.

What is important is not the erroneous vision of the equality of all beings but a more sophisticated or realistic vision, parts of which we can read from both evolutionary theory or the Bible. I have been seeking to portray in this chapter that this is a vision of the hierarchy of being in the cosmos and an understanding of the good for each being is defined by the requirements for each subsystem that arise from the total reality that impinges upon it.

This reality picture stresses that creatures, their situations, and their goals or values are not equal. Rather we are good and have life only insofar as we embody and act in accord with what the cosmic (and hence the local) ecosystem ultimately requires of us in our unique ecological niches.

What is clearly implied (in traditional theology as well as in evolutionary theories) is that God (or the nature and operations of cosmic reality, only infinitesimally known by either religion or by the sciences) is the monarch in charge of all things, including our creation and destiny as well as the other evolving animate and pre-animate kingdoms from which, on earth, we have been selected as a new and higher form.

What is good for us to do, or what is required of us if we are to exist at all, or to have life and have it more abundantly, is obedience to a set of objective (if not yet fully known) requirements, requirements we commonly define as sacred or divine. I have pointed out that in evolutionary theory as well as in biblical understanding, this set of objective requirements is a creative and ever changing set, especially for those creatures whose present circumstances happen to lie in the upper hierarchies of stages that are ever more rapidly advancing to higher levels. Human lives exist only as we reach the upper levels of the earth's evolutionary hierarchy and must be lived in accord with the requirements of those as well as of all lower levels which are still involved.

The special duties and opportunities of our level in the hierarchy of being become a sacred concern. Religions have been and must always be selected to inform us of, and effectively motivate us toward, what is indeed sacred for us. Sacrality has evolved under divine (or natural) selection to provide us with suitable information and motivation at all levels of our being. Our levels run from the biophysical and molecular chemistry up to that of savants and saints. During our long evolution and during our life cycle we build pyramidal levels from DNA in zygotes, through various levels of embryology, childhood, adulthood, and various levels of cultural and religious information or wisdom. Our capacities, duties, and opportunities change with our level of being.

I have pointed out that genetically and culturally the internal cores of our wills, desires, or loves have been shaped to conform to the sacred law, since by grace such a love or goal has been selected and transmitted to us as basic for our being. This has been done effectively through religions when they are good: in phase with, or coadapted to, the existing conditions of their places and times.

Evil is the measure of the extent to which our genes and religions (and hence we) have thus far failed to want to do what the ultimate ecosystem defines as the good. This picture of good and evil implies a universal goal or purpose for us and any living system: to seek coadaptation with whatever elements of the ultimate ecosystem that become essential conditions of our ecological niche. For me this purpose is equally well phrased: gladly to seek, find, and obey the will of God.

I argue for the genuineness of the above equality of scientific and religious statements of purpose on the basis of my examination of the central messages of various levels and categories of long-evolved religious cultures, but most particularly the Judeo-Christian tradition, where I find a proper translation of religious views of our relationship to the ultimate system of power into modern scientific concepts comes close to the above phrasing of our dependence upon our ecosystem. Of course, one should not impute to earlier theologians or still earlier contributors to religious myths or rituals any prescience of modern evolutionary theory. But one may properly impute a natural selection of wisdom in the coadapted, symbiotic packages of a religion's culture-type and gene pool. Hence such a wisdom may properly be said to be "given by the grace of God."

The evil, less virtuous, or less well-adapted behavioral patterns are continually being judged and weeded out by the reigning power of the kingdom of reality, whether we call it God or natural selection. This view confirms that we are not to regard the behavior patterns of all things, all creatures, or all humans as of equal merit. There are objective or real standards for all our values. It is especially important to note the objectivity of sacred values: a perspective on values that has faded with the loss of faith in the Christian God and the rise of humanistic hedonisms that imply the human being is the ultimate judge of all things.

We need more objective grounds for distinguishing what is good or better from what is worse—under the judgments of a supreme reality—both in ourselves and in any elements of the local ecosystems around us. Moreover, as systems around us evolve there is likelihood that our system must co-evolve. Even though at one level of analysis nothing remains the same, nevertheless we can abstract from all this flux a stable and universal rule: the highest value for all creatures is forever to seek and enact what our history requires.

It is important to realize that when our values, desires, and behaviors are shaped ultimately by the requirements of the eco-system, this circumstance applies to every phase of our behaviors, whether to human neighbors or to environment. Since all things which touch us are a part of our ecological niche, it also should be clear that our place in the Garden of Eden or the ecosystem of earth, as we become increasingly sophisticated and powerful, becomes increasingly a position of sacred custodianship. If we have no objectively sacred convictions of our duty and hope in doing the will of that in which we live and move, but have only a naively informed human hedonism to guide us, we are bound to abuse the welfare of our local environment, our fellow humans, and other elements of our ecological niche: hence abuse our own true selves.

The task of the custodian of the Garden of Eden or of the local ecosystem, as defined both in the Christian tradition and by evo-lutionary theory, is the task of finding and carrying out God's (nature's) will, which includes the requirements of the context of God's creation within which we find ourselves. Of course, to carry out the ultimate will or requirements of all creation would be an impossible task for humans. We can correctly note that *that* is God's task, and that natural selection will take care of it. We really know very little about it and could not consciously operate more than a trivial part of what goes on inside our own bodies to give us life, to say nothing of the world or cosmic ecosystem.

But the task of finding the sovereign reality's requirements in small tentative, new steps, nearby in our own changing ecological niches, is the task the Lord of History has set before each of us. This automatically requires and insures that in the end our beha-vior will be fitting to the sovereign reality, since an objective judg-ment or selection will prevail as it has for several billion years. We can be human beings only to the extent that we fit the ultimate requirements of such being. We have no power whatsoever to avoid this reality of our destiny as portrayed by religion or evolu-tionary theory. But we need revised and revitalized help from the religious sector of our culture.

A new union of scientific and theological understanding could greatly help us to believe deeply in the Lord of our history. It could help us to appreciate the heritage it has given us to know what is good and evil for our lives. It could again kindle in us proper fears and hopes for our futures. Through the successively selected levels of genes and religiously guided cultures, the Lord has revealed successively higher levels of truths by which we can be motivated internally (in our hearts) to know and to want to do good rather than evil.

Separated from the sacralizing functions and long-evolved, coadapted genetic and cultural wisdom of religion, science does not have adequate power to motivate seeking the good and avoiding the evil. But the underlying wisdom of religion for binding human sociocultural and genetic wisdom with the ultimate system of power, when revitalized by renewed convictions in the light of recent scientific revelations, would have a newly integrated power for motivating human good that a science isolated from religion does not have.

Moreover, it is clear from the history of religions and from evolutionary theory that we now can, as our ancestors and all living creatures before us did, through the grace of the reality system that is sovereign over our lives, learn (at all our levels for acquiring new information, from genes, to neural patterns, to cultures, and cognition) ever more about the will of the Lord and the higher stages promised for our future. The new sciences can greatly enhance and speed our learning or adaptation to the sovereign requirements and opportunities, where in our rapid evolution our initial desires seldom suffice as our final desires.

> "O Lord, thou hast searched me, and known me. Thou knowest my downsitting and mine uprising; thou understandest my thought afar off. Thou compassed my path and my lying down, and art acquainted with all my ways. . . . Search me, O God, and know my heart: try me, and know my thoughts: and see if there be any wicked way in me, and lead me in the way everlasting." Psalm 139

> "It may be said that natural selection is daily and hourly scrutinizing, throughout the world, every variation, even the slightest; rejecting that which is bad, preserving and adding up all that is good; silently and insensibly working, whenever and whereever opportunity offers, at the improvement of each organic being in relation to its organic and inorganic conditions of life." Darwin, *Origin of Species*, ch. 4.

Notes

1a. Lynn White Jr., "The Historical Roots of Our Ecological Crisis," *Science* 155 (10 Mar 1967): pp. 1203-07.

1b. *Information* has received a number of new and confusing meanings in the past few decades. I find that important new usages often become clearer if I recall the literal, physical meaning of the Latin root of *inform*—to mold or shape physically. It is easy to picture how the banks or boundary conditions of a river determine the way the water flows. These boundary conditions that shape the flow patterns of river waters are readily distinguished from the water that flows. In a similar way we can distinguish information in the template structures of the DNA molecules that shape the flow patterns of amino-acid and other molecules that constitute living cells and organisms. What is important for reading my paper is to understand this meaning of information as the relatively stable structures or informing boundary conditions that shape the flow patterns of less stable or more dynamic flows that pass by them. Such information structures not only shape the flow patterns of river water, living cells, and organisms, but also—at the level of ritual transmission of patterns of words and other symbols (within as well as to and from brains)—shape human attitudes and behaviors.

2. This new evolutionary theory, embracing all events about which we can know, may be found in many places, including my *Toward a Scientific Theology* (Belfast: Christian Journals Ltd. 1981—distributed in the United States by the *Zygon* Office, Rollins College, Winter Park, FL 32789), hereafter referred to as *Twd Sci Theol*. For brief accounts of bridging physical and biological matters see pp. 131-32; biological and human, pp. 84-102.

2a. An early work exploring bridges between biological and human affairs by a number of distinguished scientists is found in *Evolution and Man's Progress*, edited jointly by Hudson Hoagland and me (New York: Columbia University Press, 1962)—the published part of a series of three symposia of the American Academy of Arts and Sciences in 1960, convened by Hoagland and me, and seeking to generate new thinking on the relations among the various stages of evolution. It was first published as an issue of the Academy's *Daedalus*, summer 1961.

2b. G. Ledyard Stebbins, *Darwin to DNA, Molecules to Humanity* (San Francisco: W. H. Freeman and Co., 1982), I cite here, because he has written an excellent chapter for this book and because in *Darwin to DNA* he has presented one of the most comprehensive and soundest representations of this new evolutionary synthesis as well as of biological evolution in particular. For the links between cosmic-chemical and the genetic-biological domains, see pp. 173ff.

For links between the genetic and human-cultural domains, see pp. 397ff.

3a. The concept of the *wisdom* (conscious or unconscious) of the religions and cultural mores selected in cultural evolution (consciously or unconsciously, but in any event ultimately by its fit or viability as a system in the context of a surrounding reality) is a cultural analogue of *The Wisdom of the Body* (Walter B. Cannon [New York: W. W. Norton & Co., 1932]). The wisdom of the body is largely unconscious, stored in selected DNA codes, and transmitted by the genes. The wisdom of religious culture is largely conscious, though seldom much cognized, stored in neural patterns in the brain, and transmitted by the resulting behavior, including especially communication by ritual and myth. Selection of both genes and religious culture is simply the viability of one sociocultural system or "organism" as compared with others. A brief but sound analysis of why our salvation hangs on a religion, rather than upon science, is given by Stebbins in *Darwin to DNA*, n. 2b, p. 444. I shall be supplying more evidence on this in the following pages. Among other key scientists who have written on the important role of religion in human evolution, we can note the following two:

3b. Donald T. Campbell in his presidential address to the American Psychological Association, "On the Conflicts between Biological and Social Evolution and Between Psychology and Moral Tradition" (first published in *The American Psychologist* 30 [1975], pp. 1103-20, and a year later republished as part of a symposium in *Zygon* 11 [Sept. 1976], pp. 167-208) presented a summation of many years involved in discovering and reporting scientific grounds for cultural selection parallel to but different in detail from genetic selection, in which he suggested there is "validity in recipes for living [including the religious] that have been evolved, tested, and winnowed through hundreds of generations of human social history. On purely scientific grounds, these recipes for living might be regarded as better tested than the best of psychology's and psychiatry's speculations on how lives should be lived. This argument comes from a natural-selectionist theory of social evolution . . . ."

3c. Edward O. Wilson in *Sociobiology: the New Synthesis* (Cambridge, Mass: Harvard University Press, 1975) devotes a section of his concluding Chap. 27 to "Culture, Ritual, and Religion," pp. 559-562; and in his *On Human Nature* (Cambridge, Mass: Harvard University Press, 1978) devotes a whole chap. (8) to "Religion."

4. That scientists appreciate religion on scientific grounds does not mean they view traditional theology as science.

5a(1). *Coadaptation* is an evolutionary concept not very well-known, especially my use of the concept in explaining the relation of culture (especially religion) to the human gene pool. I. M. Lerner, in his *Heredity, Evolution, and Society* (San Francisco: W. H. Freeman & Co., 1968), p. 133, defines coadaptation as "The evolutionary process of selection for a balanced combination of genes in an individual, and of individuals in a population. . . . Darwin used this term to describe correlated modifications of different structures in the course of the evolution of an organism to produce a harmonious living being. Its meaning, however, can now be extended to the genic level, on the one hand, and to the species level, on the other."

5a(2). Stebbins in his *Darwin to DNA* (cf n. 2b), while *coadaptation* is not in his index, well describes one phase of how it comes about (p. 69): "all mutations, even before they can be incorporated into the genetic information of a single individual, must run the gauntlet of the internal or cellular environment, which can be likened to a room full of complex machinery whose parts are related to each other in a pattern of enormously detailed, exquisite harmony. The activity of the cell itself provides a finely graded sieve through which most mutations cannot pass, and thus they are rejected soon after they occur. Every change in the DNA blueprint must add to the efficiency of the operations of the celular machinery or at least not detract from it." Coadaptation of various species in an ecosystem he describes on p. 115 and elsewhere, calling it *coevolution.*

5a(3). *Coadaptation* staggers human imagination when contemplated as the billions of bits of information in the genes of a group of cells or of a fantastic number (more than 10^{100}) of bits of information that have in some measure been coadapted to make possible a viable ecosystem; a selective fine tuning of the information in a gene or collection of them has been selected to provide fitness with respect to the other genes in the same genotype or to be viably adapted to the genetically produced phenomena of other species in its potential habitats so as to produce a stable, viable, ecosystem; this has been the task of selection over the billions of years of the history of life.

5b. The theory that selection for *coadaptation* applies also to the relationship of the information bits in our sociocultural heritage to one another and more particularly to the *interspecific* relation of human *culturetypes* (analogues of *genotypes*) to our DNA genotypes was, so far as I know, pioneered by me. It was particularly stimulated in me by many conversations since the mid 1950s with Alfred Emerson about the evidences for the mutual symbioses that have been selected for in termites and several other species which cooperate so closely that they have often been supposed to

be a single organism. An excellent technical summary of this part
of Alfred E. Emerson's life's work is found in his *Tertiary Fossil
Species of the Rhinotermitidae (Isoptera), Phylogeny of Genera,
and Reciprocal Phylogeny of Associated Flagellata (Protozoa),
and the Staphylinidae (Coleoptera)*, Bull. Amer. Mus. Natural
History, 146 (3), New York: 1071.

5c. Recent biology seems increasingly to be recognizing that what we
formerly thought of as a single organism of a single species is in fact
an ecosystem of many cooperating, coadapted organisms of several
species. Recently this has been shown to be true of a human
organism in terms of different genetic species. We could not be a
member of *Homo* apart from a number of earlier bacteria-like
creatures that thrive in cooperation with the advanced genetic
nucleus of *Homo*. A variety of these tiny pre-human species carry
on various functions inside each of our cells, a notion which Lewis
Thomas began popularizing in the *New England Journal of
Medicine* beginning in 1971 and later published in *The Lives of a
Cell: Notes of Biology Watcher* (New York: Viking Press, 1974 and
several later printings).

5d. My theory of culture as a new symbiont in human nature will be
found in my *Toward a Scientific Theology* (n.2), pp. 18-22, 155,
166-70, 183-85, 189-96, 202, 214-16, 221. For illumination of the
distinction between the sociocultural organism (with its *culturetypic* information pattern) and the pre-encultured organisms of
Homo (with their primarily ape-man genotypic information pattern), see especially chs. 6 and 7 in my *Twd Sci Theol*. This
hypothesis is crucial for my account of human nature since, without symbiosis of the human gene pool with an independently
selected but highly coadapted culturetype, and the role of religion
in bonding the gene pool to the culturetype, *Homo* could not have
become altruistically cooperative beyond close kin, and hence
civilized.

6a. See chs. 7 and 4 in *Twd Sc Theol*.

6b(1). Paul D. MacLean, "The Brain's Generation Gap: Some Human Implications, *Zygon* 8 (June 1973), pp. 113-27, presents evidence of
the close genetic control of lower brain, including motivation and
the foundations of religious ritual . . .

6b(2). John Bowker, *The Sense of God: Sociological, Anthropological,
and Psychological Approaches to the Origin of the Sense of God*
(Oxford:, Clarendon Press, 1973) presents a pioneering synthesis
of cultural and organic sources of the religious sense of God.

6b(3). Eugene G. d'Aquili, in "The Neurobiological Basis of Myth and
Concepts of Deity," *Zygon* 13 (Dec. 1978), pp. 257-75, and many
other papers and books, has provided fundamental new hypotheses and evidences for biocultural understandings of the persist-
ence and power of religion.

6c. The necessity and possibility for developing voluntary motivation from the conditions required by the genetically programmed structures and functions of the brain are set forth in numerous places, including:

6c(1). Burhoe, "Pleasure and Reason as Adaptations to Nature's Requirements," *Zygon* 17 (June 1982), pp. 113-31, provides a review of how religion's coadaptations with the gene pool allows cooperative human social behavior to be internally generated or volunteered rather than coerced.

6c(2). George Edgin Pugh, *The Biological Origin of Human Values* (New York: Basic Books, 1977), is another source on human motivation.

6c(3). B. F. Skinner, *Science and Human Behavior* (New York: Macmillan, Free Press, 1965), includes a basic finding on non-coerced behavior, e.g.: "The maximal strength of the manpower born to a group usually requires conditions which are described roughly with such terms as freedom, security, happiness, and knowledge. . . It is much more difficult to use [coercive] power to achieve certain ultimate consequences," pp. 443-44.

6d. That organic behavior cannot violate its genetic requirements is as true for humans as for bacteria, worms, and monkeys. In humans as well as animals, however, learning, training, behavioral modification, enculturation, etc. may take place in two modes, attention to which was called by B. F. Skinner as positive and negative reinforcement. He early discovered and reported that negative or coercive reinforcement or conditioning, which motivated behavior by causing the creature to avoid certain consequences (consequences which, now it is clear, are those which the genes have programmed to be recognized as dangerous, uncomfortable, etc.), was not as lasting or as stable as positive reinforcement, which "taught" the creature to want to do again something that innately pleased it. In a number of my papers I have pointed out that the empirical facts, including history, show how religions, by giving greater viability to genes (as well as to culture), is primarily an agency of positive reinforcement. This art is more delicate than coercion. The state arose as coercive defense against genetically programmed threats to the society that cannot be handled by enculturation. The state can thrive or exist only so far as a religious base has generated sufficient internal or voluntary (genetically grounded) social goals. States lacking a religious base get one or fall.

7. Reported in *Evolution and Man's Progress*, n. 2a.

8. Campbell, who unfortunately had not been associated with our conferences, quite independently came up with notions of cultural evolution quite similar to mine, which later were summarized in his "On the Conflicts. . ." (n.3b); pp. 169-178, in "The Case for Sociocultural Evolution."

9. *Ritual in Human Adaptation, Symposium on, Zygon* 18 (Sept. 1983).

10. The facts of the evolution of human wisdom without necessarily involving human consciousness in no way precludes the evolutionary theory from accounting for the same natural selection operating to produce wisdom by using human consciousness as its agent. I refer you to W. Ross Ashby, *Design for a Brain* (New York: Wiley, 2nd rev. ed., 1960 [1st ed. was 1952]) for a pioneering exposition of how selection operates at all levels of the brain's functions on principles that are universal for systems including levels of the brain's functions on principles that are universal for systems including levels from the basic physical to the highest human. For the relation of five different stages of the evolution of information, from the times prior to the natural selection of genes to recent and contemporary selection by nature of culture, brain states, feelings, thoughts, theologies, and sciences, see Burhoe, *Twd Sci Theol.*, ch. 3, pp. 49-71. You will find there that I am in close agreement with Donald T. Campbell's and also B. F. Skinner's views on the cultural evolution of human behavior generally as the product of varied trials and selection of the fittest. However, I go further in specifying *fittest* in a somewhat larger context, involving the total ecosystem over a long period, as well as the relations among the spatially and temporally local conditions of genes, brains, cultures, etc. Moreover, I ascribe the final selection not to these temporary and local successes, but to what are the most stable or viable, or longest-lasting patterns in the ultimate ecosystem. If we merge Campbell's model of the pre-selected wisdom of cultural heritages (replication programs, see his "On the Conflicts," n. 3b, pp. 169-178) with Skinner's sociocultural reinforcement programs (see his "Selection by Consequences," *Science* 213 (31 Jul. 1981), pp. 501-04, we have some basics for a fair model of major aspects of sociocultural evolution.

11. Burhoe, *Twd Sci Theol* (n. 2), pp. 117-118, 136-44.

12a,b. A primary philosophical-historical concurrence with what I am saying here will be found in F. S. C. Northrop, "The Methods and Grounds of Religious Knowledge," *Zygon* 12 (Dec. 1977), pp. 287-88, his slightly revised classic chapter 23 in his *The Logic of the Sciences and the Humanities* (New York: Macmillan Co., 1947). For another significant concurrence with some elements, see quotations I make in following pages from Lynn White, as well as many citations I give in my own papers.

12c. Ralph Wendell Burhoe, *Science and Human Values in the 21st Century* (Philadelphia: Westminster Press, 1971). See particularly chap. 2, "Some Prophecies of 21st Century Technology and Religion," and the epilogue: "Twenty-First-Century Values from a Scientifically Based Theology that Creates a Common World

Culture."

13. Harlow Shapley, "Life, Hope, and Cosmic Evolution," *Zygon* 1 (Sept. 1966), pp. 275-89, in a section on "Cosmic Evolution and God" on pp. 278-79, shared a view similar to mine when he said: "All Nature is God and all God is Nature." 11.2

14a. Donald T. Campbell's efforts during the past few decades (cf. his "On the Conflicts," n. 3b) have been an important pioneering thrust in establishing a scientific relation between nature's ways of selecting genes and cultures but it is still not widely known.

14b. For a picture of some of the difficulties of the thrust toward understanding this relation between genes and culture, see Robert Boyd and Peter J. Richerson, "A Simple Dual Inheritance Model of the Conflict between Social and Biological Evolution," *Zygon* 11 (Sept. 1976), pp. 254-262.

15. Theories that increasingly bridge and integrate our present culture's diverse concepts of our natures have been noted above. I also commend: Roger W. Sperry, *Science and Moral Priority: Merging Mind, Brain, and Human Values* (New York: Columbia University Press, 1983) provides one of the soundest and most recent pictures of how all scientific disciplines may be integrated into understanding human nature including the mind-body and facts-values problems.

16a. For a pioneering recognition of the role of selection in all human behavior, see F. A. Hayek's classic, *The Constitution of Liberty* (Chicago, University of Chicago Press, 1960), esp. pp. 56-61.

16b. See my "Pleasure and Reason," n. 6c(1).

16c. Robert L. Heilbroner, *An Inquiry into the Human Prospect* (New York: W. W. Norton & Co., 1974) presents what I believe to be a highly probable if gloomy picture of our prospect in view of our being possessed of fantastic technological powers without the necessary powerful religious-moral self control to prevent tragic damage to our environment and ourselves. The book so impressed a number of us (some of whom have been operating on a similar analysis for three decades) that we held a symposium on it, which was published as a whole issue of *Zygon*, 10 (Sept. 1975): 214-375. My own response to this situation was set forth as the final paper in that issue, "The Human Prospect and the 'Lord of History'."

16d. My *Twd Sci Theol*, cf. n. 2, in the introductory chapter summarizes the work of a group of eminent scientists who began talking constructively about religion with theologians beginning before the middle of this century.

16e. Hoimar v. Ditfurth, *The Origins of Life, Evolution as Creation* (San Francisco: Harper & Row, 1982), a German psychiatrist, is an example, quite independent from the group reported in n. 19c, of increasing numbers of able scientists who are sensitive to a major problem for our civilization, who are using their scientific under-standing in a similar way (p. 185): "This book is an attempt to show that the world picture of modern science not only is no obstacle to a religious interpretation of the world, but actually helps religion by making it possible to reformulate certain statements so as to make them more convincing than they were in their traditional form, with their metaphors and images derived from a long-out-dated world picture."

17. My previous references provide a sample of this evidence—from the wide range of disciplines that are revealing our evolutionary creation from the dust of the earth and our new understandings of our present nature—and in this process giving scientists new appreciation for the positive values of traditional religion. How-ever, with many of the scientists, especially those who have not examined religion scientifically over a sufficiently wide range, the new appreciation may be said to have surprised them and evoked an acknowledgement of religion's virtues, somewhat begrudgingly, except perhaps for primitive religions' roles in early cultural evo-lution. But the impression given to scientists by the inability of many recent Christian theologians to communicate how religion may tie into the scientific world view (which for scientists and in-creasingly for the whole world) is taken to be our best revelation of what is "real") has not helped scientists to be sanguine about religion's value for the modern world.

18a. A stark presentation of why genes cannot make us human is by a bright young anthropologist, Richard Dawkins, *The Selfish Gene* (Oxford: Oxford University Press, 1976). The logic of the present scientific pictures of human nature made it clear to him as to many of us that there had to be a separate cultural evolution to account for our humanity. In his final chapter, 11, he struggled and came up with a quite brilliant theory of cultural evolution, including reli-gion, quite close to mine in some respects, but he closes by acknowledging that his theory still lacks an essential feature to make it fit with the *inclusive-fitness* requirements of gene theory.

18b. Stebbins in the later chapters of his *Darwin to DNA*, n. 2b, gives one of the very best accounts of the relationship of cultural and genetic evolution, with much more scope and empirical backing than that of Dawkins. But he, as well as Dawkins, seems not to be able to integrate the two kinds of evolution under the single umbrella of the *inclusive-fitness* model, which has made so much sense for genetic evolution. Stebbins acknowledges this implicitly when he seems to elect to reject the *inclusive-fitness* doctrine as applying, rather than rejecting a separate cultural evolution cap-able of raising humankind above the limited human societies al-lowed by the *selfish gene* (pp. 400-01).

18c. I think my earlier theory, e.g., "Source of Civilization," and "Religion's Role," which is very close to the excellent and brief model of sociocultural selection presented by Dawkins as well as to the larger one presented by Stebbins, has resolved their problem of explanation in terms of inclusive fitness by showing culture-types to be a new *species*, or more properly a new or fourth level of the kingdoms of life, which, because its heritage of information does not come from the human gene pool, does not evolve in competition with genes, and has emerged as a new kind of parasitic symbiont, analogous to the symbioses of certain species of protists, plants, and animals. The key is: humankind has two natures, symbiotically wedded. Evolution of symbionts (even when programmed only by genes) is selected by the viability of the eco-systemic niche they jointly constitute, upon which each of the *species* is now dependent. I have shown how the religious core of the sociocultural system has tied itself effectively and simultaneously to the flourishing of *selfish genes* and to *selfish memes*, as Dawkins names the corresponding cultural memory patterns; cultural templates as Stebbins calls them (p. 398), in analogy to the stereochemical templates of genes; or culturetypes, as I call them. This close symbiosis of one culturetype with thousands of varied genotypes for the first time allows *group selection*, selection of varied *phenotypes* of *groups of genotypes*. Evolutionary theory is not violated since the *group selection* is only apparent, not real; the *groups* are really variant *individual* phenotypes of *socio-cultural organisms each of which happens to embrace whole populations of genotypes*. The statistical distribution patterns of genotypes in such competing populations may be essentially identical relative to the diversities of the culturetypes that are selected. Such selection of populations of mixed genotypes is also true for Emerson's flagellates and their host termites (cf. n. 5b).

19a. Clyde Kluckhohn, "The Scientific Study of Values and Contemporary Civilization," *Zygon* 1 (Sept. 1966), pp. 230-243 (originally published in the *Proceedings of the American Philosophical Society*, 102 (Oct. 1958), presents the views of an anthropologist, post-World War II Harvard head of studies of the Soviet Union, and outstanding expert on the problem of human values. He presents a pioneering analysis of the sociocultural nature of humans, an analysis of the weaknesses of the Western World (for lack of faith in a good religion), and the greater weakness of the Soviet Marxist philosophy.

19b. My "Bridging the Gap between Psychiatry and Theology," *Journal of Religion and Health* 7 (July 1968), pp. 215-26, presents a brief picture, citing others sharing it, of some of the inadequacies of the Freudian programs of salvation as compared with those of traditional religions. A more powerful statement of this thesis is found in Campbell's "On the Conflicts." n. 3b.

19c. Victor Turner, "Body, Brain, and Culture," *Zygon* 18 (Sept. 1983), pp. 221-45, in expressing his radical conversion to appreciate the close interaction of biological and cultural levels in human behavior, is a recent example of the fact that there is emerging a new integration of the varied scientific information from many disciplines newly relevant for understanding human values, religion, and destiny.

20.   See, for instance S. H. Katz, M. I. Hediger, L. A. Valleroy, "Traditional Maize Processing Techniques in the New World," *Science* 184 (17 May 1974), pp. 765-73.

21.   That science cannot by itself save us, that religion is required, and that it is now possible to develop supportive interpretations of religion in the light of the sciences is a view held by most of the scientists I have been citing. But, as a summary, see Stebbins, *Darwin to DNA*, n. 2b, p. 444: In addition to "thinking and reasoning. . . some kind of religion. . . is. . . necessary. . ."; and for an historian, see White, "Historical Roots," n. 1a, p. 1206: "More science and more technology are not going to get us out of the present ecologic crisis until we find a new religion, or rethink our old one."

22a. See my "Human Prospect," n. 16c: esp. pp. 333-346.

22b. Alfred E. Emerson and Ralph Wendell Burhoe, "Evolutionary Aspects of Freedom, Death, and Dignity," *Zygon* 9 (June 1974), pp. 156-182 on the problem of freedom.

22c. See Sperry, *Science and Moral Priority*, n. 15. on the mind-brain problem. The relation of the concepts of God, soul, mind, and matter is dealt with in a scientific context in my "Concepts of 'God' and 'Soul'," n. 16c: *Twd Sci Theol*, n. 2. I have sought to show in many papers, including this one, how through a scientific theology the conflicts of religions tend to vanish as each is seen fit in its proper frame of reference.

23.   Chaisson, "Cosmic Evolution: A Synthesis of Matter and Life," *Zygon* 14 (March 1979), pp. 23-39. See esp. last sentence.

24.   cf. Mircea Eliade, *The Sacred and the Profane*, (NY, Harper Torchbook, 1961) p. 165.

25.   Ibid., pp. 165, 178.

26.   White, "The Historical Roots of Our Ecological Crisis," n. 1. All quotations in this section are from pp. 1205-07.

Chapter Twelve

INTERRELATEDNESS
Ecological Pattern of the Creation

Paul E. Lutz

The natural world is complex, interesting, and, above all, exquisitely beautiful. Even though there is beauty in such dramatic examples as an unforgetable sunset, a cascading waterfall, or a breathtaking vista, the real beauty of creation is much more subtle, more omnipresent, much more a part of each of us than we can initially comprehend. The creation is a silent partner, a subtle and delicate influence on our lives, an orchestration of great complexity, and a composite of forces and processes that are usually taken for granted but which are of major importance to our survival.

That area of human understanding that deals with the interrelatedness between living things and the non-living environment is *ecology*; it is more specifically defined as that branch of science that deals with the structure and function of nature. Since the term "ecology" is derived from the Greek *oikos* (meaning house or home), ecology may also be simply defined as a study of the household of organisms with everything that affects them there. Until the middle of the 1960s, ecology was primarily known only in academic circles, among biologists, and to crossword puzzle fans. Today, almost everyone on the North American continent and in the industrialized world uses the term; ecology has become an integral part of our culture. However, the word and what it means have sometimes been used incorrectly; I once heard of a high school bulletin board, designed to illustrate the evils of pollution, entitled "Help Fight Ecology"! I trust their aim was not to fight the study of environmental biology; what certainly needs to be attacked is environmental deterioration brought on by the carelessness and greed of human beings.

Historically, ecology has roots that may be said to qualify it as the oldest of all the sciences. Some three million years ago, the earliest human beings gradually became aware of the cyclic nature of the seasons, patterns of rainfall, dangerous animals, poisonous plants, and many other natural phenomena. The agrarian revolution of about 10,000 years ago was certainly predicated on primitive farmers having some knowledge about the ecology both of their area and of the crops they attempted to raise. Ecology began as a recognized, formal branch of biology about the turn of this century, and since that time knowledge about ecological processes has grown rapidly. Today, ecology is one of the most active fields of scientific research, and our knowledge about the environment has trebled in the last two decades. However, much ecological effort is also being spent to correct what decades of environmental neglect have imposed. Applied ecology or environmental management, a sub-branch that has also grown by leaps and bounds in the last fifteen years, is concerned with the many areas that threaten the integrity of nature—littering, pollution, population growth, bad land-use practices, erosion, and the lack of environmental planning.

This essay will attempt to set out several of the most important ecological principles, to show that environmental processes are universal in occurrence, and to indicate that our survival and well-being are fundamentally related to the orchestrated functioning of these embodied principles. This is undertaken out of the realization that one of the prime aspects of a movement to rebuild the Christian creation tradition is an informed appreciation of ecological interrelatedness within which all life is set.

One of the most important concepts of ecology is that everything in the creation is related to everything else. *Interrelatedness* or interdependence is one of the most important ecological principles, but one that is extemely difficult to conceptualize. It is very difficult, for example, to see the functional and ecological ties between the dragonfly nymphs in a lake near my home and a school of tuna in the Pacific Ocean, between the pesticides used on roses in Kansas City and a lion on the African veldt, or between deforestation in the Amazon basin and the survival of algae in a lake in Manitoba. The links between the members in each example and those among all facets of nature are certainly not obvious, but they are there, nevertheless, and have been traced. All of nature is joined together like a huge, multi-dimensional net in which any break or tear, regardless of how innocuous or insignificant it may seem, weakens the entire ecological fabric of life. Ecologists often use the appropriate expression "web of life" as a means to describe these important, functional links in the environment. Interrelatedness is obviously one of those very few concepts about which everyone should be aware. The more one knows about ecology, the more obvious are the interdependent lines on which our precious environment operates.

Homo sapiens is by far the dominant species in the environment today. We have the intellect and technological skills to alter radically and dramatically any portion of the environment, and historically most of our activities have been environmentally destructive. It would appear that human beings either do not care for or never knew about the basic lesson of the interrelatedness of nature. If this were not the case, would we continue to dump toxic wastes into our rivers, burn solid wastes indiscriminately, or embark on a massive deforestation program in the tropics? Do we not see that many of our activities, based primarily on carelessness and greed, ignore these basic lines of interrelatedness?

One of the most common and familiar examples of the way we defile our precious environment is to pollute it, introducing an insidious activity into a complexly interrelated natural system. Pollution takes a number of forms including air, water, radiation, thermal, noise, and aesthetic, to mention the most important ones. Air pollution, in the form of haze, smog, or fog, is primarily gases resulting from the combustion of fossil fuels in automobiles, factories, and homes. No one in the United States has not experienced the acrid smog (smoke + fog) over every major city, automobiles with serious exhaust emissions, or smokestacks belching tons of pollutants into the atmosphere. The principal air pollutants—oxides of sulphur, nitrogen, and carbon—often undergo a photochemical transformation in sunlight that makes them even more dangerous to human beings and other forms of life. Water pollution results from many specific point sources such as sewage treatment plants, factories, foundries, mills, and other industrial installations, and from innumerable non-point sources like erosion and run-off from rains that carry a plethora of substances into surface and subsurface waters. Eventually, we drink this same water, from which most of the pollutants have not been removed by conventional water treatments. Many different serious pollutants appear in air and water and are known to be directly correlated with a number of serious human diseases: cancer, emphysema, certain metal poisonings, genetic disorders, and embryological deformities.

Radioactive materials, potentially the most dangerous of all pollutants, may be emitted into the atmosphere or water, or onto the land. The potentiality of a nuclear war is a frightening prospect since radiation and radioactive pollutants could easily eliminate all forms of life. Thermal pollution, usually resulting from dumping heated water into a lake or river, often kills many forms of aquatic life. Noise pollution, resulting from motor vehicles, airplanes, tools, and very loud amplifiers, is known to result in hearing impairment or deafness. Aesthetic or visual pollution includes litter, debris, junkyards, and the omnipresent billboards.

It would actually appear from our flagrant, wanton ecological behavior that we believe that the environment is not important, and that somehow we can do without it. It also appears that society has determined that basic ecological principles governing the lives and activities of all plants and animals somehow don't apply to people. Though living in the environment, the human being is presumed to be exempt from the limitations and restrictions it imposes upon everything else that lives in the environment. I hope it will be kept in mind throughout this entire volume that every ecological principle applies to people as much as it does to any other living creature. It is extremely important to remember that we are both *in* and *of* the environment—not somehow apart from it.

Ecosystems

All organisms live in nature amid various inanimate conditions, and a given organism is inseparably interrelated both with other organisms and with its non-living environment. There are many complex biological, chemical, and physical interactions between the living and non-living components. When our attention is fixed upon these numerous interactions as they take place within a prescribed area, we recognize them collectively as an *ecosystem*. Examples of ecosystems are a forest, pond or lake, lawn, estuary or ocean, and even a temporary mud puddle. Ecosystems are real, dynamic entities, not some theoretical or abstract models; they are basic units of ecological study, of interrelatedness (Figure 1).

In every ecosystem, there are two basic, interdependent components that interact with each other in ranges from obligatory to casual. On the one hand are the non-living, inanimate, or *abiotic* components, that include the soil (partly living), water, chemicals, atmosphere and gases, sunlight, temperature, and many physical processes such as currents, pressures, and gradients. Everything in an ecosystem that is not alive is a part of the abiota. On the other hand are the many and diverse living organisms that collectively comprise the *biotic* component. If we inspect an ecosystem such as a forest, we quickly discover such varied living things as trees, shrubs, birds, insects, earthworms, and mammals. Upon closer examination, we would find that amid this enormous diversity, there are three different types of biota, based on their functional roles in the ecosystem. It is indeed a rare ecosystem that does not contain all three types.

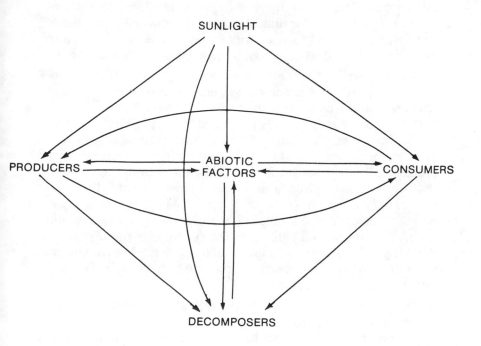

Figure 1. The components of an ecosystem and their lines of interdependent relationship.

1. Producers.   These are the green plants that may be present as large trees in a forest or as microscopic algae in a lake or ocean. They are called producers or *autotrophs* (= self-feeders) because they capture the energy of the sun and, by a series of beautifully complex chemical reactions, convert this energy into carbohydrate materials like sugars. This overall process is called *photosynthesis* and is involved in the production of food energy using raw materials from the abiotic environment (Figure 1). The photosynthetic equation is:

$$\text{carbon dioxide} + \text{water} + \text{solar energy} \xrightarrow[\substack{\text{chlorophyll} \\ \text{in plants}}]{\text{enzymes}} \text{carbohydrates} + \text{oxygen}$$

Photosynthesis is one of the most important biological processes for it alone accounts for almost the entire conversion of abiotic energy into chemical food-energy molecules. We shall return to this extremely critical process later in a discussion about energy.

2. Consumers.   These are the animals; they range from microscopic creatures in aquatic ecosystems to huge elephants and whales. They are called consumers because they use or consume chemical compounds initially produced by the producers (Figure 1). Consumers lack the capabilities of converting abiotic energy into chemical energy, and thus they are totally dependent upon producers for this process. By eating plants, or by eating animals that, in turn, ate plants, animals are appropriately called consumers or *heterotrophs* (= feeding from others). Ecologists recognize two basic types of animals: *herbivores* are plant eaters, and *carnivores* are animal eaters. As the reader can already guess, there is a definite, one-way transfer of food energy from producers to herbivores to carnivores, thus producing a food chain. We shall return to this concept later.

3. Decomposers.   These are the organisms of decay and are represented principally by the bacteria and fungi (Figure 1). Decomposers are ubiquitous in ecosystems and are particularly common, for example, at the bottom of a lake or on the forest floor. Their role in the ecosystem is to effect decay—to break down dead organisms or their parts (leaves, stems, bones, flesh) and thereby convert their constituent molecules back into the atoms of which they are built. As heterotrophs, decomposers feed on the decaying bodies of other organisms.

Although decomposers are small and often inconspicuous, they are, nonetheless, both extraordinarily numerous and important to an ecosystem. First, they function to prevent organismic remains from accumulating—an important ecological activity; if it were not for decomposers, everything that had ever lived would still be lying around. Secondly, they return to the abiotic environment the elements out of which these dead organisms were composed, a process that is remarkably significant to the interrelatedness of an ecosystem. And thirdly, elemental particles are again available to be used once more by other organisms; decomposers are essential to this elemental cycling in an ecosystem.

Every typical ecosystem contains many abiotic factors, producers, consumers, and decomposers, and each organism is totally and utterly dependent—either directly or indirectly—upon sunlight for light, warmth, and above all energy, for life processes. As diagrammed in Figure 1, the arrows connecting the various facets of an ecosystem clearly and poignantly illustrate that fundamental property of interrelatedness.

While ecosystems appear to be distinct and separate from other adjacent ecosystems, in reality the exact opposite is true. Adjacent ecosystems have important and intimate lines of mutual dependence between them. In fact, all ecosystems on our planet are tied together in marvelously beautiful and intricate patterns of interdependence. Ecologists often refer to the spherical envelope around the earth in which all of the ecosystems are located and tied together functionally, as the *biosphere*. Seeing the entire world as one huge ecosystem with innumerable connections between all the various components is truly awe-inspiring.

Mineral Cycles

There are ninety-two naturally occuring elements in our biosphere; familiar examples are silver, gold, tin, oxygen, carbon, lead, and uranium, to name only a few. Of these ninety-two elements, fewer than half are found in living organisms; the four most important ones ecologically and biologically are hydrogen, carbon, oxygen, and nitrogen. Living organisms utilize rather large quantitites of these four and lesser amounts of some other elements.

The number of elements in the biosphere is the same now as at any point since the beginning of time. We have neither gained nor lost any elements, except for a few artificially created radioactive ones, in the billions of years Earth has been in existence. Even more importantly, the number of atoms (smallest parts of an element with elemental properties) on Earth is the same now as it was a million years ago, except for a small number of radioactive atoms and a very few present in hardware discarded in space. Does this mean, then, that elements and their constituent atoms never wear out? Precisely, and over the millennia, they have been a part of millions of different organisms. A particular carbon atom present within each reader at this very moment undoubtedly has also been a part of the primeval slime, ancient worms, dinosaurs, Paleozoic clams, and Mesozoic ferns. And these same elements and atoms are today still in circulation among organisms and between organisms and the abiotic environment. In fact, all elements used by living things cycle in very definite and precise patterns within ecosystems. We shall now briefly explore the carbon cycle as an example of mineral cycles (Figure 2).

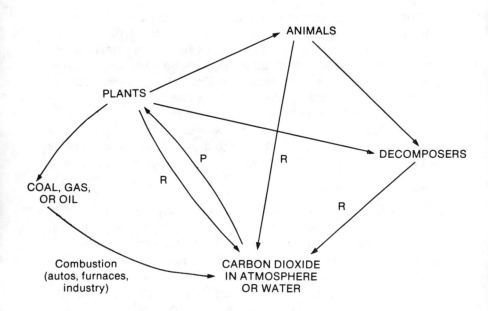

Figure 2. The carbon cycle within an ecosystem.

(P = photosynthesis; R = respiration)

Carbon, in the form of carbon dioxide, is present as a gas in the atmosphere and in water. Via *respiration*, or the process of organisms burning chemical energy to sustain the processes of life, carbon dioxide is released into the ecosystem as a gas. As already mentioned, in the process of photosynthesis carbon dioxide is utilized by green plants as an essential raw material for the production of carbohydrates. Therefore, these two great biological processes, respiration and photosynthesis, are the principal means by which carbon cycles between the abiotic and biotic portions of an ecosystem (Figure 2). In food chains, plant molecules are consumed by herbivores which, in turn, are consumed by carnivores. If not eaten, eventually both plants and animals die naturally, their bodies are decayed by decomposers, and the carbon is thus released to the atmosphere to be utilized again by plants. In the last 300 years, the industrial world has added huge amounts of carbon dioxide into the atmosphere by the combustion of fossil fuels. From this humanly-caused perturbation there is a risk of altering the global carbon cycle, a prospect that should deeply concern us all. For example, excessive combustion of fossil fuels during the last century has raised slightly the carbon dioxide level in the atmosphere. To continue this trend and even to accelerate it would be disastrous, since the atmosphere with increased amounts of carbon dioxide absorbs more infrared energy from the sun; this will trap heat near the earth's surface and create a "greenhouse effect." Eventually, rising ambient temperatures would melt the polar icecaps and thus most coastal cities would be under water. Once this ominous perturbation is in full swing, could we ever halt it?

This example shows very definitely the cyclical nature of the pathways of elements. It also shows that these atoms never wear out but are used over and over again by organisms. Finally, this example clearly illustrates the interdependent pathways in an ecosystem.

Since many of our activities are interrupting or short-circuiting these vital mineral cycles, the effects of human beings on them can be substantial. Our industrial complex is now producing many products in non-biodegradable form; this means that the particular kinds of atoms out of which such things are constructed are taken out of circulation for a protracted period. Also, many products made or refined by our technology also cycle, including such harmful substances as DDT, other pesticides, mercury, PCBs, radioactive materials, and many others. One of the most important roles

for us now and in the future is to minimize potential upsets resulting from these cycles and to promote the delicate balance and
cyclical nature of mineral uses in an ecosystem.

Energetics

One of the most important dimensions of the natural world, and
specifically regarding ecosystems, is how energy is involved. Any
system, whether a home, factory, organism, or ecosystem,
requires energy to function. *Energy* is defined as the ability to do
work; this means that whenever any work of any sort is being
performed, energy is always a part of the process. Energy is involved, for example, when anything speeds up or slows down,
when something is heated or cooled, or whenever anything moves,
changes, or is altered in structure. Energy may be present in many
different forms, including light, heat, chemical, electrical, and
mechanical.

Two laws of thermodynamics account for the ways in which
energy behaves in any system. The First Law of Thermodynamics
states that while energy can be converted from one form into
another, energy is never created or destroyed. Examples of energy
conversion are all around us: fossil fuels (chemical energy) being
converted into heat in furnaces, electricity being transformed into
mechanical energy (motion) in an electric motor, and green plants
storing the energy in sunlight as chemical energy (carbohydrates).
But in every case, energy is neither created nor destroyed; only its
form is altered. The Second Law of Thermodynamics holds that at
every energy transformation, some of the energy is always lost to
the system as heat or in some other form. For example, in the
conversion of electrical energy into light energy in a light bulb, the
bulb itself gets very warm. This is an indication that the transformation of electrical energy into light energy is not 100 percent efficient; some of the energy is inevitably lost as heat.

That energy is not destroyed (First Law) and that energy is
always lost to the system as heat at every transformation (Second
Law) are not contradictory concepts at all. The energy dissipated
as heat is not destroyed but is radiated into space as an unusable
form; while it is lost permanently and irretrievably from the system, energy is not destroyed. This means that in contrast to the
reusability of matter, energy cannot cycle because some is being
dispersed as heat continuously. Rather, energy *flows* through any
system with numerous points at which some is always lost. Logically, then, would there not have to be a continuous source of

energy for all systems? Yes, precisely, and the ultimate source of all our energy is the sun.

Energy is of vital importance to any ecosystem. Ecosystems, like all other systems, are completely and utterly dependent on the conversion of solar energy to chemical energy in photosynthesis. The photosynthetic conversion of light into chemical energy in green plants is the initial step in the flow of energy, and all subsequent steps are totally dependent upon it.

Figure 3 is a diagram of the energy flow through a given organism. It could be any organism, plant or animal, but let's use a rabbit as an example. Some of the potential energy is in an unusable form such as the roots or stems of the plants on which the rabbit feeds;

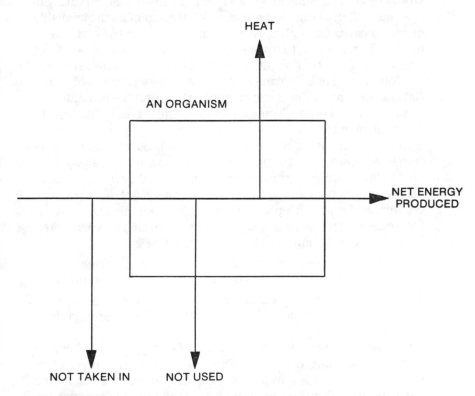

Figure 3. A diagrammatic representation of the passage of energy through an organism and the various pathways by which energy is lost.

therefore, this food energy is never available to the rabbit. Some of the energy actually taken in (eaten if it is an animal) is not used; for example, much of the cellulose in plants is not digested or used by the rabbit. Much of the plant energy that is used by the rabbit and incorporated into it is eventually lost by the rabbit as heat. In all organisms, a complex series of reactions called respiration takes place in every cell in which chemical molecules are slowly burned to release some of their energy; this energy is used by the organism to carry out its basic functions. But within every organism, much of this chemical energy is also eventually dissipated as heat. In fact, as much as 90 percent of all the energy taken in and assimilated by an organism is eventually lost as heat in respiration. The amount of energy available to a predator of rabbits (such as a fox) would be considerably less than that available to the rabbit from the grass. Why? Because about 90 to 95 percent of all the available energy passing through a given organism is lost to the system forever as heat. Doesn't this seem to be an extravagant waste of energy? At first, that might appear to be so. But further study of the functioning of an organism would indicate a plethora of essential chemical reactions going on all the time, and the ultimate loss of so much heat is only a consequence of the myriad of necessary chemical events.

Energy is involved in an ecosystem in photosynthesis, respiration, decay, and food transfer. The relationship whereby food energy is transferred from one organism to another by a process of eating and, in turn, being eaten, is called a *food chain*. Any food chain must begin with photosynthesis in green plants; then the food energy is passed along to herbivores and then to carnivores. An example of a simplified food chain would be:

grass	——▶	rabbits	——▶	foxes
(producers)		(herbivores)		(carnivores)

Actually serving as the ultimate consumers, decomposers eventually break down the molecules out of which all other organisms were constructed.

Let's now try to merge the concepts of energy and food chains into some meaningful pattern. Figure 4 will illustrate this fundamental pattern. It is a hypothetical example, but the ratios and patterns are substantially based on observed data from nature. Rather than refer to energy as Kcal./m.^{2}/min. or langleys/min., we shall call them units for the sake of convenience. To illustrate how energy is dissipated, let's assume that we begin with one million energy units, radiated toward an area where plants are growing. About half of that energy is never even available to green plants since some solar energy is absorbed by the atmosphere, and other energy units from the sun never strike the producers. Considerable amounts of energy are available to the producers, but since much of it is mostly of the wrong wavelengths, it is not used by the plants and, therefore, is lost to the system. Of the 1,000,000 units with which we began, about 98 percent (980,000 units) is lost to the ecosystem as heat even before the first unit is converted in chemical energy. In fact, only about 2 percent (20,000 units) of the total energy is transformed into chemical energy by photosynthesis. Further, about 90 percent of the 20,000 stored energy units is lost in respiration by the plants; this results in a net amount produced by the plants of only 2,000 units (Figure 4).

Some of the plant energy is not taken in (roots) or is not used (cellulose) by the herbivores, and each amount is here arbitrarily set at 100 units. With herbivore respiration releasing about 90 percent of the 1,800 units stored by these animals, the net amount from them is only 180 units (Figure 4). Parts of the rabbits (bones, fur, claws) are not ingested by the carnivores, and other rabbit energy is eaten but not used (small bones, cartilage). Fox respiration releases a large proportion of the stored energy thus leaving less than 10 net energy units. Compared to the one million units with which we started this example, only a very small fraction (8 units) remains in the food chain; the vast majority of the energy units was lost to the system as heat. Decomposers eventually break down the energy present as "not taken in," "not used," and as dead organisms, and release most of that energy as heat in their respiration (Figure 4).

One can clearly see that unlike minerals, energy *flows*. The passage of energy through an ecosystem is analogous to a charge of water into a sprinkler hose; lots of water enters the system, but very little energy reaches the end of the hose. Likewise, lots of energy is available from the sun, but very little energy is left over after it has been converted, altered, transformed, and above all, dissipated in the food chain. There are two constants in the energy flow pattern: first, a constant source of energy (the sun) is required, and secondly, a rather constant and high level of inefficiency of organisms is always observed. That organisms are inefficient is not a criticism, only a statement of fact; there is nothing that can be done about it. We cannot regulate energy loss via respiration or metabolism as we can regulate energy loss in our

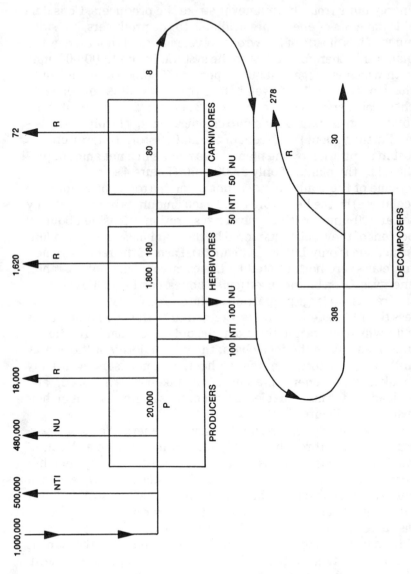

Figure 4. A diagrammatic representation of the flow of energy through an ecosystem.
(R = respiration; P = photosynthesis; NTI = not taken in; NU = not used)

homes. The apparent inefficiency in energy transfers in organisms is simply one of the costs of doing business, i.e., staying alive and performing all of the functions of life.

What do these ideas of energy flow mean to us? First, they may be seen as another example of the beauty and interrelatedness of nature. But just as important is the fact that the principles of energy flow dictate the lifestyles of about one-half of the world's population. About two billion persons live as herbivores and subsist mainly on rice, potatoes, yams, wheat, or other plants. Why? Because they cannot afford the luxury of permitting the food energy to pass through one or two consumers before they eat it; there simply would not be enough energy left. For this reason alone, one-half of the world's human population eats very little beef, pork, fowl, or other sources of animal protein. They are not herbivores by choice but by the necessities imposed by the principle of energy flow, and by the limited acreages of grazing land. And as the human population size continues to increase, more and more people must, by necessity, change their diets from that of meat consumer (carnivore) to that of plant consumer (herbivore). There are no choices in the matter; we all will have to move closer to the base of the food chain if more persons are to exist. The basic concepts of energy flow have profound and far-reaching implications for global hunger, malnutrition, new sources of food energy, population growth, and agriculture. And because of shortages of food, conflicts and even wars will ensue over precious, limited food energies. In addition to the important ecological dimensions, the political, religious, and ethical implications of energy flow now and in the future are indeed staggering.

Population Growth

One of the most important factors in the current state of the environmental crisis is the size of the human population. The population explosion, a phenomenon about which almost everyone has some ideas and reflections, is a massive, global problem. But to better understand this very complex and important issue, it will be most profitable to understand the basic ecological principles undergirding the growth of any population including our own. The reader should again be reminded that the human species is controlled by the same ecological principles that govern all other living things. A consideration of population growth applies equally well to flowers, giraffes, ferns, houseflies, and people.

A *population* is defined as a group of organisms all of which are essentially alike; therefore, they belong to the same species. Familiar examples of populations would be all the ants in an anthill, all the scarlet oaks in a forest, all the robins in a meadow, or all the dandelions in a lawn. While subtle individual differences are always present, the population as a whole is uniform in appearance.

One of the most basic properties of individuals that compose a population is the ability to reproduce more of their kind. In fact, the one parameter that always separates the living from the nonliving is the ability of the living to reproduce. What determines population size is a complex of factors, but for our purposes, population size is based on two properties—birth rate and death rate —in the following relationship:

Population Size = Birth Rate – Death Rate

When more individuals in a population are born than die, then the population grows, but when the mortality rate exceeds the birth rate, then the size of a population will decline. When birth and mortality rates are the same, then the population size is unchanging.

Many if not most organisms have a great reproductive potential. For example, a single bacterium can divide to form two new organisms every 20 minutes if conditions are optimum; if ideal conditions for reproduction are sustained, the progeny of this single initial bacterium would, in a 24-hour period, weigh in excess of 2,000 tons! As another example, an average female housefly lays about 850 eggs during her lifetime. If every egg hatched and if all the resulting females laid at the same time, the seventh generation would contain in excess of 6 trillion flies.

While these two examples illustrate the point, they are really not exceptions; all organisms possess inherent, potentially high reproductive (biotic) rates. When environmental conditions permit, population growth is almost universally manifested as a *geometric or exponential pattern* in which there is repeated doubling of the population size: 2 ——▶ 4 ——▶ 8 ——▶ 16 ——▶ 32 ——▶ 64 ——▶ 128, etc. Ecologists and population biologists talk almost reverently of the *intrinsic rate of natural increase*, the reproductive potential of a population to increase exponentially under optimal conditions.

Exponential growth proceeds incredibly fast, and the results of continued exponential growth stagger the imagination. To illustrate the effects of logarithmic growth, a fictitious story is told about an enterprising young man who wanted to get rich quickly. He persuaded a prospective employer to hire him for the paltry sum of one cent for the first day if his salary would be doubled each succeeding day. He earned two cents for the second day, four cents for the third, eight cents for the fourth day, and so on. His earnings for the 15th day were more than $160, and those for his 25th day of employment were in excess of $167,000. Had his employer been able to stay in business and uphold his end of the deal for thirty days, he would have paid his new employee total wages exceeding 10 million dollars! Repeated doubling, even beginning with a miniscule base such as a penny, produces astronomical results in a short period of time.

There are some populations of living things such as certain insects, algae, rodents, and crab grass that tend to increase exponentially for a number of generations. Numerically small and increasing at a deceptively slow rate initially, a population soon increases dramatically by repeated doublings. Its growth curve, shown in Figure 5A, is called the J-shaped growth curve, so named because of the shape of its rising segment. However, one can quickly see that continued geometric growth cannot continue for long, for if it did we would very soon be overrun by bacteria, houseflies, or by whatever is growing exponentially. Thankfully, we are never swamped by a population increasing geometrically. What invariably happens to an exponentially-growing population is that something in its environment suddenly becomes limiting like the lack of food, minerals, living space, or energy. Once these limits have been reached and exceeded and the environment can no longer support these excessive numbers, there ensues a precipitous, sudden, massive numerical decrease due to a widespread die-off. For a population growing logarithmically, a dramatic and calamitous drop in population size is both a predictable and inevitable result since there is a finite limit to what any ecosystem or the biosphere can support.

Most populations of plants and animals do not grow exponentially for very long. What happens to most growing populations is that there are forces in nature that begin to influence growth patterns long before the resulting population size becomes ecologically unsupportable. These forces, collectively referred to as *environmental resistance*, tend to push the growth curve to the right and downward, thus preventing continued logarithmic growth. What results is a sigmoid or s-shaped growth curve (Figure 5B).

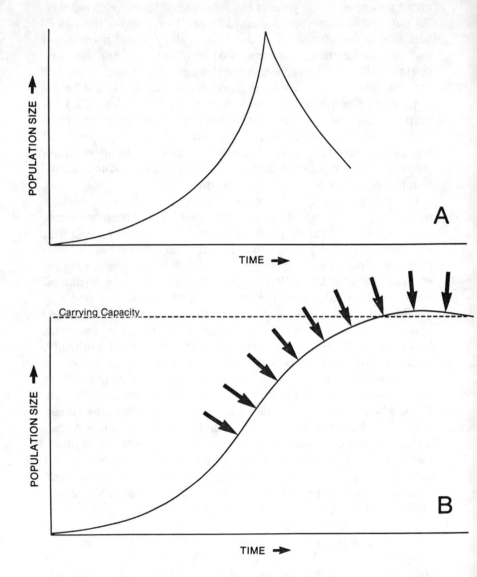

Figure 5. Two types of population growth curves. A) J-shaped with continued exponential growth until a massive die-off occurs; B) S-shaped with environmental resistance (arrows) limiting population size to the carrying capacity of the ecosystem.

Therefore, in these populations the rate of growth slows down progressively as the numbers approach what the ecosystem can bear and support. This level, called the *carrying capacity*, reflects the maximum number of individuals of a given population the ecosystem can support. The carrying capacity of an ecosystem includes all those parameters that are involved in the life support of any given organism including food and nutrients, energy, raw materials, and many other things. As the population size nears that level, the forces of environmental resistance become increasingly greater and more intense so that as this level is reached, no further growth usually takes place. At the level of the carrying capacity, population numbers are held fairly consistent by two groups of forces. On one hand are the forces of the intrinsic rate of increase —forces that continually cause more individuals to be produced and thereby drive the curve upward. This biotic or reproductive potential is constantly tending to cause the birth rate to increase. On the other hand are the forces of environmental resistance that limit population increases and push the growth curve downward; environmental resistance impairs survival and causes the mortality rate to increase. What results, then, is a fairly stable population size held in place by these two powerful, opposing, and antagonistic forces.

The Human Population

The human population is precisely governed by principles that control that of any other species. On a geological or paleontological scale, *Homo sapiens* is a very new species, having evolved in the last three to four million years. While there are no accurate data on the size of the human species until about 350 years ago, the human population has been estimated to have been about five to ten million about 10,000 years ago (Figure 6). By the time of Christ, there were an estimated 250 million persons. By the year 1650, the population had doubled to 500 million, and in 1830, just 180 years later, the population was composed of one billion persons. By 1930, the population doubled to two billion, and in the next forty-six years it doubled once again; its size in 1976 was four billion (Figure 6). The most recent figures (mid-1981) indicate that the world's population is in excess of 4.5 billion, growing at the rate of 1.7 percent annually, and will double again to nine billion in just forty-one years, if it continues at that rate.

It should be evident that the growth pattern of the human population is one of a classical, typical J-shaped curve—a curve that

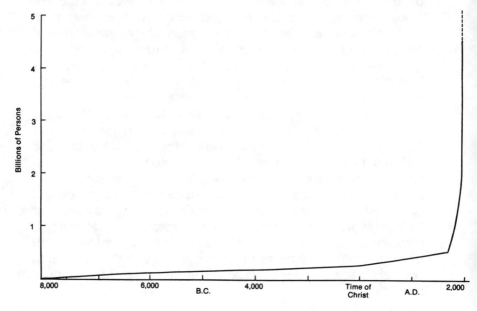

Figure 6. The growth of the world's human population for the past 10,000 years.

describes exponential growth. But there is a fundamental difference in the growth of the human population and that of most other species. In the example of the young man whose salary doubled daily, the interval between doublings was fixed to a daily basis. The interval between the doubling of the human population has actually *decreased* in the last 2,000 years; the doubling time has decreased from 1650 years to 180 years to 100 years to 46 years to 41 years. This means that our growth curve is in an exaggerated logarithmic pattern, which means that we are increasing numerically on a much faster scale than we would be by even increasing geometrically but on a fixed interval.

The numerical growth of the human species over the past several centuries is cause for great ecological concern. Growing at a steady rate of 1.7 per annum, the population will be doubling every 41 years. Contrary to some of the articles and opinions about the virtues of sustained population growth, continued exponential growth will be disastrous within a century or less. We must remember how the salary of the young man increased at an incredible rate, especially as the numbers became larger. First of all, no species can continue to increase exponentially for very long, particularly one that is exaggerated by a reduction in the time interval between doublings. Secondly, a sudden, devastating reduction in numbers can be expected if geometric growth continues.

What sort of calamity, you may ask, will happen? I am no prophet, but I do know for certain that continued exponential growth cannot continue indefinitely. I suspect shortages of food or a human-induced disaster will eventually curtail population size. Thirdly, we must seek out methods to implement the change in our growth pattern from a J-shaped curve to an S-shaped curve. Eventually, an S-shaped growth curve reaches a state of equilibrium in which birth and death rates are equal, thus producing zero population growth. And finally, we desperately need to work diligently on the plethora of social, political, economic, and religious dimensions of what zero population growth will generate. The issues of social justice will come rushing to the forefront in our efforts to curb future growth.

Some Closing Thoughts

We live in a beautiful, complex world replete with absolutely fascinating and intricate interdependent ties. I concur with the biblical writer who wrote, "And God saw everything that he had made, and behold, it was very good." Increasingly today the beauty, order, and interdependence of nature are being seen as silent but powerful witnesses to the nature of the Creator. It is my hope and dream and prayer that our society will someday see the image of God in the creation and blaze bold new trails leading to its embodiment.

Some Additional Readings

Brown, Lester R. *In the Human Interest* (New York: W. W. Norton & Co., Inc., 1974)

Clapman, W. B., Jr. *Human Ecosystems* (New York: Macmillan Publishing Co., Inc., 1981)

Ehrlich, Paul R., Anne H. Ehrlich, and John P. Holdren. *Ecoscience: Population, Resources, Environment* (San Francisco: W. H. Freeman and Co., 1977)

Kieffer, George H. *Bioethics: A Textbook of Issues* (Reading, Mass.: Addison-Wesley Publishing Co., Inc., 1979. pp. 345-409)

Lutz, Paul E. and H. Paul Santmire. *Ecological Renewal* (Philadelphia: Fortress Press, 1972)

Miller, G. Tyler. *Living in the Environment* (3rd edition. Belmont, California: Wadsworth Publishing Co., 1982)

Odum, Eugene P. *Fundamentals of Ecology* (3rd edition. Philadelphia: W.
B. Saunders Co., 1971. pp. 3-105, 161-188)

Part III

ART AND CREATION
CONSCIOUSNESS

The present ecological crisis we are facing is due in part to an impoverishment of imagination—creative solutions to admittedly complex ecological difficulties are rarely proposed and even more rarely taken seriously as "realistic." Nevertheless, it is only when we conceive of creative answers to seemingly intractible problems that we will begin to make progress toward a sustainable, replenishing world. Why? Because the problems are so massive and sprawling that anything short of new ways of envisioning environmental protection, economics, and social relations—in other words, anything less than a new understanding of world culture—will be insufficient. Old answers will not satisfy new questions.

It is for this reason that artistic resources must be an integral part in the development of genuine creation consciousness. Art works—in every medium—can symbolize for us our deepest concerns: they can be documents of what is and is not meaningful in human existence. When we are *engaged* by a work of art, we begin to participate in a new vision of the world. Art works, then, symbolically deconstruct and reconstruct our understanding of the world. They help us to *see* our world—and our place in it—in a new way. Finally, creative works spawn creative *work*. Art teaches us to become creative ourselves—to appreciate an art work fully, we must enter into its vision creatively. We must allow it to suggest new possibilities, new angles, new forms, all of which enriches the possibilities, angles, and forms of our own lives.

The arts, then, are not extraneous to a consideration of our most genuine relationship to the natural environment; instead, they can document our deepest feelings and insights about that environment. They can free us from familiar images of the environment which prevent us from truly experiencing it; and they can encourage us in our own attempts to arrive at creative solutions to ecological problems. Faced with grave and wide-ranging difficulties, creativity must become a "guiding methodology" in humanely resolving these difficulties.

Chapter Thirteen

RECLAMATION, RESACRALIZATION, AND REGENERATION
Approaches to the Environment in the Art of Smithson, Singer, and the Harrisons

Patricia Runo

Contemporaneous with the rise of the ecology and women's movements in the 1960s and 1970s was a "return to nature" impulse in the art world. This trend focused upon art as an open, interactive process, and expressed itself in earthworks, environmental sculptures, and reclamation projects—works that seemed to be ritually contracted with their environment. Although the best of these works functioned primarily to reestablish a coherent relationship between nature and culture in a civilization deracinated from its "earthy" moorings, the reasons for art's renewed interest in nature were nevertheless complex and varied. Art's re-baptism into its natural origins—that is, its rootedness in matter—may be seen as part of the "archeological impulse" in modern academic disciplines: the probing and unearthing of those "layers" that comprise psyche, society, religion, and art in an attempt to return to their original motivations. Such an art movement was, and is, an expression of anti-formalist tendencies in contemporary art—a refusal to reduce art to the merely "formal" properties of line, color, mass, and space. Further, it is an attempt—albeit a frequently unsuccessful one—to resist "commodification" in an art market whose values are infused with a "precious object syndrome" that equates worth with saleability. Finally, art's renewed interest in nature may be seen as an example of "negative entropy" in the human, cultural ecology—a tendency to reverse the processes of decay

manifested in those prevailing cultural systems which have contributed to disequilibrium in the larger eco-processes of the
planet. Good environmental art, like a waste treatment plant, is
engaged in recycling—but a recycling, in this case, of human
values back into the natural processes from which they received
their origin.

Historically, art's reaffiliation with nature may be associated
with the end of Minimalism as the pervading avant-garde trend of
the late 1960s. Minimalism was a purist style that sought to take
art "back to its beginnings" by reducing art to elementary systems
and primary structures such as the cube and the square—from
which it was thought there could be little further formal regress.
And yet regress art did: from form to process; from Euclidean
projections upon the natural world to the natural world itself. As
art sought renewed contact with nature, the conception of art as
a sleek, clean, industrialized object divorced from relationships,
free of content and context became a thing of the past. Process
entered, site entered, time entered, recreating the existential
conditions of art. The "beginnings" that minimalism sought were
not to be found in pure form, but rather in a redefinition of art as
a dynamic activity in which process, product, and context dialec-
tically interact to produce works that seek dialogue with, rather
than independence from, their environment.

Earthworks, environmental sculptures, and reclamation art may
be viewed as persistent weeds in the garden patch of contemporary art. Their wild, resilient, organic growth has consistently
uprooted and overturned every artistic overlay of stabilizing structure or definition. In site, theme, and approach, these art forms
have been as varied as the artists who have promoted them.
Remote deserts, tropical gardens, and industrial wastelands have
been their settings. Their subjects have been diverse "renderings"
of such themes as transiency and permanence, growth and decay,
entropy and regeneration, to name only a few. In the work of artists like Dennis Oppenheim and Michael Heizer, art's interaction
with nature has produced deep trench-like shapes—human punc-
tuation marks in the syntax of the earth's surface in the form of
X's, spirals, and circles. For artists Maryanne Caruthers Aiken and
Bonnie Sherk—whose works stress the interdependence of
natural, social, and cultural systems in proper intersystemic balance—"art is taking responsibility for energy in an appropriate
form."[1]

Contemporary environmental art, like contemporary culture, is ambivalent in its response to nature: the coercive as well as the yielding gesture is there; nature is both ground of value and the "field" upon which aesthetic values are written. Indeed, art and nature are presently involved in a reciprocal reclamation project in which both are being redefined through the interaction of the processes, products, and intellectual constructs which have been traditionally associated with the concepts of "nature" and "art." Consequently, there is no monolithic, overarching view of, nor approach to, nature—such as traditional Romanticism—which unifies and explains the ongoing collagistic build-up of works which have been ritually contracted with their environment. Rather, there are only representative approaches, together with their implicit definitions and valuations of nature, which, when examined, may function as heuristic models for an ecologically aware, culturally integrative response to the environment.

Three such representative approaches may be found in the art of Robert Smithson, Michael Singer, and Helen and Newton Harrison. The works of these artists typify divergent attitudes toward nature. Their thematic and formal concerns vary: Smithson's best-known pieces were earthworks; Singer's primary genre is outdoor and indoor environmental sculptures; and the Harrisons are eclectic, ecological artists whose processes and products combine an interest in life-chain systems with aesthetic, painterly concerns. And yet, in spite of these differences, their work is bound together by a common thread: an informed ecological awareness that seeks the active engagement of nature-as-subject, rather than passively acted-upon object, in the human creative enterprise.

Based upon this common thread of dialogic human-environmental interaction, it is the thesis of this paper that the works of Smithson, Singer, and the Harrisons present contemporary models of approaches to the environment that give us lenses with which to see the religious dimension of our relationship to the natural world. These models—which I have poetically termed *reclamation, re-sacralization*, and *regeneration*—function in a manner analogous to the mutual interdependence of ecosystems: they present a complex chain of processes and products (both natural and imaginal) that, when taken together, furnish us with a "web" of possible creative responses to our current ecological dilemma, responses which are both environmentally sane and religiously sound.

Robert Smithson

The work of Robert Smithson, perhaps more than that of any other artist of his generation, pioneered artistic concern for the environment and articulated the artist's awareness of her/his political responsibility for its fate. Smithson, who was accidentally killed in a small plane crash while surveying a new work in 1973, was a sculptor and earthwork artist. His major earthworks, executed between 1971-1973, merged the concerns of ecology, industry, and art into an "aesthetics of reclamation." In Smithson's work, industrial and technological waste—the slag-heaps of civilization—were recycled as art.

By self-definition, Smithson was an anti-romantic whose views of nature were decidedly complex. No paradisal Eden untouched by serpentine disruptions lurked in nature or humanity's past. Rather, nature's dialectic—of which humanity was a part—involved both gentleness and terror. The thesis of smooth rolling hills and the pastoral garden was countered by the anti-thesis of geologic cataclysm and catastrophic human waste. Like many artists of the 1960s, Smithson was fascinated with entropy—the tendency, within any system, towards randomness, chance, disorder, and the loss of available energy. His preferred sites were deserts or urban/industrial wastelands—places where "the now stilled cataclysms of remote beginnings collided with the near-futility of the industrially ruined present."[2]

Although metaphysically a pessimist, Smithson balanced his interest in entropic processes with a general benevolence towards nature. This expressed itself in a working commitment toward the endless possibilities of transformation inherent in the landscape, and in a connective symbolic association between microcosmic human processes and the macrocosmic processes of nature. Out of the disrupted landscape Smithson made art.

Smithson's best-known earthwork, "Spiral Jetty" (1970), is a reclamation of both neglected land and a neglected symbol.[3] Built at Rozel Point on the Great Salt Lake, Utah, one mile north of abandoned oil derricks, and composed of black rock, salt crystals, earth, and red water (algae), "Spiral Jetty" is a 1,500 feet long, fifteen feet wide coil which attempts to make morphological sense out of natural and industrial devastation. "Spiral Jetty" began as Smithson's search for the color red—the color that G. K. Chesterton called "the most joyful and dreadful thing in the universe . . . the fiercest note, the highest light."[4] In its present site-determined form, the red-drenched black basalt and white crystal jetty evokes the joy and dread inherent in any aesthetic presentation of the complex dialectic of creation-destruction. It is an aesthetic and cognitive map whose spiral shape makes connections between organic, stellar, and crystalline structures in their creative and destructive powers, and between the distant past (the time of primordial origins) and the near-future.

Smithson himself juxtaposed metaphors of life and death, growth and decay in order to describe the jetty. While he compared the whorling red currents of the lake to the primal life force of circulating blood "chemically analogous in composition to the primordial seas,"[5] those same currents—when swollen to the force of whirlpools—become, like flowing blood, a symbol of destruction as well as life. To Smithson, the form of the jetty suggested the spiral construction of the double helix, of the sun, of galaxies and nebulas, and of the growth of the crystal lattice. He considered the spiral jetty only "one layer within (the lake's) spiralling crystal lattice, magnified trillions of times."[6] And yet, the jetty's spiral shape—in nature associated with growth and construction—was artistically presented by Smithson in its negative, counter-clockwise aspect: the traditional destructive spiral. To the poetic imagination, the jetty's backward-turning form is a serpentine reminder that the deconstructive, entropic forces of the natural and human present, unless curtailed, threaten a return to the watery chaos from which life emerged.

Smithson's most complex work is "Broken Circle/Spiral Hill" (1971), a reclamation piece that reorganized the disrupted remains of a dredging operation at an abandoned quarry in Emmen, Holland. In both process and form, the work presents Smithson's major formal and thematic obsessions: the dialectic of creation-destruction; the telescopic collisions of time—what Smithson called "remote pasts meeting remote futures"[7]; "entropological manifestations," both natural and human; and art's potential as a human, cultural force of negative entropy.

The circle itself is a 140-foot-diameter, half-jetty, half-canal, double-mirrored, clockwise semi-circle. Paradoxically, the piece—whose form was intended to aesthetically counter the grotesque effects of dredging—was created by a means associated with the force of *natural* destructiveness, but here one which was humanly controlled: flooding. Midpoint in the circle is an "accidental center," a huge glacial boulder which was deposited during the Ice Age floods and later used by Bronze Age peoples to make prehistoric burial chambers called "Hun's beds." The boulder, uncovered during excavations and too costly to remove, took on an ambiguous, polyvalent, symbolic significance for Smithson. He saw it as a "kind of glacial Heart of Darkness—a warning from the Ice Age"[8] that symbolized the presence of chaotic, disruptive elements inherent in every act of creation. It was an "entropological manifestation," a link between the lost intentions of Bronze Age humanity and his own obstructed artistic intention to present a site "unburdened by any middle point."[9]

Smithson planned a film which would connect nearby "Hun's bed" monuments to his own. In the film there was to have been "a forward-zoom and backward-zoom that would link up the two boulders in a kind of cinematic parallel that would cover vast stretches of time."[10] Had Smithson executed it, the form of the film —like the complex, composite clockwise/counter-clockwise form of "Broken Circle/Spiral Hill"—would have presented a telescopic "collision" of past and future—a kind of cancellation of pure progressive movement, perpetrated by the essential universal force of entropy, as symbolized by the boulder center. In "Broken Circle/ Spiral Hill," as in "Spiral Jetty," no edenic or utopian future freed from what Smithson called "the dialectics of entropic change"[11] loomed on the horizon. Chaos, randomness, disruption were forces to be reckoned with. For Smithson, "The certainty of the absolute garden would never be regained."[12]

The works and writings of Robert Smithson interpret nature as an ambiguous phenomenon. Smithson affirmed the interrelatedness and mutual interdependence of all natural and cultural systems—the "web of life" model developed in the natural and physical sciences. But his artistic exegesis of the web focused upon the paradox that nature (and humanity as part of nature) at once creates and destroys. For Smithson, the sylvan landscapes of nature and the conceptual landscapes of the human mind are subject to erosion and decay even as they undergo organic growth. Any and everywhere, deconstructive, entropic forces threaten the evolutionary thrust of creative advance. "Nature, like a person, is not one-sided," said Smithson.[13] A "Hun's bed" of lost intentions— forgotten species, discarded ecological commitments, disordered aesthetic relations—burdens the entire horizon of natural and human history.

Smithson's work stands in a theological tradition that eschews primal innocence. For him the serpent—mythological symbol of the forces of chaos and disruption—is ubiquitously present from the opening chapters of creation history to any "apocalyptic completion" of the human drama. Consequently, he believed that any ecologically motivated spirituality or reclamation project that sought a return to a pre-given "ideal state" unravaged by the forces of natural cataclysm and industrial devastation fostered a "pseudo-innocence" that was hopelessly doomed to fail.

In contrast to those whom he considered beset by an "Ecological Oedipus Complex"[14]—that is, those for whom *any* manipulation of "Mother Earth" became a projection of the incest taboo into nature—Smithson sought a direct organic manipulation of the land devoid of violence and "macho" aggression.[15] He considered himself an "ecologist of the real," one who accepted the entropic situation and learned to work with it. "A bleached and fractured world surrounds the artist," said Smithson. "To organize this mess of corrosion into patterns, grids and subdivisions is an aesthetic process that has scarcely been touched."[16]

Robert Smithson engaged in an aesthetics of negative entropy that countered the ravages of natural and industrial devastation with the fertile soil of the human imagination. While his work did not seek literal regeneration of the stripped mines and minds of the urban and industrial wasteland (such was not the province of art, according to his definition), he nevertheless rendered the broken landscape aesthetically useful. The spiral form of much of his work stands as symbolic reminder that truly transformative possibilities must, of necessity, incorporate and transvalue deconstructive, entropic forces at work in the environment. Any humanly and religiously sound approach to the current ecological dilemma that is to have functional significance can never retreat to nostalgia for a lost paradise, but must inevitably reclaim the "fallen" present.

Michael Singer

Nature—and human ritual interaction with nature—is both the subject and content in the sculptures of Michael Singer. Since the early 1970s, Singer's outdoor and indoor pieces have sought to expose a view of nature as flux by evoking a sense of ritual presence in the site rather than imposing a pre-determined structure upon the environment. The primary concerns that undergird Singer's work—both the veneration of nature and the expression of transience—compel him to engage nature as active co-participant. Elements of the environment such as water, light, and wind sometimes alter the formal order of his work, allowing it to disappear into the land altogether. In the words of art critic Margaret Sheffield, "Singer's elegant and light structures (composed of materials indigenous to their surroundings) paradoxically make artistic use of the environment by *yielding* to natural forces."[17]

Singer's understanding of nature as flux, and his careful, restrained use of artistic structure to reveal or enhance natural phenomena have affinities both with oriental views of nature as cyclic change and northern romanticism's preference for the direct apprehension of unreconstructed nature.[18] For Singer, the function of art is primarily spiritual: the evocation of a "sense of ritual" inherent in a particular site through repeated actions and structures that bring the viewer/participant closer to the quintessential powers in nature. In this, Singer demonstrates affinities with the builders of the Shinto shrines, whose stately wooden entrance gates (*torris*), located at beautiful and mysterious places, were intended to display a powerful sense of the presence of gods and spirits (*kami*) in nature. Singer's work—like the ritual Japanese *torri*, or "first gate," for which much of his work is named—acts as an entrance way into the poetic qualities of phenomenal reality. The fluctuation of wind and water, the harmonious balancing of tension and compression, the perduring presence of priestly, human elements in nature—these are the themes that Singer's work ritually and symbolically evokes.

Singer's sculptural oeuvre includes both the spare, linear, calligraphic gesture and sturdier outdoor and indoor pieces whose tensive, curvilinear rhythms capture the dynamic balance of tension and compression. In calligraphic pieces such as "Sangam Ritual Series 4/76," Singer exploited the aesthetic possibilities of transience. Executed in the ten-thousand-acre Smithsonian salt marsh preserve near Chesapeake Bay and consisting of over 150 site-specific lines and elements composed of marshgrass, phragmites, and bamboo, "Sangam Ritual Series 4/76" was an example of a continuously changing horizontal structure. Not only did the structure shift ceaselessly (like the marshgrass) in poetic resonance with the site, but its chimerical visible form depended totally upon the position of the sun.[19] In the early morning, light hitting the central part of the work made it appear self-contained, like carefully executed calligraphy. By mid-afternoon, the sun's illumination of additional bamboo pieces appeared to expand the work's perimeters; rather than controlled calligraphy, its "afternoon form" resembled an exuberant space drawing executed on a

vast scale. Under the pressure of wind and rain, the original calligraphic form of Sangam Ritual 4/76 has slowly been "erased."[20]
And yet, for those who have been influenced by the work, its durative presence remains: an acquired ability to see the ephemeral
beauty of light and line immanent in an ordinary salt marsh.

Less transient than the calligraphic pieces, but equally provocative in form, are Singer's sturdier outdoor sculptures. These
works—compact, woven, wooden-mesh, curvilinear structures
constructed on ponds surrounded by hills and woods—continue
Singer's emphatic insistence upon ritual evocation of "place." In
one such piece, "First Gate Ritual Series, 1976," a horizontal two-
part work executed on the Nassau County Museum of Fine Arts'
pond in Roslyn, Long Island, Singer's intuitive delineation of
"place," and his overall attention to sculptural detail, successfully
produced a work poetically at one with its site. The work's structure of curvilinear rhythms pulls attention out to the contours of
the surrounding landscape. The mesh of bow-like diagonals connect the viewer to a sense of flow in the hills and woods.[21] And the
"grounding" vertical element—created by nearby trees—serve to
stabilize the complex dynamism of flux and flow inherent in both
sculpture and site. Like makers of the Japanese torri, Singer
employs a restrained but evocative use of sculptural form as an
aesthetic entranceway into the "spirit" of a particular site. First
Gate Ritual Series 1976 engages the viewer in an epiphany of the
natural world—a world in which wind and water, motion and
stasis—basic elements of phenomenal reality—are perceived as
alive with numina.

A central feature of Singer's outdoor sculptures is their relative
inaccessibility. Constructed at remote locations of natural beauty,
they demand pilgrimage. To "see" a Singer sculpture, viewers—
like cult devotees of a Shinto shrine—must immerse themselves in
a field of engaged vision that requires active, total participation.
To get to Sangam Ritual Series 4/76, or to the Roslyn pond piece,
the pilgrim-viewer has to risk getting wet. In such pieces the
message is clear: understanding necessitates commitment. We
must yield to nature if we are to truly perceive.

Like his outdoor pieces, Singer's indoor sculptures of the late
1970s and early 1980s continue to explore the rhythmic balance of
tension and compression. In contrast to the outdoor pieces, however, the indoor work is less linear, denser in weave, more complex.
Many of these works, again structurally and symbolically, make
reference to the *torri*, particularly in the curved, bow-like

elements nearest to the ground—elements that both "steady" the structure of the piece, while symbolically recalling the oriental idea of forces giving in to gravity.

But Singer's indoor pieces do not merely convey the restful pull of a stabilizing groundedness apart from the tug of ascent: in several indoor works, such as First Gate Ritual Series 10/78, Singer introduces the disjunctive presence of vertical elements which rise, like attenuated Giacometti figures, above the undulating configuration of shifting horizontal planes. These slim verticals, grouped at mysterious spatial intervals, functionally enrich Singer's symbolic vocabulary to include the priestly and the human. In Shinto mythology, the line between the human and the *kami* (exalted nature spirits to whom the *torri* is dedicated) is not a sharp one. The Japanese people themselves, according to the traditional myths, are descended from the *kami*.[22] By injecting a symbolic evocation of ritual human presence in his indoor work, Singer has reminded us of the deep interconnection between humans and nature in the ancient life-cycle. Part of nature and yet apart from it, his verticals rise, like hieratic human witnesses "above" the harmonious balancing of nature's ceaseless dynamism.

Michael Singer's sculpture presents an epiphany of the natural world—an aesthetic initiation into the numinous powers of phenomenal reality. His implicit metaphysic—heavily influenced by oriental thought—is processive: a dynamic world of incessant motion; of harmony and tension; and of the continuously fluctuating interrelationship of part to whole. This processive world view describes the field of mystery upon which Singer's artistic enterprise is written; his work is the calligraphic gesture, the sculpted ideogram of that view.

But nature-as-mystery is not mystification in Singer's work. Rather, his resacralization of phenomenal reality is an aesthetic and religious counter to a secularized, mechanistic exploitative view of nature that has denuded nature of its glory even as it has robbed nature of its resources. By artistically suggesting the coinherence of matter and spirit in sculptures that evoke the sacramental beauty of phenomenal reality, Singer's work posits nature's transcendent significance and reminds us that only that which can be knowingly and critically reverenced is unlikely to be disrespectfully subjugated.

In Singer's sculpture, nature is not "for humans"; rather than passively acted-upon resource, nature is active agent, the pre-given field of human values. Indeed human be-ing, when properly situated, is "for nature."

Singer's work may be read as a subversion of Western Christianity's dominant anthropocentric paradigm. Rather than a power to be "controlled," nature is primarily a process to be understood. In relation to nature and the larger cosmic process, humanity's proper posture is not "dominion over" in any coercive sense, but rather a dynamic dialectic of reverential, celebratory "yielding to" and "assertion for." Only when the human element either "gives in" to the "gravitational force" of the wisdom inherent in natural processes of motion and change (like the symbolic, lowermost curve of the *torri*), or when it rises in priestly witness to nature's quintessential power, can humans be said to be living in harmony with the earth.

Helen and Newton Harrison

Abstract Expressionist artists used to say that the blank white receptacle of the canvas was their whole world. Helen and Newton Harrison have inverted that doctrine. For them, the whole world is their canvas; algae, compost, seeds, and political proposals are their media. Their subject matter is as diverse—and as interrelated—as the life-cycle of brine shrimp and the farming systems of American Indians.

The Harrisons are ecological artists whose work is a hybrid mix of artistic, scientific, and eco-political concerns and methodologies. Schooled in minimalism, and that particular movement's concern for basic structures and elementary systems, the Harrisons have nevertheless pushed their interests in the primary beyond the formalist questions of minimalism and into the critical *material* issues of the future. Their work has variously been read as science (they were awarded a Scripp's Institute Sea Grant for successfully decoding the breeding requirements of crabs); as art (even their dead-pan political proposals are tinged in painterly sepia hues); or—as "real life." As art critic Lucy Lippard has said, their work is not simply "culture, nor horticulture, but poly-culture"[23]—an attempt to heal the anomalies that exist between the natural environment and cultural systems. In their work, art's creation of imaginary structures has been harnessed for the purpose of regenerating the earth.

And regenerate the earth they literally did. "To make earth seems a reasonable activity given the propensity of other forms of activity to make deserts," said the Harrisons.[24] At Artpark,

Lewiston, New York in 1977, Helen and Newton Harrison and their son Joshua set out to renew the barren site known as the "spoils-pile"—a disused quarry and chemical dump that covers 40 of Art-park's 70 acres. During approximately a two-year period, the Harrisons organized the spoilspile into an organic dumpsite consisting of 3,000 truckloads of earth and organic debris (leaves, tree prunings, and grass cuttings) from nearby communities.[25] The earth was intermixed and spread in what the Harrisons called a "performance piece" by state park earth-moving machinery. Native seeds were sown, a forest was planted, and—before the project was eventually halted by Artpark administrators—the beginnings of a viable meadow had begun to surface: an aesthetically fertile overlay on the deadly serious consequences of chemical waste.

The "Spoilspile Project" was cost-efficient, community-oriented, and—in the most profound sense—"ground-breaking," both ecologically and aesthetically. "What we're really doing is completing the regeneration of a quarry," said Newton.[26]

Although much of the Harrisons' art—for example, their "earth-making" activities, watershed reclamation, and "life-chain" projects—are attempts at literal regeneration, there is also a meta-phoric aspect to their work that stresses the madness of continuing eco-political and human degeneration. In works such as "The Endless Appetite Maps" and their "Meditations" series, the Harrisons have criticized the degenerative colonizing mentality prevalent in consumptive territorialism and in genocidal policies toward oppressed peoples. One large map, done in the 1970s, entitled *Wherein the Appetite is Discovered to be Endless*, illustrates a proposal—made in the real world by the Law of the Sea Conference—for dividing up the riches of the ocean floor.[27] Believing that the new division opened up a set of rules for territorial conflict—favoring seafaring nations, extending colonialism, "cutting up the whole pie for the benefit of whose who already have some"[28]—the Harrisons made a whole series of smaller maps (*More on the Endless Appetite*) which absurdly and pointedly "gridded" the ocean into microscopic squares, one for each inhabitant of the earth.

Many of the Harrisons' "Meditations" can be read as environmental-impact studies of specific sites, and as critiques of the degenerative effects of territorialism coupled with political proposals for restoring eco-political balance. In *Meditation on the Great Lakes*, a series of stark and diagrammatic drawings of maps with geometric, human-made boundaries proliferating to split up the Great Lakes basin, the Harrisons tackled water pollution by proposing "a secession and dictatorship of the ecology."[29] According to the Harrisons, their work is

a fantasy that will propose secession from both countries involved and deal with the idea of a dictatorship of the ecology. Instead of people dictating how they will use the Great Lakes, by virtue of their degeneration, their eutrophication, the lakes will dictate how people can use them . . . In the present the culture dictates, in the future the Great Lakes will dictate—so it's an ironic fantasy.[30]

Art critic Kim Levin has assessed the value of the Harrisons' Great Lakes proposal, recalling Gregory Bateson's words in *Steps to an Ecology of Mind:* "You forget that the eco-mental system called Lake Erie is part of *your* wide eco-mental system—and that if Lake Erie is driven insane, its insanity is incorporated in the larger system of *your* thought and experience."[31] When viewed through the lens of Bateson's timely words, the Harrisons' fantasy seems to be not only sound ecological reflection, but sound politics as well.

In a piece about a vanished southern California Indian tribe called *Meditation on the Gabrielino Whose Name for Themselves is No Longer Remembered Although We Know That They Farmed with Fire and Fought Wars by Singing,* the Harrisons have turned to recent discoveries in anthropology for an ecological paradigm, a cultural alternative to possession, consumption, and profit. The work is a two-part panel that balances a richly tinted sepia landscape against a dry grid of pages from a 19th century historical account. It is a study in contrasts—between the farming systems and cultural practices of the extinct Gabrielino who practiced selective burning as a means of planting and harvesting and settled disputes by singing obnoxious songs at their opponents—and the practices of the San Gabriel Mission, which took over this tribe and destroyed their way of life.[32] In textual commentary on the work, the Harrisons have drawn cogent connections between the ecocide and the accompanying genocide of the "Gabrielinos" to what we are doing to our portion of the earth today.[33] Comparing the so-called "primitivity" of early farming systems with the effects of our own, they conclude: "In terms of long-term [effect on] the environment, they turn out to be far less destructive than our own."[34] Rather than "seeing their technologies as primitive, they should be seen as appropriate."[35]

Their Lagoon Cycle series, more than any of their other works, has established the interdisciplinary, political, polycultural, and ecological nature of the Harrisons' oeuvre. Developed during the 1970s, the Lagoon Cycle series is a sequence of environmental projects concerned with marine life, whose elastic scale and diverse methodologies expanded from constructed indoor fish farms to grandiose outdoor proposals; from technological imitations of nature to projects for the regeneration of nature.

Early Lagoon cycle pieces resembled pseudo-practical engineering works or implausible natural science projects dreamed up by efficiency experts with time on their hands: there were artificial life-support systems for crabs and mollusks that had been wrested from their natural habitats; and micro-farming systems whose end results were elegant repasts of paella and bouillabaise.[36] But when the Harrisons succeeded in decoding the breeding requirements of crabs, their work seemed neither impractical nor implausible: the methodology of science was successfully being applied to mammoth projects of artistic origin. The Harrisons' hope for transforming the ecological landscape was gradually being realized.

Later Lagoon Cycle projects have shifted emphasis from individual species to the larger natural and political environs that house those species. The 5th Lagoon was a billion-dollar proposal for the regeneration of the Salton Sea in California which is dying from excess salinity.[37] The 6th and 7th Lagoon demands regeneration of a different, and potentially more costly, sort.

Following a logic inverse to that of the territorial Law of the Sea Conference, the 6th Lagoon proposes to revitalize the Sea of Cortez by returning the waters of the Colorado River to Mexico through a slight border realignment. Such a proposal, if adopted, would necessitate a shift in political consciousness tantamount to a minor adjustment in the earth's template.

An even greater adjustment would be required if the 7th Lagoon was adopted. That proposal seeks to politically and scientifically redefine the Pacific Ocean as a lagoon—a body of water here circumscribed by political, military, and economic expansionism and made brackish by the waste that such anti-ecological imperialism produces. For the Pacific Ocean the Harrisons again suggest a dictatorship of the ecology; territorial inviolability, petroleum production, and consumptive human appetite are, for the Harrisons, concerns secondary to the sanity of the eco-mental system that is the Pacific.

When art has become both an illustration of, and an answer to, ecological predicament; when its primary concern has shifted from breaking new aesthetic ground to regenerating "earthly"

ground; when it has moved from the creation of imaginary structures to the task of saving the world; then "art" has ceased to be
a separate, isolated discipline and has become instead a manifestation of negative entropy on a large cultural and ecological scale.

Such is the Harrisons' art. Their web-like work—a complex
weaving together of artistic and scientific processes and products
—is an artistic analogue for the "web of life" metaphor common in
ecological models. Indeed, few artists so cogently stress the interconnectedness and mutual interdependence of natural and cultural systems as do the Harrisons; and few artists so poignantly
illustrate the pathos inherent in the broken circuits between
nature and humanity that an ecocidal, dominantly anthropocentric world view has produced.

The Harrisons' work is a prophetic cry for cosmocentrism, an
indictment against territorialisms of the heart, mind, or landscape.
Magnification of vision has been essential for this concern, as they
have engaged in progressive movement from composing within a
frame, to framing new contexts, to creating the framework for a
new consciousness. Their work—particularly the political proposals—may be read as a quixotic battle against environmental dilemmas and human greed; certainly their post-conceptual romanticism suggests Swiftian irony and Surrealist dream. But they have
a pragmatic focus, and, like other utopian visionaries, their over-
all contribution may be judged not so much in terms of achieving
the probable as in the ability to lure us on toward the possible.
Nevertheless, let us not forget that they have, literally, "regener-
ated" the earth.

Conclusion

In an ecological apocalyptic a dictatorship of the ecology *will*
prevail—that is, failing a collective governance of the biosphere in
which human, cultural efforts contribute to the overall regeneration of disrupted ecosystems. What the Harrisons hope for is a
benevolent dictatorship. Their hybrid art, salvific in orientation,
is a post-modern aesthetic retrieval of the Genesis mandate to
"cultivate" (*ebed*) the planetary garden and "preserve" (*shamar*)
it. To return to this original mandate of stewardship demands a
rebirth of creative vision at once aware, like Smithson, that the
"certainty of the absolute garden will never be regained," yet
confidently, knowingly capable of engaging nature as active co-
participant in a dialectic of yieldingness and assertion that, like
Singer's artistic process, trusts nature's balancing movement.

Exiled from the garden of celebratory engagement with nature-as-sacrament by the flaming sword of a dualistic, anthropocentric bias, post-modern humanity is confronted with the ecological and spiritual need to reclaim an informed cosmocentrism that neither sentimentalizes nature nor exploits it. Such a cosmocentric orientation demands an "ecology of the real" capable of incorporating and transvaluing the disrupted, entropic given; as Smithson so tellingly discerned, "ecology and industry [and, we might add, religion] can no longer afford to be one-way streets. Rather, they must become crossroads."[38]

The art of Robert Smithson, Michael Singer, and Helen and Newton Harrison, and the complementary approaches to the environment (reclamation, resacralization, and regeneration) that their works exemplify, posit just such an "ecology of the real." Taken together, theirs is a web of possible creative responses that morphologically expresses the dynamic force of art as a form of negative entropy in the human, cultural ecology. In a civilization deracinated from its "earthy" moorings, their art-at-the-crossroads of science and religion seeks to heal the anomalies between natural and cultural systems. For artists, ecologists, and theologians alike, their message is clear: human creativity, in whatever form—be it religious, scientific, or artistic—must never be divorced from its organic connections.

Notes

1. Lucy R. Lippard, *Overlay: Contemporary Art and the Art of Prehistory* (New York: Pantheon Books, 1983), p. 212.
2. Ibid., p. 225.
3. Ibid., p. 32.
4. G. K. Chesterton, as quoted in Nancy Holt, ed., "Spiral Jetty," by Robert Smithson, in *The Writings of Robert Smithson* (New York: New York University Press, 1979), p. 109.
5. Ibid., p. 113.
6. Ibid., p. 112.
7. "A Sedimentation of the Mind: Earth Projects," by Robert Smithson, in *The Writings of Robert Smithson*, p. 91.
8. "The Earth, Subject to Cataclysms, Is a Cruel Master," interview with Robert Smithson by Gregorie Muller in *The Writings of Robert Smithson*, p. 182.
9. Ibid.
10. Ibid.
11. "Entropy Made Visible," interview with Robert Smithson by Alison Sky in *The Writings of Robert Smithson*, p. 191.

12. "A Sedimentation of the Mind: Earth Projects," by Robert Smithson, p. 91.
13. "Frederich Otto Olmstead and the Dialectical Landscape," by Robert Smithson in *The Writings of Robert Smithson*, p. 120.
14. Ibid., p. 122.
15. Ibid., p. 123.
16. "A Sedimentation of the Mind: Earth Projects," by Robert Smithson, p. 82.
17. Margaret Sheffield, "Natural Structures: Michael Singer's Sculpture and Drawings," *Artforum*, February 1979, p. 49.
18. Ibid.
19. Ibid.
20. Ibid.
21. Ibid.
22. Ninian Smart. *The Religious Experience of Mankind* (New York: Charles Scribner's Sons, 1976), p. 211.
23. Lucy Lippard, *Overlay*, p. 233.
24. Helen and Newton Harrison, "Notes on a Recent Project," *LAICA Journal*, October-November 1977, p. 282.
25. Kim Levin, "Helen and Newton Harrison: New Grounds for Art," *Arts*, Vol. 52: 6, February 1978, p. 126.
26. Ibid.
27. Ibid., p. 127.
28. Ibid.
29. Ibid., p. 127-128.
30. Ibid.
31. Gregory Bateson, from *Steps to an Ecology of Mind* as quoted in "Helen and Newton Harrison: New Grounds for Art," *Arts*, Vol. 52:6, February 1978, p. 128.
32. Ibid.
33. Lippard, *Overlay*, p. 233.
34. Kim Levin, "Helen and Newton Harrison: New Grounds for Art," p. 128.
35. Ibid.
36. Ibid., p. 129.
37. Ibid.
38. "Untitled, 1971," by Robert Smithson, in *The Writings of Robert Smithson*, p. 220.

Chapter Fourteen

ENVIRONMENTAL CONCERN AND IRONIC VIEWS OF AMERICAN EXPANSIONISM
Portrayed in Thomas Cole's
Religious Paintings

Doug Adams

A concern for the environment and an ironic view of American expansionism are evident in Thomas Cole's paintings when we see them, with religious understanding, in the series intended by the artist, and when we view them in the light of his letters and journal entries. But when attention is fixed on any one painting and it is then considered in isolation from the others of the series and from religious meaning, we fail to see such concern and irony. We will explore at length this isolating process in the popular and critical treatment of *Youth* from Cole's *Voyage of Life* series (1840), the most popular American painting in the nineteenth century; but first, we consider his earlier and later religious works that provide a context to understand the meaning of Cole's opus.

Cole's earliest efforts toward what he described as "a higher style of landscape" were *St. John the Baptist Preaching in the Wilderness* (1827), *The Expulsion* (from the Garden of Eden), and *Moses on the Mount*. In each of these works, he puts humans in their places; as Jane Dillenberger noted:

> Even the last of the prophets, John the Baptist, and Moses, the greatest of the prophets, are reduced in their canvases to gesticulating pigmy-like figures, whose mighty words and acts are belittled by the expanses of mountainous settings.[1]

When a human figure looms large on one of Cole's canvases, it is not a moment of human triumph but rather *The Dead Abel* (1832). Biblical background helps the viewer understand the social commentary implicit in these paintings. Moses and John the Baptist called the people out of the cities and into the wilderness for renewal. Being at home in nature (Eden) was lost by Adam and Eve's violation of the tree that was to be left undisturbed; and Abel's murderer, Cain, was the biblical founder of cities.

Consideration of much later Cole works highlights the artist's concerns within an explicit religious context. Cole's *Old Man of the Mountain* (1843), as it was incorrectly called for many years, may have struck observers as ominous or even sinister. The small shadowy figure hurries away down a mountain. What has he done? Where is he going? What is he planning to do? But when we know that the painting is *The Tempter* and that it belongs next to *Angels Ministering to Christ in the Wilderness*, it strikes us differently. With his powers of juxtaposition (that we will note again in the *Course of Empire* and *Voyage of Life* series), Cole renders the devil as something less than all powerful in the more dominant light of Christ's figure with angels. We no longer contemplate fearfully what the Devil had done or will do; but rather, we are drawn to the brightness of Christ and the portents of a new day's dawning. In Cole's words:

> Morning is as yet only wakening the heavens; the fire of the red day break is just catching along the under folds of the low sullen clouds of night, yet gloomily mantling the scene. It had great grandeur, great solemnity, great repose.[2]

The devil's effort to upset Christ's repose failed. The devil was put down. And it should be remembered that one of those temptations was earthly kingdoms. Cole's Lord rejected the temptation for kingdoms, even if Cole's country did not. In the *Pilgrim of the World* (1848), much lies between the pilgrim and the empire he seeks; for Cole noted in the original catalogue that "the path to glory lies through ruin and the battle field."[3] While John L. O'Sullivan did not write of "manifest destiny" until 1845 in his *New York Morning News* (and the United States did not fight the climactic war with Mexico until the following year), Texas had been taken from Mexico in 1835, and other aspects of American expansion were evident throughout the continent. But Cole's critique of American expansion penetrated internal as well as external manifestations; and the *Voyage of Life* and *Course of Empire* series embody this critique fully.

Youth, in the *Voyage of Life* series of four canvases, reveals a direction of nineteenth century American character not celebrated by Cole. Although Cole expressed regret at such a direction, he was not surprised; for four years earlier when he had conceived of the *Voyage of Life*, he had expressed a nearly fatalistic view of American development in his lecture on American scenery, in letters, and in the *Course of Empire* series. Ironic and religious views are expressed in these works as forces beyond any human control make short-sighted human dreams and accomplishments appear ridiculous; and the finitude of the human creature is illumined in the larger context of the Creator.

Popular overemphasis on *Youth* was evident from the earliest exhibitions of the *Voyage of Life* series. It is not surprising that the people of a growing young independent nation would identify with this painting where the confident young man "takes the helm himself." (We would not expect such people to identify with the dependence of *Childhood*, the powerlessness of *Manhood* or the utter dependence and peace of *Old Age*.) James Flexner notes that Cole's "four part *Voyage of Life* was the most popular painting in mid-century America, its second episode, *Youth*, in particular being reproduced in many engravings that inspired a flood of amateur copies."[4] Oliver Larkin writes that one-half million people viewed this series;[5] and this number appears in true proportions when we realize that the American population at the 1840 census was barely over seventeen million and at the 1860 census was only thirty-one million.[6]

A popular copy of this *Youth* episode by Hough eliminates all doubt as to the realization of the Youth's dreams of empire as the river flows straight toward the building in the sky.[7] Hough's painting is a visual parallel to William Cullen Bryant's unambiguous interpretation of *Youth*. During the Civil War, it is understandable that Bryant should demonstrate a desire for the unambiguous; but less understandable is Charles Sanford's perpetuation of this misinterpretation of Cole's *Youth* by approvingly associating Bryant's comments with Cole's intentions:

> The faraway reminded them of the future, which the promise of American life assured Americans could be nobler and better than the present. During the agonies of the Civil War, the pen of the aging Bryant was busy with futurist fantasies. During this period, too, he reviewed Cole's paintings before the National Academy of Design. One poem written in this phase, "Castles in the Air," held Cole in sentimental retrospect. The "region in the clouds" recalled the aerial mirage in Cole's second picture of *The Voyage of Life*, even to the colonnades, the architecture suggestive of "stately palaces, Gothic or Greek/or such as in the land of Mohammed/Uplift the crescent, or, in forms more strange,/Border the ancient Indus. . . ."[8]

Cole could conjure up visions of temples in America's future. (Thinking of the Hudson, he writes, "Without any great stretch of the imagination, we may anticipate the time when the ample waters shall reflect temple, and tower, and dome, in every variety of picturesqueness and magnificence.")[9] But he did not manifest Bryant's exuberance for the vision and certainly did not intend to affirm such a vision in *Youth*. Cole saw such buildings rise with an ironic eye, as we shall realize most fully in the *Course of Empire*.

Cole's *Youth* does not stand alone but falls in juxtaposition within a series. He wrote to Rev. J. F. Phillips on March 21, 1840, "Each picture I have wished to make a sort of antithesis to the other thereby the more fully to illustrate the changeable tenor of our moral existence."[10] The antithesis, evident when the paintings are viewed at one time in a series, reveals the irony of the work. In *Youth* "he . . . takes the helm himself, and in the attitude of confidence and eager expectation gazes on a cloudy pile of Architecture, an air built Castle, that rises dome above dome in the far off blue sky . . . emblematic of the day dreams of youth, its aspirations after glory and fame;"[11] but the neighboring painting reveals our confident helmsman swept along in a boat without a helm; "the helm of the boat is gone and he looks imploringly toward heaven."[12] In the heavens, the inviting castle has been replaced by demons! His thoughts of great empire have been reduced to thoughts of "Suicide, Intemperance, and Murder."[13] To superficial observation of *Youth*, the stream appears to stretch out straight toward the vision of the Castle kingdom in the sky as Hough later in fact did render the stream. "The beautiful stream flows for a distance directly toward the aerial place; but at length makes a sudden turn, and is seen in glimpses beneath the trees, until it at length descends with rapid current into a rocky ravine."[14] In *Manhood*, the stream does not allow attention to drift to distant dreams but rather cuts across the canvas in such a way as to confront the man and us with our immediate limitations. This is the reality that makes the confident youth of the previous episode appear ridiculous as Cole intended.

> Youth, in its impetuous career, is forgetful that it is embarked on the Stream of Life, and that its current sweeps along with restless force, and increases in swiftness, as it descends towards the great Ocean of Eternity.[15]

In *Manhood* we confront the full force of an American river and not a European river, tamed and managed by humans, with which we appeared to be dealing in *Childhood* and *Youth*.[16] Seeing the panels in series at one time allows us to shift our attention back and forth and makes the Youth look even more ridiculous than if we could look only forward through the series.

What we have seen and heard regarding *Voyage of Life* prepares us to approach *Course of Empire*. The two series, whose executions are separated by three or four years, are in conception much closer; for Cole conceived *Voyage of Life* as he was finishing *Course of Empire*.[17] Seeing one of the paintings alone or even all consecutively does not present the artist's intention with full force nor reveal his ironic treatment of Empire. But presenting all together in proper scale (with the third panel looming largest) presents the allegory and irony intended by the artist. In this way the full gaudiness of the Empire is the more startling. Cole did not celebrate this gaudiness. He wrote to Luman Reed on February 19, 1863, that he was "tired of the gaud and glitter of the large picture."[18] He thus began the fifth painting before undertaking the fourth, which could explain irresolvable differences of the scenes. But Cole was not primarily concerned about presenting a consistent scene. We have only to look at the paintings and listen to Cole's letters and journals in order to appreciate Cole's major concern about American development and his capacity to render such development ridiculous.

On September 7, 1836, Cole wrote to Luman Reed, the patron for whom *Course of Empire* was intended:

> My Dear Sir,—When you open this letter, you will expect to hear that the large picture is finished; but I am not yet so happy, and write to ask your patience yet a little while. . . . The figures take more time than I expected. Another reason for the length of time is, I have had to tear down some of the buildings that were nearly finished, in order to make improvements, a la mode New York.[19]

On March 26, 1836, Cole had written to Reed:

> They are cutting down all the trees in the beautiful valley on which I have looked so often with a loving eye. This throws quite a gloom over my spring anticipations. Tell this to Durand—not that I wish to give him pain, but that I want him to join with me in maledictions on all dollar-godded utilitarians.[21]

Another letter immediately followed the foregoing:

> After I had sealed my last letter, I was afraid that what I had said about tree destroyers might be understood in a more serous light than I intended. My "maledictions" are gentle ones, and I do not know that I could wish them any thing worse than that barrenness of mind, that sterile desolation of the soul, in which sensibility to

the beauty of nature cannot take root. One reason, though, why I am in so gentle a mood is that I am informed some of the trees will be saved yet. Thank them for that. If I live to be old enough, I may sit down under some bush, the last left in the utilitarian world, and feel thankful that intellect in its march has spared one vestige of the ancient forest for me to die by.[21]

But again on August 1, Cole wrote in his journal words that guide us to look more closely at the role of the rivers in both series of paintings:

I took a walk, last evening, up the valley of the Catskill, where they are now constructing the railroad. This was once my favorite walk; but now the charm of solitude and quietness is gone. It is, however still lovely: man cannot remove its craggy hills, nor well destroy all its rock rooted trees; *the rapid stream will also have its course.*[22]

His comments in an 1835 address on "American Scenery" may help us see more clearly Cole's concern as he executed the *Course of Empire*. After decrying the indifference with which the multitudes regard the beauty of nature and branding them "short lived and short sighted,"[23] Cole turned his attention to American development:

. . . Those whose days are all consumed in the low pursuits of avarice, or the gaudy frivolities of fashion, unobservant of nature's loveliness, are unconscious of the harmony of creation. . . . In this age, when a meager utilitarianism seems ready to absorb every feeling and sentiment, and what is sometimes called improvement in its march makes us fear that the bright and tender flowers of the imagination shall all be crushed beneath its iron tramp, it would be well to cultivate the oasis that yet remains to us, and thus preserve the germs of a future and a purer system. . . . And now when the sway of fashion is extending widely over our society—poisoning the healthful streams of true refinement and turning men from the love of simplicity and beauty, to a senseless idolatry of their own follies—to lead them gently into the pleasant paths of Taste would be an object worthy of the highest efforts of genius and benevolence. The spirit of our society is to contrive but not to enjoy—toiling to produce more toil—accumulating in order to aggrandize. The pleasures of the imagination, among which the love of scenery holds a conspicuous place, will alone temper the harshness of such a state.

. . . I cannot but express my sorrow that the beauties of such landscape are quickly passing away—the ravages of the axe are daily increasing—the most noble scenes are made desolate, and oftentimes with a wantonness and barbarism scarcely credible in a civilized nation. The way-side is becoming shadeless, and another generation will behold spots, now rife with beauty, desecrated by what is called improvement; which, as yet, generally destroys Nature's beauty without substituting that of Art. This is a regret rather than a complaint; such is the road society has to travel; it may lead to refinement in the end, but the traveller who sees the place of rest close at hand, dislikes the road that has so many unnecessary windings.

. . . We are still in Eden; the wall that shuts us out of the garden is our own ignorance and folly.[24]

This was a rather restrained public presentation by Cole that can be seen more forcefully throughout the *Course of Empire.* But Cole's capacity for biting humor in commenting on the building going on around him, while edited out by Louis Noble's attempts to idolize Cole, is partially restored in Elliot Vesell's "A Note on the Text." And so we learn of Cole's letter to William Adams in 1839 concerning a commission of a new public building:

I am afraid that the building when finished will be like most other buildings erected in this country, a monument of Bad Taste and Architectural Ignorance. *My only hope is in you.* My dear friend do not yield—do not I beg you give your consent to the absurdities that will be attempted nor let your name be coupled with those whose only Knowledge is conceit, whose only taste caprice. . . . As it respects my share of the design—if you cut off the mouth and ears and in their place put a proboscis or a plug—I shall not acknowledge the likeness. Regarding the alteration that your fellow commissioners and architect insist upon, I merely advise that when finished a painted cross be made in each recess. . .with the words "Rispetti la Croce" in large letters over it, or the more obvious sentence "Non si urina Qui," though in plain English, for the temptation will be very strong to all passers-by.[25]

While Sanford does not marshall the best available evidence, we must agree with his conclusion:

Cole's painting, *Course of Empire,* was a direct result of this concern for the welfare of his country, particularly as it was affected by the rising gospel of progress. His picture *Destruction* in that series was as much a reminder to the boastful young republic which liked to compare itself to the glory that was Greece and the grandeur that was Rome, ...Cole's motto for the series read: "First freedom, and then glory; when that fails, wealth, vice, corruption."[26]

A final journal entry that may provide insight into several details of the fourth and fifth paintings as well as the spirit of the final episode is dated October 10, 1835:

There is an article in the "American" addressed to the American

> people on the subject of erecting a monument to Washington.... As
> to the design of such a monument, I would say, let it not be a statue;
> for however great its size, its many parts and projections would
> render it less durable than something more simple: time would de-
> stroy the original beauty of the sculpture of the statue. I would not
> have a column; for that is an architectural member, and not a com-
> plete whole....[27]

The status *sans* head and hand in episode four may have a didactic
concern about the final form of Washington's monument; and the
single column at the center of the final episode stands as a hint
that the "final" scene is not a static one.

In Thomas Cole's paintings, we have seen how violations of the
environment are linked to the quest for empire; and the demonic
dimension permeates both activities that throw religious restraint.
Such restraint is overtly identified with religion in God's commands (The Garden of Eden and *The Expulsion*), in the angel's
presence (*Voyage of Life*), and in Christ's rejection of temptation
(*Angels Ministering to Christ in the Wilderness*). Human limitations (in perspective as well as in power) are noted throughout
Cole's works; and humans' disregard of their own finitude and
creatureliness results in enormous destruction as evidenced in
Course of Empire.

In 1946, Oliver Larkin wrote, "One reads Cole's lesson today less
earnestly than his generation did...."[28] But a decade after the
Vietnam War and in the midst of major environmental and nuclear
crises, we may read Cole's lesson more earnestly. Religious understandings help us glimpse environmental concern and ironic views
of American expansionism in Thomas Cole's paintings.

Notes

1. Jane Dillenberger, "Catalogue to the Exhibition," *The Hand and the
   Spirit* (Berkeley, 1972), p. 105.
2. Louis Legrand Noble, *The Life and Works of Thomas Cole* (Cambridge:
   Belknap Press, 1964), p. 262. These paintings were brought together
   again during the "Hand and the Spirit" exhibition in Berkeley in
   1972. How they came to be divided is noted by Jane Dillenberger in
   the catalogue of the exhibition: Dillenberger, op. cit., p.110.
3. Cf. Howard S. Merritt, *Thomas Cole* (Rochester Lithographies, 1969),
   p. 42.
4. James Flexner, *Nineteenth Century American Painting* (New York:
   Putnam's Sons, 1970), p. 54.

5. Oliver Larkin, *Art and Life in America* (New York: Holt, Rinehart and Winston, 1946), p. 204.
6. *Encyclopedia Britannica* (Chicago, 1969), Vol. 22, p. 688.
7. Cf. Flexner, op. cit., p.108.
8. Charles Sanford, *The Quest for Paradise, Europe and the American Moral Imagination* (Urbana, 1961), p. 149.
9. Thomas Cole, "Essay on American Scenery," *The American Monthly Magazine* (January 1836), Vol. 7, p.9.
10. Noble, op. cit., p. 211.
11. Ibid., p. 215.
12. Ibid., p. 216.
13. Ibid.
14. Ibid.
15. Ibid.
16. For elaboration and description of the significance of European and American rivers, consult Cole, op. cit., p. 5.
17. John Howat and John Wilmerding, *Nineteenth Century America, Paintings and Sculpture* (London: The Curwen Press, 1970), No. 45.
18. Noble, op. cit., p. 159.
19. Ibid., p. 151.
20. Ibid., p. 160.
21. Ibid., p. 161. Cole's ironic treatment of nineteenth century American idols ("reason" and "progress") has parallels in pulpit literature from Timothy Dwight to Henry Ward Beecher and in literature from Melville and Hawthorne to Twain. Cf. Doug Adams, *Humor in the American Pulpit from George Whitefield through Henry Ward Beecher* (Sharing Company, 1981) for that pulpit humor; and cf. the unpublished appendix in that book's original state as a doctoral dissertation (Graduate Theological Union, 1974) for the literary humor.
22. Ibid., p. 164. Underlining mine.
23. Cole, op. cit., p. 2.
24. Ibid., p. 12.
25. Noble, op. cit., p. 12.
26. Sanford, op. cit., p. 149. One could also see behind Cole's treatment of the city his own childhood experience and later adult associations with the city as evil: cf. Flexner, op. cit., p. 47. And in his attitudes, Cole is similar to many literati of his day: cf. Leo Marx, *The Machine in the Garden* (Oxford Press, 1967), *passim.*
27. Noble, op. cit., p. 152. *The Architect's Dream* and *Dream of Arcadia* may provide other examples of irony among Cole's works. The corpus of Cole's journals and letters edited by Nobel (but available unexpurgated in the American Archives of Art) needs to be reexamined with an eye to irony. Noble does include some hints of the

art works' ironic twist in Cole's letter to Durand (March 3, 1838): Of his encounter with the inhabitants of his Acadian dream, he notes, "I found them very *troublesome, very.* . . .But I hope to dispose of them one by one, if I have fair play, and have them hung, as a striking example, in the exhibition of the National Academy, by hangmen of our acquaintance." Ibid., p. 188.

28. Larkin, op. cit., p. 203

Cole Paintings Cited

Voyage of Life (*Childhood, Youth, Manhood,* and *Old Age*), 1840, Munson Williams Proctor Institute, Utica, New York.

Course of Empire (*The Savage State, The Arcadian or Pastoral, Consummation of Empire, Destruction, Isolation*), 1836, New York Historical Society, New York City.

John the Baptist Preaching in the Wilderness, 1827, Wadsworth Atheneum, Hartford, Connecticut.

Moses on the Mount, Shelburne Museum.

The Tempter, 1843, Baltimore Art Museum.

Angels Ministering to Christ in the Wilderness, 1843, Worchester Art Museum.

The Dead Abel, 1832, Albany Institute of the Arts.

Pilgrim of the World and *Pilgrim of the Cross,* 1848, Albany Institute.

Part IV

THEOLOGY, THEOLOGICAL ETHICS, AND SPIRITUALITY
Resources for Growth in Creation Consciousness

Theology, theological ethics, and spirituality have been three vitally important tools used in the Christian tradition to illuminate the significance, moral dimension, and embodiment of the life of faith. Descriptive, evaluative, and prescriptive, each of these takes as its province the meaning of human life lived in relation to the ground and sustainer of life, God. As the following chapters show us, theology, theological ethics, and spirituality offer us valuable resources in exploring the *meaning* of both ecological wholeness and ecological disaster for humankind—and for all the creatures of the earth—and for suggesting options and strategies for transforming the nexus of destructive attitudes which mount and prolong our contemporary environmental degradation.

Theology, theological ethics, and spirituality can, therefore, help reshape our damaging assumptions about nature—but this means that these disciplines will also have to change. All three of these "ways of knowing" have been notorious in their disregard of the natural world, if not for a positive disdain of it. Each must therefore be shaped by an awareness of the complexity, resilience, fragility, and interrelatedness of the biosphere. And each must, in its formulations, situate humankind in the midst of this flourishing, fecund world and not off to the side, as if we exist apart from it.

When theology, theological ethics, and spirituality are saturated in the patterns, cycles, and abundant proliferation of nature, they sharpen the *fundamental issues* which the present environmental crisis pointedly raises for humankind. Theology can both lift to view and critique the models which make ecological exploitation possible, and it can suggest and sketch alternative models. Ethics can analyze the hard moral choices which sooner or later we must identify and confront, notably when these models are in acute tension. And spirituality can be the intentional, centered, improvisational, dedicated "way of life" in which we put our choices into action.

The following chapters explore these possibilities from a number of perspectives. Charles S. McCoy of the Pacific School of Religion demonstrates the relevance of the rich tradition of covenantal theological ethics to environmental policy. (His Chapter 20 is positioned at the end of this section since it also anticipates the environmental policy concerns which are taken up in the opening chapters of the next section.) Theologian Conrad Bonifazi then summarizes the distinctive contribution which scientist-theologian Teilhard de Chardin has made in his writings. Process theology also has much to contribute in re-envisioning and rebuilding, and the next two statements are by scholars who have been closely identified with the vigorous development of process theology at the University of Chicago, the institution which gave the initial impetus to this field. The first piece, "A Process-Relational Conception of Creation," is by Bernard M. Loomer, former Dean of the U.C. Divinity School and leader of the early development of process theology there. It is followed by an essay by John B. Cobb, Jr., now at the Claremont School of Theology, on "Process Theology and an Ecological Model."[1]

The section concludes with Ken Butigan on Thomas Merton's assessment of the nature-human relationship and its implications for creating a "spirituality of the natural world," and Philip N. Joranson exploring the vision and structure of creation-conscious perception of the environment in "Prayer, Meditation, and Creation Consciousness."

Notes

1. In the following books, the reader will find valuable recent treatments which will more fully introduce the theological approach which is presented in the essays in this section.

   Ian G. Barbour, *Issues in Science and Religion* (Englewood Cliffs, N.J.: Prentice-Hall, 1966).
   Charles Birch and John B. Cobb, Jr., *The Liberation of Life* (New York: Cambridge University Press, 1981).
   A. R. Peacocke, *Creation and the World of Science* (Oxford: Clarendon Press, 1979).
   --------------------------------------, ed., *The Sciences and Theology in the Twentieth Century* (Notre Dame: Univ. of Notre Dame Press, 1981).
   Hoimar Von Ditfurth, *The Origins of Life, Evolution as Creation* (San Francisco: Harper and Row, 1982).
   N. Max Wildiers, *The Theologian and His Universe, Theology and Cosmology from the Middle Ages to the Present* (New York: Seabury, 1982).

Chapter Fifteen

TEILHARD AND THE NATURAL ENVIRONMENT
Pierre Teilhard de Chardin's Contribution to the Christian Understanding of the World and to Human Relationships Within the Natural Environment

Conrad Bonifazi

Teilhard de Chardin died before we were overtaken by our ecological sensitivity, so that concern for behavior patterns vis-à-vis the natural world seemed not to occupy the forefront of his mind. However, his scientific and metaphysical exploits, his observation of the earth's crust and its hidden treasures, and the religious thinking he brought to their interpretation constitute a major challenge to theological scholarship. His contribution to the Christian understanding of the world was to reject the foundation upon which it rested, and to set in its place a new world view.

Hidden beneath all scholarship, below all of our ways of thinking, lies a fundamental presupposition controlling all our thought—theological, philosophical, and scientific—about God and creation. It is our understanding of the nature of the cosmos. In *Process and Reality*, A. N. Whitehead confirms this assumption and at the same time underlines—no doubt unwittingly—Teilhard's great intellectual effort, when he says:

> The theme of Cosmology which is the basis of all religions is the story of the dynamic effort of the world passing into everlasting unity, and of the static majesty of God's vision, accomplishing its purpose of completion by absorption of the World's multiplicity of effort.[1]

A vital theology presupposes a sensitive grasp of the nature of our experience of reality, and those who "do" theology should clearly recognize the cosmological and anthropological foundations upon which their structures rest. The theological pronouncements still often rely upon a medieval world view, or reckon only partly with our modern experience of reality. Teilhard held that in this century it was not enough to show that faith and knowledge do not ultimately oppose one another. It is not a matter of reconciling a conflict, but of establishing a new synthesis. Making a few corrections here and there is of small consequence; what is needed, he believed, was a thorough rethinking of Christianity within the framework of our present understanding of the world. A favorite but suspect term with theologians has been the word "radical," but their radicality has seldom penetrated the cosmological and anthropological strata beneath their own discipline. Teilhard believed in the mutually complementary character of faith and reason, and that science and religion point ultimately in the same direction; for him this convergence opened the way to new synthesis.

Two themes seem to dominate Teilhard's work: one is the place of human beings within the totality of nature, and the other is the significance of Christ both for the human race and the entire cosmos. He recognized that humans belong to this world but that they do not always seem to be at home here. We are creatures characterized by self-consciousness and freedom, yet surrounded by a material world in which neither of these qualities may be met.

Evolution has taught us that we emerged from this planet and were not imported into it, so that we have to ask, "How can something unselfconscious produce beings who are aware of themselves, and how can freedom spring from unfreedom?" Spatially and materially, the human race occupies hardly any place at all in comparison with the whole of the cosmos. It vibrates on the surface of a planet orbiting a medium-sized star, of which there are millions! Yet how is it, paradoxically, that these humans can reach out in all directions into the cosmos and study it? Our self-consciousness, co-extensive with all that we know, differentiates us from everything else; our self-awareness is limited to our bodies, but reveals simultaneously an almost unlimited character in that it expands into all time and space.

Philosophies and theologies have tried to reconcile this duality of body and mind, and Teilhard has contributed an explanation from the viewpoint of evolution. According to him, the sciences have hitherto omitted human beings as such from their calculations. Of course, humans have been analyzed and laboriously examined, but they have been regarded as beyond the scope of science when considered as spiritual or personal wholes, as though personality were not an aspect of evolutionary change. Inasmuch as humans, in their totality, also belong to the world of phenomena, Teilhard tried to broaden our understanding of evolution to include the biological *and* the spiritual dimensions of humankind.

Attempts to explain our material origins have led to the view that we are accidentally and anomalously here, and therefore the most astounding quality in the universe has been reduced to an epiphenomenon. Consciousness and freedom are considered to be irregularities in the normal unfolding of things, fringe phenomena from which nothing may be deduced as to the nature of matter or of the world. But Teilhard gratefully recalled that some discoveries such as that of radium, at first thought to be an "interesting irregularity,"[2] turned out to provide pivotal data leading to a new estimate of the nature of the world. He therefore asks: Do the phenomena of freedom and self-awareness, which have generally been regarded as exceptional or secondary, constitute a central datum through which matter and the cosmos might be conceived of in an entirely new way? Teilhard's magnum opus, *The Phenomenon of Man*, tries to make this thesis plausible.

We have been taught by the sciences to regard the world as an evolutive event, as a process in which new phenomena continue to appear. The sciences also measure their observations and seek to express them in terms of *laws*. Recognizing that evolutive change has branched out in many directions, and developed in seemingly capricious ways, so that accidental circumstances came to play significant roles in its unfolding, Teilhard asks whether this process follows a pattern of law, or evinces a particular drift or direction. He thinks it does. On the whole it shows movement towards greater complexity of organization and an accompanying increase of consciousness. In its totality the cosmos is informed by a *law of complexity*.

This is by no means a far-fetched conclusion, but its interpretation presents us with a dilemma. Starting from matter again, we may still decide that humans are anomalous and epiphenomenal, freaks on the fringe of reality, or we can begin with self-consciousness as a fundamental datum. Teilhard started there: not that he thought evolution pursued a direct course to the human condition, but that it found justification in the intrinsic worth of self-awareness as a phenomenon surpassing all others. In his essay, *How I*

Believe, he says:

> We should use the following as an absolute principle of appraisal in
> our judgements: "It is better, no matter what the cost, to be more
> conscious than less conscious." This principle, I believe, is the
> absolute condition of the world's existence.[3]

This does not alter the course of evolution; it simply changes our
view of it. What in the former hypothesis was thought to be a basic
reality is now judged to be precursory condition; the anomalous
circumstance becomes the pivot upon which everything turns.
Teilhard did not disfigure the phenomena; he simply changed our
perspective. Then, with the help of the hypothesis that, potentially or actually, a psychic dimension is present in matter, it is possible to see evolution as a stream of events in which two dimensions are discernible: one of outwardness or growing physical complexity, and another of inwardness or growing psychism, both of
which reach a high point in human beings. And life continues; its
human form may branch into something other, or humans may
transcend their present condition—so long as collective suicide
does not cut them off—to become super-beings.

In the twentieth century the idea of "superman" has lost its
earlier attractiveness, but Teilhard discerned a mounting feeling,
despite the difficulties—such as those presented by outmoded na-
tionalisms—of human solidarity, a reaching out through international organizations and institutions towards the possibility of
global understanding and cooperation. He beheld humankind on
the threshold of a new phase of social being, already engaged in a
movement towards the highest possible unity within which our
individual awarenesses would be more clearly delineated; or, as he
succinctly stated it: "union differentiates."[4]

This is not *pure* speculation. It represents a possible trajectory
along which the momentum of the past may carry the evolutive
drive. Not every cosmology or anthropology is congenial with the
Christian understanding of human dignity within a meaningful
creation. From Copernicus on, the growth of Western society,
despite protestations to the contrary, has encouraged the devaluation of human beings. But Teilhard's effort and intention is
directed towards the integration of the total human actuality—
biological and spiritual—into the structure of the cosmos. In
human beings, he believed, the real nature of the universe is revealed, and in *them* the deepest potentiality of matter comes to
fruition. In this reassessment of humankind's place in nature, he

changed the appearance of the world.

A theory of this kind has profound implications for theology, for it touches upon the dignity of human beings and contains elements which call for a reinterpretation of Christianity. Earlier attempts at the systematic presentation of the Christian faith were informed by a concept of hierarchical order. It had been borrowed from the cosmology of the day, and doctrines were interpreted as functions of this concept of order. Because of this resonance the scholastics and their successors reasoned convincingly in their time. In our century, Teilhard did not try to build a theology upon the natural sciences; his belief in the Incarnation preceded his inquiry. But even when human beings had been excluded from the scientific world view and their place in history was no longer assured, and they had been thrown back upon themselves (as the existentialists advised), Teilhard regarded these same sciences as preparing for a new integration of humanity into the cosmos and history.

The core concept of our time is evolution (emergence, growth, development) in every sphere. Teilhard undoubtedly sought the God of a world in becoming, and not a God of static order. The Christ in whom he believed informed the universe and was guiding it to completion. Teilhard's religion was one of advance—of humanity groping its way into the future. For him it was not a matter of how Christ had contributed to the enlightenment of our existence but of the function He performed in the total structure of reality as presently understood.

Teilhard was convinced that genuine theology implies a grasp of cosmic reality—not in the sense that cosmology yields tenets which together constitute a sort of cosmic religiosity, but in the sense that any faith, regardless of origins, is efficient and relevant only when it functions in the light of our total experience of the world. It is Teilhard's view, therefore, that in the history of Christian theology one era has closed and a new period has begun. Theologians of the previous era asked: What does Christ mean for a world which, though created in perfect order, was subsequently disrupted by original sin? And to this question they replied: The original order is restored in Christ. Teilhard would not consider this theological view unworthy, but simply outmoded and irrelevant. His question is: What does Christ signify for a world in evolution, seen now through Darwinian, Marxist, and Einsteinian eyes? What sort of place is this in which any theological speculation may occur? This new question preceding all theological thinking has now been posed and must lead to new answers.

Concerned with the evolutive world whose dynamic center, in the light of the natural sciences, is represented by the human race, Teilhard believed Christ to be related to the world not accidentally, but organically and structurally, so that creation and incarnation were not two independent aspects of reality, but the one culminated in the other.

There have been indications of this view throughout the tradition. Duns Scotus shared it in the thirteenth century. In a panel of a Byzantine mosaic of creation, located in St. Mark's basilica in Venice, the globe of the earth reflects like a mirror the face of Christ. In the nineteenth century, S. T. Coleridge asked, "Might not Christ *be* the world as revealed to human knowledge?" This slender thread of opinion reaches back to St. Paul who affirmed:

> Through him [Christ] the universe has been created, and unto him, as the final goal, it is tending. . . And in him as the binding and sustaining power, universal nature coheres and consists.[5]

Teilhard's originality does not lie in this reiteration of St. Paul's viewpoint, but in his binding it closely to an evolutive world. Cosmic structure, he said, postulated a personal center without which evolution would be denied its goal. In its human phase, Teilhard maintained, the cosmos shows a convergent character pointing towards an ultimate condition of the whole process, Point Omega—a cosmic unity within which individual awarenesses would be preserved and heightened. Teilhard questions whether we could muster the courage to strive after this unity and personalization if it were not a possibility, had absolutely no guarantee of success, or if some warranty of its realization were not already present.

By virtue of the world's dynamic structure we may conjecture that within this energy-source there exists a pole of attraction. For Teilhard, that energetic center exists in the person of Christ, whose return is awaited in the end-time. Thus, *Parousia* and Point Omega coincide. Their coincidence is a keystone in Teilhard's theological edifice, and it accentuates the close relationship between Christ and the cosmos. The world for Teilhard operates on a *"christic principle"*: Christ is the principle of unity (everything holds together in him); he is the principle of its energy (the world is a christogenesis; it is christ-forming) and the principle of its completion (in him all is finally affirmed in its completeness). In a word: *Christ and the cosmos constitute one whole.*

Think of the consequences of this for theology. In a static world the significant theological moments lie in the past. Of course, the past is immensely valuable in preparing for and illumining the future and, humanly speaking, we have no absolute assurance that the goal Teilhard set forth will be achieved. Our freedom allows the possibility that the enterprise might fail. The completion of a world-in-becoming is not laid upon us as a necessity; it is offered as a possibility which is unrealizable without our cooperation. Our care must therefore be for the personal growth of humankind. Our expectations of the future dare not be purely horizontal or purely transcendent. We cannot simply dream of an earthly paradise or alternately long for another world. We have to pursue the road of human development in the direction of a personal and global togetherness and so make possible our destiny.

This destiny may lie on another plane, but it is not on that account independent of present events. The *Parousia* is meaningful only when the planet and its people, by virtue of their unity and their personal condition, are ready for transformation: "When *we* are ready, he will come."

> The Parousia will be realized in a creation that has been taken to the climax of its capacity for union.[6]

Or, to quote St. Paul again:

> and when all things are subject to him [Christ], then the Son himself will also be made subordinate to God who made all things subject to him, and thus God will be all in all [*panta en pasin*].[7]

This theological emphasis upon the end-time, or Point Omega, is capable of giving new significance to all human effort. It is geared to creating a new awareness in Christians or even a new type of Christian: someone aware, in an evolving world, that he or she has a creative role to play, not only because Christ is the goal of creation, but also because, in everyone, Christ is the center of radiation of the energies which lead the universe towards God.[8] The whole world is a divine milieu; all human activity contains a cosmic dimension and an inner religious value; indeed, "the divine omnipresence in which we find ourselves plunged, is an omnipresence of action."[9] We are co-creators of the world, and in this task every corporate group according to its genius, and every individual, has personal contributions to make to its completion.

This theology points towards a new ethic and a new humanism. For centuries prescribed behaviour patterns have rested upon a concept of world-order which was said to express the wisdom and purpose of God. It was each person's job to track it down and follow it! Humanists pursued their ideal of striking a balance between mind and body, will and reason, and of achieving an harmonious development of all their gifts and faculties, and a refinement of literary and artistic taste.

Today, ethics and humanism must be motivated by the concept of growth, effort, and creative work; commensurate with a world-in-becoming they must be marked by a constant concern with the development of humankind and the growth of the world. The value of action should no longer be gauged by its agreement or non-agreement with a prescribed order; it should be measured by what it contributes to the progress of humanity and the growth of the world—understood as being "in Christ."

A further mark of this theological draft drawn by Teilhard is a vigorous personalism. The human person stands at the center of cosmic events. Study of the evolutionary past shows that events have led *in fact* to humankind. In human beings evolution has revealed its profoundest energy and significance. It has pursued a person-making function, and human beings constitute a climax of the process to date. This characteristic is illuminated by Teilhard's claim that Christ is the personal highpoint and driving force of the universe. In Christ the universe is characterized by a personal dimension; in him it is understood as though it were a living person, and as such may become the object of our love. As our bodies share in our being persons, so the whole universe participates in the personal being of its pivot and climax:

> One can say, in the last analysis (or rather in the last synthesis) that finally, the person is for the whole and not the whole for the human person. And it is so because in this ultimate instant the whole itself has become person.[10]

We are part of a *christified* world, a whole that has become person. The cosmos *is* the pleroma, the full complement, the whole story, the completeness, the clothing and the glory, the fullness— of God. Without Christ the world is incomplete, and Christ is incomplete without the world: together they are one whole as the head and members of a body constitute one whole. The mystical body of Christ has been thought of as the church; Teilhard conceives of it as the whole world. Christ is cosmic; in him the cosmos is a "super-person."

These thoughts illumine the character of Teilhard's mysticism.

Traditionally the mystics have sought union with God by turning *from* the world in its physical and moral sense. Teilhard believes differently. Rather than an obstacle to union with God, he sees the world as an appointed way to the goal: not world-denial but world-insight and affirmation are necessary presuppositions of union. For Teilhard, therefore, work as well as contemplation opens a way to union with God. In the dedication of ourselves to labor and study, science and technology, social and political activity, to the world—we unite ourselves with Christ. Love for the world and love for God fuse into one love. Teilhard does not deny the virtue of prayer and self-denial, yet his mysticism is one of earth and action.

In this setting we are faced with a new type of Christian whose love of God is expressed in givenness to some freely chosen, earthly pursuit; a person who stands open to new thinking regardless of its origin, and is allied with fellow mortals for the realization of new knowledge, greater social justice, and the personal or spiritual growth of the human race; someone who believes firmly that the cosmos to which we belong is not an absurd and senseless reality, but that it is rational and has a grandiose destiny.

Our age is frequently thought to be atheistic; Teilhard considered it to be a time which had not yet discovered a concept of God appropriate to it, and therefore one which endured an understanding of God bound up with an antiquated world view, bequeathed to it from the past, but not in accord with its own experience of reality. For the mysterious presence we sense in the world, this "diaphany of the divine," no adequate name has been found in our day, but Teilhard's work may be understood as an attempt to disclose it. His idea of God he sometimes called a "Christian pantheism," not because he disregarded transcendence, but because he wished to emphasize the presence of God everywhere, particularly in the creative process itself. He believed that God was immersed in creation and strove for its completion, and that the incarnation, like creation, was "an act co-extensive with the duration of the world."[12] Into what had become thoroughly a-cosmic god-talk, Teilhard reintroduced the universe!

In presenting these Teilhardian views it seemed appropriate to be positive rather than critical. Many questions may be posed. If theology should acquire a dimension reflecting a contemporary world view, how valid is Teilhard's understanding of the world? Does evolution converge? Does it fold in upon itself to produce increased consciousness? Is it a "spiritualizing" process? There is evidence for such views, and Teilhard's system rests upon it, but there can be no room for dogmatism.

However, when others were *de*mythologizing, Teilhard *re*mythologized, and did so with foresight, wisdom, hope and love of the world. At a time when the planet was being dishonored, he was drawing attention to its divinity. His personal model of the creative processes as a christogenesis, and the end-time as the manifestation of a *Theosphere*[13] should be judged neither true nor false: they should be considered, at least, as a myth for the realization of the dignity and wholeness of the earth. This marriage of mythology to practicality is of vital importance to us all, and Teilhard asks us to consider the future of humankind and its lonely, cosmic habitat—a task to which Christian theology, in its own idiom, might not unwisely or fruitlessly apply itself.

Notes

In preparing this paper I wish to pay tribute to my friend Dr. N. Max Wildiers, whose interpretation of Teilhard over the years, and particularly in his *Weltbild und Theologie* (Zurich: Benzinger, 1974), has been of great value and inspiration.

1. Alfred North Whitehead, *Process and Reality: An Essay in Cosmology*, corrected edition, David Ray Griffin and Donald W. Sherburne, eds. (New York: The Free Press, 1978) part 5, a.2.,5.
2. Pierre Teilhard de Chardin, *Man's Place in Nature* (New York: Harper and Row, 1966), pp. 17-18.
3. Teilhard, *How I Believe* (New York: Harper Perennial Library, 1969) p. 35.
4. Teilhard, *The Phenomenon of Man* (New York: Harper Torchbooks, 1961), p. 262 and *Human Energy* (New York: Harcourt, Brace, Jovanovich, 1979), pp. 29-31.
5. Colossians 1.15-20 passim (translation, J. B. Lightfoot).
6. Teilhard, *Science and Christ* (New York: Harper and Row, 1969), p. 84.
7. I Corinthians 15.28.
8. Teilhard, *The Divine Milieu* (New York: Harper Torchbooks, 1968), p. 123.
9. Ibid., p. 122.
10. *Human Energy*, pp. 29-31.
11. Teilhard, *Writings in Time of War* (New York: Harper and Row, 1968), p. 60.
12. *Science and Christ*, p. 64.
13. *Human Energy*, p. 160.

Chapter Sixteen

A PROCESS-RELATIONAL CONCEPTION OF CREATION

Bernard M. Loomer

The ensuing reconception of the doctrine of creation owes much
of its formation to the philosophic labors of Henri Bergson, William
James, S. Alexander, John Dewey, A. N. Whitehead, Charles
Pierce, G. H. Mead, and Charles Hartshorne. From their writings
there has emerged, amid some important differences in method
and content, a new philosophic perspective, an alternative way of
looking at things that seems to be consonant with much of modern
scientific thought. This mode of thought may be described as process-relational in character and style. This essay is undertaken in
the spirit of this general point of view.

A brief introduction to this mode of thought is in order. It contains two elemental notions which are foundational for this recon-
structive effort. These are: (1) the ultimacy of becoming, and (2)
the givenness and primordiality of relationships. Creation can be
understood most simply as a result of the interplay of these two
elements—in a manner to be explained presently.

The principle of the ultimacy of becoming translates into the
proposition that the final actualities of the world are specific processes of becoming. These processes are individual units of energy
with varying degrees of extensiveness. These units become synthesized individuals with particular forms and structures. This
process is their becoming.

This principle can also be expressed in personalistic imagery.
Since "becoming is the becoming of experience" (Whitehead)
these instances of becoming may be called concrete occasions of
experience. These occasions may be understood as momentary instances of individuality or selfhood. They are transient and epi-
sodic in their duration. These occasions are superseded by other

instances of becoming so as to create an historic and causal route of occasions. This historic route is called an event. An event is a relatively permanent and complex organization of energy. In everyday usage, when we refer to an individual we normally have in mind an enduring person and not a self as a momentary occasion.

As units of energy these instances of becoming are the very "stuff" of existence. They constitute the "substantial" side of things. The individual process of becoming is the concrete actual reality. The actuality consists of the becoming. All else, forms, structures, and qualities, are components of processes.

There is nothing more basic or ultimate than processes of becoming. That is, events do not occur to something that is not an event. They do not "rest upon" or presuppose something more "substantial" or "real" or elemental than themselves. Becoming is the foundational category. All other categories refer either to internal aspects of occasions of becoming or to the relations between occasions (or events). Also—becomingness itself does not become.

The principle of the givenness and primordiality of relations means not only that the connections between events are given along with the events. It entails the further point that events (or occasions) are emergents from causally efficacious relations, that causal relations are constitutive components of events. Relations are the carriers whereby the energy of past events is transmitted to the present. Causal relations are the means through which one event is present in the life of another event.

This principle can be expressed in terms of what is by now a commonplace understanding within the social sciences. The relational character of these processes of becoming means that individuals are not self-existing and completely self-dependent and self-determining. They are communal individuals who are both dependent and independent, at once both free and determined.

Individuals create and are created by societies. Individuals live within societies, obviously. But equally clearly societies have their being within and amid the lives of their constitutive membership. A society has a defining characteristic because of the interrelatedness of its members wherein the defining form is derived by each member from the causal and determining influences of other members.

Also—like the condition of becoming, interrelatedness or interdependence does not become or emerge. It is a given metaphysical condition of existence. It is primordial.

In order to understand more fully the distinctiveness of this modern conception, it may be helpful to establish a basis for contrast by presenting the essentials of the traditional doctrine.

I. A Traditional View of Creation

In this older pre-evolution point of view, God created the world and all its creatures. This was the act of a God who transcends the world in much the same way that an artist transcends his paintings or a first cause transcends its many effects. The being of this God is independent of the being of the world, as the energy and resources of God are other than the energy and resources of the world.

One Greek version of this tradition holds that this creator God is like an artisan, say a potter. He creates using the materials at hand. Or he shapes the materials, but he is not the creator of the materials. His creative labors are therefore limited by the nature of the available resources.

On the other hand, some orthodox Christian theologians insist that the correct understanding of God's work as creator begins with the notion that God created the world "out of nothing." This interpretation suggests that God is responsible not only for the world that was created, but also for the nature of the materials used in the act of creating, and for the character of the conditions in which life is lived. This viewpoint is designed to buttress the contention that God is sovereign over all aspects of creation and that even the destructiveness of the forces of evil is subject to God's lordship and control. In this perspective God is still considered to be both all-good and all-powerful.

The tradition also holds to the doctrine of the "goodness of creation." This doctrine often emerges in the context of a discussion of sex. The claim concerning the goodness of creation functions to counteract judgments of the kind which contend that sex is evil because it is an expression of bodily passion.

The doctrine of the goodness of creation involves the principle that the given and unalterable conditions which permeate our natural and historical forms of life are to be understood as expressions of the wisdom and power of God. These conditions are unalterable at least to the extent that they seem to be impervious to attempted changes rooted in our own desires.

For example: In order to sustain life, species feed on other species for food. Secondly, the fact of our mortality would seem to mean it is good that we die, that death is not an affront to the human spirit, that death is not our enemy. The fact of our mortality would seem to suggest that the meaning of our lives, both as individuals and as a species, is not synonymous with life's meaning.

Thirdly, sex is an impulse or a compulsion driving us to relationships with others, usually others of the opposite sex. On the one hand, it is a relentless procreative mechanism to effect the survival of the species. On the other hand, it is a profound witness to the fact of our interrelatedness.

Fourthly, it was Reinhold Niebuhr who insisted that the dialectic of history is such that every advance in creative goodness brings with it the possibility for greater evil.

In this traditional interpretation of the goodness of creation, ambiguity is a state that bespeaks compromise. It signifies the lesser. It is a condition to be overcome or transcended. It is something to be expected but also regretted.

In traditional theology human beings seem to be viewed, by and large, as the peak of creation. We seem to be the final aim of God's purpose in creation. With our bodies we participate in nature, but with our minds and our spirits we transcend nature. Apparently only we are made in God's image. In one way or another this image reflects God's transcendence and freedom. In a secondary sense the image also reflects God's wisdom, goodness, and power. The interrelatedness of life is not part of the image of God, probably because it is not part of the reality of this traditional God.

As made in God's image, as transcendent of nature, we in the western world came to understand ourselves as having dominion over sub-human creatures. We could name them and thereby gain some control over them. Within the limits of our knowledge and power nature became a large means to our human ends. We became the measure of value.

Except for such notions as the kingdom of God, conventional understanding, and the tradition of the suffering servant, this view of creation did not give rise to a social conception of reality. The interconnectedness of life (if and when it was found to exist) apparently was interpreted as a product of love's outreach. In short, it is a non-ecological view of creation in which history has a primacy over nature, and freedom is dominant over interrelatedness.

II. Creation and the Web of Life

The process-relational mode of thought is a naturalistic interpretation of life. In this way of looking at things no resource is had

to transcendental or supernatural cause, explanations, or resources. Rather, the world of experience is regarded as self-sufficient with respect to the "hows" and "whys" of explanation. In
this outlook the "reasons" for things are found within the ways
events behave and relate. Things are as they are because. . . that's
the way they are. Since "explanation is the analysis of coordina-
tion," explanations are finally forms of description.

In contrast with the spirit and outlook of the tradition, this form
of naturalistic thought maintains that the being of the world is the
being of God, that the energy, resources, and graces of the world
are the energy, resources, and graces of God. Some may prefer to
invert these meanings. Those who do may also prefer to say that
everything is in God, rather than that God is in everything.

In the viewpoint being presented here, God is identified with
either the whole or a part of the world. The choice is not casual. It
depends on the status that one ascribes to the fact of ambiguity,
and whether one is concerned to overcome the bifurcation between good and evil. If you have a passion to guard God's purity
and if you believe that ambiguity, like tragedy, is ultimately trans-
cendable, then undoubtedly you will choose to identify God with
a segment of the world. If you believe, as I do, that the bifurcation
between good and evil should be overcome, and that goodness
without ambiguity tends to become entropic, then you will tend to
identify God and the totality of the world.

Near the beginning of this essay it was stated that, in terms of
the mode of thought being presented, creation is a function of the
interplay between becomingness and relationality (or interrelatedness), the two elemental categories of this point of view. To
put the point differently, but equally abstractly, creation is the
dynamic consequence of the interaction between the "one and the
many."

It was also said earlier that becoming is the becoming of
experience. "Experience" is a process of synthesizing into one
concrete unity the energies derived from the many events in the
immediate past of the process of unification in question. When the
process of synthesis is completed, when it has become a definite
unity and its becoming is over, then it no longer is a present event.
It is now in the past, in the immediate past. But its energy is not
thereby lost or destroyed. Rather it is now able to contribute aspects of itself toward the creation of future occasions and events.
It projects its energy in the form of causal relations which are
efficacious in the formation of occasions which supersede it. As

present events we perceive or "experience" past events as we are created by them. Each occasion comes into existence from an impulse beyond itself.

In this process of becoming synthetic unities of energies, including all the qualitative dimensions of life, we make our own contributions to our creation. This is the basis of our uniqueness. Our spirit may be defined in terms of *how* we respond to what has been given to us. We are not just *what* we are. We are also, and perhaps more significantly, *how* we are.

From this all-too-brief account of the process of creation it can be seen that all creatures are relational organisms. The fact of our interrelatedness is inherent within the process of our creation and fulfillment. This is why the primordiality of relationships was stressed in characterizing this mode of thought.

By generalizing these notions we arrive at the conception that the world is an indefinitely extended web of interrelated events. This web includes all forms of life and levels of existence. This web of life, including its possibilities, contains the energies, the resources, and the graces of existence. The web is the context of all creation. It is the widest and most inclusive meaning of "nature." The web grows but it does not become. It is primordiality given. It is the cosmic embodiment of the primordial covenant between God and all of creation.

III. Some Contrasts

Given this conception of creation and of the web, there are some entailments of this position which provide some interesting contrasts between the older and the newer views of creation.

In the first place, and contrary to certain strong emphasis within the tradition, interdependence is not grounded upon love. Rather the reverse is the case—at least to an appreciable degree. Our interrelatedness derives from our common membership within the web of life. Love may create relationships of interdependence in concrete instances, but love does not create the elemental condition of interdependence. That is given within our inner constitutions.

Love is binding upon us for the same reason, namely that we are all birthright members of the web. We are to love others because they are "other" and valuable and because our lives are bound up with theirs. Their fulfillment is also our enrichment, and their impoverishment is also our diminution.

Without interdependence love is not binding or obligatory—at least not fully so. The idea that we are to love another simply because he or she is bound up with the lives of others and the life of God, is an inadequate notion. Without membership within the web of life, John Donne's teaching that we should "never ask for whom the bells tolls" is without adequate warrant.

Secondly, there is the contrast between interrelatedness and order. Some people maintain that there is one world because there is a common order. This is analogous to saying that a society is composed of those who exhibit the same defining characteristic. This statement is true as a very abstract rendering of what is involved. The members of a society exhibit the same defining characteristic because each member has been shaped by causal relations derived from other members. This description constitutes a more concrete account of the nature of a society. The members of the society belong together because they require each other and because they create each other.

Analogously, a world bound together under a common order has an abstract kind of unity. A world bound by the ties of causal interrelationships in a web of interdependence has a more concrete unity.

Interconnectedness is the concrete condition. Order, whether physical, rational, moral, or aesthetic, is an abstraction from interrelatedness. The God who (or which) is correlated with order is a static form, an abstract entity. The God correlated with interrelatedness is a dynamic efficacious actuality.

Thirdly, the presence of the web implies that our primary self-definition as human beings should not be in terms of our transcendence of nature. Obviously we have capacities and qualities and freedoms that other creatures do not possess. Yet we can exist only within the web and we need to acknowledge that "nature" includes us.

The further implication is that we are not the measure of meaning and value. The web in its dynamic evolution is the full criterion, difficult as it may be to make sense of that proposition. To put the point a little differently, to insist on attempting to justify the ways of God (or the web) to man is probably an idolatrous undertaking. It is to subsume the web under the human. A trust in the web involves a commitment to life and not to our conception of the meaning of life.

Fourthly, the identification of God with the web of life, and the notion that creation occurs within the context of the web, suggests that creation is ambiguous and not simply "good." The effort to overcome the bifurcation between good and evil, in order to help create individuals and societies of greater stature, leads us to reconsider the role of ambiguity.

There is ambiguity within the web because: (1) the strength that created our virtues is over-played and our virtues become vices; (2) our motives are mixed; and (3) our "dark side" is an important component of the total self.

Ambiguity can be viewed in a wholly negative manner, as a state of affairs to be overcome. There is not the space to develop the topic here, but ambiguity can be understood as a creative functioning. It confounds the good and yet prevents the good from becoming entropic.

Without providing an adequate warrant, I yet suggest the tentative conclusion that the principle of ambiguity needs to be placed close to the center of ecological thought.

Chapter Seventeen

PROCESS THEOLOGY AND AN ECOLOGICAL MODEL

John B. Cobb, Jr.

During the past decade people have become aware of the dangers to the human future resulting from exploitation of the environment. This exploitation has been consistent with both the dominant economic theories and the dominant theologies of the nineteenth and twentieth centuries. Ideally these theories called for treatment of all human beings as ends rather than as means, but the power of the dominant theories has been such that their objectifying categories are readily extended to human beings. People, too, become resources, and the term human resources has become prevalent. In practice powerless human beings and powerless societies have been treated as resources for exploitation by those who have the economic and political power to establish goals and to pursue them. In response to this situation, the task cannot be simply to improve practice in light of existing theory. It must be to change the theory. And because our theory, both in economics and theology, has both shaped and expressed our dominant perceptions and sensibility, it is necessary to change our vision of reality as well.

Process thought has been protesting for some time against some of the features of our dominant practice, theory, and sensibility which are now more widely recognized as damaging. In particular, process thought has offered an alternative to the dominant dualisms of soul and body, spirit and nature, mind and matter, self and other. It should be able to speak with some relevance to the contemporary situation. The theology which has appropriated these contributions of process thought is often called "process theology."

The dominant thinker behind the distinctive approach of process theology is the English mathematician-philosopher Alfred North Whitehead (1861-1947). He taught at Harvard University during his later years and has had his largest following in the United States. In his most important book, his Gifford Lectures of 1927-1928, entitled *Process and Reality,* he proposed a "philosophy of organism." By this he meant that the actual entities of which the world is ultimately made up are better thought of as organisms than as material or mental substances.

The main significance of the idea of organism here is that each entity exists only in its relation to its environment. One cannot think first of an entity and then, incidentally, of its relation to the rest of the world. On the contrary, every entity is relational in its most fundamental nature. It is constituted by its relations. Even in thought it cannot be abstracted from them.

Professor L. Charles Birch, an Australian biologist active in the World Council of Churches, and I authored *The Liberation of Life* (Cambridge University Press, 1981), in which we develop this point. We call ours an ecological model of living things, and we show that this model fits the evidence of biological science better than the substantialist, the materialist, and mechanist models that have dominated their development. The ecological model is also more appropriate to field, relativity, and quantum theory in physics. There are a number of converging trends in the natural sciences that support a Whiteheadian, ecological understanding of nature.

If process thought accepted a dualism between humanity and nature, a changed world view would not seem very important theologically. But those who follow Whitehead understand human beings as part of nature. The ecological model applies to us as well. Human experience, too, is constituted by its relations with the body, with other people, and with nonhuman creatures.

Three further clarifications of the meaning of these assertions for theology, as well as for the natural sciences, are needed. First, the ecological model depicts the actual entities as events rather than as objects that exist through time. An event occurs in its fullness and is over. Whereas our previous models have usually explained events by the motions of atoms and particles, the ecological model explains atoms and particles as well as tables and mountains, in terms of events. The explanation is finally sought at the level of the ultimate, individual unit events into which larger events can be analyzed. These include subatomic events but also momentary human experiences. Whitehead called these unit events "actual occasions" or "occasions of experience." The world is a vast field of actual occasions within which there emerge relatively enduring patterns of many varieties. The atom, the subatomic particle, the table, and the mountain are all societies of actual occasions with relatively enduring patterns. A human person is too.

Second, our usual ideas of such dualities as mental and physical or subjective and objective are derived from reflection about societies of actual occasions, such as atoms and mountains, wrongly supposed to be substances. These ideas cannot be applied to events or occasions. Mind and matter, as conceived according to these usual ideas, do not exist. But understood more loosely, "mental" and "physical" aspects can be found in every occasion whatsoever. Every occasion is a synthesis of features derived from its environing world. In this sense it is physical. Because this synthesis is not merely the mechanical product of the forces that impinge upon it, because it includes an element of selectivity and self-determination, we can also say that the occasion has a mental aspect. There are no purely mental occasions and no purely physical ones. There are only occasions in which the element of self-origination is relatively important and others in which it is negligible.

Similarly, when we think of subjects and objects in the usual way, we cannot say that an event or occasion is a subject or that it is an object. As it takes place it is the locus of subjectivity, that is, it receives the activity of the past, and it, in its turn, acts. It is subject to the action of other events, and it is an agent determining its response to these influences and, thereby, its effects upon the world. It actively takes account of its world. When it has taken place, it becomes part of the objective world in which other occasions occur. All occasions are "subjects" in the moment of their occurrence and "objects" for other occasions as soon as they are over.

Third, every occasion in some measure transcends its world. It transcends it, first, simply by being a new occasion. No occasion can recur. However similar an occasion may be to antecedent ones, it is a different entity. In addition, no occasion is qualitatively identical with any other. It cannot be, because no two occasions have the same spatio-temporal locus, and every locus defines a different environment or world. Since this world enters constitutively into the occasion, the occasion must be qualitatively unique.

Further, as already noted, no occasion is the mere product of its world. However much the world of the occasion determines its character, the exact form of the occasion is decided only when it happens. Every occasion transcends its world by determining just how it constitutes itself out of that world. And, finally, many occasions, indeed, all living occasions, constitute themselves not only out of the world of past occasions, but also out of the world of possibility of the Not Yet. They transcend their world by incorporating possibilities derived, not from it, but from God. This need not involve conscious choice, but it can, and in the human case it often does. This is the context in which we can speak meaningfully of freedom.

Those who are accustomed to contrast material or merely phenomenal nature with human existence as spiritual may be shocked by the insistence of process thought that human beings are part of an inclusive eco-system. But it is well to recall that the dualism of the human and the natural is a modern one. For the Bible there is the one world of creatures of which human beings are a part. The welfare of humanity and the welfare of other creatures are interdependent. Process theologians rejoice that Christians are beginning to recover the sense of the unity of creation against the modern philosophical dualism of spirit and nature.

Neither for the Bible nor for process theologians does the insistence that human beings are part of the world of creatures mean that we are not distinctive. Human experiences are the most valuable of all the events on this planet, but they are not the only loci of value. In Genesis God declares all other creatures good even before and apart from the creation of human beings, and process theologians share this biblical conviction. But human beings are created in the image of God, and process theologians agree that we share in God's power of creation in quite unique ways. As Genesis indicates, we exercise a unique power over all the other creatures. Hence we are responsible for the welfare of the whole created order on this planet as no other creature could be. That we are exercising that power so extensively for the degradation of the biosphere as well as the oppression of our powerless sisters and brothers expresses the depth of our betrayal of God's trust.

The doctrine of God to which this brings us is at the center of process theology. It is above all Charles Hartshorne who has developed this aspect of process thought. Process theology has been very critical of some features of classical theism. That theism often pictures God as an immutable substance, whereas process theologians see God as the most perfect exemplification of the ecological model. Divine perfection does not consist in being totally self-contained and unaffected by creaturely joy and suffering but in being totally open, totally receptive, and perfectly responsive. God, too, is constituted by relations to all things. In the case of God, these relations are complete and express the perfection of love. Through this perfection of relations, what is perpetually perishing in the world attains everlastingness in the divine life. The threat to meaning that is inherent in transience is thereby overcome.

Too often, also, classical theism has spoken of God's power in a way that suggests the control of a tyrant or a dictator. It is thought that everything that happens in the world, even an earthquake or a war, must express the will of God. Many have turned against this God, and process theologians do so, too. But process theologians do not go to the extreme of asserting that God is powerless and is to be found only in suffering. God is certainly found there, but God is found also in a child's enjoyment of play, in the joy of a happy marriage, and in the creative ecstasy of an artist. Process theology teaches that God's power is perfect and that perfect power is not coercive. Following the biblical image of parental power, we see that coercion expresses the failure of power, not its perfection. God's power lies in the gift to every occasion of some measure of transcendence or freedom and in the call to employ that freedom in love. It is this gift and call which have brought into being all that is good in our world; indeed, they have created our world. But creatures, and especially human creatures, resist the gift of freedom and abuse it. God does not will the evil which we thereby bring about.

The language of process theology about God often leads readers to suppose that process theologians are optimistic, and it is true that they are hopeful. They hope because the giver of freedom and direction is always surprising us. The future cannot be foreseen. It is not just the unfolding of the past. It is the place where the new can be received if we will accept it. However bleak the projections of past trends into the future, we hope for a new heaven and a new earth.

But we do not *expect* what we hope for. More likely appears the self-destruction of the human race. There is no God of the sort to whom we can turn to intervene and stop our headlong pursuit of death. God calls us to life, but God does not intervene to close the door of death, if that is what we choose. God suffers with us in our self-inflicted destruction, and what is of value even there gains everlasting meaning in the life of God. But our self-destruction will deny to God all that the ongoing of human history might have contributed. The evil of our willful refusal to follow God's call has consequences of ultimate importance for us, for our fellow creatures, and for God.

Process theologians believe that this understanding of a God of persuasive love who calls us to freedom and concern for one another is the one to which we are drawn in Jesus Christ. But there is no one Christological formulation that is required by this vision. Some seek to clarify the distinctiveness of the way God was present in the human Jesus and uniqueness of the power of the Christ-event in shaping history. Others think that interest in the human Jesus is misplaced and that Christians should affirm the truth that is given to them through the kerygma without seeking to go behind it.

This illustrates the nature of process theology. It is not a specific doctrinal position. On most doctrines process theologians differ widely. In this respect it is to be compared with "idealist theology" or "existentialist theology" rather than with Calvinist theology or Anglican theology. It brings to bear on the whole range of theological doctrines a certain approach and a certain way of understanding God, human beings, and other creatures—a way it believes responsibly translates the biblical vision in the modern world. It invites theologians with varied confessional commitments to work out their doctrines in the context.

Process theology developed chiefly at the Divinity School of the University of Chicago. During the first three decades of this century that school was committed to socio-historical research in the service of the social gospel. During the 1930s it became more philosophical, and the influence of Alfred North Whitehead grew. The concerns for political freedom, peace, and justice did not disappear, but they ceased to control the theological program. The dominant emphasis among the theologians was on empirical, rational, and speculative approaches to understanding God and God's relationship to human beings. The label, "process theology," came to be used during the sixties to emphasize the rejection of static and substantial modes of thought.

When the 1960s brought renewed concern for human liberation as the focus of Christian theology, most process theologians recognized that their work had become too theoretical and abstract. During the past decade they have made efforts to display the relevance of their cosmological vision to the practical needs of the church. Thus far success has been greatest in relation to interfaith dialogue, ecology, feminism, and pastoral work. Much remains to be done especially in relation to the world of politics, although a beginning has been made there as well.

The claim of process theology is not that it offers a completed position in which the theological quest can come to rest. Instead the claim is that the Newtonian world view has too much shaped the habits of mind of natural scientists, economist philosophers, and theologians, and that contemporarty natural science and philosophy offer promise of a much more supportive context within which Christian faith can come to expression. Indeed, the sharp boundaries between theologies and other disciplines, forced on theology by the Newtonian world view and an accompanying historicism, can be replaced by a collaborative quest for truth in the service of life.

Process theologians feel great urgency about the issues they raise. There is real danger that most theology is growing increasingly out of touch with the cutting edge of thought in other disciplines and the new sensibility in Western culture. Theology is becoming a bulwark of an anthropocentric thinking that is no longer persuasive or positive in its effects. It is likely to remain "modern" when the more sensitive portions of our society have become "post-modern." Yet the faith to which it is responsible is far more congenial to the post-modern sensibility than to the modern one. To process theologians it seems ironic and painful that the church is now being rejected for its commitments to a modernity which is uncongenial to its own spirit.

But the problem is not only one of the church's increasingly making itself irrelevant in a context in which it could thrive. It is also that the church's efforts to express its faith in action are often partly misdirected. One example must suffice.

Christians are rightly concerned to stand with the weak and to support the aspirations of the oppressed. But the dominant modern Christian perception of the weak and oppressed reflects the commitment of Christian theology to "history," understood in terms of the rise of civilization, that is, of cities and, in modern times, of urban-industrial development. The dualism of history and nature relegates agriculture to the nature which is exploited for the sake of history. Along with agriculture we relegate the peasant villages in which even now the majority of the world's poor and oppressed still live. When we think of rural development we still conceive of industrializing agriculture to produce surplus for export. Subsistence farming is not even counted when we measure gross national product. It is not surprising that the lot of the masses of neglected peasants grows more desperate. Their only hope is to migrate to the slums of the vast cities; for only there is their existence even noticed.

Process theology asks the church to attend to the soil and the whole life system apart from which the great superstructure of industrial society cannot exist. As it attends to the soil, it will attend also to those who live closest to the soil. Our faith should prevent us from treating these people and their village life as obstacles to industrial development or as resources to be exploited for such development. They need help in growing firewood and using it effectively so that they can continue to cook their food. They need help in improving their farming methods so that they can not only feed themselves but also others. They need help rejecting the lure of fast profits at the expense of the sustainability of their farms. They need education for the improvement of village life rather than as a means of escape to the "true" life of government and business. They need to be given a sense of hopeful future in their villages and empowered to realize it, so that they will not simply swell the masses of the unemployed in the cities. We will recognize the high priority of such help only as we recover an Old Testament sense of the community of humanity with other living beings.

Process theology does not see itself as in competition with all other forms of theology. It hopes to contribute to political theology and liberation theology—not to oppose them. It has learned much from existentialist theology and hopes only to set its contributions in a larger context. It recognizes affinities with Indian and Chinese modes of thought and hopes to enrich Christianity by interpreting the insights of the Orient in a way that Christians can appreciate and employ. In general it hopes to serve the church by showing that faith in Christ can free us to draw together the many diverse, and too often competing, truths that divide people of good will in our world.

Chapter Eighteen

THOMAS MERTON'S VISION OF THE NATURAL WORLD

Ken Butigan

The works of the American Cistercian monk Thomas Merton, written over the course of nearly three decades, reveal a continually maturing vision of the life of spirit. Seeking increasingly to acknowledge and respond to the infinite source of this life, Merton's evolving spirituality became a creative activity which took a wide range of human concerns as its raw materials. A gifted diagnostician, Merton analyzed and interpreted numerous spiritual, philosophical, literary, cultural, and political issues, often exploring the fundamental *religious* questions which they posed for contemporary humanity. Existentialism, war, social injustice, the history of monasticism, William Faulkner and Flannery O'Connor and Boris Pasternak, the mass society, nonviolence, South American poets, nuclear weapons, and so on—Merton took up each of these subjects with great energy and frequently with astonishing insight.

It is with the same enthusiasm that Merton wrote of the physical environment. Though he never produced a fully articulated "theology of nature," Merton exhibited a strong interest in the natural world and in humankind's relationship to that world. Natural symbolism abounds in Merton's poetry, and often his prose essays draw and reflect on environmental images and settings, especially those which are explicitly autobiographical (e.g., his article, "Day of a Stranger").

The repeated presence of such imagery in Merton's writings certainly indicates his attentiveness to the physical world. These images function in Merton's work neither to "dress up" his works nor to cast them in a romantic or pastoral light. Though Merton was a poet and had been influenced by Romanticism, his primary aim was not to create a "nature mystique." Rather, his natural symbolism nearly always focused one of his "foundational insights" about human existence. Put another way, it means that Merton's use of such imagery was shaped by that vision—a vision which, in turn, grounded what might be called Merton's "spirituality of the environment."

For Thomas Merton, the universe is radically mysterious. Its immensity, depth, ceaseless transformation, its patterns of life and death disclose the inexhaustible mystery of Being. This mystery, embedded in the heart of all things, both signifies and participates in the gracious mystery of God's life, and draws its final value from that life. Born in the midst of this mystery—and fundamentally constituted by it—human beings continually encounter the mysterious character of their lives. Change, interpretation and transpersonal relationships, the origins of thought and imagination, existence itself—each of these is rooted in mystery and therefore confronts human persons with the "faces" of mystery, including novelty, fecundity, radical strangeness *and* radical familiarity, and overwhelming abundance.

The natural world, Merton maintains, is just such a bearer of mystery. When, in the early 1950s, he led the campaign within his monastery (The Abbey of Gethsemani in Kentucky) to rescind the rule which prevented the monks from venturing out into the surrounding woods, he did so fully aware of the sacramental character of the forest and the religious experience of the encounter of being-with-Being that contemplative prayer in a natural *milieu* can yield. Conducive to meditation, the natural world confronts the human person with its freshness, abundance, irreducible immediacy, its intimacy *and* alienness—and therefore in turn confronts the persons with his or her *own* immediacy, fullness, emptiness, holiness. These dimensions of human existence, Merton maintains, can be revealed in a sustained encounter with the natural world, the world which conditions, shapes, and sustains our life.

Much of Thomas Merton's work involved direct or indirect meditation on the mysterious character of the cosmos, especially as sign or sacrament of the gracious mystery of God. The world is, as Merton writes in *Love and Living*, willed and held in being by God's love and is therefore infinitely precious in his sight.[1] The cosmos is thus a revelation of the infinite love of the God who is "Maker, Lover, and Keeper."[2] Merton repeatedly writes about the sacredness of this ongoing revelation which, as Gerard Manley

Hopkins contends (and which Merton explicitly affirms with Hopkins in several places[3]), "inscapes" all of reality. "There is in all things," Merton holds, "an invisible fecundity, a dimmed light, a meek namelessness, a hidden wholeness."[4]

Thus, for Merton, the natural world conveys (and, in a sense, is conveyed by) the presence of God. This mysterious presence— mysterious because it is "everywhere and nowhere," at the heart of all things and yet not anywhere "located"—was recognized by Merton in his experience of the fundamental goodness of creation. The physical world, for Merton, shares in and makes transparent the goodness of God. The palpable immediacy of the landscape and horizons of the good Earth disclose both the immediacy *and* the mystery of God. Merton was frequently led to comment on this mysterious depth that is printed in the lining and texture—the surfaces and the hidden structures—of all life.

But Merton was drawn to comment perhaps even more frequently on the *human response* to this mysterious depth. This response shaped one of the key questions he addressed in his writings—that is, what do humans make of this mystery which they encounter within and without themselves?

Merton's fundamental intuition about this—confirmed by the thinking of a long and ancient line of "diagnosticians of the spirit" both inside and outside the monastic tradition—was that human beings generally respond to the mystery of the cosmos, not by acknowledging, participating in, and in some way "embodying" it, but by attempting to evade or deny it. The overwhelmingness of the mystery of life can elicit in human beings wonder, awe, and deep reverence—or it can become a source of fear, dread, and anxiety. Faced with such feelings, human persons often deny this radical *mysterium* in one or several ways. One of the most common is the attempt *to substitute a humanly created "world" for the unhumanly constituted cosmos.*

One of the recurring themes in Merton's work—which emerges from his ongoing struggle with one of Western monasticism's strongest "received ideas"—is the concept of "the flight from the world" (*fugia mundi*). When he first became a monk, Merton saw this issue in clear-cut terms. The "world," a network of fictions which legitimated greed, abuses of power, and even murder, was "out there" while he and his brothers, safely behind monastery walls, were "in here." They were not subject to "the world's" set of social arrangements which blotted out the light of God. He was no longer "in the world" and therefore the presence and life of

God was accessible and relatively immediate. The world, in the New Testament sense, was for the young Merton easily defined and located.

It was only when Merton became aware of the fact that the monastic environment was itself a "world"—a construct of social arrangements which institutionalized its own necessarily partial interpretation of reality—that he no longer so facilely divided the cosmos into world and non-world. Instead, he began to analyze how nearly all of humanity tends to participate in its own "flight from the world"; a flight from, an evasion or denial of, *the true world*, and a flight into a set of fictions and cultural agreements which are subject to human manipulation. At its most literal level, this leads humanity to deny the physical world. The natural world confronts the person with his or her limitation. (This ranges from the limitations of physical strength when compared to the un-fathomable power of nature to the psychic limitation implicit in the fact that the physical world, in its totality, always exceeds any human conception or interpretation of it and thus is not ultimately graspable intellectually.) Faced with this, human beings tend to side-step such troubling awarenesses—they seek mental and/or physical distance from the natural world. In its most literal sense, this is a fundamental separation by human beings from the physical environment which, in its totality, exceeds general human perceptions of it.

This flight or separation from the physical environment—a denial of its overwhelming mystery and therefore both its abundant strangeness and its life-giving power—generates and is generated by certain "organizing ideas" about nature, Merton maintains. These include, among others, the concept that *nature is an enemy bent on devouring or enslaving human beings;* the notion that *nature is irrelevant to the life and experience of human beings;* or the assumption that *nature is a commodity to be manipulated, "recreated," and consumed by human beings.*

Such concepts mystify the true human/environment relationship; worse still, they create frameworks within which whole *counter-worlds* are created. Thus, the first idea generates a situation in which the linear structure of human cities subtly neutralizes the dynamism of the natural world by imposing an alien logic on the manifold expressions of the natural. The physical environment becomes a residue or, worse, a vague memory—the mystery of the natural world is "fenced out." Mystery is packaged, conceptualized, and thus subject to human management.

Or, following the concept that nature is irrelevant, human beings tend to treat the physical environment with an arrogant disdain as if the connection between themselves and the cosmos were, at best, a trivial abstraction or, at worst, nonexistent. We are "above" nature, "beyond" nature. Nature is, at times, an intrusion—but we are working on ways of eliminating this nuisance.

Or, in line with the third concept, the world is a vast consumable object meant to be ingested, digested, and exhausted with increasing rapidity. The world's meaning, if such a thing is to be taken seriously at all, is located in this perpetual exhaustion.

Back of these ideas, Merton maintains, is the human penchant for controlling and managing the world—the world which has itself fostered humanity. By controlling that which confers life, the human beings create the illusion of conferring life on themselves by means of their own power, and thus are finally not subject to the overwhelming ambiguity, uncertainty, contingency, and finitude with which nature's mystery confronts them. Proceeding from these ideas, then, is a desire to control the means of life which, in the most basic sense, means the physical *milieu*.

Merton's skepticism about human misuse of the natural order springs from a basic conviction that humankind tends to deal with its own mystery and the mystery of the world by creating a *world-within-a-world* which is susceptible to human control, management, and manipulation. He suggests this idea in his essay "Rain and the Rhinoceros" in which, after describing the sound of a rain shower deep in the night, he writes:

> The time will come when they will sell you even your rain. By "they" I mean the people who cannot appreciate its gratuity, who think that what has no price has no value, that what cannot be sold is not real. . .The time will come when they will sell you even your rain. At the moment it is still free, and I am in it.[5]

For Merton, the natural world is first and foremost *not* an "object" with a "price-tag"; it is *not* an element in an overarching system of production, consumption, and elimination. It is, instead, source, presence, and sustaining friend: friend who is Other, friend who is Intimate. There *is* unexpected fury and destructiveness, from a human point of view, in nature, and the overwhelming magnitude of this at times requires human response and modification. Merton acknowledges this wildness, but he argues that our numerous attempts to systematize and, in our own way, "institutionalize" nature deny to human awareness the profound implications of that abundance of power and seeming chaos or discontinuity. We have, Merton claims, so absolutized our management and subjugation of the physical environment that we are no longer conscious of the difference between the natural world and our own complicated, subtle, and even neurotic interpretation of the world. These, in our minds, have become identical—and, as far as Merton is concerned, this is a dangerous tendency. Our inclination to reduce the cosmos to our necessarily limited conception of it—and to mistake one for the other—keeps us from seeing and genuinely responding to the world as a whole and therefore encourages us to degrade, abuse, and systematically destroy that world.

"The world I am sore at on paper is perhaps a figment of my own imagination," Thomas Merton admitted in *The Sign of Jonas*.[6] Elsewhere he argued that an hypostasized world "is a dangerous fiction."[7] Merton was interested, he wrote at the time, not in rejecting a reality, but only in unmasking an illusion.[8] To that end, he asks in *Love and Living*,

> What then is the world? Simply the human and the non-human environment in which man [sic] finds himself and to which he is called to establish a certain definite relationship.
>
>   It is true that most men [sic] are content to accept a ready-made relationship which the world itself offers them, but in theory we are all free to stand back from the world, to judge it, and even to come to certain decisions about remaking it.[9]

Not content with the ready-made relationship—because it "demands our total submission"[10] and confirms us in deeply rooted patterns of mystification and exploitation—Merton explored alternatives to the predominant social model which sought to control and, in turn, trivialize the natural world by conceiving of it only in terms of the grid, the void, or the consumable resource. Merton held that this process of mystification required in response to it a process of de-mystification—a process centered in a commitment to seeing, in increasingly more comprehensive ways, the world before us.

The monastic tradition, at its most genuine, seeks to become aware of how reality is constituted by means of the experience of contemplation. For Merton, contemplation is a process of plunging below the surface of human life in order to discover its roots, its ground, its center. Self and world dance, exchange places, become aware of each other's warm presence—there is a growing consciousness of the interrelatedness of being, as suggested in Merton's poem, "Elias—Variations on a Theme":

Under the blunt pine
I who am not sent
remain. The pathway dies,
the journey has begun.
Here the bird abides
and sings on top of the forgotten
storm. The ground is warm.
He sings no particular message.
His hymn has one pattern, no more planned,
no less perfectly planned
and no more arbitrary
than the pattern in the seed, the salt,
the snow, the cell, the drop of rain.[10]

"Contemplation," Merton wrote, "is life itself, fully awake, fully active, fully aware that it is alive. It is spiritual wonder."[11] Proceeding from this, Merton invites us to look—*really look*. To gaze on reality—and to sense how, in its own way, *reality gazes on us*. The first step in the move away from the trivialization of world is to see it, to "attend to" the environment and its contours, its many faces, to contemplate its processes of death and life, to discover, and be discovered by, the mystery which is its and our deepest reality.

The second step which Merton counsels is that we recreate our understanding of environment. Often we tend to create environments which *parody* the mystery of the overarching environment. To reverse this tendency, we must hallow the environment in which we find ourselves by becoming aware of how such places are constituted by a vast network of interrelationships. The environment is not created by shuffling certain "objects" alongside other "objects"—environment is, instead, "presence" encountering and linked to "presence." In one of his written prayers, Merton stresses both this kind of presentness and the experience of linkage which it creates:

> You have made us together, you have made us one and many, you have placed me in the midst as witness, as awareness, as joy. Here I am. In me the world is present, and you are present. I am a link in the chain of light and of presence. You have made me a kind of center, but a center that is nowhere.[12]

Awareness of the vast interrelatedness of beings yields a commitment to "living together"—beings of all form creating an environment with increasingly wider horizons, what Merton called a *convivium*, a "mystery of the sharing of life."[13] Such a commitment means becoming increasingly aware of, and participating in, the rhythm and "cadence" of the natural world. It means discovering our selves in the selves of nature. It means discovering our niche among the niches of the physical environment.

Merton described the niche he gradually discovered when, in the middle 1960s, he moved to a cabin a mile from the monastery to take up life as a hermit. This place, hidden in the woods, encouraged the death of inflated notions about human beings and led Merton to a new simplicity and modesty. He writes:

> I exist under trees, I walk in the woods out of necessity. . . .This is not a hermitage—it is a house. What I wear is pants. What I do is live. How I pray is breathe. . .Up here in the woods is seen the New Testament: that is to say, the wind comes through the trees and you breathe it.[14]

Merton describes in this essay as elsewhere the physical and spiritual ecology of this corner of the woods. Here Merton lived side by side with "the others"—animals, trees, the Kentucky sky—and shared in the spirit of the place, a spirit created and saturated by the convergence of these myriad forms of life. This setting became —as all settings, with time and attention, become—a kind of center *and* margin. At the edge of the world, it was also its center, and therefore symbol and expression of, at once, the emptiness and fullness (the "all" and "no-thing") of God.

In the 1960s, Thomas Merton turned his attention increasingly to *issues of survival*. With greater and greater frequency, his writings addressed the threat posed by the existence of thermonuclear weapons, the devastating war in Indochina, the suppression of human rights of blacks and Native Americans in this country and those of peoples in the Third World. Merton's concern for human survival led him to become increasingly concerned about the survival of the biosphere, and thus all the creatures of the earth who depend on that biosphere for their own survival. With this concern in mind, Merton indicated that we humans must stress at least two things in our relationship with the physical environment. First, we must learn *from nature* how to participate in the replenishing of the world. One of the strongest images in Merton's *Conjectures of a Guilty Bystander* is that of the physical environment organically reconstituting and rehabilitating itself at *night* after the ravages it has suffered at the hands of humankind during the *day*.[15] In the depth of night, so Merton envisions it, creation re-creates itself—the fecundity of nature spends itself luxuriously, salving the wounds it has received in the daytime. Merton cautions us that the destructiveness wreaked against the physical order is becoming too much for it, and that even this ritual healing—rooted in its life as a marvelous and complex organism—is being overwhelmed by the onslaught of ecological damage. We must, Merton holds, learn to become partners *with* the natural world in the healing *of* the natural world.

Secondly, Merton counsels us to become conscious in a new way that our motivation for *survival* emerges out of a greater awareness of the *meaning* survival holds for us. We must meditate on the significance of the survival of the whole of the earth and be rededicated to that meaning. For Merton, this involves becoming increasingly aware of the cosmos as ongoing revelation of God *and* the worthwhileness of *our* acknowledging and participating in this miraculous process. "Here is the unspeakable secret: paradise is all around us and we do not understand. It is wide open," Merton writes, and thus points to the mystery which grounds our lives and which urges our involvement in the earth's survival—which is to say, the ongoing unfolding of its life and the lives of the creatures it havens.

Notes

1. *Love and Living* (New York: Bantam Books, 1979), p. 159.
2. Ibid.
3. *The Behavior of Titans* (New York: New Directions, 1958), pp. 91-92; *New Seeds of Contemplation* (New York: New Directions, 1961), p. 30; and tape recording "Prayer and Meditation and the Meaning of Life" (1/28/64), #A-142, Thomas Merton Studies Center, Bellarmine College, Louisville, Kentucky.
4. "Hagia Sophia," *The Thomas Merton Reader* (New York: Image Books, 1974), p. 506.
5. "Rain and the Rhinoceros," *Raids on the Unspeakable* (New York: New Directions, 1966), p. 9.
6. *The Sign of Jonas* (Garden City: Image Books), p. 163.
7. *Contemplation in a World of Action* (Garden City: Doubleday, 1971), p. 154.
8. Ibid.
9. *Love and Living*, p. 107-08.

10. *The Collected Poems of Thomas Merton* (New York: New Directions, 1977), p. 244.
11. *New Seeds of Contemplation*, p. 1.
12. *Conjectures of a Guilty Bystander* (Garden City: Doubleday, 1966), p. 160.
13. Ibid.
14. "Day of a Stranger," *Thomas Merton Reader*, pp. 432-33.
15. *Conjectures of a Guilty Bystander*, p. 122-23.

Chapter Nineteen

PRAYER, MEDITATION, AND CREATION CONSCIOUSNESS

Philip N. Joranson

One of the fundamental dimensions of genuine spirituality is an increasingly developed awareness of things as they really exist. Spirituality—a *way of life* into truth and freedom via love—is an ongoing process in which illusion is challenged and critiqued. Conrad Bonifazi, in *The Soul of the World*, points out that "the great majority of us are children of our age and tend to accept without question its main presuppositions."[1] Cultural assumptions, rigid stereotypes, and uncritical habits of thought prevent us from experiencing the depths of existence; they bind us to a narrow, and finally dehumanizing, vision. By simply accepting our shared presuppositions, we often fail to grasp the engaging reality of the world around us. Spirituality which stresses intentionality, awareness, prayerful openness, and relationality to all that exists, questions and gradually transforms patterns of habituation that keep us from seeing, feeling, tasting, touching, and hearing God's cosmos.

Such spirituality shatters anthropocentrism; this transformation of consciousness leads us to experience, in a new way, the bond that ties all creatures—indeed, the entire universe—together. Such spirituality stresses the particularly religious insight that the fundamental connection between all things is the love that God lavishes on them; the whole creation is loved by God. Because God loves nature, nature also deserves our love. The ongoing experience of prayer and meditation informs our reflection on, and participation in, the life of the natural world when we gradually see that this divine love for the world is the best model offered us for our own relationship with the environment.

The Contribution of Thomas Kelly

Probably no one in the Western Christian tradition has communicated the nature of such experience with greater clarity and present-day appeal than the great twentieth century Quaker mystic, Thomas E. Kelly. Though himself a professor of philosophy and a scholar observing the most rigorous standards, Kelly writes about his experience of the Spirit in the last three years of his life in simple, direct, beautiful language for which fellow seekers have been deeply grateful. In the following, from his *Testament of Devotion*, we are privileged to share in a kind of perception and liberation that has been slow in coming and which we see here engendered by his radical openness to the Spirit. (The italics are Kelly's.)

> ". . . the experience of an inflooding, all-enfolding Love, which is at the center of Divine Presence, is of a love which *embraces all creation*, not just our little, petty selves. . . Not only does all creation have a new smell, as Fox found, but it has a new value as enwrapped in the infinite Love of God, wherein not a sparrow falls to the ground without the Father. This is not just Jesus' experience. Nor is it his *inference about God's* tender love; it is *the record of his experience in God*. There is a tendering of the soul, toward *everything* in creation, from the sparrow's fall to the slave under the lash."[2]

The tendering of the soul is both toward humankind and toward all other kind. Kelly speaks of it again in another place, where he reports his experience of

> ". . . prolonged days and even weeks of sense of Presence wherein . . . there is a vast background of cosmic Love and tender care for all things (plants included, I find for myself), but in the foreground arise special objects of love and concern and tender responsibility. The people we know best, see oftenest, have most to do with, these are *reloved* in a new and deeper way. Would that we could re-love the whole world!"[3]

One of the values of Kelly's contribution is its demonstration, seen here, that the *same* pattern of disciplined commitment opened his consciousness to feelings of love and tender care for *both* humankind and all other kind. This total inclusiveness which Kelly receives from the Spirit may be seen as a reflection of the basic oneness of the creation as stressed in the biblical vision of reality and also in modern findings of the sciences.

Kelly's emphasis on interrelationships between all that exists is a clear basis for coordinated and balanced emphasis upon two objectives that in the past have been either neglected or, at best, in competition with each other: (1) "ecojustice"—the equal access of the world's peoples and diverse income groups to natural resources and environmental benefits; and (2) the care and healing of the environment. In the past two decades, individuals and groups have tended to swing strongly toward one or the other. At the present time there is a great need for a balance between and integration of these objectives, both in our consciousness and in public policy.

Other Builders of Creation-Conscious Faith

The builders of the minority tradition of Christian creation consciousness have found each other and depended upon each other's writings down through the centuries. Outstanding among them, besides Kelly, are St. Francis of Assisi[4]; Meister Eckhart[5]; Nikolai Berdyaev; Pierre Teilhard de Chardin[6]; Thomas Merton.[7] Besides some basic common elements which they share, there are distinctive features in the careers of each which have influenced their spiritualities. The contribution of St. Francis of Assisi is discussed by several of the contributors to this volume, and of Teilhard (Chapter 15) by Bonifazi. In Chapter 18, Butigan characterizes the environmental concerns of Thomas Merton.

A very active scholar and educator (see Chapter 25) on creation-centered spirituality and author of Chapter 4 of this book is Matthew Fox.[8] Berdyaev,[9] Fox, and Wilkinson[10] have described and evalutated the creation-centered mysticism of the Eastern Orthodox Church, which needs to be much better known today. Woods (Chapter 3), and also Schmiel[11] and Fox[12] have also traced the important influence of the Celtic Christian tradition on Meister Eckhart and others of his age.

Several characteristic features of creation-conscious faith are often stressed in the thought of these and other figures, including:

1. An arresting sense of Presence in the being(s) of which one has been made especially aware.

2. Consciousness of participation in a community of being that is much wider or more significant than is experienced at more accustomed levels of consciousness.

3. Experience of love for other creatures as warm, completely trusting, delighted enjoyment.

4. A humbling sense of confrontation with mystery—mystery which is also Presence.

Emphases among these and other characteristics vary from one writer to another, but there is more consensus than one might expect from a comparison of their vocations and pathways of life. This consensus applies not only to the *fruits* of their commitment but also to the *roots* that have nourished these results, among which at least the following are characteristic:

1. Willingness to give one's self completely to God, rejecting utterly and seeking forgiveness for the sinful ways that separate and cripple.

2. The coming of the Spirit as freely offered gift of God, not as meritorious response to assiduous human effort.

3. Complete relaxation of body and mind, and expectant response.

4. Assurance that the loving Spirit of God, sometimes recognized as Christ, is manifest throughout all the creation, and can be experienced.

5. Understanding that the opportunity to enjoy such experience depends upon the frequent exercise of prayer of some duration, using selected biblical and other resources, of which some may—but do not need to—have special bearing upon relating to God's creation.

In the years immediately ahead, it is to be hoped that many will begin to follow the lead of the great teachers and will make their own deeply founded and delighted discoveries. One morning when I was thinking along the lines of these remarks, I had walked up into the hills near my home east of Berkeley, California and had such an experience, which came entirely by surprise. Sitting in the savannah-type grassland there and leaning up against one of the valley white oaks, I had just finished with prayer. As I opened my eyes, I found myself immediately in active encounter with another white oak tree about twenty yards in front of me. I was fascinated, and gave the tree my full attention. Its widely spreading branches reached down almost to the ground, and the whole tree was communicating in a very direct fashion. This is what the tree seemed to be saying, and I wrote it down soon afterwards on some note cards I was carrying:

> "Here I am . . . *I am. Look straight at me.* . . try to understand what I am doing here . . . try to understand how both you and I got here . . . how intricately, how interdependently we are both woven into all that surrounds us! . . . Incidentally, . . . what are *you* about . . . what is it that *you* do?"

My sense was that through the Spirit of Christ, which had prepared my spirit and rendered me receptive in the course of the prayer that had just preceded, the tree was able to seize my attention; the tree and I, both creatures of God, in that brief interval of breakthrough were sharing in the Love of God that does indeed bind all things together and is their source.

The Dynamics of Creation Consciousness

The prayer-engendered level of engagement with God's creation can greatly increase during the next several decades. Its cultivation is a growth process, and takes time.

Creation consciousness will be promoted by much wider recognition of its reality. Thus, for some, a first step will be to recognize the reality of spiritual encounter of *any* kind, moving beyond doubt through personal experience to the point where the Spirit of God begins to validate itself as the source of the most real things we know. Then a further step—and another crucial one—is to become aware that through our openness in prayer and beyond into all our living, the Spirit is able to change radically our perception and valuation of all the beings of God's otherkind, so that more and more we find ourselves actually participating in God's universal love for the creation.

All other kinds *deserve* to be perceived and valued in this way: this must be at least part of the meaning of Paul's great insight (Romans 8:19) where he declares, "For the created universe waits with eager anticipation for God's sons to be revealed."

The Spirit of God illumines, interprets, endears, and motivates in encounters with the other beings of the creation. God is still there, we find to our delight, and we can count on this "God-is-still-thereness," for the sense of it grows as our experience and commitment grow. This is prayer-supported creation consciousness-in-the-making, and it must now become a part of the future-in-the-making.

In the Judeo-Christian tradition, disciplined prayer is benefitted by reading from the Bible, from the writings of great religious teachers, and from many other sources. But the nurture of creation consciousness will also benefit from particular creation-oriented passages from the Bible and from contributors to the literature of creation consciousness such as those we have particularly noticed. There is a great need for published collections of discriminating selections that may be used in this way. In Christian healing, selected brief biblical and other affirmations are repeated over and over through the day. Growth in creation consciousness will also be promoted by repetitions of appropriate affirmations, including some composed by oneself.

Prayer and public worship in the out-of-doors offer great opportunities. In commencing a prayer, we may cradle in our hands the leaves of a favorite plant, let go as the prayer proceeds in its course—not too brief a course—and then, upon the conclusion of the prayer, but still with its openness and quietness and with some sense of expectancy and eyes now open, let the plant express to us its special kind of plantness as a fellow creature of God. Let us sometime try this with a pet, too, in this new kind of openness— and be prepared perhaps to be overwhelmed by a feeling that nothing else matters then like the suddenly new quality of relationship to that animal! In forming a prayer circle outdoors, we should sometimes try asking our group if they would like to include a tree or a flower or an animal or several of these fellow creatures in the hand-clasping circle of prayer—not as a surprise, but with good preparation for this new quality of relationship. In getting started, each of these kinds of engagement with other creatures should probably be ventured more than once. Their value may be expected to increase as one's experience in the prayer support of creation consciousness grows.

As we advance in creation-conscious experience, we may find ourselves also consciously growing in closeness to Christ, whom John and Paul perceived to be so intimately and ultimately related to the entire creation. Listen to Paul. ". . . the whole universe has been created through him and for him. And he exists before everything, and all things are held together in him . . . Through him God chose to reconcile the whole universe to himself, making peace through the shedding of his blood upon the cross—to reconcile all things, whether on earth or in heaven, through him alone" (Col. 1:16c-17, 20).

As our Spirit-infused nearness to the otherkind grows, we may find ourselves *expecting* that Christ would speak as he did of the wild flowers. . .of the sparrows. . .of the stones that he declared would have shouted out loud if, as the Pharisees demanded, he had silenced the joyful singing of the disciples in anticipation of the triumphal descent of the Mount of Olives. Creation consciousness is involved with the fullness of being that Paul saw in Christ, and this appreciation helps us to understand a little better that boldness-beyond-all-bounds of Paul's great charge to the Ephesians (Eph. 3:19); "May you attain the fullness of being, the fullness of God himself."!

In the experience of the Spirit-instructed masters, the world as most of us have known it is not the most real world there is. With their help, the means are now much closer at hand for coming to know the world more and more as God knows it and has made it. That world must not remain forever out of our reach because our faith has been minimal and our spirit-consciousness undeveloped.

God has made the world a theater for a much finer human enterprise than the one we presently have under way—so dangerously close to massive nuclear destruction! We must understand that it is now up to us, of the human species, to demonstrate to God and to all otherkind that we *belong* in God's creation! We must let our ways be guided by the insight of the hymn writer, Walter C. Smith, when he wrote,

> "In all life Thou livest, the true life of all."[13]

Here is the *real* world, in process toward glorious fulfillment, and union with God.

Notes

1. Conrad Bonifazi, *The Soul of the World: An Account of the Inwardness of Things* (Washington, D.C.: University Press of America, 1978), p. vi.
2. Thomas R. Kelly, *A Testament of Devotion*, with a Biographical Memoir by Douglas V. Steere (New York: Harper, 1941), p. 106.
3. Kelly, pp. 99-100.
4. The literature on Assisi is voluminous, but highly variable in quality. In addition to the *Omnibus* and the Fortini volume cited by Weigand in Chapter 6, consult the following for its particular relevance: Eloi Leclerc, O.F.M., *The Canticle of Creatures, Symbols of Union: An Analysis of St. Francis of Assisi* (Chicago: Franciscan Herald Press, 1977).
5. See especially: (1) Matthew Fox, "Meister Eckhart and the Fourfold Path of a Creation-Centered Spiritual Journey," in Matthew Fox, ed., *Western Spirituality: Historical Roots, Ecumenical Routes* (Santa Fe: Bear & Company, 1981), pp. 215-248; and (2) Matthew Fox, *Breakthrough, Meister Eckhart's Creation Spirituality, in New Translation*, Introduction and Commentaries by Matthew Fox (Garden City, N.Y.: Doubleday, 1980).
6. Chapter 15 of this book, by Conrad Bonifazi, deals in part with the spirituality of Teilhard. For readers who wish to make further study of Teilhard's contribution to creation-conscious spirituality, the following works are recommended:
   (1) Pierre Teilhard de Chardin, *The Phenomenon of Man*, tr. Bernard Wall (New York: Harper Torchbook, 1959).

(2) _____, *Hymn of the Universe* (New York: Harper and Row, 1961).

(3) _____, *Human Energy* (New York: Harcourt, Brace Jovanovich, 1962).

(4) W. Henry Kenney, *A Path through Teilhard's Phenomenon* (Dayton, Ohio: Pflaum Press, 1970).

7. See Chapter 18, by Ken Butigan, "Thomas Merton and the Environment."

8. See especially the following titles:

(1) Matthew Fox, *On Becoming a Musical, Mystical Bear: Spirituality American Style* (New York: Paulist Press/Deus Book, 1976).

(2) _____, ed., *Western Spirituality*.

(3) _____, *A Spirituality Named Compassion and the Healing of the Global Village, Humpty Dumpty and Us* (Minneapolis: Winston, 1979).

(4) _____, *Breakthrough*.

(5) _____, *Original Blessing, A Primer in Creation Spirituality* (Santa Fe: Bear & Co., 1983).

9. Nicolas Berdyaev, "Salvation and Creativity: Two Understandings of Christianity," tr. and notes by Carolyn Gifford, in Matthew Fox, ed., *Western Spirituality*, pp. 115-139.

10. Loren Wilkinson, ed., *Earthkeeping: Christian Stewardship of Natural Resources* (Grand Rapids: Eerdmans, 1980), pp. 221-223.

11. Mary Aileen Schmiel, "The Finest Music in the World: Exploring Celtic Spiritual Legacies," in Matthew Fox, ed., *Western Spirituality*, pp. 164-192.

12. Matthew Fox, *Breakthrough*, pp. 30-35.

13. Walter C. Smith, Hymn: "Immortal, Invisible, God Only Wise," *Pilgrim Hymnal* (Boston: Pilgrim Press, 1958), no. 7.

Chapter Twenty

COVENANT, CREATION, AND ETHICS
A Federal Vision for
Humanity and the Environment

Charles S. McCoy

The twentieth century opened with great optimism, bright with
the promises of science and technology to bring humanity into an
enduring era of peace, plenty, and security. The century draws to
a close with humanity and the world in peril, caught between
prosperity and poverty, between unprecedented possibilities and
total destruction. As the rising demands for justice combine with
the dangers of nuclear holocaust and environmental catastrophe,
the crisis deepens. Faith in scientific method has proved to be as
illusory a dogma as earlier versions of such sectarian triumphal-
ism. It is imperative that we seek a wider vision, one capable of
including humanity and the whole environment of nature and
history in their interdependency.

   In this chapter, I suggest that encompassing vision by exploring
an understanding of the created order within the covenant of God
and the meaning of this perspective for environmental ethics.

1. The Covenant: Resource for Ethics

   Within the traditions informed by the Hebrew-Christian scriptures, one strand in particular stands out as a striking alternative
to the view that humanity is apart from and above nature and
should dominate and exploit the natural world. This alternative is
faith shaped by covenantal vision. The covenant and covenantal
faith are central in the Bible, continue as important elements in
the early church and medieval period, and emerge as powerful
components in the modern world.

The importance of the covenant for modern society can best be grasped with the insight that the covenantal tradition can be called the federal tradition. "Covenant" usually is related to the Bible, "federalism" to politics. The inseparable relation becomes clear when it is remembered that the word *federal* comes from the Latin *foedus*, which means *covenant*. Covenantal and federal are alternative ways of naming a central stream of the Judeo-Christian tradition. When the covenantal character of contemporary federal society is remembered, the covenant becomes a major resource for developing a meaningful environmental ethics today.

The pervasiveness of covenant thought in the Bible is generally recognized. The idea of covenant is central in both the Old Testament and the New. Indeed, the word "testament" comes from the Latin *testamentum*, which is the way the Vulgate translates the Hebrew *berith* (covenant). Walther Eichrodt focuses his *Theologie des alten Testaments* on the covenant and bases the first of the three volumes on the notion of Yahweh as the Covenant God. The covenant, Eichrodt says, is "the critical term for Israelite thought" and "the basic principle of the relationship to God."[1] Just as God in Hebrew faith is the Covenant God, so also are other terms in the Old Testament to be understood in terms of the covenant, e.g. *mishpat* as covenant justice, *hesed* as covenant loving-kindness, etc.[2] Martin Buber asserts that it is impossible to grasp the inner coherence of the faith of Israel without understanding the covenant.[3]

God makes covenant in creation with the whole of the natural order (Jeremiah 33:20, 25). Humanity is created within the same covenant of creation, a covenant that Adam breaks, beginning the faithlessness of humans to God (Hosea 6:7). God upholds the covenant and makes it anew with Noah (Genesis 9:8ff.), with Abraham (Genesis 15:17f.; 17:7), with Isaac (Genesis 17:19), and with Jacob (Genesis 28:18ff.; 35:9ff.). Whatever humans may do, the covenant from God's side remains firm. The covenant with Israel can no more be broken from the divine side than can God's covenant with the day and with the night, that is, with the natural order (Jeremiah 33:20).

The covenant of God is historical and communal. Bernhard Anderson writes: "The peculiar nature of the Hebrew community is expressed in the covenant relationship between Yahweh and the people of Israel, and the Laws and the institutions by which this relationship is expressed is. . .the core of the life of these people."[4] The Hebrew nation is founded on the covenant made at Sinai

(Horeb) (Exodus 19:5; 24:7ff., etc.) after the liberation from Egyptian bondage. This covenant with God becomes the constitution of their life as a people, the basis of their theology and ethics, and the pattern for understanding the whole of creation and history. It is renewed repeatedly despite the faithlessness of Israel.

The covenant is projected forward from Sinai toward the consummation of God's purposes and backward from Sinai to the creation. Sinai is the place where God renews the covenant made with Abraham; the covenant with Abraham is a continuation of the covenant made with Noah; and that covenant with Noah is rooted in God's creation of the world. The core of Israel's story is summed up as follows: "You stand this day all of you before the Lord your God . . . that you may enter into the sworn covenant of the Lord your God, which the Lord your God makes with you this day" (Deuteronomy 29:10ff.).

The prophets speak from this covenantal context and call a faithless Israel back to God. Jeremiah declares a new covenant (Jeremiah 31:33) that Jesus affirms in saying, "This cup which is poured out for you is the new covenant in my blood" (Luke 22:20), a theme taken up again and again throughout the New Testament (e.g. I Corinthians 11:25, Romans 11:27, II Corinthians 3:4-6, 12-17, Galatian 4:22-26, Ephesians 2:12, 13, and virtually the entirety of Hebrews).

2. The Covenantal/Federal View of Creation

What resources are available in the covenantal or federal tradition for disentangling Christian faith from exploitative forces and renewing the Christian understanding of the created order? In this tradition, covenant signifies an inclusive view of God as the Faithful One and of God's faithful will as embodied in the wholeness of creation.

The Meaning of Covenant.   In biblical perspective, covenant means an unconditional agreeement of community, friendship, peace, and justice. Covenant can be contrasted with what we usually call contract. A contract is a conditional agreement with the stipulation understood: obligation to carry out the terms of a contractual agreement derives from the performance of certain contractual obligations by the other party; contract means *quid pro quo*. Covenant as unconditional agreement is not dependent upon the performance or nonperformance of the parties. The commitment fundamentally is to one another. Covenant, therefore, means gift. It signifies a relation based on grace. Parties in a covenant are unconditionally committed to one another. In addition to community, friendship, peace, and justice, covenant implies a means for overcoming enmity, alienation, conflict, and injustice.

In the ancient semitic world, covenants might be from a superior to an inferior or between equals. The first was a suzerainty covenant imposed by conquerors on the conquered, or extended from God to the creation (Genesis 9:13). The second was an agreement of friendship, common purpose, and peace among humans, as the covenant between Abraham and Abimelech (Genesis 21:27). Hebrew faith includes both forms, uniting their meaning and transforming them by referring the final meaning of covenant to God's covenant. God makes covenant with Israel as the continuation of the covenant God has already made with the created order, including nature and all humanity. God's covenant with Abram fits into this sequence (Genesis 15:18). But David and Jonathan also make a covenant with one another, so there is friendship between them deep enough to overcome the enmity that threatens to divide them. And "the soul of Jonathan was knit to the soul of David" (I Samuel 18:1).

God is understood through covenant, not by any final name, but as the One who is faithful, who makes covenant and keeps covenant. Lines from what may be an early Christian hymn convey this Hebrew view: "If we are faithless, God remains faithful, for God cannot deny God's very own selfhood" (II Timothy 2:13).

Covenant reaches back to creation and depicts the origin of the world in God's faithful action. Covenant points forward toward the consummation of the process initiated in creation. The wholeness of creation, coming to focus in the coherent pattern and responsibility of every present, is covenantal, is faithful. Nature no less than history is understood through covenant. The covenant of the rainbow after the flood reminds us of the inclusion of nature: "While earth remains, seedtime and harvest, cold and heat, summer and winter, day and night, shall not cease. . . . Behold I establish my covenant with you and your descendants after you, and with every living creature that is with you. . . . I set my bow in the cloud, and it shall be a sign of the covenant between me and the earth" (Genesis 8:22; 9:9,10,13). And Jeremiah affirms the same: "Thus says the Lord: If you can break my covenant with the day and my covenant with the night, so that day and night will not come at their appointed time, then also my covenant with my servant David may be broken" (Jeremiah 33:20,21).

The Symbiotic Relation of All Creation.   In covenantal perspective, the entire created order is within the covenant of God—
nature, history, and humanity. By creation they are in community
and friendship with God and with one another. Peace and justice
are constitutive elements of the world as created. All parts are
joined together in symbiotic relation, mutually interdependent
and together dependent upon the faithful will of God.

Violation of the covenant is an attack upon the created order of
the world and is rebellion against God. Injustice, conflict, enmity,
and alienation result from unfaithfulness to the covenant; such
faithlessness disturbs the ordered relation and process of nature,
history, and humanity. Actions that violate the covenant do harm
to every part of the symbiotically related creation. When humans
treat other humans unjustly or exploit nature, they are acting
against God, the covenant, and themselves. Faithlessness harms
the exploiter as well as the exploited. The symbiotic nature of creation means, therefore, that all action has a boomerang effect,
going out toward goals intended but turning back upon the agent
originating the action.

Johannes Althusius (1557-1638), author of the first federal or
covenantal political philosophy, speaks of politics as the art of
associating in societal life and upbuilding all within it. Thus, he
says, politics is called "symbiotics." And humans are known as
"symbiotes" because of their symbiotic relation with one another,
with the entire creation, and with God.[5]

Sin means faithlessness to the covenant of God. It is rebellion
against and an attempt to violate the integral wholeness of creation. Sin is, therefore, unfaithfulness toward God, toward nature,
toward humanity, and toward the self, for all are bound together
in the symbiotic relationship of covenant.

Because of the pervasiveness of sin, it should not be a shock to
find that nature has been abused and exploited, even as the
human story is one of continuing inhumanity of humans to one
another. The covenantal view of the environmental crisis emphasizes that when we violate any part of the created order, it is harmful to the whole. That is precisely what we are discovering painfully today: when we are unfaithful to the covenant with nature,
nature snaps back at us, and we see the results in ecological disruption, that is, in the disturbance of the symbiotic relations of the
covenant.

Covenant, thus, includes command, promise, and threat. God's
covenant as embodied in nature and history contains the command

to live in community, friendship, peace, and justice. The promise of the covenant is the enjoyment of well-being through the relations established and growing in creation. The threat of the covenant is that violation leads to the fragmentation of community, to alienation, to conflicts, and to injustice. In federal perspective, theology and ethics are bound together inseparably in covenantal relation.

Nature and History in Process toward Fulfillment.   In the light of the covenant of God, we may say that nature has a history no less than that history is embedded in nature and is natural. Both are integrally related aspects of God's covenant in creation. Nature and history, therefore, are not static but are in process toward a consummation given by God and ultimately hidden in God.

Covenantal theology and ethics have a distinctive way for understanding creation as historical. The created order as created by God "in the beginning" through covenant is not complete. The world is created in process toward increasing fulfillment and toward final consummation. Humanity as part of this created order is also created incomplete and in process toward further growth and toward fulfillment.

This federal view is not to be identified with recent process theologies based on philosophical metaphysical systems. Covenant thought derives its process elements from the biblical understanding of creation within the covenantal purposes of God that contain a process of fulfillment. Indeed, it is highly probable that the process philosophies of the nineteenth and twentieth centuries emerged from contexts influenced by the covenantal or federal tradition and thus are in part intellectual progeny of covenant theology and ethics.

Theological federalism stands also in contrast to the Augustinian views of creation, history, and humanity, a view widely influential in Western theology. Creation, including humanity, for Augustine, is from God and is as good as can be. Only God is perfect. In the fall into sin, humanity declines from that creational goodness. As a result, humans and all their deeds are corrupt in that they seek lesser goods than God. Jesus Christ redeems humanity and the entire creation from their fallenness and restores them to their created goodness.

Covenant theology and ethics offer a different theology of history and understanding of the fall. Creation is good but incomplete, in process toward fulfillment. Nature and humanity by cre-

ation are undergoing change, as history unfolds, toward completion in God. There is a greater goodness lying ahead as creation
moves toward consummation. Humans know themselves to be
developing toward fulfillment, yet they do not know what their
full potentialities are. In all human aspiration, there is a nagging
"not yet" of hope and anticipation. The fall into sin, for federalism, is a fall from that mutability in which humans develop toward
their fulfillment into immutability, into a static state that is resist-
ant to change, that seeks to avoid the process of growth toward the
fulfillment that is our covenant destiny in God.

The "unquiet heart," the restlessness of human existence, is not
the result of the fall as in the Augustinian view but rather is built
into humans with their creation. Humanity is created with a restless heart, a striving beyond the incompleteness of creation toward
the fulfillment of the potentiality given by God. Humans do not
know completely what their full potentiality is, but they look forward in hope, knowing through covenant faith that the final consummation is community and unity of the entire creation in God.

The redeeming word of Christ for federalism is twofold. First,
whether humanity had fallen or not, Christ is the pioneer of this
developmental, covenantal order moving toward consummation.
Without the fall, for Augustine, the work of Christ is problematical. Second, because of the fall of humanity into immutability and
resistance to change, Christ restores mutability to humanity, that
ability to respond to God's call to grow and change toward fulfillment.

In this meaning of covenant, in the symbiotic relations of nature
and humanity, and in the incompleteness of the world as it develops toward its fulfillment, the basis for a renewal of the Christian
understanding of the created order takes shape. The covenant of
God in creation points to the pattern of nature and history as faithfulness. Creation relates every part to every other part. Creation
is an interdependent whole, based upon and related through the
covenantal will of God. By origin and nature, humans belong to
one another and to nature. The created order in covenant is characterized by community, friendship, peace, and justice. Any violation of covenant harms all parts of the creation. The breaking of
community, acts of enmity, conflict, and injustice are violations of
the covenant and of the relationships of creation.

Faithfulness to the covenant of God is the way of continuing
development toward the fulfillment intended for the world and all
its parts in creation. Faithlessness means a retreat into stasis, a

resistance to change. Faithlessness violates the covenant and harms the object of the action as well as the agent.

In covenant, creation is known to be incomplete, to place nature and humanity in process toward their fulfillment. Community, friendship, peace, and justice, understood through the love of God and guaranteed in Jesus Christ, who is our covenant, provide the key to the creating, judging, and redeeming activity of the covenant God.

From the covenant tradition can come the resources for a renewal of the Christian understanding of the creation and for a new environmental ethics. It is a tradition with deep roots in the Bible and in the Western heritage of theology and ethics. Covenantal or federal thought, though its biblical and theological background is often forgotten, remains woven into the fabric of the modern world. Drawing on this tradition thus offers a means also for renewing the relationship of Christian faith to the patterns of human community and developing a covenantal ethics comprehensive enough for the cultural, environmental problems endangering humanity today.

3. The Meaning of Ethics

Ethics can be understood most comprehensively as reflection within a community of interpretation on the moral significance of human action. Codes of conduct, laws, and styles of living may be regarded as related to ethics insofar as they represent the results of ethical reflection. Reflection in a more general sense or as careful reasoning takes place in particular human locations and receives its warrants of validation from specific historical, societal contexts of commitment. Ethics is not necessarily relativistic because it takes place within social locations, but such reflection emerges within and is dependent upon a particular community of interpretation and commitment.

Though many hope otherwise, ethics does not suddenly disclose a realm of absolute right and wrong not previously visible. Instead, ethics can help us see more clearly and steer with greater precision through the environment of values, moral directives, and behavioral valences that surround us.

Morality as "Natural."   We emerge as human beings immersed in social contexts permeated by values. Moral directives are given to us from the time we are born. Not much later, we have internalized enough of these directives to participate in shaping the moral climate of society. From womb to tomb, humans exist in relations of intense moral valence. The fabric and varying strength of the particular factors will differ somewhat from one location to another within the same society and will differ greatly from one culture to another. But the presence of values, directives, and moral valences will be a constant.

Morals and behavioral expectations are as "natural" in human social environments as physical objects and biological needs. Varied dietary practices in different cultures do not lead to the conclusion that the need for food is unreal, unnatural, or "merely" emotive. Nor do different colors and shapes of bodies persuade us that physical existence is epiphenomenal to culture. The world as experienced has a wholeness in which the parts are symbiotically related. It is a dubious practice to presuppose the priority of one part and assume the presupposing to be adequate demonstration. Moral meaning is a pervasive and ineradicable part of the whole that constitutes human living.

Through overt directives and laws and in a myriad of subtle ways of approval, disapproval, and nuanced response, humans communicate values and valences of behavior to one another. From parents, peers, preachers, police, and teachers—from home, school, government, and religious community—the moral directives come and the behavioral valence is enunciated. Communal and ecclesiastical rituals convey and reinforce societal values. And the patterns of intimate human relationship evoke profound impulses to internalize these values.

Plural Moralities and the Rise of Ethical Reflection.   Insofar as the framework of explanation and legitimation for moral meaning and action form a coherent totality, we may speak of a religious/cultural system. But there is never complete coherence, certainly not in developed societies and probably not even in societies called "underdeveloped" or "primitive." In our own lives, we become aware early of uneven valences and conflicting moral directives. It is to deal with the directives demanding contradictory actions that we are compelled to engage in ethical reflection. At first ethics takes the form of seeking a way to deal with the contrasting directives of parents and siblings, of home and community. Later we find decisively different traditions within our society grasping for our loyalty and commitment. Finding criteria and meaning to make our own in steering through cultural cross-currents is the process of forging our ethics and our identity in a context of plural values and moral directives.

When the plurality of religious/cultural systems around the globe comes into view, the problems of ethics are compounded. The differing moral directives to be found within the fairly coherent heritage of Western culture are difficult enough. Finding adequate criteria for action within the cultural plurality that includes the Ayatollah Khomeini's version of Islam, the varieties of Buddhism and Hinduism, the Marxisms of Lenin and Mao, and widely differing sectors of Christianity, varying with cultural location, may seem impossible for those who must manage policy for nations and transnational social organizations. Ethics can provide important guidance, but not a single, absolute way of "right action" in such a global context. Within particular social enclaves, adherents of Special Revelation or Tradition or Reason may claim to possess a final authority for ethics. But the diversity of moral meaning and action in the wider human community discloses the inadequacy of such absolutisms and demonstrates the extent to which ethics depends on particular historical and social locations.

Such recognition in no way entails relativism. It does involve taking account of differences in values and purposes. Only then can persons and organizations operate outside the limits of particular communities in the wider world arena where plural cultural systems meet.[6]

Ethics as Social.   In this perspective, ethics is no less social than it is individual. From the context of moral directives and valent relationships that shape our lives, it is clear that ethics is a profoundly social and deeply necessary human undertaking.

As reflection on the moral significance of human action, ethics takes place on different levels of agency. First, there is the individual level of agency. So accustomed have some become to thinking of ethics only in individual terms that they regard this as the only level on which ethical reflection takes place. Such a limited view of ethics is inadequate.

Second, there is the organizational/institutional level of agency. Policymakers in organized groups discuss and deliberate about alternative courses of action for the organization. As diverse values are weighed and priorities set, ethical reflection is taking place. Policy ethics is a way to characterize the ethics of an organization. Illustrations of this level of agency are business corporations, governmental departments, hospitals, labor unions, churches, social service agencies and community groups of all kinds.

Third, there is the level of agency best described as a social sector. Professional groups such as physicians, dentists, lawyers, artists, clergy fit here, as also do banking, religious groups, health services, government, agriculture, the entertainment industry, the communications media, etc.

Fourth, there is the societal level of agency. Here we consider the total society, the political economy, the religious/cultural system, etc. The development of criteria takes place gradually and changes slowly. Traditions that have become embedded in societal action represent reflection of an ethical nature. Once developed, this more encompassing level of action exercises great influence over the others. On all these levels, ethics pertains to social groups and organizations as well as to individuals.

As culture and societal interaction emerge on a global scale, a fifth level of moral agency is taking shape.

Ethics is social also in the sense that moral agency and ethical reflection take place in an ongoing context of interaction among individual and organizational agents. Reflection on the moral significance of action is thus not only about the past or what is right in the present but also concerns the results of action and the anticipations of responses to action in a continuing pattern.

Still further, ethics is social in that moral agents draw criteria for action not primarily from individual reasoning but more from traditions, faiths, and communities of interpretation and commitment that permeate the society surrounding agents. These sources of ethical criteria are communicated as humans touch one another through story and social ritual, as morals are transmuted into law, and as social valence is transformed into internalized values by individual and organizational agents.

4. Ethics and the Environment in Christian Perspective

Keeping this wider meaning of ethics in mind, we turn now to drawing more explicitly on the Christian tradition for resources in recovering a sense of responsibility toward the environment and for a renewed appreciation of humanity as part of the created order. We shall do this under three headings: creation, creativity, and covenant.[7]

Creation. In keeping with its biblical origins, Christian ethics is an ethics of creation, an understanding that can serve as a primary resource for environmental ethics today. A Christian ethics of creation means, first, that any criteria for human action in Christian faith derive from an understanding of the world as created and valued by God. When God looks upon the creation and declares it good (Genesis 1:31), the inseparability of reality and value is affirmed for ethics and for human action. The created order is good, and goodness is built into the reality of creation.

A Christian ethics of creation, second, does not involve the notion, however, that "nature knows best," as environmentalists like Barry Commoner appear to be saying. The ground and judge of what is and what is of value is God, not nature or humanity in themselves. Yet what is good, insofar as humans can understand and respond to it, is present through human experience and through nature.

Nor, third, does a Christian ethics of creation imply that human values eclipse the value of the natural order. Humanity is created within nature as a part of nature. No meaning of "dominion" and "subdue" can make sense when it ignores God's valuation of the entire created order and the relation established in creation between the environment and humanity. Humans are enjoined to use the abundance within which they have been created but not to misuse or abuse it. Neither nature nor humanity is the center of value. God is. And in virtue of that source of value, the entire created order, including humans, shares a goodness permeating its interrelated parts.

Fourth, a Christian ethics of creation derives criteria of human action from *what is*. Ethics is rooted in the reality of creation and in the wholeness of that reality. On the one hand, the welfare of humanity is bound up with the welfare of the whole. On the other hand, human violation of the created order is as much a peril to the well-being of humanity as of nature. Christian ethics is axiological, that is, concerned with what is valuable. But Christian ethics is equally ontological, that is, concerned with the reality of the created order within which human life emerges and has its context of existence and action.

Christian ethics, fifth, is theocentric. This should already be clear, but it bears emphasis and clarification. Christian ethics displaces meaning, purpose, and value away from humanity in any original or final sense. Human life is part of the created natural order. Even more important, however, for the biblical perspective, meaning, purpose, and value derive from God as creator and inhere in the created order only in a secondary sense. To say that Christian ethics is theocentric does not suggest that it is theocentric in the sense that humans can somehow achieve the perspective of God. Such a view, for biblical faith, would be patently idolatrous. The meaning of theocentric for Christian ethics, therefore, cannot be a meaning defined as the opposite of anthropocentric. Any human believing, any human attempt to understand the will of God will inevitably take place from particular human locations and will in that way be anthropocentric. Copernicus did not leave his human location and earth-centered perspective when he proclaimed a heliocentric solar system; he was using his human imagination to construct a different way of understanding our human location. To the extent that Christians believe themselves created by God, they know that they live by faith and not by a certainty derived from occupying the place of God and viewing reality and value from that center. A theocentricity defined as the opposite is both contradictory and impossible within a Christian ethics of creation. Though aware that their reflection as moral beings takes place within historical, social, and natural location, Christians believe in the deepest sense that the source of reality and value is God. As an ethics of creation, Christian ethics points beyond human location for its validation, its limitations, and its possibility for change and renewal. This kind of anthropocentric understanding is what is meant by theocentric in Christian ethics.

Sixth, a Christian ethics of creation involves awareness of the wholeness of the world and the interdependence of all its constituent parts. Christian ethics, when faithful to the biblical teaching of creation, cannot be other than committed to environmental integrity. This is required by the value given the created order by God as well as the knowledge that the well being of humanity is symbiotically linked to the well being of nature. For policy ethics, this wholeness reminds us that issues are closely related and cannot be separated out and dealt with one by one as scientific rationality would prefer. Policy in its implied wholeness corresponds well to the wholeness of a Christian ethics of creation.

Creativity. To speak of ethics and the environment in Christian perspective involves also an ethics of creativity. Creation is not a static, once-for-all occurrence but rather refers to the making of something that is new. Creation, as it is understood in the Bible, is a process involving change and the continuing emergence of the new. Creation means ongoing renewal toward a consummation hidden in God. Genesis reports God declaring the creation good, and Revelation affirms that God is making all things new (Revelation 21:59). It is not a contradiction but rather an illustration of the creativity of God's activity in creation.

A Christian ethics of creativity, first, means understanding the world and humanity as created and existing in process. Reflection about the moral significance of action and the criteria for guiding human response to God must take account of change. God did not create a perfect world but rather a good world in process toward a greater completeness, toward an ever-emerging goodness the course and end of which are shrouded in mystery. We know in bits and pieces, but as we move toward that consummation we shall know in the wholeness with which we have been known all along (I Corinthians 13:12). In this perspective, we cannot say that we know with certainty where we are headed. We make projections and we plan on the basis of imagination and information. But reality unfolds in unanticipated ways. We are aware only that we are called in faith toward a future in the hands of God the Faithful One. Rather than a process theology and ethics based on upon the "right" philosophy and upon a rational metaphysics, a Christian ethics of creativity is based upon a process theology drawn from the Bible and its teaching of the unfolding and development of nature and history through God's covenant.[8]

A Christian ethics of creativity, second, means that creational process involves creating the new and continuing renewal. On the one hand, humans come upon the stage of the world that provides compelling evidence of a past filled with emergence of the new. Creation exhibits creativity and calls humans to responsibility in freedom that requires participating in the creativity of the world. New problems calling for new solutions are constantly emerging on the horizons of human experience. The creativity of the Creator is reflected in the responsive creative of the creatures. On the other hand, humanity rebels against the goodness and faithfulness of God. Humans resist the creational process and turn from the possibilities inherent in creativity. God's renewing and redeeming work through Christ is crucial if creativity is to continue and humans have the possibility of rejoining God's creative process.

Third, a Christian ethics of creativity involves also a sense of purpose, projection, and goal. Responsibility means responding not just to what is happening at the moment but to the unfolding future. Creativity means dreaming forward toward real possibilities no less than careful attention to the present. Because Christians believe that the sovereign reality as created by God is in process toward fulfillment, Christian ethics as ontological must also be teleological. Humans are called to have goals and to make plans to accomplish them. The movement from old to new in the Bible embodies the newness and renewing power of God's love and also points forward to a more encompassing consummation. Jesus speaks of the newness when he says, "You have heard it said of old . . . but I say unto you" (Matthew 5:21-22,27-28,31-32,33-34, 38-39,43-44). He proclaims the new in relation to customs, by his own treatment of and relation to women, and in his dealing with the law. It is not a doing away with the past or with the law but a fulfillment of them (Matthew 5:17). Paul underscores this teleological element that Jesus represents: "For Christ is the end (*telos*) of the law, that everyone who has faith may be justified" (Romans 10:4).

A Christian ethics of creativity, fourth, with its teleology of nature and history does not involve a belief in progress either as inevitable or probable. The future holds unfolding possibilities that we perceive dimly. Those possibilities insofar as we can judge them contain a mixture of good and evil. From both natural occurrences and human action, good and evil come, and rain falls on the just and on the unjust. Jesus is crucified. Prophets and prophetic minorities are persecuted. Leaders of movements for justice are assassinated. Every human accomplishment stands forever on the razor's edge of danger, both in the possibility of being swept away and in the possibility of producing bad rather than good results. The ethics of creativity offers no historical guarantees. But such an ethic does offer guidelines helpful in understanding our creation within, submersion in, and responsibility for the created order and our environment. The ultimate hope of Christian ethics lies in the resurrection of Christ, in possibilities beyond tragedy, and in the faithful action of God bringing all things to consummation with faithfulness.

Covenant. A Christian ethics of creation and creativity require completion in and ethics of covenant. The entire created order is within the covenant of God and therefore to be valued and respected in itself. The covenant emphasizes the bond among all parts of creation making them interdependent. The covenant provides the basis and bounds of creativity, while creativity underscores that God's covenant is not static but rather shapes a process with purpose and possibility. A Christian ethics of covenant understands humanity as social and symbiotically related to the environment; morally responsible to God for other humans and for nature; and called to act in faithfulness and fittingness.

First, Christian ethics as covenantal involves an understanding of humanity as existing in relationship to society, nature, and God.

Humans can be viewed in covenantal perspective neither as separate nor as autonomous individuals. Humans are born into natural and social relationships and exist by means of a web of interdependency. To be an individual is to be in symbiotic relationship with nature and with particular human communities. The natural order and history have a dynamic quality of change, yet there are also in our experience strong elements of stability and dependability. Experience discloses a covenant world of change within steadfast patterns. Philosophers may presuppose a static substance underlying the ordered flow of events, but nothing of that static substructure appears in human experiencing. Or scientific positivists may adhere to the dogma of static "facts" waiting to be uncovered and described, but their seeking for "objective reality" never escapes its involvement with their "subjective interpretations." A covenanted wholeness provides a more adequate metaphor for our world than do the fragmented results of critical rationality or metaphors of organism and society alone. Covenant encompasses the parts, restores the relatedness of the whole environment, and adds dimensions of commitment and loyalty to the created order and to God.

Second, therefore, Christian ethics as covenantal includes the moral responsibility of humans within and through the fabric of relationships in an environment that is at once natural, social, and divine. The covenantal call of the Hebrew prophets for justice in the political economy and for liberation from oppression, the command of Jesus that we love one another as he has loved us, and the demand flowing through all the Bible for faithful response in all our actions to the faithfulness of God—all these and the vivid narratives in which they are conveyed give content and valence to covenantal ethics.

Third, Christian ethics as covenantal reminds us that fittingness and faithfulness through Jesus Christ, who is our covenant, are central for Christian faith and action. Fittingness means that human action must correspond to the need of the context and be appropriate within the pattern of prior and subsequent action. In one sense, fittingness underscores the importance of particularity —responding to particular persons, situations, and issues. In a larger sense, fittingness requires taking account of the encompassing context of the social and natural environment, so that what is done fits in with everything else that is happening and avoids causing more problems than it solves. Faithfulness means loyalty to the cause of God, whatever the consequences. In extreme cases, it could involve a martyr's death. In the more usual sense, however, faithfulness means loyalty to our companions on life's journey, to our world, and through these to God. In seeking justice for the downtrodden, liberation for the oppressed, food for the hungry, clothes for the naked, ways to avoid nuclear holocaust, and sound ecological policies, we are being faithful not only to our neighbors in society and to the larger environment but also to God the Faithful One, who in covenant creates a symbiotic order and continually judges, redeems, and renews this bent and battered world.

Christian ethics as an ethics of creation, creativity, and covenant provides an encompassing and rigorous pattern for recovering the Christian awareness of the created order and developing a meaningful environmental ethics for today. It remains now to suggest the policy implications inherent in this perspective.

5. Implications for Policy Ethics

The renewal of the Christian awareness of and concern for the created order has far-reaching significance for policy relating to a wide spectrum of issues and on all levels of human agency. Christian ethics, understood as outlined above as part of the renewed Christian creation consciousness, requires the inclusion of policy ethics in relation to all arenas of human action. We shall explore the implications for policy ethics under two headings: the interrelation of issues, and the significance for levels of human action.

Interrelation of Issues. Because the Christian understanding of creation seen in the perspective provided above emphasizes the interdependency of the entire created order within the covenant of God, it is not possible to consider one social or environmental issue in isolation from others. Every sector of the world is related to every other sector.

In the mid-70s, the staff of the Center for Ethics and Social Policy began developing curricular materials on world hunger. It soon became clear that hunger must be related to issues of agriculture, population, development, and ecological care for the natural environment. We looked at many treatments of justice. We found elegant theories. But justice is not a theory but rather relations among real human beings in the actualities of political economies and social/natural environments. Problems of injustice arise in particular situations and cannot be detached from issues of power and ecology. In the world as created, all parts have a mutuality of relation and responsibility to one another given by

God in the creational covenant. Justice and love inhere in these covenantal relations, not as rational theories but as actualities permeating all particular contexts.

The study material on hunger, therefore, developed into what we called *Ethics for a Crowded World.*[9] Built around issues related to world hunger, the study volume contained units on world population, world income distribution, world agriculture, international development, ecology and development, energy and development, a discussion of limits to growth, and, to keep us close to real human situations, case studies in development. As a framework for ethical analysis, we used one with three elements: self interest, responsibility for others, and social vision. These correspond to criteria operative in human situations and are applicable to varied levels of human agency. These criteria relate well to a Christian ethic of covenantal interdependency. And they open the way for emphasizing the interrelation of issues.

Significance for Different Levels of Agency.   Just as issues cannot be separated from one another if they are viewed in the wholeness of creation, so also action on behalf of creation justice and well-being must be related to the various levels of human agency. We have discussed these earlier as the individual level of agency, the organizational level, the social sector level, and the macro socio-cultural level. As an example of a way to deal with a current problem in this wider social and environmental perspective, let us look at energy.

The ethical issues associated with energy policy are rooted in the extraordinary global interdependency exemplified in energy production and use. Present patterns of production and utilization demonstrate how decisions on different levels in the United States have an impact on justice and human well-being around the globe. Americans live in a society organized around high energy use. Our massive use of energy resources limits what is available to other parts of the world and has enormous influence on social patterns elsewhere. Policies in the U.S. have for decades encouraged the profligate use of energy—gasoline for big automobiles, natural gas and oil to heat poorly insulated buildings, electricity to cool offices whose windows will not open, energy-intensive agriculture, etc. The challenging questions today relate to social justice, to hunger and poverty, to the prospects of depletion of energy sources, and to environmental damage. What avenues of responsible action are open in the light of these challenges?

Three patterns of response seem possible: conservation, restitution, and global cooperation. Each of these must be considered in relation to the levels of human agency. Individual action is appropriate but insufficient. The perspective of Christian creational wholeness requires action on organizational and societal levels and, therefore, the development of policy ethics.

Conservation of energy is an immediate need. Reduction of our wasteful use of energy is the first front. Actions of individuals can have important and direct impact on energy conservation. Each person can examine his/her life style and modify behavior on a day-to-day basis. We can buy automobiles that use lower amounts of fuel, consider more carefully whether trips are necessary, and take public transportation more often. We can insulate our homes and other buildings better in order to decrease the need for fuel to heat in the winter and to cool in the summer. We can shift to renewable energy sources, such as solar and wind energy. But these must not be left and are not being left to voluntary and individual action. It is important that the organizational level of agency be utilized. The policies of corporations, educational institutions, hospitals, community groups, churches, agriculture, and labor need to be revised to carry out conservation along the lines suggested for individual action. Even more entire social sectors need to take action to conserve. And, of course, governmental action in the form of laws and incentives impinging on all levels of the political economy need to be carried out.

Restitution is a further form of action needed. This approach acknowledges that the energy drain from and pressure upon developing nations is, in part at least, the result of inadequately responsible action in the industrialized nations. The United States has benefitted in greater proportion and European nations to a lesser extent from past patterns of energy use. As actions of restitution, we need to consider greater individual efforts and contributions to aid developing nations, through churches and community agencies. Organizations such as corporations, banks, and agricultural agencies need to develop programs that will aid the developing world. As the Third and Fourth World loom larger on the global scene, such aid may serve the purposes of survival and continued growth for Western corporations as well as the increase of justice and well-being for other peoples. Governmental action is especially important for purposes of restitution. Loans, better schedules for repayments, lower interest, and grants of money and technical assistance are ways that action on the level of governmental/societal agency can be improved. Increased technical assistance that emphasizes low investment, low cost, decentralized forms of energy development and conversion is imperative. Such an approach requires research and development commitments by Western nations to solar, wind, water, and biological energy sources using intermediate technologies applicable to less developed economies.

Global cooperation represents a continuing agenda for policy ethics. It begins with an acknowledgment of the highly interdependent nature of peoples, nations, and nature, and the massive problems that inadequate global cooperation is causing today. Not only is action needed at every level of human agency, but we must have increased information about the values and purposes of other cultural systems. No amount of aid that does not fit in with other national contexts can be effective. And no dealing with energy apart from other problems will produce real solutions. Policies by Western governments that gear into the feudal political economies of Third World nations will not further the cause of justice and thus will be inadequate with reference to hunger, population, or energy.

This illustration suggests the direction of energy policy that recognizes the wholeness of the created order. All reality is valuable because valued by God. Christian ethics rooted in creation awareness reminds us from first to last of the interdependence woven into the very fabric of creation, a fabric shaped by the covenant of God so that humanity and nature, and every issue of our large environment must be seen as existing in symbiotic relationship.

The power to affect policy at any particular level or with reference to specific organizations and issues is limited for everyone. But it is our responsibility within the Christian community to take seriously the dimensions of ethical concern informed by creation, creativity, and covenant. We then can take action as persons and as participants in the policy processes of society at various levels of agency in the light of Christian faith.

Notes

1. D. Walther Eichrodt, *Theologie des alten Testaments*. Three volumes. (Leipzig: J. C. Hinrichs, 1933), Vol. I, p. 6.
2. See Norman H. Snaith, *The Distinctive Ideas of the Old Testament*. (London: Epworth Press, 1944); and Otto J. Baab, *The Theology of the Old Testament*. (New York: Abingdon-Cokesbury Press, 1949).

3. Martin Buber, *The Prophetic Faith*. (New York: Macmillan, 1949), passim.

4. Bernhard H. Anderson, *Understanding the Old Testament*. (Englewood Cliffs: Prentice-Hall, 1958), p. 51.

5. Johannes Althusius, *Politics*, Translated by Frederick S. Carney. (Boston: Beacon Press, 1964), I, 1.

6. See Charles S. McCoy, *When Gods Change: Hope for Theology*. (Nashville: Abingdon, 1980).

7. For a somewhat different but compatible treatment, see H. Paul Santmire, *Brother Earth: Nature, God, and Ecology in Time of Crisis*. (New York: Thomas Nelson & Co., 1970).

8. See *When Gods Change* for a biblical process theology based on covenant.

9. (Berkeley: Center for Ethics and Social Policy, Second Edition, 1978.) See also Ian G. Barbour, *Technology, Environment, and Human Values*. (New York: Praeger, 1980.).

Part V

MODELS FOR
THE EXPANSION OF
CREATION CONSCIOUSNESS
TODAY

The expansion of creation consciousness must take place in ways that enhance the quality of every type of human relationship. In the essays that follow, the development of these relationships is visualized in terms of different kinds of models, each contributing to the transformation of the culture and the extension of the Kingdom of God. Charles McCoy, earlier in Chapter 20, and Alan Miller, here in Chapter 21, focus upon the kinds of changes that an expanding creation consciousness may be expected to bring about in attitudes toward the environment, in motivation for environmental action, and through policy building. These chapters and portions of others that follow in this section are written in response to the frustration that was first felt so keenly in the 1960s over the patent inadequacy of the main body of the inherited Christian creation tradition to deal with the rising tide of abuse of the environment.

Additionally, in Chapter 22 Ted Peters describes a recently emphasized style of Christian anticipation of the future that has roots earlier in the tradition. In Chapter 25, the leaders of four recently initiated educational programs describe how these programs implement the new concern to understand and relate to the "otherkinds" in terms of a Christian faith that is finding its way into a creation-embracing relevance and depth.

Douglas Adams' exploration of "Sacramental Worship for Creation Consciousness" in Chapter 23 reflects his interest in worship that manifests awareness and that is open and expressive enough to be truly creative.

In Chapter 24, Philip Joranson and Ken Butigan offer suggestions for the building of creation-conscious life styles, valued for their instrumentality in personal growth and for their contribution to the dynamics of creation-wide fulfillment of the Kingdom of God.

Chapter Twenty-One

THE ENVIRONMENTAL AND OTHER BIOETHICAL CHALLENGES FOR CHRISTIAN CREATION CONSCIOUSNESS

Alan S. Miller

If environmental planner Ian McHarg is even close to correct in his now classic book, *Design with Nature*, Judeo-Christian religion stands much in need of an updating of its creation tradition. Criticizing the radically anthropocentric perspectives of the tradition, McHarg states that Christianity,

> in its insistence upon dominion and subjugation of nature, encourages the most exploitative and destructive instincts in man rather than those that are deferential and creative. Indeed, if one seeks license for those who would increase radioactivity, create canals and harbors with atomic bombs, carry poisons without constraint, or give consent to the bulldozer mentality, there could be no better injunction than this biblical creation text. Here can be found the injunction to conquer nature—the enemy, the threat to Jehovah.[1]

Although stating the case, as many feel, too unequivocally, he nonetheless points to the central dilemma confronting those who are sensitive both to the Judeo-Christian tradition and to the insights of the natural sciences. Traditional theism has always had trouble explaining the importance of the created orders. God, cosmologically separate from and independent of the natural world in so much of this tradition, is forever more concerned for humankind than for nature. The problem was posed precisely in a recent study of the relationship between Christianity and the stewardship of natural resources:

> . . .Christians have traditionally seen the rest of the world merely as the background for the human drama of salvation.[2]

But however we may distinguish *Homo sapiens* from the rest of the creation, the biological disciplines are clear about our close relationship to other living organisms. Whether we view our species with the Psalmist as being only ". . .a little lower than the angels" or with the Church Fathers as ". . .created in the image of God," we now understand correctly that beneath our respective membranes, living things from bacteria to humans are biochemically very much the same. DNA is DNA whether we like it or not! Throughout the billions of years of evolution, the biological process has indeed made one family of all living creatures on this earth.

Having cut my own theological eye teeth, however, on the staunchly emphatic and anti-ecological "no" of Karl Barth and most of the neo-orthodox theologians to any form of natural theology, I now must protest that tradition which suggests that the history of the cosmos must be seen as having only subsidiary importance to the salvation history of the human species. Protestant orthodoxy, for example, has for too long viewed nature and the biological process as permanent, unchanging, and essentially separate from the other, more spiritual forces affecting humankind. Nature's function was to provide a cornucopia of "resources" for the use of Adam and Eve and their successor generations. In such a tradition of instrumentalist ethics, where earth's bounties had only a "use" value, with the creation viewed as essentially a means to other and greater ends, the only realm of the really real has been human history. The only portion of that history with real consequence for believers was its salvation history. Eschatologically, nothing else really mattered.

But the environmentalist—religious or otherwise—has to make a choice. Either our combination of reflection and action—the praxis of our common life—has to be focused on the special history of our own species or on the entire creation. What has been called "Christian environmentalism" has too often been pre-empted by the premise that, after all, "this world is passing away." Accordingly, such efforts have too often represented little more than liberally chic efforts to tidy up the global house a bit before the millenium arrives. Those who as Christians are more intellectually centered in the functioning of nature than in the formulas of special revelation may perhaps be forgiven for wondering how a state of grace for modern humanity can have much to do with ecological survival.

At the Turning Point. During the past decade, three major studies, each sponsored by the Club of Rome[3], have provided a continuing analysis of the primary environmental dilemmas of the era. Although criticized by both ends of the political spectrum, the conclusions of *The Limits to Growth; Mankind at the Turning Point;* and *RIO: Reshaping the International Order* suggest the problems requiring resolution if there is to be whole earth survival.[4] Analyzing the five key factors in the crisis (resource use, pollution, food per capita, industrial output per capita and population growth), the authors of these studies develop a variety of futurist scenarios based on the implications of a continuance of exponential growth rates in these areas. Their conclusions were upsetting both to Western industrialists and to planners in the Socialist countries who, interestingly enough, project remarkably similar economic growth models based on unlimited increases in resource use and overall industrialization.

In *The Limits to Growth*, an attempt is made to describe the biospheric limits to environmental degradation and to suggest the consequences of continued growth.

> One of the most commonly accepted myths in our present society is the promise that a continuation of our present patterns of growth will lead to human equality. . .

> Present patterns of population and capital growth are actually increasing the gap between the rich and the poor on a world-wide basis, and. . . the ultimate result of a continued attempt to grow according to the present pattern will be a disastrous collapse. . . .

> If the present growth trends in world population, industrialization, pollution, food production, and resource depletion continue unchanged, the limits to growth on this planet will be reached within the next hundred years. The most probable result will be a sudden and uncontrollable decline in both population and industrial capacity.[5]

Taking off from the rather dire predictions of this first Club of Rome study, *Mankind at the Turning Point* suggests the importance of viewing the globe as a mixture of overdeveloped and underdeveloped regions, each with special needs requiring economic and environmental policies formulated to accord with the particular strengths and problems of the region. This report was prepared primarily at the request of leaders in the developing world who understood the irrelevance of attempting to apply a single model for growth and development to countries rich and poor. One of the compelling features of the study, based on a recognition of the disparate economic and social realities throughout the world, was the development of a theory of "organic growth" as an alternative for developing countries to the more traditional patterns of exponential increases in the exploitation and uses of natural resources. Organic growth models assume a more rational movement toward stable economic development patterns after basic social needs of particular societies have been met. The kind of rapacious overdevelopment so characteristic of most industrial nations is specifically rejected.

Attempting to practically implement some of the suggestions in these two studies, the third Club of Rome publication, *RIO: Reshaping the International Order*, suggests new and often controversial means for implementing "eco-development." Agreeing with *The Limits to Growth* that the patterns of industrial growth in the overdeveloped world provide the single greatest problem in the environmental crisis, the study essentially affirms the recommendations of the United Nations' New International Economic Order: protecting developing nations from the predations of the global market system, providing back-up support programs for the poorest nations, affirming the importance of local control over basic public utilities, encouraging special taxation programs to redistribute wealth from the wealthiest to the poorest, plus commodity indexing and the creation of new international control organizations to curb the economic power of the overdeveloped nations.[6]

However one views these suggestions and the analysis in the Club of Rome studies, it is generally agreed that the five problems outlined are absolutely critical to our collective future. Some further analysis of the issues, however, needs to be made to put these problems in perspective.

Population.   Although Western policy in confronting the global population problem has focused on exporting contraceptive technology to the developing world, the data is fast accumulating to document the more comprehensive population theory that only a fundamental redistribution of the wealth in the poorest countries of the world can check the global population explosion. As many demographers have noted, people are not poor because they have large families; on the contrary, they have large families because they are poor.

The critical point of demographic transition (the statistical movement from higher to lower birth and death rates and the consequent stabilization of population growth) has been reached only in those countries where food, housing, education, and health care have been reasonably distributed among all classes in the society. The guarantee of social security, assured employment, and a steadily rising standard of living seems to be required to move developing nations toward population stability. In fact, of course, population densities in most parts of the Third World are far less than those in, for example, Western Europe. But population growth rates have shown substantial increases in recent decades and family planning services have proven to be completely inadequate substitutes for needed economic and social change. While birth control clinics have been more palatable to most of these governments than efforts to internally redistribute wealth, most of the world's poor have discovered that the only way to survive and the only possible hope for old age security is to have many children.

Food Distribution.   Food production and distribution continues to be one of the overwhelming problems facing the people of the world. This year, world-wide, twenty to fifty million people will starve or will die as a direct result of inadequate nourishment. More than one-third of all people alive today suffer chronic protein and caloric malnutrition. The World Bank has documented the fact that infant mortality in the Third World (Asia, Africa, Latin America) is now more than eight times higher than that in the developed world. Life expectancy is one-third lower. The nutritional level of one hundred million children is not sufficient to permit optimum brain development. Seven hundred and fifty million people have a per capita income of less than $100 per year and another billion earn less than $500 per year. What is clear is that, tragic as it is, famine is only the spotlight on the stage of the world's food problem. Of more basic concern to the two billion have-nots are chronic hunger, the diseases induced by malnutrition, and the continuing competition for food supplies with the richer nations. Unbelievably, the Third World is a net exporter of protein to the overdeveloped world, a trade imbalance further complicating the already harsh conditions of suffering people.

Most experts would agree with the blunt appraisal that food is generally available throughout the world, but only to those who have the means to buy it. As Earl Butz, (then U.S. Secretary of Agriculture) stated to the developing nations in 1974 at the Rome Food Conference, in a paraphrase of the U.S. position on food policy, "If you've got the money, we've got the food." Income, particularly within the existing world inflationary spiral, determines who shall live and who shall die. Already, the nations of the world produce sufficient food to provide each person with more than 3,000 calories per day. Until collective decisions can be reached, however, to change the patterns of land ownership and global food production and distribution, the all too-common-cycle of malnutrition, infection, and death at an early age will continue to be the unconscionable norm of the planet Earth.

Resource Use, Industrialization, Pollution   The people of the earth face a double dilemma in their use of natural resources: maldistribution of resources and shortages of critical materials. That, however, is only part of the overall problem. No longer does anyone—even the worst offender—deny that the developed world has irrationally exploited the material stocks of the planet. As every American school child knows, North America with six percent of the world's population now consumes almost forty percent of total world resources. Per capita, Americans consume up to fifty times as much of the primary materials and fuels as people in the poorest countries. To suggest that such a pattern of unbalanced and irrational use of resources can continue much longer into the future is to ignore the survival requirements of the species. While some may argue that the resource base is much greater than estimates usually indicate, requiring only technological sophistication and the pricing mechanisms of the market to open up new supplies, the environmental limiting factors of the planet suggest that there are indeed absolute limits to growth. So long as the rich consume the great part of the earth's resources in a consumption binge that escalates year by year, people everywhere must look to alternative economic and political systems to guarantee fairer consumption patterns.

It is hard to be optimistic about the possibility of new standards of self control ever being invoked by the offending nations. The usual American targets of increases in the Gross National Product of five to six percent per year guarantee that resources will continue to be extravagantly exploited. Such annual increases imply doubling times of ten to fifteen years—even at the lower end of the growth scale. With ten-year doubling times in economic growth comes similar doubling in the use of raw materials, consumption patterns that clearly cannot long be sustained. Unfortunately, alternative models of economic growth and industrialization are not easy to find. Both capitalist and socialist economic orders seem to share a common irrational belief in the beneficence of nature and in materials policies that affirm the propriety of exploiting whatever is needed to meet national economic goals.

In a world with unlimited demand, finite resources, and enormous inequities in economic and political power, the question of who gets what and why — the historic problem of distributive justice — is at the heart of any system of resource planning. Given the tradition in all societies that the well placed or well to do always get the most and the best of everything, the question of how to properly deliver both the essentials required to maintain even minimum life quality (food, shelter, education) and needed health services demands attention. Distributive justice is at the very center of environmental ethics.

Even though every social system from the beginning of time has given at least some form of lip service to the issue of fairness in sharing resources of all kinds, the practice has always come far short of the theoretical mark. Even in advanced and "enlightened" countries like the United States, the pretense of being able to effect equity in delivering the goods of society was given up long ago.

Even though a particular country may be able to moderately resolve its own dilemma of distributive justice in the delivery of needed goods and services — and perhaps cannot be expected to do much more — such a resolution may prove out to be basically irrelevant to the rest of the global population. Distributive justice, because it involves the parceling out of a relatively fixed supply of resources amongst all members of the society, is clearly a social issue. But it is also a macroallocation problem global in scope requiring global rather than local or regional solutions. Joseph Fletcher states the point clearly:

> Ethics is perforce "social ethics" now. It is no longer. . .what we might call interpersonal morality. The world is so tied together. . .that we are caught in a tight web of radical interconnectivity. This is an age of macroethical rather than microethical analysis.[7]

The First World—the overdeveloped world of Europe, Japan and North America—still consumes 67 percent of all the global grain supply, 75 percent of the fish, and 80 percent of all the protein produced by the nations of the world. If the United States should develop a medical nutrition program to resolve the dietary problems of America's "have-nots," one-third of the total population of Africa and Asia would still suffer debilitating malnutrition. If the two great health problems of the developed world, cancer and cardio-vascular disease, could be resolved, the immensely larger problems of infectious disease in the poorer nations of the Third World would still not be touched. In spite of all good intentions, therefore, it is obvious that solutions to human and environmental survival problems go beyond the drawing boards of the distributional planners. Notwithstanding our sophisticated political and economic systems, choices are made daily over who shall live and who shall die. It has recently been estimated that if only 18 percent of the world's population (instead of the current 6 percent) consumed goods at the rate North America deems appropriate, absolutely nothing would be left for the remaining 82 percent of the world's population. According to United Nations estimates, 450 million people now alive may starve to death. To solve that basic starvation problem would require only about 50 million tons of wheat per year, an amount equal to only 3-5 percent of our total global production of cereal grains and only 10-15 percent of the cereals currently fed to cattle alone in the developed world.[8]

Of at least equal long-range importance to human survival and to distributive justice is the fact that destruction of renewable natural resources continues to escalate. While most of the international focus centers on the depletion of non-renewables (oil, natural gas, coal, minerals), production has already begun a sharp decline in the four key areas of renewable resources: forests, fisheries, grasslands, and croplands. Internal nation-by-nation efforts to deal with the economic realities of resource preservation seem to affect the overall calculus very little. Economist Herman E. Daly, arguing that it is both an ecological and a moral necessity to limit economic growth in the developed world, suggests the need to formulate an "impossibility" theorem.

> The starting point in our thinking about economic development should be an impossibility theorem: that a U.S. style high mass consumption economy for a world of four billion people is impossible to achieve, and even if it could be achieved it would be very short-lived.

> Even less possible is an ever-growing standard of consumption for an ever-growing population.

> But, it will be objected, the answer is simply to increase total world resource flows. By how much would such flows have to increase to bring world per capita levels up to U.S. per capita levels? By a factor of about 6 or 7, it turns out. But this refers only to current production. To supply the rest of the world with the average per capita accumulation or 'standing crop' of industrial metals already

embodied in existing artifacts in the ten richest nations would require more than sixty years of production of these metals at 1970 rates.[9]

Daly, and an increasing number of international economists, suggest that the total number of person-years remaining in industrially developed nations is now limited. The interface of resource use and population in such countries precludes a long-range future under such conditions of consumption. This recognition pushes us to face a series of difficult ethical decisions. How can a more equitable apportionment of resources be effected if we are to increase the number of survivable years amongst the nations of the earth. To those who respond, "only by the use of economic power and military might," we must note that most such power now rests in the hands of those rich and powerful nations who bear primary responsibility for the problem and who apparently have no intention of changing the social policies leading to such consumption norms. Attempts to internally reallocate resources in poor countries—a desperately needed requirement—have inevitably resulted in wars of revolution or national liberation. Given the political power imbalance in the world today, it is doubtful indeed if any such efforts at redressing historic inequity can succeed on any but quite local levels. Even here, however, the first and most critical step towards resolution of the problem is securing information and doing education around it.

Industrial excess and/or maldevelopment have other consequences as well. More than any other of the environmental predicaments in the Club of Rome studies, pollution is correctly seen as the most complicated effect of the interaction of technology, industrialization, production modes, and population. As the Meadows study points out, it is impossible to determine accurately the upper limits of the carrying capacity of the earth to handle global pollution. What is clear is that toxicity limits have already been exceeded in many local environments. Very little of the prior damage done to the biosphere is reversible. Urban life expectancies are changing, a host of new diseases related to pollution are now common, environmentally induced cancer seems to be growing at the astounding rate of almost one percent per year in some areas, and few people will willingly live in what are expected to be the terrifying pollution problems of Mexico City, Los Angeles, Tokyo, and other major cities of the twenty-first century. As one environmentalist commentator has stated, documenting the fact that humankind will have to live with the consequences of its polluting activities for a very long time,

If pollution is to be cured and mankind to survive in a healthy world, the individual enterprises of society have to be coordinated by a common goal directing the activity of the whole society. Only by creating such a society, which governs its actions by a social instead of a private rationality, can mankind live in affluent but non-polluting culture.[10]

Science and Technology.   The manner in which we deal with the natural orders is to a very large degree determined by the functioning of the established scientific and technological communities. Contrary to much popular opinion, scientific options do not simply flow unimpeded by bias in some neutral pursuit of absolute truth. Decisions regarding the forms and functions of science are usually made in the corridors of power by governmental and economic decision makers. Indeed, the functioning of the political and economic system is of far more consequence to the practice of science than either traditional philosophies or conceptual paradigms.

In his now classic play, *Galileo*, Bertolt Brecht reminds his audience that the only real purpose of science is to ease the burden of humanity, even though he suspects that: ". . .the best one can hope for from science today is for a race of inventive scientific dwarfs who can be hired to do anything." While most of the members of the scientific community today will protest that their arts are always ethically neutral, such in fact is rarely the case. The ruling elite of any given society determines to an almost total degree the nature of the scientific venture and the types of technological problems which require resolution. Although the practitioners like to keep a clean conceptual separation between the functions of science and technology, the two most often blend together in not always subtle fashion. Science often simply functions as the fig leaf for technology, less concerned for serving truth than for cloaking the development of new and potentially profitable tools for those in positions of power.

As Joseph Schumpeter long ago pointed out, corporate activity is usually the key in advanced market economics to unlock the door to scientific and technological innovation. And although Thomas Kuhn might protest, it does appear today that the emergent scientific paradigms reflect more the needs of capital and the bottom line of profitability than the new conceptual apparatus historically required to inaugurate scientific revolutions. Since industrial research is most often geared directly to the satisfaction of either the requirements of state policy (e.g., military research) or the satisfaction of manipulated consumer desires, the bias within the research endeavor inevitably tilts toward meeting private or governmental requirements rather than social needs.

With the emergence of the new knowledge industries within government (in education, health, energy, national security) which now control both the decision making and the mechanics of scientific funding, the bias in science and technology in this direction becomes reinforced. Indeed, politics and economics are now considered the legitimate parents of science, ministered to by a managerial class neither equipped nor normally interested in asking the requisite value questions. The ethical dilemma becomes immediately apparently, for example, when one helplessly notes that two-thirds of the federal budget for research and development is earmarked for the military and that all energy research policy is determined by industry and rubber-stamped by governmental functionaries.

Similarly, science and technology always carry certain marks that are imprinted by the nature of the production system within which they must operate. Characterizing our American industrial system—whether in the production of consumer goods or the goods of science—are tendencies toward capital intensive, centralized, hierarchically organized, large-scale and labor specialized forms of production. An illustration that leaps to mind has been this nation's official advocacy of nuclear energy as our primary alternative energy source for the future. Only reluctantly in recent years have energy planners had to face the shattering of the nuclear dream.[11]

In accord with our basic prerequisites for production, nuclear plants are capital rather than labor intensive, both because of the requirements of capital and the difficulties industrialists experience in managing a labor force. Machines are always more docile (but sometimes more dangerous) than people. Construction and maintenance costs of nuclear plants far exceed those of conventional fossil fuel generating systems, thus providing continual opportunities for reinvestment. The control and management of nuclear facilities (especially as they have grown in scale) have become more and more centralized. Plants are larger—never below 1,000 megawatts—with nuclear visionaries projecting "atomic parks" of ten to fifteen plants in a cluster mode. Should nuclear fusion ever become reality (an even more remote possibility than economically sound nuclear fission power generation), authorities agree that such tendencies will be reinforced with an entire energy industry controlled by very small numbers of people. With production largely controlled by automated processes and cybernated systems, decision-making must be hierarchial and authoritative. When dealing with fissioning atoms and ionizing radiation, too many cooks might indeed spoil the broth. Technological specialization is now a formal requirement of advanced industrial systems. The old popular dreams of humanized labor and worker autonomy no longer fit within the mode of accepted industrial development or scientific progress.

The end result of this form of science and technology is a deepening of the social constraints that operate in the society. The worker becomes an appendage of the machine (with the exception of the "new class" of technicians) and loses any sense of a direct role in the course of production. In human terms alone, energy systems relying on labor intensive, decentralized, small-scale and democratically organized production seem to be at least one primary base for an energy ethic for the future.

Perception and images of the environment are always reinforced (or changed) by cultural, economic, and scientific perspectives. New images of the creation will likely be determined by the emergence of the new ethical paradigms. This must include a redefinition of the concept of scarcity. Most of the popular reporting on the environmental crisis details aspects of the scarcity problem: scarcity of food, of mineral resources, and of energy. But scarcity is never an absolute concept: rather, it is inextricably tied to social, scientific, economic, and cultural ends. Switzerland, for example, currently uses less than thirty percent of the energy per capita used in the United States. But for anyone who has traveled in Switzerland, it is clear that energy is in no sense scarce. If we were to transpose Swiss consumption to this country, however, an abundance in one situation would quickly become a shortage—a "scarcity"—in this. Few of our scarcities arise out of nature itself. Most are created and managed by forces within the society and either "solved" or exacerbated by the existing economic, scientific, and technological apparatus.

So it is that the patterns of industrial production in this country, the usually "for profit" functioning of the scientific establishment, and the manipulation of consumer demand by the corporate sector have contributed to a profligate use of resources and an increasingly rapacious attitude toward the creation. Called to be stewards, we both consume materials at rates many times those of most countries in the world and ignore the conservationist imperative. Burdened by manipulated expectations, we accept the mythologies of scarcity and are unknowingly used to further goals inimical to the welfare of the world's people. For when connotations of absolute limits come to surround the debate over resource scarcity, then functional limits of one kind of another have to be determined. Unfortunately, but inevitably, such definitions of limits tend to be directed toward formal constraints on population growth rather than to the primary issue of increasing and redistributing existing resources in order to increase the global population carrying capacity. Within the arena of population demographics, for example, science can be directed either toward promoting contraceptive technologies or to ending economic inequity and distributive injustice.

The psychologist John Watson—father of psychological behaviorism—was wrong when he said, "Give me a child and I will make it into whatever I wish." But those who today propose the questions which the scientific community is called upon to answer and who pay the bills for the responses, quite clearly influence the behavioral patterns of the scientists involved and tend to turn the scientific establishment into "whatever they wish." Those who are concerned for the creation must evidence a deep concern for the development of a new and more humane paradigm for a genuine science for the people.

Biological Ethics.   Within the past decade, the new discipline of bioethics has risen to a place of visibility within sections of the American health sciences community. Bioethics is essentially the field of study which attempts to evaluate the ethical implications of trends and developments within the biological and behavioral sciences. Methodologically, one seeks to apply general ethical theory to current biological reality. Theories of justice as well as the moral implications of molecular biology and *in vitro* fertilization are topics within the province of bioethics.

Reflecting the popular concern and interest in such issues, National Public Television in 1981, for example, inaugurated a six-program series entitled *Hard Choices*. Subjects covered in the programs included genetic screening and genetic engineering, human experimentation, behavior control, death and dying and the problem of equity in health care delivery. Increasingly, both popular and scientific concern is mounting over these and a host of other issues in biological ethics.

The bioethicist has several important tasks: identifying the key issues that arise from developments in the general field; attempting to work out a systematic framework for analyzing the issues; and finally, doing whatever is possible to help the scientific community make good decisions and to assist the public in evaluating those decisions.

The questions posed by bioethical discussions are generic to all science today but focus on specific implications for human welfare. Does science have the right to do whatever it finds possible to do? Are there things that should not be done even though they can be done? Is it still possible for any rational control to be exercised over biological research by persons outside the scientific community? Should such controls be exercised? What are the long-range implications of the social rearrangements which have been occasioned by developments in science and technology? Are there new and deepening social constraints imposed on the population at large by the hierarchically organized and increasingly specialized practitioners within the health sciences today? What does it mean to be a "normal" human being? Are there dangers that can emerge from the establishment of biological norms? Should we try to eradicate all genetic "abnormalities"?

The ethical issues arising from the answers we give to these questions are clear and disturbing. The three most common systems of evaluating ethical acts today continue to be those of the Kantian deontologists (who believe that moral acts are always related to one's innate sense of duty and obligation and that humans must always be treated with absolute respect), the utilitarians who evaluate the relative good in an action by virtue of its contribution to the general well-being of the group, and the natural law theorists (inspired by Aristotle and Aquinas) who insist that human actions are morally appropriate so long as such actions are fully in accord with our understanding of both human nature and our end goals as human beings.

Each perspective can provide assistance in attempting to assess the consequences of scientific determination. In a recent and well-publicized case, for example, medical researchers requested authorization to use still viable but voluntarily aborted fetuses for research on the development of an artificial placenta. The fetuses, already legally "dead," could be kept viable for two weeks following the abortion. Although most observers will have an immediate negative response to the merits of such research, it is instructive to note how differing systems of ethics would view the case.

Thomas Aquinas would, of course, be emphatic on two grounds: his essential opposition to abortion and, of more importance, his belief that every natural creature should seek the kind of well-being related to what it is as a species and to the appropriate life and end goal of that species. Under such a moral calculus, research using a fetus in the same ways as others might use a guinea pig would be both abhorrent and immoral. The utilitarian (from Jeremy Bentham and his godson John S. Mill through bioethicist Joseph Fletcher) would affirm the principle of utility in ethical decision-making and suggest that no act is intrinsically right or wrong but should be evaluated strictly on the basis of whether or not it has good consequences and redounds to the real or potential benefit of the greatest number of people. Deontologists—from Immanuel Kant to Paul Ramsey—would emphasize motivation in ethical action rather than consequences and the terrible importance of treating every living being as an end in itself and never to be used as a means to other ends—good as they might be. In this case, the experimental research would cease.

The kind of ethical relativism that has so characterized much modern philosophy seems to this writer singularly inappropriate to deal with issues of the magnitude of those emerging from the biological sciences today. To simply state that in spite of the possible misuse of the new information from recombinant DNA research, we must completely trust the scientific community to make the right decisions (as a renowned molecular biologist said in a bioethics class taught by this author)—is to affirm a kind of moral neutrality that is always coopted by those with other less wholesome intentions. It may well be that humankind for survival's sake today requires a new kind of limitation on scientific inquiry that will limit our explorations into the unknown until such time as our values catch up with our technical expertise. The earth, after all, is in a literal sense the ground of our collective being. Faithfulness to creator and creation requires a particularly cautionary stance today.

In more dramatic fashion than ever before, the Promethean problem and the box of Pandora now reside on the doorstep of every human being. Although a little learning is not a dangerous thing, the legends of the past hold particular warnings for us today. To a larger degree than ever before, the arts and sciences do enable us to have control over our personal and collective destinies and over the planet Earth. Like Pandora's box—but accelerated by many orders of magnitude—our collective wisdom in the sciences coupled with our global ignorance in ethics and morality pose unprecedented possibilities for both good and evil. Choices have become more difficult than ever because the new learning has given us more power to do things both to and for people than we could have imagined just a decade or two ago.

> These consequences may include dramatic changes in our sense of
> what is possible with respect to the determination of human be-
> havior, the manipulation of human genetics and the alteration of life
> forms. What is possible is a matter of scientific discovery, of knowl-
> edge and technology. Its limits are yet to be determined. But beyond
> what is possible, there is another question to ponder: what is desir-
> able? The answers to that question are more definite, more problem-
> atic, more closely related to choices about what we value, what we
> cherish as the most important and critical aspects of human life.[12]

There is certainly no greater issue in bioethics than that of the
possibility of nuclear war. Unhappily, the sanguinity of the political leadership on the issue has blunted our common understanding of the absolute terror of nuclear war. We need to be reminded
of the human and ecological consequences posed by the alternative nuclear scenarios.

In two national conferences in 1980, Physicians for Social Responsibility compiled the data, provided experts to defend it, and
then published their findings in a small volume entitled *The Final
Epidemic*.[13] The statistical profiles of "moderate" nuclear attacks
on Boston and San Francisco are instructive. One twenty-megaton
bomb (only one of the more than 50,000 nuclear weapons now in
existence) exploding at ground level in Boston would destroy all
buildings within fifteen miles of the blast. Blindness would be
occasioned by retinal burning for up to forty miles away. There
would be 2.2 million immediate fatalities with millions of others
badly burned, blinded, or otherwise seriously wounded. Radiation
sickness would kill many of the wounded in later weeks and
months. Water and food will be either destroyed or so badly irradi-
ated as to make it useless. Medical facilities will be essentially destroyed and medical services almost totally wiped out. In New
York the scenario would change to ten million immediately killed
or with mortal wounds. In San Francisco, the same twenty-megaton bomb would kill 1.9 million and seriously injure another
874,000. The number of burn casualties just in San Francisco alone
would require ten to twenty times the capacity of all burn care
centers throughout the United States.

Virtually all animal life except for insects will be destroyed and
all ecological relationships in the biosphere massively disrupted.

> Over the first two to four weeks after the attack, thousands of short-
> term survivors will die of radiation sickness. The problem of mass
> infection is particularly ugly. Even assuming that a firestorm

conveniently incinerates 500,000 of the dead in a one megaton attack, there will remain some 300,000 or more decomposing corpses in the Bay area.[14]

But even this vision of the holocaust is an unreal projection. For instead of a one or twenty-megaton attack, it is estimated that in an all-out assault, the United States will undergo a 6,559-megaton attack throughout the country.

Moments after the attack 86 million—nearly forty percent of the population—will be dead. An additional 34 million . . . will be severely injured. Fifty million additional fatalities are anticipated during the shelter period, for a total of 133 million deaths. 60 million (Americans) may survive.[15]

To continue the operative dualism of much philosophical and religious teaching (e.g., the traditional Christian separation of nature from history) in the face of such overwhelming threats to humankind and all other life forms by our own species will be to define a radically new form of the demonic in the structure of human thought. Happily, the recent emergence of a global nuclear freeze movement demanding bilateral nuclear arms reduction has begun to change the popular consciousness of the danger of nuclear war, if not official state policies. As dramatic in its impact as any social movement in recent decades, the nuclear freeze consensus may yet move political decision makers to rethink their policies which continue to depend on strategies of "mutually assured destruction." The freeze movement, visible and growing in the United States, has been most militant in Europe where people are more directly exposed to nuclear destruction. It remains, of course, to be seen as to whether even overwhelming majorities opposed to the policies of the political, economic, and military leadership can still have any effect in changing established defense expenditures. While the majority of the American people have opposed the Reagan administration's decision to add another 17,000 nuclear weapons to the existing arsenal of 30,000, it is clear that this plea has fallen on deaf ears in the nation's capital. As has been suggested, however, those who continue to be concerned for the greater creation—for both humankind and nature—must always be in the vanguard of the struggle for positive social change.

Summary

Each generation, we are told, is convinced that its problems are the gravest of any preceding generation and its collective wisdom

more advanced than any before. Having thus relativized any current threat to survival, we are urged by those wishing only to
maintain the *status quo* to relax in the knowledge that many have
similarly cried wolf before us. Surely he will not come this time
either! But, as noted, the changes this time around are qualitatively different from earlier threats. And religion over-all has been
as one-dimensional in its general indifference to environmental
survival as most other primary institutions. This tendency in
Christianity to focus on creedal affirmation and *Heilsgeschichte*
has been most crudely summed up by former U.S. Secretary of the
Interior James Watt:

> I believe there is a life hereafter, and we are to be here to follow the
> teachings of Jesus Christ. One of the charges he's given is to occupy
> the land until He returns. We don't know when He is coming, so we
> have a stewardship responsibility. . . to see that people are provided
> for until He does come and a new order is put in place.[16]

Other more sophisticated commentators, like historian Lynn
White, Jr. have criticized what they feel to be a more common
reflection of the Christian attitude toward the creation.

> Our science and our technology have grown out of Christian atti-
> tudes towards man's relation to nature which are almost universally
> held not only by Christians and neo-Christians but also by those who
> fondly regard themselves as post-Christian. Despite Copernicus, all
> the cosmos rotates around our little globe. Despite Darwin, we are
> not, in our hearts, part of the natural process. We are superior to
> nature, contemptuous of it, willing to use it for our slightest whim.[17]

To move from our past preoccupation with eschatology into a
truer perception of present responsibility may require a new set of
symbols. As Paul Tillich reminded some of us many years ago, that
which concerns us ultimately can be expressed symbolically.[18]
Symbols point to current realities, participating in that to which
they point and opening up levels of reality otherwise closed. They
are not invented but emerge from the historical context. Like
living things, they grow and—on occasion—die. The fundamental
symbol will, of course, be that which for the individual defines
ultimacy: God, Unity, Being. But, in addition to such a primary
symbol, we need today some other living images which can point
to (and enable us to participate in) a reengagement with the earth
and all the fullness that surrounds us. For many religious persons,
for example, the era of the sixties found the symbol of the Cross
overlaid with the struggle for civil rights. In the seventies, the

intersection was with peace and justice. As important—and in all probability of even more consequence for human harmony and welfare—will be the themes of environmental participation and ecological health for the rest of this century. Our newer, integrative symbols must be like those of the sculpture of some tribes in East Africa, each reflecting the inseparability of humankind and the other natural orders—the linking of plant and animal, time and eternity, mind and body, heaven and earth—defining anew the quality of life for every person.

Environmental survival and the development of a new ecological ethic require basic and quite radical changes in human societies around the world. Cosmetic transformations will do no good. Such change—revolutionary for most of us—will require transitions in our economic, political, and social relationships of a kind unconstrained by established ideological formulas. Philosopher-saint Simone Weil speaks to the reality:

> One cannot be a revolutionary if one does not love life. Revolution is a struggle against all that which forms an obstacle to life. It has no meaning except as a means; if the end pursued is vain, the means loses its value.[19]

Those who would rethink the creation tradition should note that always the reform of the individual consciousness will go hand in hand with social transformation. Practices capable of facilitating individual self-transformation must seek to place the individual in collective situations wherein the problems of solitude and individualist frustration can be at least tempered by group support. The New Age must seek to undercut the triple pillars of inequity and repression referred to earlier: hierarchy, specialization, and non-communication. To reconcile social purpose and individual need is the primary task of this disturbing time. Structures to enable both individual self-acceptance and the development of new forms of community emphasizing integrated earth symbols from which to work out new dimensions of political and economic life will be required if the ancient alienations are to be overcome.

Similarly, any meaningful restatement of the human/nature relationship will require a reaffirmation of certain priorities within the religious community. These will include:

- an effort to work toward the restoration of the integrity of global ecosystems
- the conservation and ethical management of material and energy resources

- the struggle against all forms of nuclear weapons
- efforts to control the pollution-creating activities of our species
- a more proper utilization of land and the ownership of the agricultural means of production in order to assure the equitable distribution and management of global food resources
- the development of responsible population policies
- the proper management of the total global commons
- the humane application of the newer discoveries in science in order that the lives of human beings may be enhanced

And in between the times of analysis and action, whenever that shall be required, the priorities for those concerned for God's creation in the midst of ecological crisis have been anticipated by St. Bonaventure:

> He, therefore, who is not illumined by such great splendor of created things is blind; he who is not awakened by such great clamor is deaf; he who does not praise God because of all these effects is dumb; he who does not note the first principle from such great signs is foolish. Open your lips and apply your heart, that you may see our God in all creatures.[20]

Notes

1. Ian L. McHarg, *Design with Nature* (Garden City, N.Y.: Natural History Press, 1969), p. 24.
2. Loren Wilkinson, ed., *Earthkeeping: Christian Stewardship of Natural Resources* (Grand Rapids, Michigan: Eerdmans, 1980), p. 3.
3. The Club of Rome is an international consortium of industrial and political leaders sponsoring studies on the future of humankind. Key actors in the organization have included the Volkswagen and Ford Foundations.
4. Donella H. Meadows, et al., *The Limits to Growth* (New York: Universe Books, 1972); Mihajlo Mesarovic and Eduard Pestel, *Mankind at the Turning Point* (New York: E.P. Dutton, 1974); Jan Tingbergen, *RIO: Reshaping the International Order* (New York: E.P. Dutton, 1976).
5. Donella H. Meadows, et al., *The Limits to Growth*, p. 178.
6. Tingbergen, *RIO: Reshaping International Order.*
7. Joseph Fletcher, *Humanhood* (Buffalo: Prometheus Books, 1979), p. 355.
8. Herman E. Daly, "The Economic and Moral Necessity for Limiting Economic Growth," in *Faith and Science in an Unjust World,* Roger L. Shinn, editor (Philadelphia: Fortress Press, 1980), p. 215.
9. Herman E. Daly, op. cit., pp. 214-215.

10. Harry Rothman, *Murderous Providence: A Study of Pollution in Industrial Societies* (New York: Bobbs Merrill, 1972), p. xi.

11. While the Reagan administration continues to tout the nuclear alternative (wiping out all expenditures for conservation and most alternative energy programs while dramatically increasing the budget for nuclear research and development), it remains uncertain as to whether the new economic realities of nuclear electricity generation will permit such an emphasis. Because of greatly accelerated construction costs, more than 200 orders for new nuclear plants have been cancelled in the past five years.

12. Joseph Duffey, *An Introduction to Hard Choices* (Boston: Office of Radio and Television, 1980).

13. Ruth Adams and Susan Cullen, eds., *The Final Epidemic* (Chicago: University of Chicago Press, 1981), statistics from pages 169-176.

14. H. J. Geiger, "Illusion of Survival," Ibid., p. 180.

15. H. L. Abrams, "Infection and Communicable Diseases," Ibid., pp. 192-94.

16. James Watt, "Interview with James Watt," *The New Yorker* (May 4, 1981).

17. Lynn White, Jr., "The Historic Roots of Our Ecological Crisis," *Science* 155 (March 10, 1967).

18. Paul Tillich, *The Dynamics of Faith* (New York: Harper & Brothers, 1957), pp. 41-54.

19. Simone Weil, as quoted in Simone Petrement, *Simone Weil: A Life* (New York: Pantheon Books, 1976), p. 210.

20. St. Bonaventure, *The Mind's Road to God.*

Chapter Twenty-Two

CREATION, CONSUMMATION, AND THE ETHICAL IMAGINATION

Ted F. Peters

Has the time come to reconceptualize the Christian concept of creation and ethical responsibility in light of contemporary future consciousness? The future consciousness which has become pervasive over the last decade raises Shakespeare's question in behalf of our planet and not just for Hamlet alone: "To be, or not to be?" As we try to map the path of earth's future we become conscious of a possible end to its evolutionary journey. If modern industrial civilization continues to career recklessly down the road of unlimited growth and expansion, we may soon be stopped by a fatal accident. We may run out of the nonrenewable resources needed to fuel civilized life as we know it. We may swerve into our own ditches of polluting agricultural and industrial waste. We may sideswipe either the scylla of overpopulation or the charybdis of famine. Or the head-on collision of two nuclear powers may incinerate both ourselves and our environment in a final blaze of atomic warfare. Future consciousness includes the awareness that tomorrow may be radically different from today, and that there just may be no tomorrow that can remember today.

The future is contingent. It always has been. The very existence of a contingent future and its possibilities is the result of God's creative activity. It is God's creative power that releases us from the deterministic constraints of the past, opens the future to a variety of possibilities, and places on us in the present moment the joy and burden of freedom.

Futurist prognostications regarding the ecological crisis raise two interrelated questions, one theological and one ethical. First, how ought we to understand God and creation in light of our consciousness of temporal projections and future realities? Future consciousness leads us to ask this very comprehensive question because we can envision a future so very different from the present and past. It becomes obvious that life in this world has not been given an immutable nature. It is subject to rather significant change. Therefore, the notion of divine creation as a once-and-for-all-act requires rethinking. This essay is an attempt at such rethinking. In it I will suggest that we ought to think of God as the ontological power of the future drawing the present moment into freedom and all things toward a final and consummate fulfillment.

This gives rise to a second question: how does a futurist orientation to reality and concern for the ecological crisis influence our ethical understanding and responsibility? In this essay I will suggest that the point of departure for ethical thinking consists in the imaginative projection of a vision of future fulfillment followed by work toward its actualization in the present. We begin with a wholistic vision of the ultimate future and then seek to thwart the fragmenting and destructive prospects of the near and medium range futures.

I call this position 'proleptic eschatology' because it seeks to anticipate—to pre-actualize—the future. Proleptic eschatology has three principles. We will look at them in turn.

Principle #1: God Creates from the Future, not the Past

This first principle—that God creates from the future, not the past—may seem to contradict the commonly accepted Christian view as well as common sense understandings of causality. But I believe this principle provides a rich interpretation of the scriptural understanding of God and actually makes more sense than the common sense view of efficient causality because it accounts for human freedom.

Our common sense view of time and causality—at least in Western culture—is that time consists of a linear one-way passage from the past, through the present, toward the future. The power of being in this scheme is thought of as coming from the past, i.e., a past cause and a present effect. Within this framework God's creative activity is assumed to be a single event that happened once upon a time—at the beginning of time—long ago. God created all things once and for all *ex nihilo*. That is, out of abject nothingness he built a lovely machine complete with parts and principles of operation, then wound it up, and it has been operating ever since.

According to this scheme, the power of being is presumed to be a push from the past. The state of affairs today is the result of yesterday's causes, which in turn are the result of the previous day's causes, on back to the divine first cause on the first day. I like to call this the 'bowling ball' theory of creation. The image is that of a divine bowler providing the power of being by hurling the creation down the alley of time. We at present are somewhere on the alley, having left the divine hand behind but not yet colliding with the eschatological strike still ahead of us. As for human decision and responsibility, because we can contribute a modest influence on the course and direction of the roll, we strive to keep ourselves in line with God's original aim so as to avoid a gutter ball.

But does this image adequately describe how we experience time and the power of being? I suggest not. The power to be does not reside in the past. It belongs rather to the future. To be is to have a future. To lose one's future and to have only a past is to die. The dynamic perdurance of the present moment is contingent on the power of the future to draw us into it.

The power of the future is also the source of freedom. When in the present moment we feel overwhelmed by trends set in motion by past causes, we feel cramped and contained and restrained. To look at a future we believe to be predetermined is to feel that life has been lost. The power of God, however, comes to us not as a brute determination from the past but as that which counters such determinations. Each moment God exerts God's power to relieve us from past constraints so as to open up a field for free action, for responsible living.

In light of current future consciousness and the ecological crisis, what appears to be the power of being giving us a push from the past is not the bowl toward God's foreordained 1-3 pocket. The thrust of ecologically destructive trends already set in motion by industrial society have put us on a trajectory headed for the gutter. If we continue in the direction set by our past, our destination will be destruction.[1] But we must acknowledge that we have a certain freedom and responsibility in the present moment. The sense of freedom which we feel is the sense that our past has not foredoomed us. The future is sufficiently open so that responsible action on the part of the present generaton may yet result in a just and sustainable and fulfilling tomorrow. Our desire is to change course and re-aim our trajectory toward the divine target. Does it not make sense to think of the power of God's creative work as coming to us from the future, releasing us from the past and for freedom? I believe it does.

Instead of a push from the past, I suggest we think of God's creative power as a pull from the future. Instead of a bowling ball thrown from behind, I suggest the equally inelegant image of the eschatological vacuum cleaner. Here the power of the future is drawing all things toward itself. We in the present moment are caught in the carpet, deciding whether to cling to the present or to give ourselves over to the divine draw.

According to this view, creation is not a single event that happened once in the past. Rather, it is a constant durative process. God is every moment drawing reality out of the nonbeing of the past into the actual existence of the present moment and reestablishing his trajectory toward his own as yet unrealized purposes for the consummate future. He is constantly providing all of nature and all of history with a call forward, with a divine lure toward greater reality. To be is to have a future. If you do not have a future, you drop into the nonbeing of the dead past. God—the power of the future—is the source of life and being.

In developing this understanding of constant creation and the fluidlike flow of events we need a wholistic image that overcomes the traditional substantialist and the modern mechanist picture of reality. This picture views the world as broken down into atomic units, and each unit is a substantial and localized object relating to all other objects by external laws of cause and effect. On Isaac Newton's billiard table where each ball represents an atomic unit, an event consists in the collision of two balls. The movement of a given ball has as its *causa proxima* a bump from a ball moving immediately prior to it in a chain of such bumps. The ultimate *causa remota* is the initiating power of the cosmic cue stick. All relations here are external relations.

Temporal passage can be apprehended better via synthetic thinking, I believe, i.e., by picturing events in terms of organismic or wholistic models. Here relations are internal as well as external. The experience of eating and digesting an apple, for example, is an event in which the existence of the now past apple is drawn up and synthesized into the present and future life processes of a human being. The apple once hanging on the tree is given a new meaning by its future. Everything present will be given new meaning when taken up into our future; yet the identity of that future will be determined in part by the past which it synthesizes into itself. What we are is determined by what we shall be, by how we are related to what lies beyond us.

A past experience can be remembered in such a way as to inform and give shape to future experience, while that future experience in turn will reinterpret and reshape that enduring memory. The past as past has no independent ontological status. Only the power of its future—the now present—sustains it. The durative present is continually drawing the past up into itself and thereby sustaining while redefining it. And the meaning of the present is similarly contingent upon its future. The process is a continuing fluidlike movement, more akin to a river than to a sequence of billiard ball collisions. Rather than a staccato chain of causal bumps down the alley of history, the non-substantialist and supra-mechanist view I suggest here envisions the continuing draw of apparent atomic particles through a process of synthetic incorporation into new actualities. This current process itself is dependent for its power of operation on the ultimate synthesis, the eschatological consummation.

It is the power of the ultimate future that creates freedom in the present to decide in behalf of the near future. We are not yet in the vacuum bag, to press this inelegant metaphor perhaps a bit too far. What we now experience is the power of the draw necessary to release us from being caught in the fibers where the past has placed us. We can decide for something new, for transformation. We can decide to cling or we can decide to allow the divine draw to carry us forward.

Evil and Redemption.   What about evil? What about the problems of ecological disruption, fragmentation, conflict, destruction, and death? Evil, according to this scheme, would be the desire to stop the drawing duration, to substantialize and to particularize oneself in the present moment. It would be to resist further synthesis by insisting upon only external relations with one's environment. Evil is the attempt to deny life and experience to the future by making choices that will produce only a dead past. A sinful act is the result of a choice that seeks to absolutize one's premature being, to cut oneself off from the divinely intended unity of all things, to favor oneself to the exclusion of others and of the world around. Living for the moment is to choose a present that will soon become only a dead past. Evil produces a disruption within the single flow of the creative process, a process which upon completion will have overcome this disruption.

To account for this disruption the traditional theology of creation and redemption drew a dualistic picture. First, there was the creative act of God, after which God declared, "Behold, it is very good." We lived in primeval paradise. Then, unfortunately, humankind introduced sin and the whole created order fell away from the divine aim. It was necessary for God to act salvifically to retrieve a creation gone astray. The eschatological future was thought of as a second paradise, as a return to a pre-fallen harmony.

According to the proleptic eschatology I am proposing here, in contrast, creation is not done yet. Consequently, the eschatological future is not a return to a previous state of affairs. It is rather advent, the arrival of something new. The completion of the creative process and the final eschaton coincide. Only upon consummate fulfillment can God say with honesty, "Behold, it *is* very good." From our perspective today, we can only say, "it *will be* very good." In the final eschatological synthesis the disruptive tendencies of self-absolutizing events will cease to have a future. Only the wholistic harmony of all things will perdure. Hence, creation and redemption are a single process culminating in a single destiny.

Proleptic Eschatology and Process Theism.   This concept of eschatological redemption providing the power and direction for continuing creation differs somewhat from parallel notions found among the theological disciples of Alfred North Whitehead. Although both positions affirm continuing creation, members of the Whiteheadian process school object to the very notion of an eschaton, to the idea of a single final fulfillment of all things. They object for three reasons: because (a) they believe a final end implies a static homeostasis with a cessation of human freedom and creative movement;[2] (b) in the process view God is not omnipotent, i.e., not strong enough finally to accomplish his will;[3] and (c) wholism can be established through ecological images such as the "web of life" without recourse to eschatological redemption.[4]

With regard to the first objection, the process theologians employ good reasons but only to commit the straw man fallacy. They are right in maintaining that the eschaton ought not to be conceived as static. But to my knowledge it never has been. One of the prominent biblical symbols for the eschatological kingdom of God is 'eternal life.' If the eschaton were to mean the cessation of duration and the elimination of a still outstanding future, then it would be eternal death, not life. Hence what characterizes the end time is not simply the end of time but rather the end to disruptive evi¹ and to the deadness of the past. It is the fulfillment of St. Paul's promise that "creation itself will be set free from its bondage to decay." (Rom. 8:21a) Whatever the eschaton means, it means life and not death.[5]

With regard to the second objection, process metaphysicians opt for a divine figure that is not the omnipotent deity of classical Christianity. Their faith is not in a deity that can provide us with the assurance that his will will finally be done. Free human decisions to actualize evil and death may go on forever and ever, frustrating the announced plan God has for God's creation.[6] The chief problem with this view is methodological, i.e., it is a doctrine of God developed in conscious independence of any Hebrew or Christian revelation. Whitehead, while admiring the dispassionate and nonreligious approach of Aristotle in establishing a metaphysical doctrine of God, proceeds himself to construct a notion of God as the "principle of concretion" and "principle of limitation."[7] Despite what he says elsewhere, Whitehead's god is a strict construction invoked to save the metaphysical system from collapse. A nonomnipotent deity fits the Whiteheadian system well. The requirements of the metaphysical system take precedence over biblical revelation.

The God portrayed in the revelatory foundation of Israel's faith is quite different from Whitehead's deity. God is spoken of in passionate religious symbols as the one who has heaven as a throne and the earth as a footstool (Isaiah 66:1), who will crush the power of Satan under our feet (Rom. 16:20), and who promises a new heaven and a new earth (Rev. 21:1). God is confessed in the creeds as "the almighty." It is never sufficient, of course, to answer an opposing position by simply hurling Bible verses and creedal phrases. But the methodological point is that the source for Christian confidence in the omnipotent God of the future is the encounter with divine power in the past and the promise of future fulfillment. It was an encounter with the God who raised Jesus Christ from the dead and who promised the advent of God's eschatological kingdom that yielded the revelation upon which Christian thinking about God is based. Christian faith has for two millenia taken the risk of living out of trust in this promise. Should the promise never be fulfilled, then perhaps we may look back and say the Whiteheadians were right and our faith was in vain.

The third objection to eschatological thinking is a bit more subtle. It is seldom articulated in quite this way. It takes the form of an affirmation of wholeness at the present time. John Cobb along with biologist Charles Birch, for example, seem to assume it is sufficient to establish a wholistic vision by simply making the

case for internal relations. Their ecological model is rightly contrasted with the Newtonian mechanistic model because it pictures
all living things on earth as inseparably interconnected with their
environment. To believe one's own existence is atomic and independent and has only external relations with other things is to
believe an illusion. The truth is that everything belongs to the
single web of life. But what Birch and Cobb have achieved here is
a wholism of the mind, not necessarily a wholism of the actual
world. That they have liberated "the conception of life" from ob-
jectivist thinking seems to be sufficient for establishing the whole.
But what they have achieved is a formal or structural wholism, a
mental construct that may misleadingly equate interdependence
with cooperation and harmony. The establishment of an ecological
vision does not itself constitute the healing of a broken ecosphere.
It is one thing to acknowledge interdependence and internal relations, but a giant step remains to be taken toward a wholism that
implies healing.

To be sure, Cobb and Birch argue eloquently and forcefully for
an ethical posture parallel to that by proleptic eschatology.

> Because all are interdependent, all are necessary. Humans should
> recognize that their arrogance and their efforts to manipulate their
> environment are destructive of the web of life. In this perspective
> the need is for a deep spiritual transformation that will lead human
> beings to experience themselves simply as part of the whole web
> and not as agents of purposive change.[8]

Like Birch and Cobb, proleptic ethics seeks a spiritual transformation that will dissuade us from destroying the web of life. But the
method is different. Birch and Cobb seem to assume that it is good
enough simply to "experience" ourselves as part of the whole web
and on the basis of this experience to stop acting purposefully. The
proleptic position, in contrast, is that the whole—at least the
whole understood as the healed and redeemed whole—does not
exist at present. It is still future. It cannot be experienced. It can
only be believed in. It can only be responded to in faith. What is required is purposeful action based upon our faith in a whole which
is yet to come.

In contrast to the position of process theists, then, the wholism
affirmed in proleptic eschatology refers to divine redemption in
the future, to the actual putting together what is now broken and
still breaking. Present experience of brokenness and threatened
destruction is authentic experience. There really is denial of the

web of life. There really is separation, competition, violence, and death. The actual world in which we live is in fact not whole, i.e., not yet whole. A conceptual wholism is at best a nice ideal. Without the promised eschatological redemption, however, such a belief in wholism is belief in an illusion.

The Creative Word in Genesis 1:1-2: 4a. How do we reconcile my proposal of durative creation with the Genesis account wherein God creates the cosmos out of nothing by speaking his word? Genesis, chapter one, is traditionally interpreted as referring to a single week's activities which occurred only once a long time ago. God labored for six days and on the seventh God took a vacation. Is God still on vacation? If creation happened only once, then God might as well be.

But if we conceive of creation as a process continuing today, then it might be helpful to think of Genesis as describing the present, not just the past. God is not yet resting, nor will God rest until God's creative work is done. We today are still somewhere within the first six days and looking forward to the seventh. The first book of Moses, then, might be speaking not about what happened once upon a time but rather about what is happening now and what will yet be.

How about the concept of the Word of God? Let us first observe something about spoken words in general. Human words are transient, ephemeral. They are immediately replaced by silence or by other words. They may be forgotten or they may be remembered and repeated, but they themselves do not endure.

When we speak of God's Word, however, we think of an eternal word. It is not ephemeral or evanescent. It has a future. It is not subject to the perpetual perishing of temporal passage. Could we on this basis indulge in a bit of anthropomorphic imagination and think of God as having opened God's mouth and as still speaking? Perhaps God has not yet finished the primal performative utterance: "Let there be. . .a cosmos!" The sentence is not yet finished. We today stand in the midst of God's holy and creative speaking, somewhere between the first syllable and the final period. And God will not close God's mouth until all things are fulfilled, until all reality is consummated into God's everlasting kingdom.[9]

Principle #2: Jesus Christ is the Future Made Present

If we think of the Word of God as the creative power of the cosmos continually drawing all things toward their final and definitive actuality in the one consummate future, then how should we think of Christ, the incarnate *logos?* The answer to this constitutes the prolepsis in proleptic eschatology: Jesus Christ is the future made present. The key biblical passage, of course, is the New Testament counterpart to the Genesis creation account, namely, the prologue to the Gospel according to John.

> In the beginning was the Word, and the Word was with God, and the Word was God. He was in the beginning with God; all things were made through him, and without him was not anything made that was made. . . . And the Word became flesh and dwelt among us, full of grace and truth; we have beheld his glory, glory as of the only Son from the Father.—John 1:1-3, 14 (RSV)

The Greek word for 'word' here is *logos,* which refers to the rational principle within the order of things that organizes all reality. It connotes the very mind of God. The Gospel of John identifies Jesus Christ the redeemer with the selfsame Word or *logos* of God that calls reality into existence and imparts God's will to it. Here is attested the continuity between God's creative and redemptive activity, between origination and consummation, between alpha and omega.

The paradoxical presence of the incarnate *logos* in Jesus of Nazareth means that here in this time and place we have the universal will of God at work under the finite conditions of human personality. On the one hand, he is subject to transiency, to the evil designs of others, to the power of present fixation and denial of futurity, to death. Jesus is a part, not the whole, of creation. The cross signifies that God's will is not "done on earth as it is in heaven." On the other hand, Jesus' own unyielding faith in God means the *logos* never broke relationship with God's future. Even when facing death and praying in Gethsemene, Jesus said, "Thy will be done." The Easter resurrection was God's act wherein the faith of Jesus was vindicated and his oneness with consummate fulfillment affirmed.

Jesus Christ is proleptically at one with everything that finally will be. By 'prolepsis' here I mean anticipation of future reality in a concrete pre-actualization of it. Jesus Christ proleptically reveals the destiny of the whole world because he embodies it in his own personal faith and destiny.[10]

The imagery attached to the traditional picture of the incarnation is that of a heavenly being coming down to take up residence on earth below. It is spatial imagery. What happens when we temporalize incarnation imagery and locate God's creative power at the consummation? We get prolepsis. Jesus Christ is the future made present. He is the first fruits (I. Cor. 15:20), a foretaste of the great banquet yet to be enjoyed in the consummate kingdom of God.

This understanding of Jesus is derived by examining his Easter resurrection in light of the interpretive context in which it was first understood, namely, Jewish apocalypticism. Many in Jesus' time were expecting the course of world history to erupt into uncontrolled violence and catastrophes, with those loyal to God suffering unjustly at the hands of the enemies of God. Jesus himself experienced this in his own person as the mob and government brought him to a cruel and unjust death on the cross. Many were also expecting a resurrection from the dead and a vindication of righteousness. Jesus experienced this too in his own person in a way that loosely fit the expectation. By raising Jesus from the dead God was confirming as valid the widespread hope for the future kingdom of God. To hope for God's future kingdom and for the vindication of righteousness is not to hope in vain. The future of all things has happened ahead of time in Jesus; and that happening becomes for us a promise regarding our own future. The New Testament message, then, proclaims that as Jesus rose so also will all of us who are tied to his destiny rise in the future. It becomes a message of joy and hope even when great calamities threaten to engulf us as they apparently do now.[11]

Principle #3: Eschatology Implies Ethics

Does this advocacy in behalf of a strong eschatology necessarily result in a pie-in-the-sky, bye-and-bye, take-me-to-heaven-when-I-die escapism? Is this a version of pre-millenialist fundamentalism that seems to endorse the bourgeois status quo while awaiting the rapture? Is this a return to the religion rejected by the Marxists as the opiate of the people? No, it is not. The eschatological vision is not a sedative; it is stimulus to action.

Lenin thought of religion as a sedative innoculating the believer against creative activity. Karl Marx, however, saw the eschatological element within religion as consciousness of the need for change, as the "sigh of the oppressed" and the "protest against real distress."[12]

It is important to note how in the Christian versions of liberation theology spreading so rapidly about the world that eschatology is an essential element. Letty Russell uses the term 'advent shock' to refer to the sense of maladjustment in the present when compared to the anticipated future fulfillment. "Because of advent shock we seek to anticipate the future in what we do, opening ourselves to the working of God's spirit and expecting the impossible."[13] Gustavo Gutierrez reports that "the attraction of 'what is to come' is the driving force of history. The attraction of Yahweh in history and his action at the end of history are inseparable."[14] Or, in the words of Wolfhart Pannenberg, ". . . the striving for God as the ultimate good beyond the world is turned into concern for the world."[15]

Carl Braaten refers to ethics in this context as *eschatopraxis*, i.e., doing the future ahead of time. He writes, ". . . in proleptic ethics it may truly be said that the end justifies the means, because the end is proleptically present and operative beforehand, rehearsing the qualities of the eschatological kingdom—peace, love, joy, freedom, equality, unity—in the course of history's forward movement.[16] We are saying here that not only does eschatology stimulate action, it is the very foundation of ethics. Once we apprehend God's will for the consummate future, we seek to incarnate that future proleptically in present human action.

Recognizing our advent shock and the need for eschatopraxis, we need to think in terms of an action program, in terms of middle axioms that will move us from the comprehensive vision to the challenges we face amidst current future consciousness. Jürgen Moltmann says such action planning in church circles is too often oriented toward the past, thinking in the category of "re": e.g., *re*volution, *re*turn, *re*newal, *re*vival, *re*formation. He advocates using the future-oriented category of the "pro", e.g., replacing '*re*volution' with '*pro*volution.' Moltmann maintains that "in provolution, the human dream turned forward is combined with the new possibility of the future and begins consciously to direct the course of human history as well as the evolution of nature."[17] Taking our cue from Moltmann, let us draw out some further "pros" for Christian provolutionary strategy. We will list seven such pros.

1. Project a vision of the coming new order.   This is the prophetic task of the Christian church. The redemption of the historical and the natural order is coming and someone needs to say so. This first *pro* is perhaps the single most important element in the strategy of *pro*leptic ethics. It reflects faith in the divine promise as well as provides the starting point for significant human action.

The key to resolving the world problematique on the human side of the kingdom is found in our adherence to a vision of new reality. Visions are akin to ideas or ideals, and many practical minds are reluctant to embrace great ideals. The fact is, however, that projecting visions and ideals is the first and necessary step to any significant cooperative action. Dutch sociologist and pioneer futurist Fred L. Polak contends that positive images of the future are the primary causal factor in cultural change.[18] Such positive images pull a civilization together and unite its people in a single task. Nothing is more practical than a good idea, an idea that inspires and directs.

What is our image of what is to come? It is the vision of Isaiah 58:6-9, where the rich share their bread with the hungry. It is the promise of natural harmony in Isaiah 11:6, where "the wolf shall dwell with the lamb." It is the vision of Amos 5:24, where justice and righteousness roll down upon us like an everflowing stream. It is Micah's vision of no more war, where swords are beaten into plowshares and spears into pruning hooks. It is John's vision in the Apocalypse, where God wipes away every tear from our eyes, and where death and mourning will have passed away. (Rev.21:4) Our hope flows from such visionary symbols and is based not on unfounded wishes for an idealist utopia but upon the promise of God confirmed in the proleptic revelation of the future in Jesus Christ.

The projecting of such visions creates advent shock. The contrast between what is promised for tomorrow and the actuality of today creates tension. If in God's future there will be no more war, then why have war now? If in God's future the hungry will be fed and the mourning comforted, then our proleptic task is to minister to the hungry and the mourning today. If in God's future the lion will lie down with the lamb, then perhaps now we should seek to the degree possible to live in the realization that human harmony depends upon harmony throughout all of nature.

And can we go still further? On the basis of this promise and on the basis of what we know to be the crying needs of our present world threatened as it is with an ominous near future, can we project a tailor-made vision? I believe we can say prophetically that there is a new world coming which includes among other things:

— a single world-wide planetary society;
— united in devotion to the will of God;
— sustainable within the biological carrying capacity of the planet and harmonized with the principles of the ecosphere;
— organized politically so as to preserve the just rights and voluntary contributions of all individuals;

— organized economically so as to guarantee the basic
survival needs of each person;
— organized socially so that dignity and freedom are
respected and protected in every quarter;
— and dedicated to advancing the quality of life in behalf of
our future generations.

This is the schematic outline of a constructed vision. It is rational
and terse, to be sure. But if it could be amplified and molded with
beauty and drama by committed artists into symbols, songs,
poems, pictures, and architecture, then its heuristic power would
be increased and it could become an inspiration and guide.

With regard to a theological concern that might arise when making such a proposal, let me add that I believe there is no irreconcilable conflict here between divine action and human imagination.
There is no hidden pelagian agenda. The ethical action being
proposed here is a response to God's promise; it is not itself the
fulfillment of that promise. While retaining his sublime mystery,
God has promised *that* his kingdom will come. Exactly *what* that
kingdom will look like we humans can only imagine. And imagine
we must! Our imaginative projections of the perfect society are
influenced by our sensitivity to the needs of our present context,
to the crisis posed by future consciousness. Our thoughts are
conditioned and finite, to be sure. Nonetheless, we understand
God's salvation as fulfillment, as meeting the actual needs of his
creatures as experienced historically. This means that the content
of God's eschatological kingdom—*who* and *what* will be there—
will be made up of the very course of historical events in which
you and I are presently engaged. The *what* of the kingdom is us.
Therefore, the projection of future fulfillment based upon present
understandings is as theologically legitimate as it is morally
necessary. Our only caution is to avoid the premature absolutizing
of our vision, i.e., to retain the proleptic and provisional character
of anticipatory visions.

2. Promote a sense of global Gemeinschaft.   The second of
our proleptic principles is an extension of the first. A significant
element in the vision we project is the sense of unity. The type of
unity we speak of here is not an amorphous cosmic oneness but
rather *com*-unity, i.e., unity with ('com' means 'with'). It is a unity
we humans share with one another, with the world of nature in
which we are enmeshed, and with God. We need to replace "we-
they" thinking with "us" thinking. The German term for community, *Gemeinschaft*, connotes intimacy and loyalty within a

group of people. It connotes the qualities one would expect to find in a close family unit wherein each member's identity is so tied up with the *Gemeinschaft* that the success and happiness of the group is simultaneously the success and happiness of the individual. Can we think of the whole world this way?

Futurists are accustomed to thinking wholistically, recognizing that the various peoples of the world no matter where they live are becoming increasingly interdependent. International trade is no longer a luxury. Natural resources and agricultural production are in constant movement, and this movement is necessary for each civilization simply to be itself. In addition, trends such as continued depletion of nonrenewable natural resources and environmental pollution impoverish the whole world. Their effects crisscross borders and ignore the separation of continents. We are all in this together. Localism, parochialism, and nationalism are all forms of ostrichism. There is only one future for all of us. The promotion of a sense of worldwide community places a high value on the futurist observation that everything is interconnected, that no part is divorced from the whole. Any attempt at aggrandizement of the part—any attempt by a portion of the world to garner more than its share of terrestrial blessing—is disintegrative for the whole and will finally result in self-destruction. The way to express *Gemeinschaft* in our present circumstance is to care; it is to treat quarters and peoples previously thought foreign as parts of one's own family. Such caring today proleptically anticipates the divine unity of tomorrow.

It is important in this regard to emphasize that *Gemeinschaft* need not refer solely to interhuman relationships. We share community with nature as well. The traditional neighbor ethic is here being swept up into a more comprehensive ecology ethic.

It has become somewhat fashionable recently to blame the Judeo-Christian tradition for the ecological crisis we face. Lynn White, for example, is notorious for his castigation of religious people who believe what is said in Genesis 1:26-28, wherein God commands humans to have "dominion" over the earth. White argues that our crisis is rooted in a dualism between humanity and nature promoted by Genesis, a dualism that interprets "dominion" to mean a divine mandate for wanton exploitation.[19]

The eco-ethic I am advancing here positively appropriates this Genesis passage and contends that Lynn White has misinterpreted the Christian position. The Hebrew verb *radah* translated "have dominion," appears elsewhere in the scriptures. It may indicate the rule of a master over a hired servant or a chief officer over laborers. The stress is always on humane treatment: a Hebrew master is charged that he not rule over his hired servant "with harshness" (Lev.25:43, 46, 53).

Of particular interest are a number of occurances of the verb that appear in contexts having to do with the dominion a king holds over his subjects. The king rules not for himself but for God. He represents the dominion of Yahweh. Perhaps it would be helpful to get a picture of how the Bible understands this form of kingship. The verb *radah* appears in Psalm 72, along with these passages describing the Hebrew king:

> May he judge thy people with righteousness,
>   and thy poor with justice! (vs.2) . . .
> May he defend the cause of the poor of the people,
>   give deliverance to the needy,
>   and crush the oppressor! (vs.4) . . .
> For he delivers the needy when he calls,
>   the poor and him who has no helper.
> He has pity on the weak and the needy,
>   and saves the lives of the needy.
> From oppression and violence he
>   redeems their lives. (vss.12-14)

This enthronement psalm in no way suggests that the king is permitted—let alone mandated—to engage in unencumbered exploitation of his subjects. Similarly, the humans of Genesis, chapter one, are given *radah* not to destroy the creation but to care for it as the king in God's stead cares for God's people, especially the needy.

This notion of dominion reflects, of course, the patriarchal and monarchical hierarchy endemic to the ancient orient. We cannot expect it to reflect our occidental post-Enlightenment egalitarianism. What is important to note nevertheless is that the Israelite king is expected to care for those over whom he rules. Caring is contrasted to exploitation. In fact whenever the king began to exploit his subjects for his own selfish interests—e.g., King David taking Bathsheba and killing her husband (II Sam. 11), King Ahab's confiscation of Naboth's vineyard (I Kings 21)—a prophet of God appeared to accuse the king of failing to exercise proper dominion (Ezek. 34: 2-4). To exploit rather than to care is to misrule. If it is on the ideal model of Hebrew kingship that the author of Genesis conceived of human dominion over earth, it was clearly a model of fostering *Gemeinschaft* through caring and supporting the weak and needy.

We might expand this by pointing to the wholistic qualities of the biblical world view. Nature itself tells of God's presence in it (Ps. 10:1; 89:11). The popular hymn, "This is my Father's world," written near the turn of the present century, picks up this theme and depicts nature as alive with the presence of the divine: God "shines in all that's fair; in the rustling grass I hear him pass; He speaks to me everywhere." There is nothing here that authorizes exploitation. Far more does it connote reverence.

In Genesis 2, the human race being created is pictured as radically dependent on both nature and God. We are formed from the dust of the ground, making us a part of nature. But being thus formed, God breathes into us the breath of life, and we become living beings. (Gen. 2:7) We are not truly human except as we express the metaxic tension of being at one both with God and with the natural world. God, humanity, and the world together make up the whole of reality as the Bible sees it.

It is not the Bible then that justifies the rape of the earth. It requires anthropocentrism for that. The era of greatest exploitation and ruin is the era of industrialization, which stands in the wake of the Enlightenment and the rise of humanism. To view the human as the source and end of all valuing is to cut the tie between our species and the whole; it is to reinterpret representative dominion as mastery.[20] Lynn White's grievance should be taken to modern humanism, not to the ancient Hebrew or Christian religions.

Global *Gemeinschaft* means, among other things, a revered sense of the oneness we share with nature and of the call to care in behalf of God. The World Council of Churches, which first gave attention to futurology at Geneva in 1966 and later sponsored an international conference on the theme "Faith, Science, and the Future" at MIT in 1979, has astutely characterized the global *Gemeinschaft* as a "just" and "sustainable" society. Justice points to the necessity of correcting the maldistribution of the products of the earth and of bridging the gap between rich and poor countries. Ecological sustainability points to humanity's dependence on earth. An ecologically sustainable society which is unjust can hardly be worth sustaining socially. A just society which is ecologically unsustainable is self-defeating. Proleptic ethics means that the *imago dei* within us, i.e., the *radah* we have been given, be employed so as to bring justice to the needy and sustainability to the biosphere and thereby anticipate ahead of time the consummate whole toward which we are being drawn.

3. Provide for our posterity.   The unity sought in global *Gemeinschaft* implies a community over space, a worldwide community. But what about community through time? What is our relationship to future generations whom we ourselves will not live to see? Given the prognostications of futurists regarding depletion of nonrenewable resources and uncontrolled pollution of the biosphere, we pose the ethical question this way: does the present generation have the right to go on one last gluttonous technological fling, using up all of mother earth's fecund ability to support life, and then leave our grandchildren with only a cesspool of pollution for a home? Unless decisions are made to alter current trends, this is just what will happen.

Perhaps the most representative test case regarding our ecoethic over time is the use of nuclear fission power by the present generation. "What's the matter with a little nukey?" read the tee shirts of its supporters. Well, there is something that matters. Apart from the awesome threats of sabotage and nuclear blackmail by terrorists who gain access to power plants, the legacy of radioactive waste may result in the bequeathal of an uninhabitable environment to our descendants.

If we look just at High Level Wastes (HLWs), we ask about what should be done with the nonuseful remainder produced by nuclear power plants in the form of spent fuel rods and liquids of highly intense and penetrating radioactivity. HLWs generate considerable heat and must be handled remotely without human contact. One member of the Environmental Protection Agency forecasts that the U.S. will have accumulated 200 million gallons of HLWs by the year 2000. The American people are now confronted with an important moral decision: how should we dispose of—i.e., how should we care for—this radioactive debris? Should we continue producing it? If so, how much?

The relevant technical data include the fact that the potential danger from nuclear waste will endure beyond the life-span of all those making disposal decisions. The time it takes for most fission products to decay to manageable levels of toxicity is about 700 to 1000 years. Staggering in its implications, however, is the fact that long-lived actinides such as plutonium 239 will not decay to safe levels for 250,000 years. Permanent disposal would mean isolation from the biosphere for this entire period. No human beings to this point have had sufficient long-term experience with such containment processes as to be able to guarantee with integrity that our proposed disposal plans will be permanently safe. Hence, we must operate on the presumption that we are risking the health and safety of our descendants for hundreds of millenia to come.

And even if it be possible to achieve safety for an indefinite period, the achievement will not be easy or automatic. Tomorrow's residents will have to care for today's waste in order to protect themselves. How long will the repositories have to be monitored? Opinions vary. Some believe that if nothing goes wrong within the first 10 to 30 years after disposal then nothing is ever likely to happen. Other believe we need institutional arrangements for monitoring for as long as 200,000 years at sites where plutonium is buried. Finally, there is an intermediate position which sees the necessity for monitoring during the first 100 to 700 years. (This is roughly the time it takes for most HLWs to decay to levels of toxicity equivalent to that of natural uranium ore.) After that time information posted at the site could prevent accidental intrusion into the repository. Regardless of which estimate contains the most truth, it appears vigilance will be required of our descendants for extensive periods of time to protect themselves from dangers we have created. How much vigilance the present generation can rightly require of them is a moral question.[21]

If we were to call a moratorium on fission energy production today, what we have already done will require considerable vigilance on the part of our children. High level radioactive waste is presently being poured into stainless steel or concrete tanks which have an effective containment life of 30 years. After 30 years the contents must be transferred to other tanks. Because of the relentless activity of HLWs, such as its tendency to boil at 1200 to 1400 degrees Fahrenheit, some of these tanks must be continuously cooled. Where water is available it is used for cooling. At the nuclear processing plant at La Hague, France, air conditioners are employed. To prevent the steel containers from melting and spilling their contents, the air conditioners must run constantly 24 hours per day, 365 days per year, for perhaps hundreds or even thousands of years to come. On one occasion the electricity went out for a period of six minutes, stopping the cooling units. The community was stricken with fear until power was restored. We must hope that the earth's crust for the next 700 or more years will agree to treat our radioactive pollution gingerly and not quake, fold, thrust, or break, thereby spilling these poisons into the biosphere. There is no disposal of HLWs in any final sense. There is only perpetual care. To what extent we can ask our descendants centuries into the future to keep the plug in on the air conditioners and to pay the electric bill is an ethical question that presses for an answer.

This concern for protecting posterity led small-is-beautiful economist E.F. Schumacher to write in 1973:

> No degree of prosperity could justify the accumulation of large amounts of highly toxic substances which nobody knows how to make "safe" and which remain an incalculable danger to the whole of creation for historical or even geological ages. . . . The idea that a civilization could sustain itself on the basis of such a transgression is an ethical, spiritual, and metaphysical monstrosity.[22]

Stretching the global *Gemeinschaft* over time would replace the current "we/they" thinking with a form of "us" thinking that would foster a sense of unity between the present and future generations. It would enjoin us to try to protect our posterity.

4. Protect human dignity.   By 'dignity' here we mean what Immanuel Kant meant, namely, that we treat each person as an end and not as a means. Dignity in this sense is at present basically an ideal; it does not fully exist. The industrial society in which we live is organized around hierarchical structures and job descriptions, which makes persons interchangeable with one another due to their work skills. Value is derived from a giant economic machine, and persons function as cogs in the wheels that keep this machine rolling. And to compound the indignity, whatever cog one becomes is often due to discrimination on the basis of one's race, age, or gender, all impersonal factors irrelevant to the integrity or value of the person. Dignity is not a widespread present actuality.

Dignity is future-dependent. In the wake of the Enlightenment we have come to think of dignity as being inherent. But this is not quite true. Our experience tells us that before dignity can be inherent, it must be conferred. Dignity must first be bestowed; then it becomes owned. Dignity has a grace or giftedness quality to it. This is because it is a social phenomenon. To experience self-worth through being respected, honored, loved, or served, i.e., to be treated as an end and not as a means. And this self-worth is gained through intercourse with a world of meaning that confers this worth. Dignity is dependent upon the web of interconnectedness that will finally unite all things, upon the anticipated whole of redeemed reality wrought by a God whose love for us makes us ends rather than means.

The proleptic position I am developing here differs in part with the ecological ethic proposed by John Cobb in concert with

Charles Birch. What the two proposals have in common is a sense of wholism, a sense of dependence upon the interconnectedness of the web of life. The difference is that Cobb places the locus of value in the experience of biological life in general, thereby subordinating human dignity to a further end. ". . . the locus of intrinsic value is, not in person as such," Cobb writes, "but in experience. All experience has intrinsic value."[23] Cobb's position is an experiential hedonism which holds that value is intrinsic to life because life experiences. This leads to gradations of value due to the relative "richness of experience" within life. The greater the richness the greater the life and, hence, the greater the value. "To have richer experience is to be more alive."[24]

One ominous implication for human life is that we may raise again the question of comparative intrinsic worth. Belief in human dignity had eliminated this question, positing human equality on the grounds that every person has equal dignity. In the Cobb scheme, however, we may now discriminate between human persons, valuing more highly those with richer experience and valuing more lowly those whose experience is restricted. "There is no substantial reason to believe that all persons have equal intrinsic value," write Cobb and Birch.[25] Although Cobb and Birch are quick to deny it, it seems inevitable that an ethic of triage would follow from these premises. One could devise a scale of richness of experience against which we could measure every person we know. In time of crisis due to limited resources we would have a ready-made calculus for eliminating those people with relatively less richness up to the point of bringing resources and population back into balance. This is certainly not the intention of Cobb and Birch who are seeking a wholistic ethic that can meet the needs of the ecological concerns which we have. But any position which withdraws support for human dignity risks a dangerous setback.

Whatever ecological wholism we aim for must include human dignity, even if it goes beyond it. Dignity is not just an aberration of the Enlightenment; it has a biblical foundation on three counts. First, although God through God's wisdom creates the whole cosmos, there is a special "delight" in humanity.

> When he (the Lord) set the heavens in their place I (Wisdom) was there,
>> when he girdled the ocean with the horizon,
>> when he fixed the canopy of clouds overhead
>>> and set the springs of oceans firm in their place,
>> when he prescribed the limits for the sea

and knit together earth's foundations.
Then I was at his side each day,
  his darling and delight,
playing in his presence continually,
playing on the earth, when he had finished it,
  while my delight was in mankind.
        —Proverbs 8:27-31 (NEB)

Second, God delights enough in humanity to sacrifice for it. The incarnation and the atonement amount to a divine conferring of dignity, to a divine act wherein we are treated as an end and Christ as the means. Third, we are created in the image of God. In light of what was said earlier about proleptic eschatology and creation from the future, what we mean by the *imago dei* is Christ, the second Adam. Who we as humans are is dependent upon who we will be, namely, new creatures in Christ. Our dignity today anticipates and is dependent upon who we will actually be tomorrow. Today dignity is conferred. Tomorrow it will be inherent.

Such a proleptic ethic is necessary to ground a movement to liberate the oppressed in our world. The first step in the liberation process is the conferring of dignity where it does not presently exist. Victims of injustice and poverty lack dignity in the sense that they are not ends—and may be simply the exploited means—of the world economic system as a whole. The millions if not billions of poor people in our world can be defined almost by their deprivation of rich experience, or at least their deprivation of the experience of richness. They lack actual dignity because, as the forgotten and exploited ones, they are not the end of the dominant social value. The dignity of the poor and the oppressed is a dignity that is conferred upon them—that is imputed to them—even though it runs contrary to their and our experience. The basis for conferring such dignity is faith, faith in a future where this dignity will become actual and inherent. The basis of this faith is God's promise. Without such a divine promise, the whole enterprise of striving for liberation would consist of an empty ideal that flies in the face of our current experience of injustice and oppression. As promise, however, the tension between the ideal and the present reality becomes the very inspiration for vigorous work.

The dignity we are supporting here is not intended to justify an anthropocentrism that in turn justifies the wanton destruction of nature. It does imply, however, that any dignity ascribed to the natural order at large is derived from human dignity. We need to resist current sentimental and romantic appeals to an alleged wholism in nature that would exist apart from contamination by human exploitation, an ecologist's version of the noble savage. The fact is that violence and destruction occur every moment in the biosphere, as life feeds on life: blood "red in tooth and claw" (Tennyson). The current interdependence of various strands within the single web of life is a competitive and violent interdependence. One living thing is not an end for another living thing; it is a means. It is devoured. That the whole of life in all its complexity can be viewed as beautiful and revered depends upon the viewer. The only viewer who can do this as far as we know is the human being. Amidst the constant violence and destruction that characterizes natural life we can confer dignity on the biosphere only because of God's promise that some day the lion will lie down with the lamb. We live proleptically when we say grace at table, showing thankfulness for the life sacrificed so that we can eat, and when we seek to live in a global *Gemeinschaft* wherein we care for the earth as we would care for our own family.

5. Proffer the distinction between needs and wants.   One of the reasons the wealthy First World overconsumes and is slow to share with the Third World is that it blurs the distinction between *needs* and *wants*.[26] We pretend that everything we desire has the status of a need. Needs are what all people require just to be human: food, shelter, sleep, exercise, protection from danger, etc. These are the survival and security requirements at the bottom of Abraham Maslow's hierarchy of human needs.[27] They are satiable. Once they are met, we do not need them any more.

Wants, on the other hand, have to do with our desire to be unique or superior. They are insatiable. The more we get the more we want. An ancient Upanishadic saying puts it this way: to believe you can cure a person's desire for wealth by giving him or her money is like thinking you can put out a fire by pouring butterfat on it.

Basic needs have a certain moral priority over wants and desires. Ian Barbour says that ". . . all persons have *a right to life and therefore a right to the basic necessities of life*, including adequate food for survival."[28] Given the maldistribution of wealth in our world, this could mean that the rich will have to live more simply if the poor are simply to live.[29] Unless we can distinguish our wants from our needs—as long as we wrongly call them all "needs"—it will not make moral sense to think of our responsibility to meet first the needs of all and only then meet the wants of some.

6. Propose alliances between Christians and non-Christians who share visions of a truly human future.   Pope John XXIII wrote in *Pacem in terris* that Catholics could cooperate with "all men of good will" in working for world peace. So also should Christians of every stripe link arms with all women and men who share a positive vision of the future and who are willing to exert effort toward making it a present actuality. We should be willing to form alliances with whomever shares our commitment to all or any part of our vision of a planetary *Gemeinschaft* and of living at peace with nature.

At the same time the critical power of the Christian vision of God's ultimate future will remind us that all human approximations to it are—though good and meaningful—still provisional and not absolute. We must always be on guard against fanaticism, the unflagging belief in one's own rightness that idolatrously absolutizes one human individual or institution. No present political system or even the church itself should ever be identified isomorphically with the as yet transcendent kingdom of God. To claim prematurely such ultimacy within the confines of human finitude leads to totalitarianism, a demonic unity at the expense of personal dignity. Proleptically speaking, that which we value now as a right or a good is done only in the light of the as yet coming absolute good, that is, dependent for its goodness on the future eschaton.

Because of this situation, society needs the preaching of the church. Such preaching does two things. First it reinforces the already healthy visions of a positive future produced by secular visionaries. Second, it reminds secular society that it is secular. The church as a distinct institution is in a position to remind the present political order (and natural order too) that it is provisional.

7. Profess faith.   If we allow the forecasts of professional futurists who extrapolate from present trends to doomsday to get us down and sap our energies, then we will have surrendered our faith in God. I like to define 'faith' as trust in the God of the future, trust in the God who raised Jesus to new life on Easter and who promises to transform the present world into God's new creation.

Even if doomsday should come—as it did for Jesus on Good Friday and for the persecuted first readers of the book of Revelation— the New Testament promise is that God will not fail. He has the power of resurrection. The burden of our errors and evils, though heavy, will not last forever. The good news of the Christian evangel is that sin is met by forgiveness, that hurt is met by healing. The birth of the new humanity and new ecology for which we yearn will not ultimately be stillborn. Our visions are not vain illusions. Our praxis is not without meaning. The new world will finally come. It will come with God's power.

Professing this faith may itself help to bring the projected new order into being ahead of schedule. The professing of proleptic faith could make the faith itself contagious. Others might catch on and join the project of bringing the future reality of God's kingdom to bear on the present crisis.

Notes

1. Although the challenge of the impending globewide ecological crisis is dramatically portrayed in myriads of books, newspapers, magazines, and journals, some readings are better than others. Some of the better resources are the following: *Faith, Science, and the Future,* ed. by Paul Abrecht (Geneva: World Council of Churches, 1978); Harrison Brown, *The Human Future Revisited* (New York: W. W. Norton, 1978); *The Global 2000 Report to the President,* volume I, Summary Report, $3.50 to Superintendent of Documents, U.S. Government Printing Office, Washington, D.C. 20402; and Lester R. Brown, *Building a Sustainable Society* (New York: W. W. Norton, 1981). For an overview of the field of futurology see Edward Cornish's *The Study of the Future* (1977) and Frank Feather, ed., *Through the '80s: Thinking Globally, Acting Locally* (1980) both published by the World Future Society, Washington, D.C. 20014.

2. See Lewis S. Ford, *The Lure of God* (Philadelphia: Fortress, 1978) pp. 113f; John B. Cobb and David Ray Griffin, *Process Theology: An Introductory Exposition* (Philadelphia: Westminster, 1976) p. 117. Metaphysically this is rooted in the contention of Alfred North Whitehead that "time requires incompleteness," cited in *Philosophers of Process,* ed. by Douglas Browning (New York: Random House, 1965) p. 315; cf. Whitehead's *Process and Reality* (New York: Macmillan, 1929, 1957) p. 169. But the process objection to the eschaton may miss the mark as long as it focuses on passage rather than perfection. The attainment of the latter does not necessarily deny the former.

3. John Cobb still uses the term 'omnipotence' but with radical qualification: "We may still use the term 'omnipotence' if we like, but its meaning is quite altered. It no longer means that God exercises a monopoly of power and compels everything to be just as it is. It means instead that he exercises the optimum persuasive power in relation to whatever is. Such an optimum is a balance between urging toward

the good and maximizing the power—therefore the freedom—of the one whom God seeks to persuade." *God and the World* (Philadelphia: Westminster, 1969) p. 90. He writes elsewhere, "process theism . . .cannot provide the assurance that God's will is always done." *Process Theology*, p. 118. The position of proleptic eschatology, in contrast, is that it is not necessary to sacrifice divine omnipotence is order to acknowledge human freedom and violation of the divine will.

4. L. Charles Birch and John Cobb, *The Liberation of Life* (Cambridge: Cambridge University Press, 1981) pp. 7, 65, 89.

5. Jürgen Moltmann speaks of the eschaton as an "open system." He writes that we may ". . .assume that there will be time and history, future and possibility in the kingdom of glory as well, and that they will be present in unimpeded measure and in a way that is no longer ambivalent. Instead of timeless eternity we should therefore do better to talk about eternal time. . ." *The Future of Creation* (Philadelphia: Fortress, 1979) p. 126.

6. Lewis Ford puts it this way: "Classical Theism, for all the difficulties it might have with present evil, can be serene in the confidence that someday God will wipe out all evil. After all, he is all-powerful, and needs only to assume full control of the world to make it conform to his will. Process theism, by relinquishing the claim that God could completely control the world in order to overcome the problem of present evil, cannot have this traditional assurance about the future." *Lure of God*, p. 119. Cobb and Griffin offer up an interesting distinction as they implicitly distinguish between temporality and everlastingness. The deepest concern with evil, they say following Whitehead, is our concern over the loss of the past, over the perpetual perishing of things. Perishing tends to make life meaningless, they say. This problem is overcome by positing everlastingness in the consequent nature of God. "This divine life is neither eternal, in the sense of timeless, nor temporal, in the sense of perpetual perishing. Instead it is everlasting, constantly receiving from the world but retaining what in the world is past in the immediacy of its everlasting present." *Process Theology*, p. 122. Does this mean 'everlastingness' refers to temporal process minus the evil? This seems to be the intention here. Cobb's doctrine of providence pictures God as transforming evil into good. "God's aim is so inclusive that he can receive and synthesize into good what in worldly occasions would be mutually destructive elements, or elements incompatible with their limited aims." *Christ in a Pluralistic Age* (Philadelphia: Westminster, 1975) p. 226. Because God is inclusive, evil at the divine level is synthesized into good. Because we are limited, we must suffer the consequences of evil. According to this scheme, then, salvation is for God but not for the actual creation. It is my judgment that the Cobb and Griffin program

describes well the divine synthesis that overcomes evil, but, in contrast to Cobb and Griffin, this divine synthesis applies to the eschatological redemption of the creation and not simply to God's contemporary and ongoing memory.

7. Alfred North Whitehead, *Science and the Modern World* (New York: Macmillan, 1926) Chapter 11.

8. Birch and Cobb, *Liberation of Life*, p. 65.

9. Of course this will necessitate a radical difference in scale between the human experience of time and the cosmic process itself. But even somewhat non-literalist renderings of passages such as II Peter 3:8, ". . .with the Lord one day is as a thousand years, and a thousand years as a day," clearly opens the door to interpretations that stress the difference in scale.

10. The concept of prolepsis in relation to Christ in recent theology has been developed primarily by Wolfhart Pannenberg. "Christ's mediation of creation is not to be thought of primarily in terms of the temporal beginning of the world. It is rather to be understood in terms of the whole of the world process that receives its unity and meaning in the light of its end that has appeared in advance in the history of Jesus, so that the essence of every individual occurence, whose meaning is relative to the whole to which it belongs, is first decided in light of the end." *Jesus—God and Man* (Philadelphia: Westminster, 2nd ed., 1977) p. 391. Cf. also by Pannenberg, Vol. III of *New Frontiers in Theology*, ed. by James Robinson and John Cobb (New York: Harper & Row, 1967) p. 125; Carl E. Braaten, *The Future of God* (New York: Harper & Row, 1969); and James M. Childs, Jr., *Christian Anthropology and Ethics* (Philadelphia: Fortress, 1978).

11. John Cobb offers a tempting alternative interpretation of the incarnation. His thesis is that 'Christ' is the image or name we give to "creative transformation." *Christ in a Pluralistic Age*, pp. 21, 45. He defines *logos* in terms of the universal transcendent principle of order necessary to produce novelty in the world. Ibid., p. 75. This connotes both reason and creativity, two items intrinsic to *logos*. The term 'Christ' refers to the *logos* as incarnate, i.e., anywhere and everywhere that it finds concrete actualization. Ibid., p. 77. This position has much to commend it. Cobb's boat may very well float, but before we set sail with it we should attend to a small leak. Perhaps the concept of creative transformation is a bit too abstract. Transformation for what? At least in Whiteheadian theory proper, creativity is not something actual in itself but rather a descriptive principle so abstract that it has no character of its own; it is a category of the highest generality. *Process and Reality*, p. 47. If this is what Cobb means by 'creativity', then the incarnation or actualization of creativity is not enough to constitute Christ, at least the Christ we know from scripture. Christ must also embody the subjective aim of God, the will of the creator for the redemption of all things. The term

'Christ' should refer to creativity with a specific target and to the concrete presence ahead of time of the bulls-eye. Toward the end of *Christ in a Pluralistic Eye*, after drawing upon the visions of the future projected by Soleri and Pannenberg, Cobb begins to focus on the kingdom of God as his bulls-eye. To develop this further would give the concept of creative transformation greater theological substance.

12. Karl Marx, "Contribution to the Critique of Hegel's Philosophy of Right," cited in *Marx and Engels on Religion*, intro. by Reinhold Niebuhr (New York: Schocken Books, 1964) p. 42.

13. Letty M. Russell, *The Future of Partnership* (Philadelphia: Westminster, 1979) p. 102.

14. Gustavo Gutierrez, *A Theology of Liberation* (Maryknoll, NY: Orbis, 1973) p. 164. Eschatology has a strong accent as well in the work of James H. Cone, *A Black Theology of Liberation* (New York: Lippincott, 1970) Chap. VII, and *God of the Oppressed* (New York: Seabury, 1975) pp. 159f.

15. Wolfhart Pannenberg, *Theology and the Kingdom of God* (Philadelphia: Westminster, 1969) p. 111.

16. Carl E. Braaten, *Eschatology and Ethics* (Minneapolis: Augsburg, 1974) p. 121.

17. Jürgen Moltmann, *Religion, Revolution, and the Future* (New York: Scribner's, 1969) p. 32.

18. Fred L. Polak, *The Image of the Future*, trans. and abridged by Elise Boulding (New York: Elsevier, 1973).

19. Lynn White, "The Historical Roots of Our Ecological Crisis," *Science* 155 (March 1967) pp. 1203-7; reprinted in *The Environmental Handbook*, ed. by Garret de Bell (New York: Ballantine, 1970) pp. 12-26. Cf. also the criticism of White offered by James Limburg, "What Does It Mean to Have Dominion over the Earth," *Dialog* 10 (Summer 1971) pp. 221-23.

20. Charles Hartshorne calls this brand of humanism "monomania." *Beyond Humanism* (Lincoln: University of Nebraska Press, 1937, 1969) p. 1. Cobb, Griffin, and Birch call it "anthropocentrism." They take the argument further by criticizing current liberation theologians for the limited scope of their vision. They are too anthropocentric, thereby ignoring the wider issues of ecology. John Cobb writes, "The problems of justice and human liberation must be addressed . . . But if the problems are addressed in forgetfulness of the inclusive global situation, the efforts cannot succeed. Just distribution of food, for example, will not suffice if it means only that everyone is equally deficient in proteins." "Process Theology and Environmental Issues," *Journal of Religion* (1980) p. 441. The process theologians are right on this.

21. Cf. Ted Peters, "The Ethics of Radwaste Disposal," *The Christian Century*, 99:8 (March 10, 1982) pp. 271-73; and "Ethical Considera-

tions Surrounding Nuclear Waste Repository Siting and Mitigation" in *Nuclear Waste: Socioeconomic Dimensions,* ed. by Steve H. Murdock, F. Larry Leistritz, and Rita R. Hamm (Boulder, CO: Westview Press, 1983) pp. 41-56.

22. E. F. Schumacher, *Small is Beautiful* (New York: Harper & Row, Perennial Library, 1973) p. 145.

23. Cobb, "Process Theology and Environmental Issues," p. 449.

24. Birch and Cobb, *Liberation of Life*, p. 146; cf. p. 106.

25. Ibid., p. 164.

26. Cf. Daniel Bell, *The Cultural Contradictions of Capitalism* (New York: Harper & Row, 1976) p. xiii; Ervin Laszlo, *A Strategy for the Future* (New York: George Braziller, 1974) p. 47.

27. Abraham Maslow, *Motivation and Personality* (New York: Harper, 1954) pp. 80-89.

28. Ian G. Barbour, *Technology, Environment, and Human Value* (New York: Praeger, 1980) p. 250, Barbour's italics.

29. Cf. Charles Birch, "Nature, Humanity, and God in Ecological Perspective," in *Faith and Science in an Unjust World: Report of the World Council of Churches Conference on Faith, Science, and the Future* (2 Volumes: Philadelphia: Fortress, 1980) I, 72.

Chapter Twenty-Three

SACRAMENTAL WORSHIP FOR CREATION CONSCIOUSNESS

Douglas G. Adams

At a conference with ministers, I noted that appreciation for arts in worship was grounded on the same theological foundations that help one appreciate sacraments and social concern for the environment and other political issues: i.e., God created the material world. One minister then said that he not only did not appreciate arts in worship but also did not care for either the sacraments or church political action. In his church, the connection between worship and the world is minimized: there are few body movements, few references to world political issues, and infrequent eating of bread and wine that bears any resemblance to worldly forms. Such worship forms have their consequences in minimizing the relation between worshipping and caring for the material world. Changing worship forms in more sacramental directions promises consequences that cultivate creation consciousness. Sacramental directions include not only more frequent celebrations of communion of worship but also forms of communion and other worship elements and actions that resonate with forms in daily life.

Few ministers intentionally develop worship forms antagonistic to concerns for the environment and other issues of justice; but worship forms often have their consequences in unintended and unexpected ways. For instance, when I was in the South in the 1960s, I was working with a woman of moderately progressive persuasion. But she could not understand Martin Luther King as anything but demonic. She could not see him as a voice of God, a view which I had been urging on her. I finally asked her why she viewed King so negatively; and she responded, "Because he is so noisy. He raises his voice and causes upheaval." Talking with her, I found that her experience of worship had been with pastors who had always been quiet in speech and led worship in forms that had been harmonious, sustained, symmetrical, quiet, and clean. One consequence of such forms was that she could not hear the voice or see the face of God in Martin Luther King's expressions. Worship forms have their consequences.

Christian worship has not always been limited to such forms. Such quiet, clean, formal, harmonious settings are peculiar to the last hundred years of public worship. We need a recovery of some earlier Christian worship forms; for instance, the first century worship and later periods such as early American worship had very percussive forms. All musical instruments in the early church as in Old Testament times were percussive. Even stringed instruments were plucked, not bowed. In both the early church and early American churches, sermons were followed by times when the people could speak out and disagree with what had been said; such discussion times were opportunities for dissonance in worship. In order to appreciate and sense God's presence in all settings, it helps to have some worship that is dissonant and some that is harmonious, some that is asymmetrical and some that is symmetrical, some that is noisy and some that is quiet.

Different religions have different worship forms. We generally identify the asymmetrical forms with breaking forms and emerging new forms. Such dissonant forms (that often strike the listener as noisy) usually are associated with the prophetic tradition. The prophet is concerned with new, emerging forms which shatter the old and bring about change. Well ordered, harmonious, symmetrical and sustained forms are associated more commonly with the priestly tradition, where there is a great concern for order. Judaism and Christianity are oriented toward the prophetic, although they have their priestly qualities. Other religions of the world may tilt toward the priestly and may be concerned with the sustained and harmonious. But the fact that Christianity and Judaism tilt toward the prophetic Biblical forms may not be apparent to those of us experiencing worship forms of the past hundred years when order, harmony, and cleanliness have dominated. And such forms have their consequences in our inability to link our worship lives and our lives outside of worship.

When I was at the 1973 conference on religion, art, and architecture in Jerusalem, the participants were asked to draw how they thought the Church of the Holy Sepulchre should have been designed. Everyone did drawings; in most of them there were trees and flowers, but no people. Most of the conference participants found the most congenial place to be the Dome of the Rock, a marvelous Moslem shrine with decorative floral designs. There one must always be in silence; and wherever one stands, the entire architecture and art lead one into a unitive sense with the whole place. Everyone hated the Church of the Holy Sepulchre, the Christian site traditionally thought to cover the places of Christ's crucifixion and resurrection. When one walked into that church, there was a Catholic Mass going on over at the right, an Armenian rite being celebrated in a chapel to the left, an Orthodox service also being celebrated at the left, and an Italian group coming down the street and into the church as they continued chanting. Yet, when one stepped from the Moslem shrine back into the city of Jerusalem, it was a shattering step. Most people coming home from the shrine expressed the hope to escape the city by heading for the countryside or going back into the shrine. The form had its consequences. But when one stepped from the Church of the Holy Sepulchre into the busy streets, one sensed that one was in a continuity and able to live in the city. That form had a different consequence.

There is an environmental consequence of worship forms. If one grows up experiencing God in forms that are always harmonious, clean, orderly, and quiet, then one must flee the city in order to find God. I suspect that that is one reason why people from cities flee into the countryside; but unfortunately, such flight can pollute the countryside. If people grew up with some noisy, dissonant worship, they might find God in the city. Similarly, there are those who could never find the face of God on people, because people are often making noise; but they could readily find the face of God in a tree, which never makes too much noise.

It is ironic that late nineteenth century and twentieth century worship services can encourage people to pollute what remains of the countryside when the hymns of worship are loaded with positive lyrics about trees and flowers and lack references to daily city life. Part of the problem arises from the fact that in worship people sit quietly and resemble trees and so do not cultivate a consciousness that God may be present when we are around talking, moving, working people.

By mistakenly calling Sunday "the sabbath," English-speaking Puritans since the seventeenth century have further separated worship and work; for the sabbath was a day of rest that precluded many activities characterizing the rest of the week. As we begin to understand that Christian worship was originally conceived as a day of work, then its sacramental connection to daily city life may be reestablished. Until Constantine made Sunday a holiday, it had been more like our Monday, the first work day of the week. And Christian worship was called "liturgy" (*leitourgia* in Greek) because that term meant "the work of the people," the day or two which people gave in the Greco-Roman world to build up the bridges and roads and other public works for the growth of the community. By losing the connection between Sunday worship and the rest of the week's activities, we have made it more difficult to perceive God's concern for weekday activities. And so such activities go unrestrained by any religious considerations or ethics, even if such ethical considerations are talked about on Sunday in worship; for many think such talk inappropriate if they mistakenly think that Sunday is a sabbath day of rest.

Sacramental forms in worship have the power to remind us of God's concern and presence in all of life during the week. "Sacramentum" relates to the salute given by a Roman soldier to a superior and was a reminder of one's responsibilities to a higher authority. As the communion bread and wine are to remind us of our relationship with God and Christ whenever we eat bread and drink wine during the week, so other sacramentals in worship would remind us of God's concerns whenever we see such elements or activities during the week. The rituals of Passover focus in part on the doorway; doorways remind one to be about God's business when one comes in and goes out. Similarly, salt, light, blows, doors, and other objects and activities were sacramentalized through the Bible and church worship life. The Eastern Orthodox church has systematically sacramentalized objects and activities from daily life as evidenced by the *Euchologian*, a collection of prayers keyed to every object and occasion in daily work life.

A first step in creation consciousness is recognizing ourselves and our activities and creations as part of God's creation and not alien from God's creation. When we begin to sense that our buildings are as much a part of creation as mountains and that people are as much a part of creation as trees, then we may take greater care with how we make buildings as well as how we treat mountains.

Sacramentalizing may not always mean affirming the objects

or activities included in worship. But including the objects or
activities (even if they are included only in the confession) leads
us to see them related to God's judgment and grace in the future.
Such sacramentalizing may occur through the lyrics of hymns.
Such hymns make good hymns of confession. For instance, Clarrissa Kitchen's *The Ecology Hymnal: New Words for Old Tunes*,
contain the following new lyrics to be sung to the tune of "The
Battle Hymn of the Republic:"

> Mine eyes have seen the fury of the spoiling of the earth;
> Seen the promise of a future that was dead before its birth;
> Where the heraldings of plenty were the harbingers of dearth
> As we go marching on.
> Refrain: Slowly, slowly to the future
>   Slowly, slowly to the future
>   Slowly, slowly to the future
>   We all go marching on.
> I have seen it in the forest fires that blossom on the hills,
> I have seen it in the refuse in the rivers and the rills,
> I have seen it in the dumping and the trashing of the spills,
> As we go marching on.[1]

The second stanza is more sacramentalizing than the first; for the
concrete language of the second stanza will come to mind as we
view land burned over by a forest fire or as we view a polluted
river.

Another hymn by Clarrissa Kitchen sacramentalizes many of our
hectic and wasteful daily activities to the tune of "America the
Beautiful:"

> O prodigal of ores, and trees,
>   Of amber waves of grain
> That long in piled futilities
>   Had robbed the fertile plain.
> America, America,
>   God send God's wrath on thee
> Who spent thy soil, thy workers' toil
>   Producing wastefully.
>
> O prodigal for traffic fleet
>   and eager hordes that press
> More thoroughfares to crush and beat
>   Thy shrinking wilderness;
> America, America,
>   God press the charge on thee
> That of thy soul no self control
>   Permitted this to be.

O prodigal for market place
  That bids beyond its worth
The price of what one buys and sells
  For everyone on earth.
America, America,
  God mend this dreadful flaw,
That greed and power advance the hour
  When Money shall be law.

O prodigal for patriot dream
  Still building through the years
High piled its armaments to gleam
  Memorial of its fears;
America, America,
  May God thy gold consume
And with they vain prosperities
  Thy prejudice entomb.[2]

While such lyrics are not easy to sing or hear, they are true confession and judgment that will be remembered and not easily forgotten. And seeing such activities under the judgment of God is more hopeful than seeing such activities beyond the concern and constraint of God and worship.

Notes

1. Clarrissa Kitchen, *The Ecology Hymnal: New Words for Old Tunes* (Austin: The Sharing Company, 1974), p. 11.
2. Ibid., p. 14.

Chapter Twenty-Four

ELEMENTS OF CREATION-CONSCIOUS LIFE STYLE

Philip N. Joranson and Ken Butigan

Two types of elements are fundamental in the development of creation-conscious life styles: elements which cultivate creation-conscious sensitivity and perception, and activities which express this consciousness in all relationships with God's otherkinds. These two types are described below.

A. Elements Which Cultivate Creation-Conscious Sensitivity and Perception

1. Disciplined prayer.   The experience of disciplined prayer is basic to developing this awareness. By frequently opening ourselves to the presence of God in the midst of God's world, we are joined in an intimate and meaningful way with the creatures of the world so loved by God. The experience of prayer, over time, focuses attention, intention, and perception—we become aware in a new way of the interrelationships throughout the cosmos, and, in grasping that unity, see before us unifying love embodied. Our seeing leads to loving—this intentional prayer, this explicit communion with all that exists, can lead us to fall in love with all that exists.

2. Prayer's process.   Prayer opens us to, and allows us to glimpse in ways "ordinary consciousness" does not, the *horizon* and ultimate *context* of our lives as individuals and as members of the "community of creatures." Prayer leads us to grasp the meaning of our life-experience by helping us to assimilate and integrate that experience in the wider context of our existence. It prompts us to perceive the connections between ourselves and the entire creation, and to consider a number of primary issues, including:

a. How much do we love *people*—ourselves[1] and others? The love that we bear for our own species will serve as a foundation for our love for all creation. Prayer tends, over time, to blur the edges between "classes" of creatures—the affection, sympathy, compassion, and unity we feel with other human beings can lead us to feel strongly for the whole cosmos. Without human love, our love for creation will be stunted and diminished.

b. Our prayers will be enriched by a lifelong pattern of first-hand experience of the creation. We should become thoroughly at home in at least one place in the landscape by becoming well acquainted with plant and animal life there, and by developing a "sense" for that unique, specially configured location. This sense should be saturated with the awareness that we are in the midst of this *particular* part of the cosmos. Our cities have, by and large, broken the connection between "meaning" and "natural environment"—one location is as meaningful as the next. This attitude denies the fundamental importance of "place" and our relationship to it, especially the natural contours of the land, the sea, the sky, and all the creatures—and not only human creatures—who inhabit them. The unique, natural "place" deserves our full attention and affection—we must have easy access to natural environments which reveal the flow and structure of a cosmos in continual creation. Such relationships ground our prayers—our prayer of praise and celebration which we take up with the author of Psalm 98 and with all who have marvelled at the created order.

c. Roger Tory Peterson, the great naturalist and illustrator of birds and other wildlife, has recently asked, "How can you expect people to preserve wildlife when they don't even know what they're looking at?" Let us see the natural world and be educated by that bare gaze. The Native Americans knew intimately each kind of plant and animal of the landscape. This knowledge when to the heart of their identity as a people. By failing to attend to the natural world, we have lost a significant aspect of our own self-understanding. Let us rediscover ourselves by discovering the natural environment.

One way we could do this is by creating and participating in worship services which magnify and praise the Lord by focusing on one or several creatures—a rock, a plant, an animal? A congregation could be introduced to such an event through familiarization—it could be acquainted with the evolutionary derivation, geographic distribution, ecological niche, relationship to humanity of a selected species, culminating in a liturgy of praise and thanksgiving. Such a celebration would echo in a small way the joy which the Creator took in creation for the 4½ billion years before humankind appeared on the surface of planet earth.

d.   We need to become increasingly aware of our evolutionary kinship—extending back to the origins of life and out to the limits of earth—with all beings that are now alive and that have ever lived: becoming conscious of our personal involvement in a very long and still continuing creation. By undertaking such an endeavor, we will attempt to, as theologian John Dunne urges, "pass over" into the point of view of God—to attempt to see life as God conceives and makes it, as God sees and loves it.

e.   This is, through and through, a world in process—the discoveries of the last 100 years have led us to see the evolution of the world from inorganic to organic, from organic to cultural and then spiritual self-understanding.[2] We need to develop metaphors which embrace the whole of the cosmos in the horizon of the holy. Creation-consciousness will be spurred on by all-embracing images which bring alive the truth of the interrelationships of the cosmos.[3]

f.   We must, finally, cultivate an attitude of openness. A culture which has valued the nonhuman creation so poorly cannot afford from this point forward to be anything but open to a positive relationship with the natural world. Christian creation consciousness is in its infancy. We must become aware of the obstacles which prevent that positive outreaching to the environment. As Paul Santmire has shown in *Brother Earth*[4], sentimentalism is one of its most subtle enemies. Another is an insidious Christian exclusivism which kills the spirit of a vision of universal connectedness. Our religious frames-of-reference should function as ways into awareness of the world and never as a roadblock to that world or to the understanding of the environment held by another religious tradition. The Christian vision of the environment must not block out the vision of the environment which other major world religions engender. What is needed is a great inter-religious adventure in developing a constructive, reverential, and fully compassionate relationship with the cosmos.

B. Activities Which Express Creation Consciousness

Creation consciousness is fully realized only when it is embodied—that is, only when it finds application in the concrete relationship between humankind and the environment. Personal and communal involvement in the development of this consciousness includes:

1. Engaging in ecological practices— recycling of household materials and promotion of municipal recycling and energy-recovery programs; conservation of energy through insulation and other means, and development of home alternative energy sources (solar, wind, biomass); and reshaping consumption patterns.

2. Maintaining familiarity with, and personal involvement in at least one of the major environmental trouble areas.

3. Involvement—through time, energy, money, our very lives —in organizations working on: nuclear weapons policy; population policy; global social justice, involving access to resources, local food production and distribution, and transforming the present world economic order; reversing trends in the withdrawal of farmland from production; energy policy and energy research support; environmental degradation in all forms, including soil erosion; a halt to the extinction of species; wilderness and recreational land policy; toxic waste disposal; and the danger of "acid rain."

4. Promoting creation consciousness in religious education, in Christian worship, and in the arts.

5. Pure enjoyment of the creation in many ways—as a major theme of life. Joseph Meeker[5] has called for the rediscovery among environmentalists of the enjoyment ("comedy", in the sense of the Greek drama) of the environment, a quality which should not only inform our appreciation of the natural world, but also shape our approach to the way we defend and preserve that world.

Creation consciousness is not merely a multi-dimensional commitment; it is a way of being calling for, and generating, wisdom— wisdom about the ways to be engendered not only in the individual, but also in many communities. One hundred lives in a Christian community, each developing a unique and increasingly mature creation-conscious style of life, will become one hundred points of entry for the luminous Creator-Spirit of God, revealing humankind and all other kind to each other, and will create a new understanding of the environmental dimension of what Jesus called the Kingdom of God.

Chapter Twenty-Five

EDUCATIONAL MODELS: FOUR CURRENT PROGRAMS

In several centers where there has been interest in the expression and nurturance of creation consciousness as an inherent dimension of the life of faith, substantial educational programs have taken shape. Four of these programs are described by their facilitators in the following statements.

The religious communities sponsoring the programs are Roman Catholic, evangelical Protestant and, in two instances, ecumenical. All of the programs are ecumenical in operating policy. A move toward the cooperation of a wide number of groups committed to this work, including the four described here, was taken in December 1982 when a year-long Consultation on Faith, Science and Technology—sponsored by the National Council of Churches of Christ—was initiated.

1. THE INSTITUTE IN CULTURE AND CREATION SPIRITUALITY

by Brian Swimme

To introduce the Institute in Culture and Creation Spirituality (ICCS) I have chosen a number of ideas that are intrinsic to our thinking and work. I hope in these short reflections to provide some understanding of the educational processes at ICCS.

Collapse

We take the reality of a major collapse for granted. The only argument now is how huge it will be. Some people think it's just western consumptive society that will go down. Many fear that all

the advanced life forms will go. But what scientists agree upon are
these grim forecasts: hundreds of millions of humans will die of
starvation in the next ten years; and at least a third of the planet's
arable land will be changed into desert; and no fewer than half a
million species will be removed from the planet forever.[1]

Causes

We all want to know the causes. If we can nail them down perhaps we can alter things to limit the damage. The suffering is going
to be tremendous regardless, but perhaps with insight we will be
able to stem some of the needless destruction before it engulfs us
completely.

At ICCS we see the homocentrism of modern society as the principal defect, the flaw that has led to our dead end. By homocentrism I mean the way in which our civilization is centered totally
on the human. By taking our ultimate context as the human world
we have limited our thinking severely, which is reflected in our
consequent activities. Thus, for modern society, progress means
human progress and wealth means human wealth. Focussed on
this myopic goal of human wealth we change the rivers to sewers
and the soils to poisons and only now realize that human benefits
all depend on the natural world and its inherent vitality. Blinded
by our homocentric thinking we desire wealth but create pervasive ecological poverty.

Benign Culprits

We need to ask ourselves how this all happened. How did modern scientific-technological society fixate on the human? Why did
we fail to develop a more cosmic or planetary viewpoint?

The source of our world view is the creative turbulence of the
seventeenth century. We had scientists enthralled with the new
power and knowledge that was foaming into their midst. And we
had theologians and political figures anxious about the possible
assaults on the established order in society. Was anything of value
in the old order? Should it all be thrown out *en masse*? Or should
society, instead, curb the new scientific knowledge and power?

A compromise was suggested by various thinkers who wanted to
provide for a strong science in a secure social order. It worked out
to this: the earth and universe are made of matter which is inert,
dead, without intrinsic value. Thus anything we learn about it
through science can not possibly conflict with traditional religious

concerns since these concerns in a fall/redemption theology pertain to values from an other-worldly realm. Science could now proceed, and religious authority was momentarily shored up. But the price for this social stability was rather dear. We had to fork over the ancient intuition that the universe was alive, that the earth was a magical womb of life and existence.[3]

Once a society convinces itself that matter and the earth are intrinsically dead and inert it sets out on the tracks that lead to a dedicated transformation of the planet into cesspools and asphalt. For if the nonhuman earth has no meaning, no value, no inalienable rights, then nothing matters but the economic and political programs of humans. The earth then is seen as future consumer products.

Not Just Wrong, But Lonely Too

We need to reflect on the following observation of western scholars. In all the dozens of civilizations, in all the hundred tribal communities we have studied, only *one* adopted the viewpoint that the earth was a dustball of dead matter. Only one managed to convince itself that the earth was nothing but potential resources for a human economy. It was our modern society that tried to build a world on this flawed conception. Start off with a mistake and it will show up sooner or later in your work. If you are clever enough to avoid correcting this mistake for several centuries, when it does show up it will do so with a vengeance.[4]

Cosmos As Referent

We escape the homocentrism of the past few centuries by taking the cosmos as our primary referent. Our thinking and our working must have the earth and the universe as its central context. In that domain our thoughts begin to reflect some of the fullness of our destiny. In that spaciousness we begin to see our way out of the impasse.[5]

Death and Rebirth

From a cosmic perspective, the essential nature of our situation can be appreciated. What we discover when we examine the twenty billion years of the universe's development are a series of crises where one order collapses for the birth of a new order of existence. For instance, the fireball that filled every point of the universe during its first million years broke apart, but only through this collapse could the great galactic systems emerge. From the perspective of life on earth, the most stable society in four billion years was that of the prokaryotic organisms. After two billion years this society broke apart in the increased concentration of oxygen. But only with this collapse could a new world of more complex organisms establish itself. Within the human story we see the same sequence in the breakdown of the tribal communities and the simultaneous emergence of the great civilizations; or in the breakdown of these classical civilizations under the pressure of the advancing scientific-technological phase of human development.

So now the modern scientific mode of humanity breaks apart. We live in this transition time. This collapse enables another phase of human existence to establish itself, and it is the task and delight of education to assist in this transformation and rebirth.

Central Conviction

At ICCS we are convinced that the central intuition of the emerging order is the sacrality of the earth. All creation is divine, sacred, and worthy of our deepest reverence.

Transmitting Conviction

ICCS exists to ignite and transmit this conviction. That alone would be enough. For if this intuition is felt deeply all the rest follows, all the revisioning of our forms of thought and culture and life.

How does one transmit conviction? Especially if this conviction differs radically from the dominant viewpoint of contemporary society? Here are some answers:

1. By studying the spiritual traditions that are steeped in the intuition that all creation is divine. At ICCS we concentrate on the creation-centered tradition within western religions. In particular we study Hildegard of Bingen, Mechtild of Magdeburg, Meister Eckhart, Julian of Norwich, Dante, Nicolas of Cusa and the wisdom and prophetic literature of the Bible out of which they develop their cosmic world views. We also celebrate the traditions of the native peoples of America, Europe, and Africa.

Creation-centered western religion begins with the conviction that all existence is a blessing. This is the spirituality of the earliest author of Hebrew scriptures and has been lived and affirmed by men and women throughout three thousand years of our history. From this perspective each thing reveals the Creator of all, since each thing is a word spoken by the Creator. Such a viewpoint rejects completely the notion that the earth is dead or fallen. All of earth is divine because isness is already the very essence of God. ("Isness is God," says Meister Eckhart.)[7]

The native traditions in America and Europe and Africa have persisted tens of thousands of years with the central conviction that the earth is sacred, is the source of all being, all life, all that is good. The earth is a mother that sustains and nurtures, and is worthy of our deepest gratitude and respect. For these traditions, any suggestion that the earth is just dead matter is seen as ridiculous. Life for a human centers on enjoying the many gifts that are bestowed upon us and in passing these gifts on to bless all creatures just as we have been blessed.[8]

2. By studying the feminist thinkers who articulate the oppression intrinsic to our sociopolitical structures. It can no longer be a question of capitalism vs. socialism when both insist on excluding whole groups from central social decisions. The exclusion of females and nonwhite races from positions of power has been especially dangerous. By so doing we have largely eliminated from our world-making the feminine principle and its intuitive feeling for life. Instead of creating communities dedicated to mutual empowerment and the enhanced vitality of our bioregions, we have assembled the great industrial machine with its sustained degradation of all life forms.[9]

3. By studying the universe and the planet Earth through the organic evolutionary perspective of recent scientific thought. This understanding shows how the same stuff of the fireball is organized into the stars and planets and lifeforms: that everything is interconnected. From this tradition's perspective, life and even consciousness can be understood as permeating all that exists in a potential manner. This scientific tradition rejects as outdated the Newtonian position that matter is without intrinsic intentionality. The stuff of the fireball is permeated with self-organizing dynamics. The Earth is a self-assembling, self-actualizing reality, and the human plays a vital role in this overall emergence of life and intelligence.[10]

Transmitting Conviction Through Art As Meditation

To know is half the journey. All knowledge at ICCS aims at activating creativity.

To know how the universe can be understood as an emerging

reality is crucial. To feel this organizing energy in one's center completes the learning process. To know how the creation-centered traditions affirm the ongoing presence of God's Word in all of nature is vital. To feel this energetic presence surge into one's immediate awareness deepens the learning.

ICCS presents a cosmology where feeling and awareness permeate the universe, where sentience wells up in forests and mountains and stars as well as in mammals. The encounter with clay or plants or dance or music in the art-as-meditation courses is an encounter with this divine immanence that floods everything in the universe. To engage in clay is to engage in the mystical presence that fashioned the universe. In the process one realizes in an indestructible way that this creative presence that forged the stars is at work in our own hands.[11]

Education

Education is something the universe does. The Earth, for instance, was involved with its own education for billions of years before any humans happened on the scene. And this educational venture has been singularly successful. The elements have learned the intricacies of the first proteins. The earliest organisms learned the genetic code, without pencil and paper, and invented all the genes that we employ so nonchalantly. The processes of hibernation, the invention of the eye and of photosynthesis were tremendous accomplishments in education, and each proceeded as naturally as water making its way to the sea.[12]

We trust that humans will learn, once again, what it means to be human in this new era of humanity. Learning is the core of biology, the essence of what it means to be alive. We are learning just as our ancestors did in the eras of human evolution before us. That which guided them, that which guided the inventors of photosynthesis, and the inventors of the eye, will guide all of us engaged in recreaating the human in the emerging era of the Earth Community.

Programs

ICCS was founded seven years ago by Matthew Fox, who serves as director of the various programs. Presently ICCS consists of several different educational ventures. There is the nine-month degree program leading to a Masters of Arts in Culture and Spirituality. There is the nine-month Certificate Program. There are the fall and spring Sabbatical Programs. There are week-long summer programs at various colleges across the continent. There are week-end programs. And there are video tapes that present some of the main ideas of ICCS.

For further information contact:
Brendan Doyle, Administrative Assistant
ICCS/Holy Names College
3500 Mountain Blvd
Oakland, CA 94619
415/436-0111

2. THE AU SABLE INSTITUTE
A New Venture in Creation Consciousness
by Calvin DeWitt

Consciousness of the creation and human responsibility for its stewardship recently have taken new form as the Au Sable Trails Institute of Environmental Studies. This Institute promotes care and concern for the creation and is located near Mancelona, in the northern part of Michigan's lower peninsula.

In 1980, the Au Sable trustees resolved that the Institute become "a center for study and experiences which will integrate environmental information with Christian thought for the purpose of bringing the Christian community and general public to a better understanding of the Creator and of the stewardship of His creation." By 1982, the Institute was providing college-level certification programs in cooperation with nineteen evangelical Christian colleges, programs which are a combination of courses taken at the home college and at the Institute. In addition, the Institute and the colleges have supported a national Christian Environmental Forum and provide environmental stewardship education for 3,000 children in area schools.

The Institute is located in an unusually favorable environmental setting. College-level programs make full use of the abundant resources and opportunities of the region. These include a designated wild river, hundreds of lakes and bogs, a variety of forest ecosystems, sand dune communities, varied climatic and topographic features, and an abundant and diverse flora and fauna.

Areas that have suffered eco-damage are also studied. Among these are the PPB burial pit (endpoint for the slaughtered animals from Michigans PPB crisis), wells contaminated with brine from oil well operations, and sterile savannahs remaining from the deforestation and fires of the great white pine lumbering era of the 1890s. The services of numerous regional government agencies and institutions involved in natural resource use and protection, planning, and management are used, and the Institute program also serves some of these agencies and institutions in various ways.

All of the educational activities are developed from a stewardship perspective on the creation, and cultivate respect and care for the lands, waters, air and creatures of the earth. College students from participating evangelical Christian colleges earn vocational certification by the Institute in four areas—interpretive natural history, land resources analysis, water resources analysis, and environmental analysis—under programs licensed by the State of Michigan Department of Education. Students learning and practicing environmental stewardship at Au Sable also take courses at their home colleges to fulfill certificate requirements, and are awarded certificates upon graduation from the home college. Thus, a student might combine a college degree in chemistry with an Institute certification in water analysis, a degree in political science with a certificate in land resources analysis, or a degree in biology with a certificate in environmental analysis.

The term "vocational," as applied to Institute certification, has religious reference to the Christian "calling" to be stewards of the creation. It connotes also that particular stewardship skills have been acquired which qualify the student for certain kinds of employment and tasks in society that call for stewarding. Depending upon the program, these skills may include ecosystem analysis by remote sensing; computer applications to ecosystem modeling and management; surveying and mapping techniques, species and community identification, and planning procedures.

Stewardship is the theme of the Institute, with focus on the environment. Programs and activities are conducted for the promotion of Christian stewardship both in style of operation and in over-all programming. This theme is thus reflected in the buildings the Institute builds, in the equipment it purchases, in the management of the natural resources with which it is entrusted, and in its programs of service to the colleges, to the local community, and to the Christian community at large. The main Institute building is a new earth-sheltered structure of high heat energy efficiency.

Au Sable's mission is based upon the conviction that the Bible is the sole authority for faith and practice. Participating colleges require their faculty members to be confessing evangelical Christians who share this commitment. In one of the planning documents is this statement: "We have concluded, based on Scripture, that humans have been given dominion over nature and that they are to use that dominion to serve nature and humanity. Such service is the will of Him who charged us with dominion; its purpose is to preserve, enhance and glorify the creation, and in so doing, to glorify the Creator. In short, we are STEWARDS of God, managers of this particular part of his household . . . our authority is more characteristic of a trustee than an owner—the use and care of nature is entrusted to us. The Creator retains ownership. . . in order to manage correctly—with all the intricate decisions which such managing requires—the stewards must have ecological knowledge . . . Otherwise we shall be ignorant of the effects on nature of our own use of it, and will not be able to act responsibly in the sustaining, renewing, and preserving of the rich diversity of that creation."[1]

Where essential ecological and stewardship knowledge is not yet available or not yet organized, the Institute seeks to use its resources in promoting development and organization of such knowledge. One important program supporting this objective has been the Au Sable Forum, a conference or writers' workshop involving a number of persons with expertise, experience and interests in developing stewardly approaches to the care of the creation. Au Sable Forum presentations are published in several formats, including reference books, handbooks and articles. The proceedings of the 1980 Forum on environmental ethics is the first Forum product and among other uses has been adopted as a supplemental text in college courses.[2]

For further information contact:

Calvin B. DeWitt, Director
Au Sable Institute of Environmental Studies
Route 2
Mancelona, MI 49659

3. THE CENTER FOR THEOLOGY
AND THE NATURAL SCIENCES
Robert J. Russell

The Center for Theology and the Natural Sciences is located in Berkeley, California as an affiliate of the Graduate Theological Union. The purpose of the Center is to encourage research and teaching in the relationships between theology and science. Primary emphasis is placed on philosophical, methodological and historical dimensions. Additional areas include the ethics of technology and the interactions between humans and the environment. The Center provides an ecumenical and interreligious context in which persons with a diversity of religious commitments can work together on vital questions of faith and science.

   Currently, the Center sponsors:

   —research in religion and science;
   —professional and academic courses at the
        doctoral and masters level;
   —fellowships for distinguished scholars in
        religion and science;
   —graduate student assistantships;
   —conferences, colloquia and forums;
   —church workshops and seminars;
   —newsletters and occasional papers.

Design and Vision of the Center

   The idea of forming a new GTU center to study the relationship between theology and the natural sciences has emerged over the last decade. In the fall of 1981, the Center was officially launched by a board of directors including women and men from the seminary, university, parish, and industrial communities. CTNS was located in GTU because of the unique ecumenical structure and outstanding commitment for excellence of this community of scholars and students. From the outset, the Center was designed along interreligious and ecumenical lines, with a commitment to openness and inclusiveness respecting the enormous variety of religious, professional, and personal views of persons in GTU and the Bay Area.

There are five principal dimensions to CTNS:

—The heart of the Center is the individual and shared research of scholars within GTU whose work involves theology, philosophy, and science. The new J. K. Russell Fellowship in Religion and Science brings distinguished scholars to this 'think-tank' forum.

—Growing out of their research, these faculty teach both in the graduate school at the masters and doctoral levels, and in the participating seminaries offering courses for ministry in churches involved in faith and science issues and for clergy returning through the doctor of ministry programs for continued education.

—The Center is active throughout the Bay Area with communities concerned to relate religion and science; it sponsors workshops, seminars, and forums designed for industry, church, and university and college audiences.

—CTNS participates in national and international groups dealing with the global problems of energy, food, population, technology, and environmental values.

—The Center is engaged in developing new resources in written, audio-visual, and computerized form, dealing with the problems of faith, science, technology, and values for church, college, and university curriculum, and for the NCCC and WCC.

Clearly these five areas are integrally interrelated, since theoretical research cannot be broadly adequate if isolated from the learning process of higher education or from the communities that these students will ultimately serve; yet without foundational work, ministry in the wider community will be undernourished and ill-prepared. Local, national, and global concerns are intricately related, as are foundational areas of theology and science with applied issues in technology, ecology, values, and human need. These areas form the vision and vocation of the Center.

Research

A number of GTU faculty are involved in research in theology and science and in related ethical areas. Topics draw from contemporary physics with an emphasis on cosmology, quantum nature, spacetime dynamics, entropy, and thermodynamics;

modern biology, focusing on genetic and population evolution, ecology; the philosophy of science, with primary emphasis on scientific methodology, including the thought of Popper, Kuhn, Lakatos, Feyerabend; and from contemporary theology, including the writings of Barbour, Cobb, Hefner, McFague, McMullin, Moltmann, Pannenberg, Peacocke, Teilhard, and Torrance.

The formation of CTNS triggered the funding of the new J. K. Russell Fellowship in Religion and Science, whose purpose is to promote creative research and teaching in science and religion at GTU. The Fellowship supports the research of a senior scholar while in residency for one semester at GTU. Recipients of this Fellowship include:

1981-83, Professor Andy Dufner, S.J.
1983-84, Professor Ian G. Barbour.

Future recipients include:

1984-85, Professor Philip J. Hefner,
1985-86, Professor Arthur R. Peacocke.

Teaching

Since the inception of CTNS in 1981, some thirty courses in religion and science have been given in both religion and science, and in ethics and technology. Many of these have been conceived and developed by Dr. Russell as new components in the GTU curriculum. The resident CTNS Fellow normally offers one or two new courses at an advanced level, while a series of related offerings are available throughout the seminaries. In the first year alone, more than 100 students and faculty participated in these courses.

Courses include theology and science in historical and current perspectives; physics and Eastern thought; the contemporary mind; philosophy of nature; readings in Whitehead; religion and science in process modes of thought; mathematical models in theology; method in science and theology; technology, environment, and human values; biomedical ethics; ethics of an information society; Christian faith and the environment; the theology of Thomas Torrance; sociobiology and ethics.

Bay Area Interaction

CTNS seeks to involve in its program a broad range of persons from scientific and religious communities, enabling dialogue between people in science whose interests are in religion and theologians whose interests are in science. The geographical location of the Center is therefore particularly significant. The University of California, Berkeley, and other institutions of higher learning are nearby, as well as a variety of industries and religious communities including Catholic, Protestant, Jewish, and Orthodox traditions, all of which are intentionally included in the purposes and goals of CTNS. Consequently the conferences, seminars, forums, and workshops sponsored by CTNS are geared at providing an opportunity for lay and clergy, technologists, scientists, industrialists, faculty, students, to work together on faith and science issues.

Three major conferences have been held involving faculty and students from regional and national campuses, and from church and industry. As a follow-up to the World Council of Churches' 1979 MIT conference, a West Coast consultation on the impact of computers on society was organized featuring speakers from MIT, UC Berkeley, Lawrence Berkeley Laboratory, Stanford, Mills College, Xerox, and the GTU. About 500 people attended the afternoon general session, and workshops continued the next day with 50 invited participants from Bay Area churches and parishes. In the fall of 1982, physicist Freeman J. Dyson spoke at the GTU to an audience of over four hundred on theological implications of the origins of life; respondents included faculty and students from UC Berkeley and GTU. In the spring of 1983, British physicist David Bohm was the featured speaker at a conference on his work in quantum physics and philosophy, at which six invited papers were presented and discussed by faculty and students from GTU, UC Berkeley, Stanford, University of Notre Dame, and the Center for Process Studies in Claremont.

Two extended church seminar series were held in the Bay Area during 1983. These seminars were sponsored by CTNS in conjunction with the Presbyterian Task Force on Theology and Cosmology and with the National Council of Churches of Christ Task Force on Faith and Science.

In addition, CTNS provides student assistantships to support graduate students pursuing advanced studies in religion and science, either in preparation for the doctorate or for ministerial vocations. Membership in CTNS is available for persons interested in receiving the Center's newsletter and participating in the activities.

For further information contact:

Robert J. Russell, Director
The Center for Theology and the Natural Sciences
c/o Graduate Theological Union
2465 LeConte Ave.
Berkeley, CA 94709

4. THE ENVIRONMENT AND THE CHRISTIAN CREATION TRADITION
A Project of the Center for Ethics and Social Policy

by Philip N. Joranson

The present volume is an outgrowth of a graduate course developed by the Center for Ethics and Social Policy, and first offered in the curriculum of the Graduate Theological Union (GTU) in the 1981 spring quarter. The Graduate Theological Union is a consortium in graduate education in which nine seminaries and institutes—Protestant, Roman Catholic, Eastern Orthodox, and Jewish—participate, in liaison with the University of California, Berkeley. Two members of the sponsoring Center for Ethics and Social Policy and nine specialists from a broad range of contributing fields cooperated in offering the course. The students registered represented half of the GTU member seminaries.

A second offering in the 1983 spring quarter was jointly sponsored by the Center and the Pacific School of Religion, through the appointment of Philip Joranson as course director to the adjunct faculty of the School and the participation of 12 other professors and a performing arts group. Registration was open to students in the Master of Divinity and advanced degree programs.

In the summer of 1984, the Center and the Pacific School of Religion offered to area clergy and interested lay people a similar course on the environment and the rebuilding of the Christian creation tradition. The Center is now also anticipating cooperation with an interested group in a church congregation, to learn how to establish a focus in a local church for creation-conscious education, nurturing, and expression in many-dimensional life encounter.

Progress toward accomplishment of the many kinds of transformation which the sponsored courses and the present volume are intended to stimulate will depend heavily upon interdisciplinary research on a broad scale, and the Center seeks to encourage and facilitate such research.

The Center hopes soon to move beyond its inital focus on the creation in Judeo-Christian tradition to a comparative and interacting consideration of beliefs about, attitudes toward, and ways of relating to nature in other world religions. Each religious tradition—and Christianity not the least—is regarded as certain to benefit from such open interchange and mutual exploration.

Since its founding in 1974, the Center for Ethics and Social Policy has majored in the exploration of the ethics of organizations, as a new field of social ethics. In a "triadic" approach, it has brought policy-makers, social scientists, and ethicists together to illumine the ways policy is formulated and the ethical dimensions of policy. In addition to the project on the environment and the Christian creation tradition, other currently active projects concern social implications of religious concepts of justice, corporate ethics, the ethics of churches and hospitals, and an analysis of the economic, environmental, medical, political, and psychological costs of the nuclear arms race.

For further information contact:
Philip N. Joranson, Director
Project on the Environment and the Christian Creation Tradition
Center for Ethics and Social Policy
Graduate Theological Union
2465 LeConte Ave.
Berkeley, CA 94709

Notes

1. The Institute in Culture and Creation Spirituality

1. Samuel S. Epstein et al., *Hazardous Waste in America* (San Francisco: Sierra Club, 1982).
   Paul and Anne Ehrlich, *Extinction* (New York: Random, 1981).
2. Brian Swimme, "New Natural Selection" *Teilhard Studies*, Number 10 (Chambersburg, PA: Anima, 1983).
3. Morris Berman, *The Reenchantment of the World* (Ithaca: Cornell University Press, 1981).
4. Huston Smith, *Forgotten Truth* (New York: Harper and Row, 1976).
5. Thomas Berry, "The New Story" *Teilhard Studies*, Number 1 (Chambersburg, PA: Anima, 1978).
6. Erich Jantsch, *The Self-Organizing Universe* (New York: Pergamon, 1980).
7. Matthew Fox, *Original Blessing* (Santa Fe: Bear & Co., 1983); Matthew Fox, *Breakthrough: Meister Eckhart's Creation Spirituality in New Translation* (Garden City, New York: 1980). See also: Matthew Fox, ed., *Western Spirituality: Historical Roots, Ecumenical Routes* (Santa Fe: Bear & Co., 1981).

8. Patrick Twohy, SJ, *Finding a Way Home* (Spokane: The University Press, 1983).
9. Rosemary Ruether, *New Woman New Earth:* (New York: Seabury, 1975).
10. Brian Swimme, *The Universe is a Green Dragon* (Santa Fe: Bear & Co., 1984).
11. M.C. Richards, *Centering in Pottery, Poetry, and the Person* (Middletown, Ct.: 1964); Matthew Fox, *A Spirituality Named Compassion* (Minneapolis: Winston, 1979), chapter four on "Creativity and Compassion," pp. 104-139.
12. Thomas Berry, *Earth Community* (New York: Riverdale Press, 1982).

2. The Au Sable Institute of Environmental Studies

1. This quote from Institute planning documents is taken from: Loren Wilkinson, Peter DeVos, Calvin DeWitt, Eugene Dykema, Vernon Ehlers, Derk Pereboom, and Aileen Van Beilen, *Earthkeeping: Christian Stewardship of Natural Resources* (Grand Rapids: Eerdmans, 1980).
2. These proceedings are available from the Institute at a cost of $6.95, under the title *The Environmental Crisis: The Ethical Dilemma,* E. R. Squiers, Editor.

Conclusion

THE NEW ROAD AHEAD

Philip N. Joranson and Ken Butigan

Given the checkered relationship between the Christian tradition and the natural environment—and the present urgent need to transform that relationship—what kind of agenda of thought and action suggests itself for the immediate future?

Our encounter with analysis from a host of relevant disciplines clearly indicates that we face a far-reaching challenge. To take up this task, we require new vision, wisdom, methods and expertise which deal stringently with the real issues. Vision must be commensurate with both the potential for mass environmental destruction and, more importantly, the potential for humankind to avert that catastrophe by beginning to live in symbiotic relationship with the whole of the created order as a sign of our faithfulness to the author and source of that order.

A realistic agenda will include:

1. Clear Recognition of the Problem and the Goal

The problem: The inherited creation tradition in the West offers, on balance, an extremely poor grasp of creation-related biblical faith and vision. There have been alternative approaches to this biblical perspective within the tradition—represented by the work of St. Francis, Meister Eckhart, Teilhard de Chardin, and Thomas Merton—which remain potential, valuable resources in developing a constructive Christian approach to the natural world. Nevertheless, the dominant approach, saturated in a grossly inadequate theological understanding of creation, has largely ignored this *rapprochement* with nature and has therefore legitimated widespread ecological disaster.

The goal: To retrieve the biblical vision of the environment and, in light of the rich theological, scientific, artistic, and political resources available today, to rebuild the Christian creation tradition in order that we will recover a sense of the value of the biosphere and that we will be mobilized to radically improve the human relationship to the environment. Such awareness will be aided by greater knowledge and understanding of the entire ecosystem and the resources which are available to achieve that understanding.

2. Emerging Emphases and Qualities

The foregoing essays indicate the essentially *religious* transformation which this task requires. A number of emphases and qualities will be stressed in this activity, including:

a. *Focus* upon processes which truly engage the passion and imagination of the human community, including ecosystem functioning and patterning; evolution; the vastness, structure and dynamics of the physical universe.

b. *Attention* to our partners in the cosmos, the nonhuman creatures which inhabit the world.

c. Cultivating *imagination* as a way of shedding our "environmental stereotypes and clichés", as a way of appreciating the infinite complexity of the world's natural processes, and as a way of conceiving of ways to heal and/or prevent ecological damage.

d. Loving *care* and *respect* for creatures and systems of the nonhuman creation.

e. Disciplined *prayer* and *meditation.*

f. *Celebration* of the privilege and glory of existing in the midst of God's wonderfully complex and various world.

g. A grounded *commitment* and *fidelity* to preserving and reverencing the natural world.

Our commitment to the task of rebuilding the creation tradition is made clearer when we become increasingly aware of the diverse eco-communities we are part of, and we are prompted to discover a new answer to an old question: "What is our place in the world?" In our vision of a new creation tradition, we are members of one great "master" community which includes several interacting communities.

Thus, we are born into an *all-creational ecosystem of the Spirit of God* which embraces all that God has made and is making. This is the homeland to which I make my master commitment. Within this community are several interrelated communities, including:

—**The entire human species:** a species like all others in having a distinctive role to play in dynamics of the over-all cosmos, but different from all other species in the highly endowed creative potential of its role, and in its *self-conscious* relationship to all other species and forms of being;

—**The world-wide Judeo-Christian Community:** a community which stresses the relationship of the Spirit to all the creation.

—**The entire world religious community:** a community of communities which recognize the role of the life of nature in awareness, action, life styles, rituals, and traditions;

—**The local Christian community:** a community in which we participate as beneficiary and as agent; and

—**The local ecosystem:** a community in which our lives are involved directly, including the now-disturbed *local natural ecosystem* and the particular *city ecosystem* in which I may live with its far-flung dependencies on natural ecosystems for food, energy, and materials.

This conscious awareness of this network of communities can serve as the foundation for a new, realistic location of ourselves in our environment, and can therefore help structure our response as Christians to the "cry of the environment."

3. First Priority: Cultivating, and Being Cultivated By, The Spirit

Much depends on recognizing, at an early stage, that Christian creation consciousness shaped by prayer and meditation is a radically different, yet much more real way of perceiving the world than "ordinary" awareness. The intimacy of fellow creaturehood, a precious gift of the Spirit, is essential in developing this awareness; this consciousness will be more important than mere accumulated information or analysis. Though technical data will be central to the process of encouraging a reconstruction of the creation tradition—and in implementing that transformation—it must itself be grounded in the overarching vision of a world in harmony, a vision which emerges from our openness to the Spirit. It is this form of perception which will create a communal perspective for evaluating, prioritizing, and employing the information derived from technical analysis.

Through the communion of prayer, God invites us to become co-workers in the processes of a very great consummation, a fulfilling realization of the cosmos, which continues and, in a sense, begins again in the present. We are invited, in this process, to participate in embodying the unbounded love with which, through which, and for which the entire creation is founded.

Spirituality, long a valuable part of the Christian tradition, has re-emerged with great vitality in all the churches in the last decade. Catholic and Protestant churches and seminaries have embraced in a new way the commitment to prayer as an essential aspect of their fundamental identities, and increasingly this "prayer of the community" has taken as its content the marvelous processes of the natural world which disclose the depth of God's presence and love among us. We need to continue to encourage this—to take to the center of our meditation the presence of the Spirit moving among us in the life of the earth, the waters, and the sky.

Creation consciousness is not meant as a substitute for the other concerns of Christian faith—it is not meant to be competitive with the great work which is going on concerning social justice, international disarmament, or relieving great public or personal suffering. On the contrary, creation consciousness becomes a lens through which these other issues can be understood and evaluated—a vision of the anguish of the earth leads us to a vision of the anguish of its people. The one does not exclude the other—indeed they complement and strengthen each other. We focus on creation consciousness here only because it has been so neglected as a "way of the faithful life"—as a channel through which the life and light of the Infinitely Self-Surpassing Self, as Charles Hartshorne has described God, can shower into our existence and the existence of this fragile yet resilient planet. Creation consciousness widens our horizons, and therefore blows into our lives like a wind which can heal our perverse tendency toward a narrow and self-indulgent religious narcissism which we, consciously or unconsciously, pit against a miraculous, abundant, and flourishing cosmic order. Our awareness of this will be heightened with the development of more creation-celebrating music, visual arts, and literature which will confront us with both the ambiguity and immediacy of the natural world and our relationship to it.

4. The Vision That Sustains— And Sustaining the Vision

Once experiencing the reality and promise of creation-conscious living, we yearn to become a part of a larger human community which likewise shares a profound sense of participation in the whole evolving world of God. It is time for us to dream of, and concretely develop, an intentional creation-conscious culture, one which cries out against the violence of environmental and human abuse as one—for they emerge from the same impulse of exploitation and unacceptable death—and which lives an alternative by creating structures of care, concern, respect, and compassion for a battered earth. Let us intuit and conceptualize a map for ourselves which, when followed with discipline, will lead us from our attitudes of indifference toward the natural world into a province of sympathy for the planet and all its creatures where we demonstrate daily our solidarity with the cosmos and, in loving it so, be united that much more with its Creator who has so tenderly fashioned it. Mystic, scientist, artist, worker, theologian, policy-maker, and minister—each has her or his role to play in drafting a vision of a world which is no longer simply dying under our feet, but is being replenished and liberated, even at the cost of our expectations and ambitions. Anything of value costs—does not the world deserve our sacrifice, the price we must pay to heal it and give it life again?

5. Cultivating Creation Consciousness in Local Parishes and Congregations

Some of the alternative communities which were formed in the 1960s were committed to ecological life styles which included practices of recycling, raising small crops, generating energy from renewable sources, and other measures. Today, interest in creation-conscious living will spur the formation of groups in local congregations which will develop similar practices. The churches are really quite natural places for this to take place—their structures are already in place; they share a creation tradition which, though undervalued and often twisted out of recognition through history, nevertheless promises to offer church-goers a common frame-of-reference for making a strong commitment to a constructive vision and program of championing the natural environment against the present onslaught of environmental degradation; and they could become a resource center for the local community, focusing on both regional and global environmental problems.

In most churches, people who share this vision—especially when it has been lifted to explicit self-awareness within the church structure itself—will have little difficulty in finding each other. One can imagine with great excitement the activities which may emerge from a "community of concern" composed of people from diverse backgrounds and perspectives: scientists, gardeners, government employees, artists. . . . We might call these "God's World" groups, which would both stress solidarity between humankind and the natural order and promote concrete activities which make that solidarity come alive. Such activity will result in greater solidarity among churchmembers, as well. The churches desperately need a widening of their self-understanding to begin to create ongoing grass-roots centers for the rebuilding of the creation tradition.

6. The Creation-Conscious Shaping of Public Policy

Governmental and corporate policy which has ramifications for the life of the natural environment—toxic waste management, nuclear waste disposal, strip mining, air pollution standards, sale of federal lands to multi-national corporations, and so on—will be critiqued, challenged, and reformulated only when there is a *constituency of environmental advocates* which is bringing a strong voice to policy debates. The churches can begin to play a larger role in creating that constituency by encouraging the development of a consensus within American congregations that policies which threaten the environment threaten the life of faith and therefore are no longer acceptable. This involves undertaking a project of widespread environmental education squarely situated in a faith context, of mobilizing large numbers of people to clamor for change, and to promote activities which can lead to direct changes in policy, including boycotts and nonviolent direct actions against flagrant violators of both environmental laws and the laws of nature.

The environment and energy policy statements issued by the National Council of Churches and by some of the specific church denominations recently are first steps in this direction. But the theology and ethics developed in these statements now need the support of committed, cultivated spirituality which can inform, illumine, and strengthen a culture-wide transformation of the nature-human relationship.

The role of the churches in the ongoing discussion about, and action around, these issues will become increasingly more important in the coming years as citizens and policy-makers grope for a moral vision of "right relationship" with the natural world. An indication of this was seen recently when, for example, community leaders in Hartford, Connecticut declared in a prepared statement that the churches and synagogues of the area have "special credibility and authority" qualifying them to participate in the formulation of public policy. Three special assets were noted: (1) the concern of religion for the whole of life; (2) ability to approach individual issues within a larger ethical framework; and (3) possession of resources and flexibility that other institutions lack.[1] All three apply to congregations throughout the country, and can be brought to bear on the complex issues of environmental policy. Just as the Catholic and Protestant churches in America have focused on the thorny moral issues raised by nuclear weapons policy—including the threatened, unimaginable creation-cide of world-wide nuclear war—there is a great potential for the explicit raising of the ethical questions prompted by irresponsible and threatening environmental abuse. The churches could develop programs which would acquaint people of the background information necessary for understanding specific environmental issues, develop ethical analysis, and develop concrete programs of action. By following such a course, the religious community would take its legitimate place in both understanding and transforming the peril which threatens the natural world and its inhabitants.

As we become increasingly aware of the host of dangers which threaten the integrity of planet earth, we must remind ourselves again and again that the great creation is, in fact, an immense, inexhaustible, creative enterprise of the Spirit of God who is in love with every living being, every landscape, every wave length and electron, every star and galaxy, and with all processes and interrelationships. Our hand-in-handedness with the creation must grow with joyous love in a progressive fulfillment of creaturely community within the horizon of the divine spirit.

Out of prayer and worship relearned, and through the difficult sacrifices that will be necessary to take up this concern and respect for all of life, our vision of a redeemed world will become a great, shared work of art which, when entered, heals and replenishes a tortured planet. Love will teach love—the environment will be, as Thomas Kelly urged, re-loved, for we will have learned to see, *and everything will begin to look different!*

Notes

1. Martha Gotwals, "Religious Leadership: Survey Says it Is Needed in Public Policy Arena," *A.D. Magazine,* United Church of Christ (February 1982), p. 35.

ABOUT THE AUTHORS

Douglas G. Adams , Professor of "Christianity and the Arts" at the Pacific School of Religion, and Chairman of the doctoral faculty in "Theology and the Arts" at the Graduate Theological Union. Recently Associate Professor of Worship and Preaching, PSR. Did research on Thomas Cole's paintings when he served as post-doctoral Smithsonian Fellow in Art History at the National Museum of Art, 1974-75. Fellow, North American Academy of Liturgy. Editor of six books, author of six others.

Bernhard W. Anderson, Emeritus Professor of Old Testament Theology, Princeton Theological Seminary. A well-known figure in Old Testament studies, Dr. Anderson has had a long-standing interest in creation theology in the Old and New Testaments, and has published extensively in this and other fields. Three of his many books are *Understanding the Old Testament* (1957), *Creation vs. Chaos: The Reinterpretation of Mythical Symbolism in the Bible* (1967), and as editor, *Creation in the Old Testament* (1984).

Conrad Bonifazi, Emeritus Professor of Interdisciplinary Studies, Humboldt State University, Arcata, CA. Dr. Bonifazi is a highly regarded Teilhard de Chardin scholar and has published *A Theology of Things: A Study of Man in His Physical Environment* (1967), and *The Soul of the World: An Account of the Inwardness of Things* (1978).

Ralph Wendell Burhoe, Emeritus Professor, Meadville/Lombard Theological School, Chicago. Executive Officer, American Academy of Arts and Sciences, 1947-64. Founding Editor of *Zygon, Journal of Science and Religion.* 1980 Recipient of the Templeton Award for Excellence in Religion. Author of *Toward a Scientific Theology* (1981) and contributor of many articles to professional journals.

Ken Butigan, staff member of the Center for Ethics and Social Policy, is a writer, editor, and social activist. He has recently edited *The Present Nuclear War: The Economic, Environmental, Medical, Political and Psychological Costs of the Arms Race.*

John B. Cobb, Jr., Ingraham Professor of Theology at Claremont School of Theology. Author of numerous articles and books, including *The Liberation of Life* (with Charles Birch—1981), *Beyond*

Dialogue: Toward a Mutual Transformation of Christianity and Buddhism (1982), *Living Options in Protestant Theology: A Summary of Methods* (1973), and *Is It Too Late? A Theology of Ecology* (1972).

Calvin B. DeWitt, Director of Au Sable Institute of Environmental Studies, University of Wisconsin, Madison. Taught previously at Calvin College and the University of Michigan. Fellow, Calvin College Center for Christian Scholarship (Christian Stewardship and Natural Resources), 1977-78. Author of many papers and co-auther (with the Calvin Fellows) of the book, *Earthkeeping: Christian Stewardship of Natural Resources* (1980).

Andrew J. Dufner, S.J., Seattle University, Former Dean, Jesuit School of Theology, Berkeley, and Fellow, Center for Theology and The Natural Sciences, Graduate Theological Union. A physicist, Dr. Dufner has contributed many articles to professional journals.

Matthew Fox, O.P., Director of the Institute in Culture and Creation Spirituality at Holy Names College, Oakland, which he founded in 1977 at Mundelein College in Chicago. A featured lecturer at universities, religious, and cultural conferences and congresses, where he has delivered over 250 addresses. Author of nine books on spirituality and culture which seek to share the aims and resources of spirituality with the general reader; his recent *Original Blessing: A Primer in Creation Spirituality* is a comprehensive development of his thought. Fox is a Dominican who has taught at many colleges and received a doctorate in spirituality *summa cum laude* from the Institute Catholique de Paris.

Philip Hefner, Professor of Systematic Theology at the Lutheran School of Theology in Chicago. Author of *The Promise of Teilhard*, many papers, and a frequent speaker at conferences. Associate Editor of *Zygon, Journal of Science and Religion*.

Philip N. Joranson, Director of the Environment and Christian Creation Tradition Project of the Center for Ethics and Social Policy, Graduate Theological Union, and Adjunct Lecturer, Pacific School of Religion. Leadership responsibilities since 1964 in three programs addressed to religious reconstruction for the environmental future. Earlier teaching in biological sciences and environmental studies; research and administrative experience in forest science. Many articles in professional journals.

Bernard M. Loomer, former Dean of the Divinity School of the University of Chicago and leader there in the early development of process theology. More recently, Professor of Philosophical Theology at the Graduate Theological Union. Author of many journal articles.

Paul E. Lutz, Professor of Ecology and Invertebrate Zoology, University of North Carolina at Greensboro. Co-author with H. Paul Santmire of *Ecological Renewal* (1972).

Charles S. McCoy, Robert Gordon Sproul Professor of Theological Ethics, Pacific School of Religion and Graduate Theological Union, and Senior Fellow, Center for Ethics and Social Policy, has led many projects and written numerous articles and books, including *The Meaning of Theological Reflection* (1963), *The Covenant Theology of Johannes Cocceius* (1965), *The Responsible Campus* (1972), and *When Gods Change: Hope for Theology* (1980; German translation, 1983).

Marjorie Casebier McCoy, Pacific School of Religion, author, actress. Dr. McCoy has written books on living and dying, and on theology and drama. Recent titles include *To Die with Style!*, *The Transforming Cross* (with Charles McCoy), and *Mary the Mother of Jesus.*

Alan S. Miller, Academic Coordinator and Lecturer, Department of Conservation and Resource Studies, University of California, Berkeley. Dr. Miller is author of more than 50 articles and the book *A Planet to Choose: Value Studies in Political Ecology.*

Ted F. Peters, Associate Professor of Systematic Theology, Pacific Lutheran Theological Seminary, Berkeley. Dr. Peters has written many articles and books on futurist themes, including the two recent volumes, *Futures, Human and Divine* (1978) and *Fear, Faith and the Future: Hope in the Face of Doomsday Prophecies* (1980).

Patricia Runo, is a feminist writer, artist, and social activist. She is presently pursuing graduate studies with an emphasis on women's spirituality at the Graduate Theological Union.

Robert John Russell, Executive Director of the Center for Theology and the Natural Sciences, affiliated with the Graduate Theological Union, and Assistant Professor of Theology and Science in Residence, GTU, Berkeley.

G. Ledyard Stebbins, Emeritus Professor of Genetics, University of California, Davis. A world authority on evolutionary science, Dr. Stebbins has served as president of several major national scientific societies, and was recently Regents' Fellow at the National Museum of Natural History, Smithsonian Institution. He has published extensively, including three books of high reputation: *Variation and Evolution in Plants* (1950), *Processes of Organic Evolution* (1977), and *Darwin to DNA: Molecules to Humanity* (1982).

Claude Y. Stewart, Jr., Associate Professor of Theology, Southeastern Baptist Theological Seminary, Wake Forest, N.C. In 1983, Dr. Stewart published *Nature in Grace: A Study in the Theology of Nature*.

Brian Swimme, a physicist, is co-director of the Institute in Culture and Creation Spirituality at Holy Names College, Oakland, CA. He is co-author, with Matthew Fox, of *Manifesto for a Global Civilization* (1982), and author of *The Universe is a Green Dragon* (1984).

Paul Wiegand is a recent graduate at the Franciscan School of Theology and the Graduate Theological Union, and works in Franciscan studies and in the field of Religion and Society.

Richard J. Woods, O.P. is Professor of Philosophy at the College of St. Thomas, St. Paul, Minn. He is author of *Mysterion: An Approach to Mystical Spirituality* (1981) and *Symbion: Spirituality for a Possible Future* (1983).

The Voyage of Life: Childhood (1842), Thomas Cole; National Gallery of Art, Washington, D.C.; Ailsa Mellon Bruce Fund 1971.

The Voyage of Life: Youth (1842), Thomas Cole; National Gallery of Art, Washington, D.C.; Ailsa Mellon Bruce Fund 1971.

471

The Voyage of Life: Manhood (1842), Thomas Cole; National Gallery of Art, Washington, D.C.; Ailsa Mellon Bruce Fund 1971.

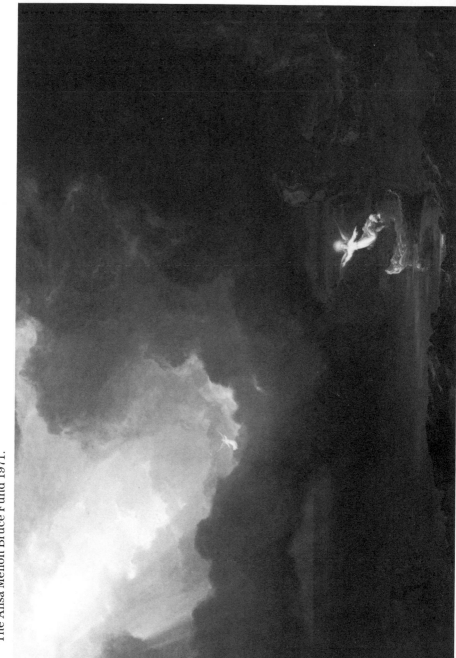

The Voyage of Life: Old Age (1842), Thomas Cole; National Gallery of Art, Washington, D.C.; The Ailsa Mellon Bruce Fund 1971.

The Course of Empire: The Arcadian (undated), Thomas Cole; Courtesy of The New-York Historical Society, New York City.

The Course of Empire: Savage State (undated), Courtesy of The New-York Historical Society, New York City.

The Course of Empire: The Consummation of Empire (1835–36), Courtesy of The New-York Historical Society, New York City.

The Course of Empire: Destruction (1836), Courtesy of The New-York Historical Society.